OUTSIDE THE FOLD

Frontispiece. Annie Besant, socialist turned theosophist, c. 1880s

OUTSIDE THE FOLD

CONVERSION, MODERNITY, AND BELIEF

Gauri Viswanathan

PRINCETON UNIVERSITY PRESS   PRINCETON, NEW JERSEY

Copyright ©1998 by Princeton University Press
Published by Princeton University Press, 41 William Street,
Princeton, New Jersey 08540
In the United Kingdom: Princeton University Press,
Chichester, West Sussex
All Rights Reserved.

Library of Congress Cataloging-in-Publication Data
Viswanathan, Gauri.
Outside the fold : conversion, modernity, and belief / Gauri Viswanathan.
p.   cm.
Includes bibliographical references and index.
ISBN 0-691-05898-9 (alk. paper).—
ISBN 0-691-05899-7 (pb : alk. paper)
1. Conversion—Comparative studies. 2. India—Religion—
19th century. 3. India—Religion—20th century. 4. England—Religion.
5. Religion and politics—Comparative studies. 6. Religion and
culture—Comparative studies.   I. Title.
BL639.V57 1998   291.4′2—dc21   97-34908   CIP

This book has been composed in Times Roman

Princeton University Press books are printed
on acid-free paper and meet the guidelines
for permanence and durability of the Committee
on Production Guidelines for Book Longevity
of the Council on Library Resources

http://pup.princeton.edu

Printed in the United States of America

1   3   5   7   9   10   8   6   4   2

1   3   5   7   9   10   8   6   4   2

(pbk.)

To the Memory of My Brother

Contents

Illustrations

Preface

IN ITS MOST transparent meaning as a change of religion, conversion is arguably one of the most unsettling political events in the life of a society. This is
irrespective of whether conversion involves a single individual or an entire
community, whether it is forced or voluntary, or whether it is the result of
proselytization or inner spiritual illumination. Not only does conversion alter
the demographic equation within a society and produce numerical imbalances,
but it also challenges an established community's assent to religious doctrines
and practices. With the departure of members from the fold, the cohesion of a
community is under threat just as forcefully as if its beliefs had been turned
into heresies.

Modern history has borne witness to the violent reactions to such perceived
threats. In 1981, the mass conversions of noncaste Hindus to Islam in south
India unleashed right-wing Hindu militant forces, whose main platform consisted of whipping up fear of the "foreign hand." The mobilization of Hindu
groups like the Vishwa Hindu Parishad around this issue contributed in no
small measure to the rapid ascendancy of paramilitary Hindu extremism.[1] But
what is worth recalling is that an identical rhetoric of paranoia marked the
response of nineteenth-century Anglican England to a spate of Catholic conversions, which were interpreted as almost certain confirmation of the imperial
reach of Rome as well as of the inexorable onslaught of Irish immigration.
These identical responses, separated by time and place, as well as culture and
circumstance, indicate the degree to which national boundaries are made con-
tinous with uniform religious and social composition.

If the conferral of citizenship rights on religious minorities has never been
more urgently debated nor its realization more infuriatingly elusive than it is
today, a great deal of the difficulty centers on the incompatibility of two opposing goals. How are minority religious groups to be brought into the modern
nation and protection extended to their claims to certain rights and privileges
guaranteed to all members of that nation, without at the same time effacing
either their unique religious differences or the content of their religious beliefs? The vexing problem of militant Hinduism in India, for example, which
has been stridently seeking to integrate Indian Muslims and other religious
minorities by requiring them to forego their own civil laws, is only one among
many instances of a tendency in contemporary cultural politics to blur the
boundaries between national and religious identity and declare the practice of
other customary laws separatist and antinational. The shading of religious
identity into the artificial fabrication of a *secular* India, made interchangeable
with *Hindu* India, has given further impetus to Hindu extremist forces to install
an absolutist state based on a single religion with which the state is to be fully
and exclusively identified.

At the same time, if modern secularism has responded to the challenge of religious absolutism by insisting on the autonomy of national identity, such assertions have created problems of another kind. Foremost among them is the placing of religious identity at a stage of historical development prior to the emergence of the nation. Although modern cultural studies have benefited from analyses of the sort provided by the anthropologist Johannes Fabian, who has shown that terms like "primitive" and "savage" have temporal resonances that reflect their origins in world-historical models developed during European colonialism,[2] these sorts of insights have not extended their reach to question the temporality of, say, Freud's assessment of religion as equivalent to the stage of childhood in historical development, "to be outgrown in a civilising adolescence."[3] If religion survives at all in the "mature" phase of civilization, after having jettisoned the content of its belief systems, it does so largely as a function of legal administration, bureaucratic rationality, and governance.

Subordinated to the legal and administrative will of the nation, religion in the modern secular state is less a marker of the subjectivity of belief systems than a category of identification. Religion shares features with the analytical categories of race and class in that each assumes certain established criteria for determining rank, position, and membership in a national community. The commuting of religious identity into a subcategory of social composition is facilitated by such instruments of administrative classification as census reports, which, in assigning groups or communities to predetermined categories, often overrule the indeterminate beliefs and practices by which people may choose to live their lives. However, the intransigent nature of such beliefs, reflecting inchoate ways of life and suggesting a different order of relationality, refuses to be made pliable by determined acts of classification. Political psychologist Ashis Nandy cites as an example the Gujarat census of 1911, in which two hundred thousand Indians declared themselves oxymoronically as "Mohammedan Hindus."[4] Such types of self-declarations, asserting fluid and overlapping identities, throw doubt on the usefulness of census categories, especially since the people who make up those categories insist on scrambling them when asked to identify themselves.

The reduction of religion to a mode of social organization finds one of its most poignant moments in the modern history of partition—the breakup of nations along religious lines—forcing individuals who have lived in contiguous relations with members of diverse communities to reconceptualize those same relations now as antagonistic ones. As Barbara Harlow among other critics has argued, partition, in the tragic experience of formerly colonized states as diverse as Palestine, Ireland, and India, connotes far more than the truncation of territory recorded by official historiography. It is the truncation of identity itself and the alienation of individuals not only from each other but also in their ways of defining themselves according to their own worldviews,

understandings, and beliefs—a right henceforth usurped by official discourse.[5]
Some of the most moving testimonies of the dramatic differences between
self-perceptions and bureaucratic determinations appear in—and undercut—
the records of recovery operations undertaken by state agencies to return displaced peoples to their native homes. In the partition of the Indian subcontinent, the attempt to nullify forcible conversions of abducted Hindu women to
Islam and restore them to the culture and land of their origin reestablishes
"Hindu" and "Muslim" as fixed categories, quite at variance with the ways
these women define themselves at the moment of both rupture and recovery.
A social worker assigned to the refugee camps is quoted as saying, "The identification [of recovered women] was done according to the countries they belonged to, this one is Indian, this one a Pakistani. Partition was internally
connected with Islam, the individual, and the demand for a separate homeland.
And since this label was attached, how could the women be free from it?"[6] The
imbrication of gender in a state-sponsored religious nationalism makes room
for neither choice nor will, even when an act of restoration is intended to undo
the effects of rupture—a motive one "recovered" woman angrily challenged
when she confronted her rescuer with these words:

> You say abduction is immoral and so you are trying to save us. Well, now it is too
> late. One marries only once—willingly or by force. We are now married—what
> are you going to do with us? Ask us to get married again? Is that not immoral?
> What happened to our relatives when we were abducted? Where were they? . . .
> You may do your worst if you insist, but remember, you can kill us, but we will
> not go.[7]

Social theorist Veena Das has documented the skeptical and often angry
questioning of national repatriation schemes by the abducted women she inter-
viewed, whose testimony of forcible conversion and separation is structured
more precisely around desire and need rather than feelings of victimhood or
alienation. In a third-person narrative that Das describes as a "metonymic displacement" of the narrator Manjeet's own story, forced separations from the
homeland are evaluated in relation to forms of gratification not immediately
accessible to historiographical interpretation. Manjeet's telegraphic and under-
stated plot summary of her life—"She became a Muslim and she did well"[8]—
constitutes a counternarrative to the official version of national history as a
history of consolidation of religious ideologies into social units.

Correspondingly, the fixing of religion for classificatory purposes establishes aspects of religious behavior as invariant. These may not necessarily
relate to beliefs actually held which, when expressed, are so far outside the
identifiable, accepted categories that their nonrecognizability makes them appear dangerous, threatening, "other." Clearly, the move describing certain
types of religious behavior as fanatical, militant, or cultish does not involve a
great leap. If religious belief in contemporary parlance has become moder-

nity's estranged self, our acknowledging the history of its representation opens up what is undoubtedly much needed, if potentially explosive, discussions of how the "othering" of religious difference and belief contributes to the discursive construction of such things as religious fundamentalism. In an important article Susan Harding has recently argued that modernity's invention of religious fundamentalism as its necessary antithesis is systematically ignored by antiorientalist critiques, which otherwise have had little hesitation in taking up issues involving race, class, and gender, and asking questions in what are now fairly "routine theoretical moves" about assumed categories in narrative representations and who presumes to speak for whom. Harding writes, "It seems that antiorientalizing tools of cultural criticism are better suited for some 'others' and not other 'others'—specifically, for cultural 'others' constituted by discourses of race/sex/class/ethnicity/colonialism but not religion."[9]

Harding puts her finger squarely on what I believe is a principal difficulty in contemporary cultural studies: to engage in discussions about belief, conviction, or religious identity in a secular age of postmodern skepticism is already fraught with infinite hazards, not least of which is the absence of an adequate vocabulary or language. Rustom Bharucha in *The Question of Faith* has eloquently written "that apart from the low priority given to representations of faith in theories of oppression and resistance, there are no adequate languages in the social sciences to deal with its contradictions in the first place."[10] He makes a sustained critique of one of the most radical and significant historiographical interventions in recent years—the school of subaltern studies scholars—to reveal the extent to which even the most innovative historical methods have failed to come up with ways of studying belief systems as an essential component of subaltern consciousness. With the possible exception of Ranajit Guha who, Bharucha admits, has acknowledged the inability of the historian to "conceptualise insurgent mentality" outside of "an unadulterated secularism,"[11] Bharucha charges that subaltern historians have continued to polarize worldly and otherworldly consciousness as descriptive of the divide between secularism and religion. And if shifts in attitude to religious consciousness are beginning to emerge in the work of younger historians, Bharucha is right to express certain reservations that these newer formulations should not lead simply to "an instrumentalist reading of religion as an adjunct to political activity," but should enable a recognition of the "experiential contexts of religion providing new possibilities of representing 'resistance' and 'transcendence.' "[12]

Despite the obvious differences in purpose, philosophy, ideology, and political alignments of scholars looking for legitimate ways of talking about religion in their intellectual work,[13] the ultimate significance of such work lies in its being a vehicle for secular intellectuals to express the difficulties of communicating the idea of religious belief—as distinct from religious ideology—

in and for a secular community. Ashis Nandy, who has tirelessly written on the polarization of intellectual discourse into secularism and religious ideology, refuses even to concede that he is writing for a secular audience and declares himself, somewhat perversely, to be "anti-secular."[14] Although his cantankerous, polemical style may not be entirely congenial to others who share his dissatisfaction with polarized vocabularies, there is little doubt that words like "secular" and "religious" have lost their descriptive value and function instead as signposts to given attitudes.

No recent work has more persuasively traced the genealogical shifts of religion—from a knowledge-producing activity to an otherworldly, passive repository of beliefs—than Talal Asad's *Genealogies of Religion*.[15] One of the most provocative arguments emerging from his book suggests that the removal of religion from the public space of discussion may be a construction that itself follows upon another construction: namely, the concept of religion as transhistorical, transcultural essence. The tension between religion's claims to universalism, on one hand, and, on the other, the demand that religion be kept separate from the rational articulations of modernity (in such institutions as politics, law, and science) cannot be reduced simply to the product of a secular outlook, but must be considered as a tension internal to the ways religion has been constituted in the world. If this self-generated conflict has tended to be resolved on the ground of individual subjectivity—as the lone space for the continued practice of and assent to belief—Asad's historical reading that "the only legitimate space allowed to Christianity by post-Enlightenment society is the right to individual belief"[16] enables one to rethink western secularism, not as a linear successor to religious culture but as its necessary complement within the same time frame.

Asad's rendering of this complex history begins in the seventeenth century with Lord Herbert's *De veritate* and its formulation of a "Natural Religion" commanding universal assent. He demonstrates that Herbert's search for a common denominator for all religions in an era of early colonial expansion led him to represent religion as a set of propositions to which believers give their assent—propositions that would hence be known as beliefs. Asad then delineates the progressive demarcation between Natural Science and Natural Religion as corresponding to the distinctions between acts of knowledge and states of belief, experience, and feeling. The durability of these distinctions, he points out, can be seen in the fact that even sympathetic anthropologists like Clifford Geertz continue to describe belief as a state of mind rather than a constituting activity in the world. Asad goes on to argue that

> the suggestion that religion has a universal function in belief is one indication of how marginal religion has become in modern industrial society as the site for producing disciplined knowledge and personal discipline. As such, it comes to

resemble the conception Marx had of religion as ideology—a mode of consciousness which is other than consciousness of reality, external to the relations of
production, producing no knowledge, but expressing at once the anguish of the
oppressed and a spurious consolation.[17]

Central to the diminished role of religion in modernity is the process by which,
according to Asad, the weight of religion has shifted "more and more onto the
moods and motivations of the individual believer."[18] Within this description,
it is already possible to discern the sources of the divide between believer and
secular society, individual subjectivity and institutional rationality.

If, as the above observations further enable one to conclude, the marginalization of belief in history is constitutively linked to the lack of an adequate
vocabulary to deal with its worldliness, I suggest that by recovering this history one may also begin the search for corrective ways of talking and writing
about belief in terms other than "fundamentalist," "premodern," or "prehis-
tory." (Ernest Gellner's recent book, *Postmodernism, Reason, and Religion*, is
a perfect example of how the absence of an adequate language in modern
scholarship confines discussion of Islamic societies to a category of premodernity and Islam in general to an incorrigibly fundamentalist identity.)[19] But
I would add that the search for an alternative mode of intellectual engagement
with the question of belief requires one to rethink not only the discursive construction of religious fundamentalism but also the pressing claims of religious
minorities. In much the same way that religious belief is placed outside public
discourse, it is also evident that, in a parallel historical process, the content of
minority religions is placed outside the space of national culture. If the right to
individual belief is the surviving—indeed, permissible—form of religion in
modernity, the question of how that right may be protected, without reducing
to sentiment or affect the subjectivity upon which belief is formed, raises once
again the issue of worldliness, or what I describe as the position of belief in
self-constitution.

I shall offer as the principal argument of this book that conversion ranks
among the most destabilizing activities in modern society, altering not only
demographic patterns but also the characterization of belief as communally
sanctioned assent to religious ideology. Although it is true that, in the context
of majority-minority relations, conversion is typically regarded as an assimilative act—a form of incorporation into a dominant culture of belief—conversion's role in restoring belief from the margins of secular society to a more
worldly function is less readily conceded. The worldiness I have in mind relates to civil and political rights. Why, for instance, does history throw up so
many instances of conversion movements accompanying the fight against rac-
ism, sexism, and colonialism? What might be the link between the struggle for
basic rights and the adoption of religions typically characterized as minority
religions? What limitations of secular ideologies in ensuring these rights do

acts of conversion reveal? Does that act of exposure align conversion more closely with cultural criticism? And finally, what possibilities for alternative politics of identity might be offered by conversion as a gesture that crosses fixed boundaries between communities and identities? These questions frame the terms of my inquiry in the ensuing pages, and are suggestive of both the comprehensive, inexhaustible scope of meanings attached to conversion and its location at the nexus of spiritual and material interests.

Chapter One, "Cross Currents," provides a genealogical account of the construction of the English "tolerant" state from its colonial provenance, drawing on significant literary works to elucidate the problematic, dual characterization of conversion as assimilation and dissent. Chapter Two, "A Grammar of Dissent," focuses on John Henry Newman's conversion to Catholicism as an expression of political resistance to English secular nationalism. Chapter Three, "Rights of Passage," shifts to colonial India and examines court testimonies by converts as exemplary texts that render problematic the neat separation between belief and law attempted by British secular policy. Chapter Four, "Silencing Heresy," offers a close study of a female convert to Christianity, Pandita Ramabai, whose spirited questioning of Christian creeds led the English missionaries who sponsored her stay in England to interpret her feminist stance as essentially heretical.

Moving from gender to race theory, Chapter Five, "Ethnographic Plots," juxtaposes two genres—the census report and the romance novel—in order to trace the contribution of the conversion narrative to discourses of race and national origin in colonial India. Chapter Six, "Conversion, Theosophy, and Race Theory," focuses on Annie Besant's conversion to theosophy and examines more broadly how alternative spiritual movements, which proclaimed a universal brotherhood of man yet were concurrent with theories of racial hierarchy, prepared the ground for a commonwealth model displacing empire. Chapter Seven, "Conversion to Equality," describes the Indian untouchable leader B. R. Ambedkar's strategy of fighting caste oppression, not by turning to the secular state for protection but by converting to Buddhism. The epilogue, constituting Chapter Eight, extends the preceding discussions on the claims of individual belief into the contested terrain of contemporary forms of blasphemy and heresy. In sum, the book as a whole establishes the need to historicize conversion not only as a spiritual but also a political activity, the narrativization of which crucially elucidates the momentous transitions to secular societies.

Acknowledgments

IT IS my pleasure to thank the institutions and people who helped me complete this book. Research was made possible by fellowships from the John Simon Guggenheim Memorial Foundation, the National Endowment for the Humanities, the American Institute of Indian Studies, and the Columbia Council for Research in the Humanities and Social Sciences. My travels took me to various archival collections, among which the major ones were at the British Library, the India Office Library and Records (London), the National Archives of India (Delhi), the Tamil Nadu Archives (Madras), and the Research Library of the Theosophical Society (Madras). I am grateful to the research staff at all these places for their unfailing courtesy and assistance.

A number of institutions have invited me over the past few years to give lectures based on this book. To friends and colleagues at the following places I offer thanks for the opportunity given to refine and clarify my ideas: Princeton, Michigan, Wisconsin, Pennsylvania, Rutgers, Berkeley, Santa Barbara, Santa Cruz, Wesleyan, Amsterdam, Warwick, Oberlin, Emory, Hawaii, Sussex, Sydney, Australian National University (Canberra), Witwatersrand (Johannesburg), among others. I am especially indebted to those who, through an innocuous question or bemused look, set me furiously thinking in ways that I had not anticipated earlier. I am grateful to Phyllis Mack for inviting me to a year-long seminar on religion at the Rutgers Center for Historical Analysis; the animated weekly discussions did much to buoy my spirits.

Earlier, condensed versions of the following chapters appeared in various publications: Chapter Three in *After Colonialism: Imperial Histories and Postcolonial Displacements*, edited by Gyan Prakash (Princeton: Princeton University Press, 1995); Chapters Two and Seven in *Conversion to Modernities: The Globalization of Christianity*, edited by Peter van der Veer (New York and London: Routledge, 1996); and Chapter Eight in *Comparative Studies in Society and History* (April 1995): 399–412.

For the deep pleasure of their friendship, for their steadfast encouragement and support, and for their stimulating example, I thank my colleagues Ann Douglas, John Rosenberg, Edward Said, and Gayatri Chakravorty Spivak. Peter van der Veer read the whole manuscript with exemplary thoughtfulness; our shared interests have opened up what I hope will be a lasting conversation. Sara Suleri also read the manuscript with her characteristic grace and generosity. For valuable insights, it is a special pleasure to acknowledge David Ludden, Ranajit Guha, and Robert Young. Some of the ideas in this book found their way into my graduate seminars at Columbia. I was fortunate to have wonderful students who kept the level of discussions consistently high and helped me refine my thoughts. Particular appreciation goes to Elaine Freedgood, Amy Martin, Tim Watson, and Neville Hoad. Madeleine Adams, Mary Murrell, and other editorial staff at Princeton University Press provided assistance at various stages. I am indebted to Margaret Case for her careful reading of the manuscript.

Writing a book about conversion can itself be a changeful activity, just as it can also mean being outside the fold for long stretches of time. But I am happy to say that the constancy of the following friends gave a continuous flow to life's events, and for that I am truly grateful: Meena Alexander, Una Chaudhuri, Elaine Freedgood (again), Lynn Mulkey, Kirin Narayan, Anne McClintock, Rob Nixon, and Priscilla Wald. In the time that it takes to finish a book, losses also occur: I have many regrets that neither my brother nor my father lived to see this. To my mother I owe a debt which I am only now beginning to comprehend.

Part One

DISSENT AND THE NATION

CHAPTER ONE

Cross Currents

RELIGIOUS MINORITIES AND CITIZENSHIP

On the assumption that genealogy is often a function of historical narrative and that the history of cultural developments can best be told through the stories (both historical and literary) that chart their transitions, this chapter offers a genealogical account of the construction of the English tolerant state from its colonial provenance. Although conversion remains, as it does for the rest of the book, the lens through which cultural formations (including the factors shaping secular culture and religious identity) are observed, historicized, and analyzed, it is also evident that the book's main thesis—that conversion is a subversion of secular power—can best be grasped as an outcome of a particular historical conjuncture.

That conjuncture, I suggest, does not consist exclusively of Britain's domestic transition from a religious to a secular order, or from church authority to the authority of law. Rather, the expanded international context of Britain's history and culture reveals that ecclesiastical history is as subject to the notations of an imperial history as are other spheres of English culture. For example, as I have argued elsewhere, the realignments between religious and secular culture in England were affected by such apparently distant events as the introduction of British education in the colonies.[1] The challenges posed by managing far-flung colonies from a metropolitan center plainly showed the advantages of secular governance over the more risk-laden goal of Christianizing colonial subjects. The official promotion of missionary activity was especially perilous in British colonies like India, which had entrenched religious traditions and laws that derived in turn from these traditions.

Rule by the efficient machinery of bureaucracy (which Max Weber describes as a form of administrative rationality),[2] unsanctioned by church authority, may appear to be the natural result of England's internal evolution from an exclusionary Anglican culture into a "tolerant" civil society comprising a plurality of religious groups. Yet Britain's successful experimentation with secular policy in the colonies places the negotiations between religious and secular cultures in a perspective that reaches far beyond the limited domestic purview of England. Not simply internal to English culture but strategically affected by the mode of governing England's colonial subjects, these negotiations cannot be adequately analyzed solely in terms of theories of secularization that draw exclusively upon European history.[3] Rather, working in the narrative interstices between metropolitan and colonial histories, secularity is as much a function of England's imperial expansiveness as it is that of altered church-state relations within Britain. For this reason, only a transcultural perspective can fully illuminate the international dimensions of secularization.

The organizing principle of this book draws upon the dictionary definition of "cross current" as a "current of air or water moving across a main stream; a conflict of feeling or opinion." Reading works from metropolitan and colonial cultures together, or reading them contrapuntally, to use Edward Said's resonant term, is virtually to experience not only the interdependence of histories and cultures—the "overlapping territories" that Said describes in *Culture and Imperialism*—but also the ripples and currents that interrupt, retard, reverse, or accelerate what would otherwise be an undisturbed flow of history, ideas, movements, and lives. Such a reading strategy produces discordances where there might be a will to hear only tonality and harmony. This is vastly different from reading one culture in terms of another, a feature of Orientalist scholarship and knowledge that has left a legacy of diminished understanding of other cultures and their right to be known on their own terms. Rather, a changed picture emerges when one culture is studied as at once the condition and the effect of the other. If cultural histories can be understood as woven together in an intricate design, cultural criticism then becomes an act of disentangling them from their knotted past. What might thus appear as interdependence will be more accurately understood as mutual limitation.

Strikingly, interweaving and disentangling are the metaphors that most accurately describe the conversion experience, which meshes two worlds, two cultures, and two religions, only to unravel their various strands and cast upon each strand the estranged light of unfamiliarity. Viewed thus, conversion is primarily an interpretive act, an index of material and social conflicts. Such an approach does not reject the Jamesian model of conversion as epiphany or sudden "turning," but rather locates religious subjectivity more precisely in relation to the culture that produces, inhibits, or modifies it. If spiritual autobiography shades into critiques (or, in other instances, defenses) of such things as national consolidation, racial/caste/gender hierarchy, and bureaucratic rationality, it does so during the crucial transitions to secular societies in the nineteenth century, shaping the particular forms of conversion narratives produced in this period.

By juxtaposing narratives representing both metropolitan and colonial locations, we may detect a noteworthy fact: the period between 1780 and 1850 (that is, between the time of the Gordon riots in England over Catholic emancipation and of the disempowerment of ecclesiastical authority following the Gorham judgment) marks the simultaneous growth of English colonial influence in India. The English parliament's decision to assume responsibility for

Indian education enabled England to incorporate colonial subjects into the civil structures of governance at precisely the same time that, at home, it was deliberating legislation to admit religious minorities and relieve them of their civil disabilities. By undertaking the education of its subjects in Western sciences, languages, and literature, England was able to insert Indians into the colonial administrative apparatus and make them useful servants of empire. The delicate balance sought by English educational policy in India was essentially a secular project to transform Indians into deracinated replicas of Englishmen, even while they remained affiliated to their own religious culture. The colonial project, however, did not necessarily imply giving English-educated Indians a place in the English political system. The strategic objective of turning Hindus into non-Hindu Hindus, or Muslims into non-Muslim Muslims,[4] has been memorialized in Macaulay's infamous pronouncement on the goal of an English education to produce Indians who would be "Indian in blood and colour, but English in taste, in opinions, in morals, and in intellect."[5] Less noted, however, is that by 1850 there occurred a parallel process in English social and political life that aimed to turn Jews into non-Jewish Jews, Catholics into non-Catholic Catholics, Dissenters into non-Dissenters, Nonconformists into non-Nonconformists, and so forth.

At first glance, these two developments—the lifting of religious discriminations against non-Anglicans in England and the Anglicization of Indians—would appear to bear little or no relation to each other. Indeed, they almost have the semblance of contrary developments. In fact, the mid-nineteenth-century relaxation of penalties against non-Anglicans is more in tune with the East India Company policy of involvement with India in the late eighteenth century. This policy coincides with the Orientalist phase of scholarship, when indigenous systems of learning, culture, and religion were allowed to flourish without any interference from the company officials.[6] So it might seem that civil relief in England has more in common with the Orientalist encouragement of Indian learning. The bills to enfranchise Jews, Dissenters, and Catholics in England, however, were far closer to Macaulay's Anglicization of Indians than they were to Orientalist policy. If religious tolerance and emancipation won grudging acceptance by even the most die-hard Tories and Anglicans, it had a great deal to do with the appeal of securing a nation of good Englishmen promised by such legislation, a goal shared by Macaulay's avid program of cultural assimilation. After all, the Catholic Emancipation Bill of 1828 was sponsored by Tories under Robert Peel, driven by unease over Irish restiveness. The Tory support of the bill was motivated in part by the conviction that aiming for a nation of good Englishmen was a more realistic goal than achieving a nation of good Anglicans. Similarly, in the expectation that Indians were more acceptable if they were no longer practicing Hindus or Muslims, it was considered profitable to make good Englishmen of them, even if it was unlikely or even undesirable for them to be good Christians. In these ways the Macaulayan educational project coalesced imperceptibly into the emancipatory legislation admitting excluded religious minorities into the English nation.

The more than speculative link between these two events lies in Macaulay himself. As the figure most closely identified with the English education of Indians, Macaulay also fought strenuously for the lifting of restrictions against Jews in England and for absorbing them as citizens of the English state. It is no accident that the figure responsible for the Anglicization of Indians also happened to be one of the most strident voices in the English parliament for the removal of Jewish disabilities. If the making of good Englishmen privileged national over religious identity, this was no doubt Macaulay's pragmatic concession to the fact that it was impracticable to aim for the making of either good Christians in India or good Anglicans in England. As Israel Finestein points out, Macaulay's "robust advocacy" of the cause of Jewish civil emancipation blended indistinguishably with the radical agenda of the Whigs to enfranchise the Jews as a necessary step in the teleological progress of English liberalism.[7] That the Anglicization of Indians was crafted from the same political philosophy that advocated the emancipation of religious minorities in England establishes Macaulay's colonizing mission of humanistic education as the international counterpart to his domestic revision of criteria for citizenship.

Macaulay's formal involvement with Jewish emancipation began with his strong support of a parliamentary measure introduced in 1830 by Sir Robert Grant to remove the civil disabilities of Jews. In an 1830 article published in the *Edinburgh Review* (about which I will have more to say), Macaulay pleaded eloquently for the removal of restrictions against Jews and threw the weight of his prestige as a Whig spokesman to persuade the English public to reconsider the criteria of citizenship that had thus far prevailed. However, Grant's bill, which would have placed Jews largely in the same legal position as Catholics, was defeated in the House of Commons. In April 1833 Grant introduced another bill, which came to be regarded as "the classic presentation by a Gentile" of the case for opening municipal office and parliament to professing Jews.[8] This time the bill had more success in the House of Commons, but it was decisively rejected by the House of Lords. Not until the 1840s was the Jewish question taken up again, this time successfully. In 1845 the Tory government of Sir Robert Peel passed legislation that opened municipal office to Jews. Ironically, the momentum for Jewish emancipation that had begun under liberal auspices reached fruition only under a conservative regime.

Macaulay's espousal of Jewish civil relief inevitably brought him into conflict with the family of Clapham Evangelicals in which he grew up. Their eagerness to reclaim Jews as converts to Christianity led the Evangelicals initially to oppose Jewish emancipation. Yet there were within this missionary community certain reformist tendencies that Macaulay had imbibed, even though many of these tendencies divided the Clapham Evangelicals on several fronts. One aspect of Evangelical reform was decidedly conservative. The approval of Jewish emancipation was based on the understanding that it would facilitate Christian conversions, since the absorption of Jews as English citizens would presumably diminish their alienation from Anglican culture—an alienation that Anglo-Jews had turned into forms of group cohesion and community consolidation. From a conversionist point of view, England's long-standing exclusionary politics had the deleterious effect of creating a separatist consciousness and pride in Jews that Christian missionaries were unable to penetrate or undo. When, therefore, in the 1830s, Sir Robert Grant presented a series of bills in parliament urging Jewish civil emancipation, support from Evangelicals was not entirely grudging, and Lord Bexley, former chancellor of the exchequer, declared that admitting Jews fully into public life "will be a great step to bring them back from the Talmud to Moses and the Prophets—from there to Christ the transition is comparatively easy."[9]

But for his part Macaulay was completely unmoved by Evangelical efforts to yoke Jewish emancipation to Christian conversion. Driven less by conversionist zeal than expediency, he had a pragmatic sense of the political gains to be reaped by merging his liberal agenda with that of the Radicals, who called for the extension of the franchise and the elimination of religious disabilities. Though historians cite Macaulay's spirited defense of the natural rights of all native-born Englishmen, irrespective of their religious orientation, as evidence of his "plain fairness and justice,"[10] his *History of England* offers clues to another set of motivations. In this work he underscored his acute perception of Britain's expanding imperial and commercial power by evolving a doctrine of political liberalism to explain English growth. In developing the theory that civic equality gave English history its incomparable monumentality, enabling England to spread its domain to the far corners of the earth, Macaulay expressed a classic Whig position on the constitutive role of liberalism in British ascendancy.

In essence, this allowed him to argue for domestic reforms on the principle that they were consistent with the destined international course of English history. He elaborated this argument more systematically in an extraordinary essay, "Civil Disabilities of the Jews," published in 1830 in the *Edinburgh Review*. In a period when Englishmen were breaking out of their crippling parochialism, settling in places of the world far outside England's borders and calling themselves "British residents" in the colonies they ruled, it was foolish, argued Macaulay, to believe that the nationalism spurring Englishmen to extend England's borders could be sustained for long if English society continued to be run on exclusionary principles. Invoking a long history of religious persecution in Europe that forever complicated national loyalties, Macaulay pointedly observed that oppressed groups had greater affinity to kindred groups outside the country than to their own countrymen—certain proof, he claimed, that policies of exclusion harmed the nation's long-term interests more than it could have imagined:

> If there be any proposition universally true in politics, it is this, that foreign attachments are the fruit of domestic misrule. It has always been the trick of bigots . . . to govern as if a section of the state were the whole and to censure the other sections of the state for their want of patriotic spirit. If the Jews have not felt towards England like children, it is because she has treated them like a stepmother. . . . Till we have carried the experiment, we are not entitled to conclude that they cannot be made Englishmen altogether. The English Jews are, as far as we can see, precisely what our government has made them.[11]

In this passionate call for admitting Jews, Macaulay turns the tables around by denouncing as unpatriotic not the Jews but rather the English state for failing to extend the virtues of good government to all sections of society. If Jews were imbued with a greater sense of their religious than their national identity, Macaulay tried to rationalize Jews' apparent lack of English feeling by arguing that their disloyalty was state-produced. By shifting the Jews' insularity to an effect of state policy, rather than a cause of their exclusion from citizenship, Macaulay brilliantly undermined the rhetoric of patriotism cushioning the English state, which found it convenient to condemn the very behavior it created.

At the same time, Macaulay's interest in Jewish emancipation was not driven solely by his wish to see the liberal promise of the English state fulfilled. The language he employed in arguing for Jewish civil relief on the grounds of administrative efficiency had a strongly utilitarian dimension, echoing his Anglicist philosophy of making colonized Indians "good subjects of the empire":

> On our principles all civil disabilities on account of religious opinions are indefensible. For all such disabilities make government less efficient for its main end; they limit the choice of able men for the administration and defense of the State; they alienate it from the hearts of the sufferers; they deprive it of a part of its operative strength in all contests with foreign nations.[12]

When this passage is compared with Macaulay's proposed program to educate Indians in English language and literature, the strength of his belief in the power of secular governance appears almost uncanny in hindsight:

> In India, English is the language spoken by the ruling class. It is spoken by the higher class of natives at the seats of Government. It is likely to become the

language of commerce throughout the seas of the East. . . . There is now in that country a large educated class, abounding with persons fit to serve the state in the highest functions, and in no wise inferior to the most accomplished men who adorn the best circles of Paris and London. There is reason to hope that this vast empire, which in the time of our grandfathers was probably behind the Punjab, may, in the time of our grandchildren, be pressing close on France and Britain in the career of improvement.[13]

The debate on citizenship, as worked out by Macaulay in such pragmatic terms in both the Indian and English contexts, is clearly less focused on cultural adaptation than on progressively secularizing religious identity into an autonomously conceived national identity.

In the great secularization movements of the nineteenth century from which the modern state takes its present form, it is possible to discern, if not the origins of modern religious and ethnic strife, then at least prototypical enactments of the drama of citizenship. This drama unendingly complicated itself by questioning and rethinking the possibilities of dual allegiances brought on by such things as—in England, for instance—legislation to enfranchise religious minorities in the wake of national union and disestablishment: Could an Englishman be both English *and* Catholic, Jewish, Nonconformist? As a result of altered relations between church and state the concept of nationality, which had hitherto relied on an unquestioned equation of Englishness with mainstream Anglicanism, had necessarily to undergo drastic transformation. No longer characterized by formal oaths of allegiance to doctrine and creed, Englishness accretes in significance as a function of the incorporative logic of law, administrative rationality, and constitutional principles of liberty. When swearing by the Thirty Nine Articles of the Anglican creed or by parliamentary oaths ceases to be the primary condition for admission to Oxford or Cambridge, parliamentary seats, or voting rights, a new order of citizenship is called forth based on criteria of legal rather than religious inclusion.

The first phase of the movement for legal emancipation of religious minorities culminated in the legislative successes of 1828, when Protestant Dissenters, including Unitarians who repudiated the doctrine of the Trinity, won civil relief from disabling legislation—the Test and Corporation Acts—that had until then prevented them from sitting in parliament, among other restrictions. M.C.N. Salbstein comments on this moment as one of the most dramatic in the history of the English nation: "The vital Anglican principle of the constitution had been breached."[14] Yet, despite this initial breakthrough, certain disabilities still remained. Until 1830, Dissenting chapels could not be registered for marriage and Dissenters were obliged to have their marriages solemnized in the Church. Nor were Dissenters entitled to perform their own burial rites in parish churchyards until the Burial Bill of 1880 became law. Church rates, always a source of discontent, were not remedied until as late as 1868. But the parlia-

mentary repeal of the loathsome Test and Corporation acts in 1828 provided
some relief to Dissenters, and this legislation was soon followed, in 1829, by
parliamentary emancipation for Catholics.

The charge of divided loyalty leveled against Catholics in the decades prior
to the emancipatory legislation of 1829 had kept alive the specter of foreign
sources of power, such as the fear of papal supremacy that threatened to sub-
vert England's power from within. Denial of foreign allegiance and dual loyalty became an obligatory feature of Catholic arguments, so much so that
members of a committee formed in 1787 for the purpose of negotiating with
the governent to win emancipation decided to call themselves the Protesting
Catholic Dissenters. The Test Acts of the 1670s, along with the required vows
of allegiance to the tenets of Anglican England, had functioned for some time
as safety valves against the augmentation of Catholic power. By the late eighteenth century, however, some relaxation of restrictive legislation was in evidence, and though Catholics and Jews were still excluded from public office,
annual indemnity acts to Protestant Dissenters showed a new mood of permis-
sive practice that augured well for other religious groups.

In part, the concessions to Catholics in 1829 were inevitable responses by
the English government to the volatility of the Irish situation and the political
pressures created by it. Although Catholic Ireland remained associated with
external threat to British civil peace, summoning up the fearsome image of
powerful foreign enemies consolidating their strength through the covert support of England's Catholic subjects, a distinctive feature of the discourse on
dual loyalties emphasized attachments to the Irish Catholic hierarchy rather
than to Rome. This emphasis specifically linked the growth of Irish identity
with the resolution of the Catholic question. Within Ireland the movement for
Catholic emancipation served to redress social and economic ills, protest
against which had begun to shape Irish peasant nationalism. Because Irish
identity was so closely imbricated with the destiny of Catholicism—as distinct
from the papal attachments that made Catholicism so foreign in the minds of
Englishmen—the threat posed by civil dissension on religious principles substantially persuaded the English parliament to relax the entrenched disabling
legislation of the past. That the chroniclers of English parliamentary history
chose to present religious emancipation not as the result of revolutionary
change but rather as the consummation of a "liberalizing adjustment to the
constitution" has remained an abiding definition of English tolerance.[15]
Downplaying its own anxiety over the Irish question, Britain's collective
memory highlighted an emerging climate of tolerance and goodwill as the
motive-force of Catholic emancipation. To help their former opponents make
the best of a potentially humiliating situation, many English Catholics gladly
went along later with the myth that emancipation represented "not a triumph
of strength but rather a victory for abstract principles of liberality."[16]

These developments in the Dissenting and Catholic communities encouraged Anglo-Jews to believe that the time was ripe for a similar extension of

civil liberties to their own community. The Jews in Britain, like the Roman Catholics, saw themselves as part of a larger religious group having ties that superseded national boundaries. When Anglo-Jews perceived that Catholic emancipation was not stymied by the vexing problems of dual loyalty to spiritual and temporal authority, they were encouraged to believe that their claims to English citizenship too would receive a more favorable hearing than had historically been the case.

But even after the acts of 1828 and 1829 conferred substantial benefits on Dissenters and Catholics, the Jews remained the only major religious group to whom civil restrictions still applied; it took much longer, for instance, for their exclusion from municipal office and parliament to be reversed. Far from preparing the ground for Jewish emancipation, Catholic relief stiffened Anglican opposition to extending the same reform momentum to Jews. Citing the profession of Judaism as categorically disqualifying Jews from public office, Gladstone distinguished between the admission of non-Anglican Christians and the admission of professing Jews. The operative word is "professing." In 1847 Gladstone delivered an impassioned speech in support of removing Jewish disabilities, noting that such a move would develop a secular community of Jews rather than "professing" believers, who ironically thrived in a culture that practiced politics of exclusion.

By this time, of course, Gladstone had done an abrupt *volte face* and openly embarked on the road to liberalism. His earlier position, as adumbrated in *The State in Its Relations with the Church* (1839), made different claims about integrated church-state relations, which left him open to fierce attack. For instance, Macaulay's review of Gladstone's theory "that the propagation of religious truth is one of the principal ends of government, as government" is one of the most sustained critiques of this seasoned politician in nineteenth-century letters.[17] In "Gladstone on Church and State," Macaulay minutely tears apart Gladstone's effort to yoke temporal and spiritual interests and categorically asserts that "no two objects more entirely distinct can well be imagined" than "the protection of the persons and estates of citizens from injury" and "the propagation of religious truth."[18]

Not only do these two goals create a conflict of interests: Macaulay believes that Gladstone's philosophy confounds the purposes of government, obliging it to assume responsibity for the religious character of the state when its true raison d'être is the protection of its citizens' material interests. Macaulay's trenchant critique of Gladstone's moral state rests on the fear that the obligatory profession of religion reintroduces practices of exclusion and discrimination, despite Gladstone's reassurance that he was less interested in the propagation of Christianity than in the profession of religion in general, even one as unpalatable to Gladstone as Islam.

In any event, despite Gladstone's intervention in the 1840s, the formal admission of Jews to parliament came only in 1858, well after the concessions to Nonconformists and Catholics. Concurrent with attempts to admit atheists into parliament, which bore fruition only as late as 1882 when Charles Bradlaugh became the first atheist to assume a seat in parliament, Jewish admission consolidated the secular state by detaching religious qualifications from national identity. Until this time, as long as allegiance to the articles of faith remained a prerequisite to such things as a seat in parliament and education at Oxford or Cambridge, an Englishman was defined in terms of his membership in the Anglican church. Whig attempts to modify the parliamentary oath, which contained the words "on the true faith of a Christian," were repeatedly defeated in the House of Lords. When the Jewish Relief Act was finally passed in 1858, other developments were already under way in the mid-nineteenth century that facilitated the admission of Jews. In the 1850s Oxford University ceased to require submission to the Thirty-Nine Articles on matriculation. Practically speaking, however, full access to the degrees of Oxford and Cambridge was available to all non-Anglicans only after 1871, when Gladstone's government passed the Universities Tests Act, finally removing all disabilities. This act opened all degrees and offices to individuals of any religion, as well as to those who practiced none. Despite the latter clause, however, atheists still had a difficult time circumventing the residual pull of the parliamentary and promissory oaths that, by the 1880s, had acquired the weight of tradition and practice. When Charles Bradlaugh was elected from the borough of Northampton in 1880 but was debarred from sitting in parliament because he insisted on making a solemn declaration rather than taking an oath, his fight to sever the nation's ties to religious oaths took England into the last phase of the move to lift civil disabilities. On gaining his seat, Bradlaugh introduced a general affirmation bill, replacing oaths, that became law in 1888.

The incorporation of Dissenting groups, Catholics, and Jews now dispensed with the concept of heretic as defining what a true Englishman was *not*. By the mid-nineteenth century, with criteria of doctrinal allegiance no longer determining Englishness, national identity increasingly required a differentiation between political and civil society. Civil society emerged as the privatized domain onto which were displaced a variety of religious distinctions that had no place in political society, or in what came to be construed as the more transcendent plane of secularism. Secularization not only polarizes national and religious identity; it also privatizes belief and renders it subordinate to the claims of reason, logic, and evidence. Henceforth all these claims are identified with the rationality of the state and its institutions.

Not coincidentally, 1858 is also the year when the English Crown formally wrested control of India from the private East India Company. The Crown's consolidation of colonial governance, however, continued to honor the Company's policy of administering India by secular principle, for example, in such fields as education. The overlapping of a secular educational agenda for colonial subjects with the decline of ecclesiastical authority in England has several implications that become positively combustible when these developments are juxtaposed to the effects of emancipatory legislation admitting excluded religious minorities in England. First, this concurrence of events introduces a politics of identity into both English and colonial life, where the grounds for Englishness are increasingly determined by the individual's ability to become detached from the *content* of local or regional affiliations while maintaining their form. Second, the strengthening of the English state is predicated not by a single unified framework of ecclesiastical or missionizing doctrine but by the absorption of racial and religious "others" into a secular, pluralistic fabric. And third, a centralized administrative machinery is set in place whose legislative capacity displaces the authority of religious bodies to determine the criteria for membership in the community.

But the overlay also contains a number of problematic dimensions that suggest the uneven development of colonizing and colonized societies, even while both may be driven by a comparable trajectory. The difference crucially hinges on the issue of civil enfranchisement. The possibilities of religious emancipation in the English situation permit religion to be more "naturally" identified as a necessary prior stage in the progression toward nationhood. Religious differences, although present as established social categories, are neutralized as they are subsumed within a national identity. The split occurs along the axes of citizenship and subjecthood. Religious tolerance in England is, by definition, the process that emancipates religious minorities from existing civil disabilities and enables previously marginalized groups to participate in the nation state. Of course, the fact that religious enfranchisement effectively displaces the extension of the franchise across social classes creates tensions of another kind that have persisted in English social history. These social tensions are vividly exemplified by the fraught narrative structures of a number of important Victorian novels about sectarian conflict, such as Charles Dickens's *Barnaby Rudge*.

Although the modern English state is constructed on the premise that formerly excluded religious groups are duly given the rights of citizenship, such a premise can be no more than conditional in colonial societies, and religion continues to be an unassimilable and resistant marker of political difference. Secularization in the colonies remains a flawed project, even more than in England, because of the absence of an emancipatory logic that steers a once monolithic religious culture into the gradual absorption of pluralized groups into the nation state. Secularization in India has always been a fraught process driven by unresolvable tensions, due partly to the fact that parliamentary reform, which enabled religious minorities in England to be absorbed as citizens, failed to perform a comparable function in India. There, obviously, state formation is basically incorporation of subjects into a *colonial* state and, following national independence, into a hegemonic state in which the social relations sanctioned by colonialism continue virtually uninterrupted.

Furthermore, England's policy of religious neutrality had always officially resisted endorsing missionary proselytization and substituted "Englishness" for "Christianity" as the defining principle of subjecthood, even while retaining the moral foundations of Christianity. The administration of colonial law in matters involving Christian conversions is a case in point. Even when Hindus or Muslims were converting to Christianity, the decisions made by the civil courts denied that such conscious change occurred, and the Christian convert was treated as essentially someone who had *not* converted. The particular situations that brought the British resistance to religious change out into the open also challenged colonial administrators, paradoxically, to defend the rights of converts against the punitive actions of Hindu or Muslim personal law. But while seeming to protect the rights of converts, the application of English law severed Christian converts from a larger communion of Christians to which native converts erroneously believed they had been admitted. Their religious identity was subsequently recast in the form of the religion they had renounced.

The nexus between the convert as religious dissenter and the convert as colonial subject broadens the scope of conversion narratives to include a transcultural perspective not otherwise visible in nineteenth-century texts. By the mid-nineteenth century, the disempowerment of ecclesiastical authority in England gave civil courts the right to refuse judgment on the truth value of dissenting opinion or to make determinations about doctrinal meaning. Although belief is placed outside the space of public discourse in English culture, such a move is rendered problematic in the culture of the colonies. The clean separation between belief and law is less manageable when applied to converts in colonial India. For, like religious minorities in England, converts struggle against punitive restrictions imposed by their former community and seek to reverse their condition of exile and excommunication.

Yet, unlike minority groups who accepted emancipation as their right of entry into England's public life, even at the cost of renouncing the specificity of their religious identity, for colonial converts such renunciation is a denial of their conversion itself and therefore not reconcilable with the state's offer to protect them from caste disabilities. The resistances of converts to the legislated solutions worked out in colonial courts cannot be construed as local events, pertinent only to relations of colonial subordination. Rather, the appeal made by converts to the legitimacy of their religious subjectivity forced a reform-oriented English law to deal instead with the question of their rights under the law, even as it also sought to minimize the relevance of converts' religious beliefs. The norms of liberal discourse set by the alignments between state, religion, and culture in nineteenth-century England are ultimately exposed as insufficient and hollow. For although these norms propose religious subjectivity as part of a privatized realm of meaning—and therefore beyond the purview of the secular courts—the challenge of managing colonial conversions required the British government to disavow this notion and publicly adjudicate the claims of converts, often in civil courts. That a *legislated* subjectivity resulted from such adjudication introduces an even more conflictual element into the already fraught relations between belief and law.

The colonial disturbance of the categories of liberal humanism as well as of the norms of public-private transactions exposes a deeper split in English social and intellectual history. The cultural ideology within which narratives of conversion in British colonialism are interpretable is obviously not limited to the discourse of civil law, though it is within the secular structures of civil legislation that the social rewriting of conversion takes place most regularly. The liberal spirit of tolerance that entered English public life by the mid-nineteenth century did indeed enfranchise Dissenters, Roman Catholics, and Jews, whose incorporation into the structures of political governance showed an England moving toward a more open pluralism in which a multiplicity of beliefs was seemingly acknowledged. One critic describes the new public space created by enfranchisement as the "deregulated market of religious belief."[19] Certainly the ascendancy of courts of appeal—with the state's refusal to pronounce judgment on the rightness or wrongness of dissenting opinion— appeared to rob the church of its spiritual authority. The Gorham judgment of 1850 opened up a breach between church and state that Gladstone had long feared would overtake England; when the determination of doctrinal meaning was declared outside the function of a secular body like the Judicial Committee of the Privy Council, the break seemed to be complete. It is no coincidence that the Privy Council was originally intended primarily to hear appeals from the colonies, even though later, as a secular body, it came to exercise jurisdiction as a court of final appeal in ecclesiastical cases.

But what did it actually mean for civil courts to desist from deciding what was theological truth—and from placing "tariffs on dissent"[20]—and leave matters of faith to private judgment? The state's relegation of doctrine to private interpretation followed from its insistence on preserving the so-called heretic's legal rights to whatever position he or she held prior to being accused of heresy. As long as a dissenter's beliefs were basically compatible with the doctrines laid down in the Church's Articles, the question of heresy did not arise. What might have been an opinion contrary to accepted doctrinal meanings was declared nonheretical by the Privy Council according to the standards of compatibility. Accentuated by the spirit of secularization, the new tolerance may have been the first step toward separating religious belief from social identity. The abolition of tests of religious belief in parliament, the relaxation of the laws of blasphemy, and the removal of divorce from the ecclesiastical realm all combined, as Anton Lentin notes, to "shift religion to the ceremonial margins of state affairs."[21]

In a regime mediated by law, the tolerant secular state is the foundation for an English national identity in which differences of belief are effaced. While individual rights are protected—and the rectitude of law is upheld—the self-definitions and beliefs held by individuals are made irrelevant in the national incorporation of previously excluded dissenting sects. In not only rendering self-perceptions of religious identity no more than a formal subset of social classification but also leaving no place for private faith altogether, the usurpation of spiritual authority by the mid-nineteenth-century English state highlighted the failure of Anglicanism and the national church to provide such authority. The British census of 1851 placed half of England's worshiping population as Nonconformists, indicating the extent to which the language of dissent was expressed as belief.[22] If dissent is framed as a protest against the legislation and standardization of religious belief, it is just as stridently a revolt against a political society obliged to efface self-definitions in order to protect individual rights. The fact that many Tractarians were prompted to convert to Roman Catholicism following the decline of church authority reveals how steadily dissent was being consolidated as the religion of belief. The growing incidence of conversions to Roman Catholicism points to a rejection of national definitions and national institutions, even when (or perhaps because) the national spirit was expressed as tolerance and liberalism.[23]

If dissent expresses itself most powerfully as conversion, particularly to minority religions, the reasons are not hard to understand. By undoing the concept of fixed, unalterable identities, conversion unsettles the boundaries by which selfhood, citizenship, nationhood, and community are defined, exposing these as permeable borders. Shifts in religious consciousness traverse the contained order of culture and subtly dislodge its measured alignments, belying the false assurance that only change from the outside has the power to disrupt. The indeterminacy of conversion poses a radical threat to the trajectory of nationhood, and this is not only because it scrambles the categories of religious identification neatly kept in place by bureaucratic logic. Conversions to a mainstream religion are as disruptive to the state as are conversions to alternative or minority religions.

Of course, value-laden terms like "majority" and "minority" have a numerical significance, which corresponds to the power relations that produce them. On one hand, conversion to a dominant religion consolidates the making of a cohesive nation by bringing renegade individuals and disparate religious communities into a unified single tradition. It is, after all, through such a cobbled tradition that social identities are fashioned. But on the other side, conversion undoes the settled patterns of a community's composition and the certainty with which its practices are followed and regularized. These disruptions produce antagonistic relations between individuals and families, majority and minority cultures, and religious communities and their renegade offshoots.

At the same time these conflicts also constitute the necessary tensions from which the modern state derives its own identity as supreme legislator and arbitrator. Transcending the internal antagonisms set off by departures from the fold, the state acts to establish its authority as disinterested judge and protector of rights. As disruptive as it might seem, conversion also brings to a focus an essential role of the state in modernity: the restoration of a fixed, unassailable point of reference from which cleavages within communities are addressed. If conversion precipitates breaches within the fold, it also sets in motion a dynamic social process that confers a new power and role on the state.

Although conversion histories are undoubtedly a source of oppositional expression, the degree to which these potentially counterhegemonic narratives are undermined by legislative processes or economic rationality deserves much closer attention than they have thus far received. Because its threatening capacity to alter social symmetries generates the internal conflicts that bring about state intervention, conversion both as a process and an event is crucially relevant to the state's self-definition as a regulator of belief. The paradox, of course, lies in the fact that the value of conversion for the state lies not only in its assimilative but also its dissenting aspects. Dissent, as much as assimilation, is the necessary disruptive mechanism for the exercise of tolerance by the state. Incidents of conversion in society enable the state to demonstrate a unity larger than the community, splintered as the latter is by the departure of members from its fold.

For this reason, the resistances of converts to the erasure of their subjectivity are split equally between two objects: on the one hand, against their former community, which threatens to excommunicate and impose civil disabilities; and on the other, against the state, which promises to protect converts' civil rights but in exchange for subsuming converts' religious conviction and belief within predetermined official categories. This latter maneuver has been recognized in feminist scholarship, which points out the problematic nature of the modern state for women by presenting itself as both guarantor of rights and usurper of female subjectivity. But this contradiction has yet to be adequately theorized as a position of liminality created by the nature of religious dissent from prevailing class and gender codes, cultural norms, religious orthodoxies, and systems of authority. One of the most notorious cases in recent Indian history illustrates the fraught relations between the modern state and female subjectivity. In a 1986 civil suit that went up to the Indian Supreme Court, a divorced Muslim woman, Shah Bano, vainly sought maintenance support from her husband under the Criminal Procedure Code after he had divorced her, claiming the prerogatives of Muslim personal law.[24] If resistance to patriarchal authority often leads women to seek protection from the state for injustices and cruelties perpetrated on them—as did Shah Bano—the conditionality of state support closes off room for the articulation of female oppositional energies *as female*. The protection extended to women on the grounds of their constitutional rights is conceived primarily in the abstract and without regard to gendered circumstances. In the case of female converts like Huchi, whose affecting case is the core of Chapter Three, the double dislocation is even more striking, because not only female subjectivity but also religious belief is transmuted into a category of social identity. Trapped in a liminal space of nullified private experience, the female convert is banished from the public space of legislative reason and patriarchal authority, both of which combine to render her conversion experiences not only irrelevant but also subversive.

Indeed, the cooptation of oppositional voices in conversion histories by prevailing norms of national definition presents a set of textual problems that can best be studied in relation to the formative secular discourses of the state. The principal textual phenomenon is the disappearance of converts' subjectivity altogether in texts (legal as well as literary) that advocate their essential rights under the law. The peculiar challenges of self-representation are no different for converts than they are for dissenters and heretics, whose legal identity is at variance with their professed faiths. If the secular state's task is to accommodate the rights of disenfranchised religious dissenters to the proper functioning of organic communities, without diminishing either, the defense of constitutional liberty places abstract principles over and above the religious subjectivity of converts. An account of their own spiritual and material needs is virtually refined out of existence, rendering their religious identity hollow and insubstantial.

When the problem of self-representation of converts and religious dissenters appears as an issue in colonial texts, it merges with the problem of representation of colonial subjects in general in the English novel. Because the nineteenth-century English novel has considerable salience in highlighting vexing questions of voice, agency, and representation, and because these questions also dominate analysis of the textual presence of converts—a presence at times so elusive and impalpable as to turn converts into abstractions—a methodological convergence between the representation of converts and that of colonial subjects is not surprising. In a subtle Bakhtinian reading of how the novel form employs complex, multivocal systems only to deny them, Graham Pechey has argued that, though dialogism in the English novel exists as the liberal incorporation of hegemonic and subaltern voices, it finally affirms only the voice of the dominant subject as the voice of active agency.[25] The colonized, he argues, are never the second person in dialogue; in the bulk of nineteenth-century English novels, as Edward Said too has shown in *Culture and Imperialism*, the peripheral places occupied by colonial subjects are a mute testimony not only to the imperial reach but also to an imperializing literary form.[26]

If the English novel limits the essential dialogism of the material it works with into a monologism based on lines of class, gender, and racial power, this is no less true of the judicial narrative. In court cases such as the ones described in Chapter Three, testimony provided by the convert is repeatedly challenged by the dramatic structure of cross-examination, interruption, interrogation, and judicial pronouncement framing the testimony. In each case, again both historical and literary, converts are the ground rather than the subject or even object (the British records are neither of or about converts) on which the whole question of rights is worked out. The crucial point of reference is the state, which performs the dual move of effacing the religiosity of individuals and groups, while at the same time ensuring their rights to such things as property, conjugality, and guardianship. In so doing, the state ensures its own self-constitution, indeed its very genealogy, from the disinterested principles of tolerance.

Prominent in judicial records, this dual move is repeated in literary writing, though not unproblematically. Indeed, the difficulties of sustaining a seamless narrative without suppressing the voice of active agency often cause narratives to buckle under the sheer weight of insupportable contradictions. Novels about the civil emancipation of religious minorities particularly reveal the fragility of secular postures. Such novels bear comparison with narratives of conversion because both types of works are centrally concerned with exploring questions of inclusion and exclusion. If the former works more narrowly within existing religious categories, even effacing them in order to assert the supremacy of the tolerant state, the latter by definition must be capacious enough to imagine different positions within society. Such differences illuminate the generic possibilities of the conversion narrative as it, too, seeks to find a place for converts without denying the fact of their difference.

SECTARIAN FICTIONS

By working in the interstices of simultaneous developments in the English metropolis and the colonies, we may productively examine how discourses of religious identity are produced, contained, or opposed by the languages of law, reason, and classification identified with the modern secular state. Our specific challenge is to evaluate the degree to which English texts (both literary and nonliterary) participate in—as well as offer the terms for—the constructions of religious identity and selfhood in the culture at large. The critical question at hand, in other words, is how English texts reflect both the uncertainties of official definitions and the legitimacy of their operative premises.

If sectarianism can be understood as one of the effects produced by discourses of religious identity, a cross-referential approach may yield a more complex picture of intertwined histories and intertextualities. Consequently, such an approach will obviate the facile turn to a language of differential development often deployed to describe religious violence in developing societies, as for example in Ernest Gellner's recent book on the subject.[27] No doubt, sectarianism in postcolonial societies such as India has been extensively studied as a byproduct of British representational strategies, which reduced socioeconomic conflicts in indigenous societies to incidents of religious fanaticism.[28] However, the same degree of critical attention has not been given to the proposition that a convulsive history of religious dissent and discriminations in English culture functions as an interpretive grid through which religious identity is re-imagined and re-presented in colonial and post-colonial texts.

In this and the chapters that follow, I shall offer readings of several different types of narratives—literary, historical, ethnographic, and juridical—to argue, among other things, that the secular state's struggle to preserve difference while striving for religious tolerance and inclusiveness is often too over-whelming for narrative form to handle. The overburdened narrative structure of two striking nineteenth-century works—Maria Edgeworth's *Harrington* (1817) and Charles Dickens's *Barnaby Rudge* (1841)—slips into contradic-tory class and gender positions that reveal the difficulties of sustaining the logic of emancipation. The lapse occurs even as these novels attempt to work out incorporative strategies of containing religious difference while making gestures toward its recognition and protection. As responses to Jewish and Catholic relief, respectively, *Harrington* and *Barnaby Rudge* reveal that their authors were deeply conversant with the most pressing debates of the time about civil emancipation. Yet the novels also reflect a fundamental ambiva-lence about the absorption of religious minorities, as indicated by their com-mon search for a touchstone of moral values lying beyond the pluralistic com-position of the English state. Both novels aspire to acknowledge and accept Jewish and Catholic difference, while making a claim for religious tolerance as the essence of English Protestantism and an English national identity tran-scending sectarian affiliations. In the long run, Maria Edgeworth's *Harrington* and Charles Dickens's *Barnaby Rudge* end up affirming the dominant commu-nity of English Protestants, while making gestures toward extending political rights of citizenship to Jews and Catholics. Indeed, the pressures on literary form to manage conflicting social tendencies, which are often resolved by neutralizing and absorbing religious difference into a uniform social identity, uncannily reproduce the anxieties of a secular world in dealing with threaten-ing religious excess.

Edgeworth's novel is in some respects a psychological rather than political exploration of Jewish emancipation. Though *Harrington* rehearses the various political debates about the status of English Jews, its real interest lies in a discovery of the sources of anti-Semitism. Maria Edgeworth wrote the novel in 1817 primarily as a corrective to the impression of anti-Semitism conveyed by her earlier novels. Piqued by one of her readers in America, Rachel Morde-cai, who plaintively wrote a letter asking why the author allowed herself to perpetuate prevailing stereotypes of Jews, Edgeworth set out to correct both her own prior misunderstandings and the historical record in general. Absorb-ing an enormous amount of Anglo-Jewish history through her wide reading, she planned to write a novel that charted the progress of England toward the enlightened acceptance of Jews, paralleling her own gradual embrace of a more receptive attitude toward Jews.

However, at several crucial points *Harrington* belies its author's intents. Edgeworth's novel battles to preserve Jewish difference while arguing for religious tolerance and the positive virtues of Jewish naturalization. At the same time *Harrington* strives uncomfortably to accommodate the concept of an English Jew: a rich Spanish Jew, however, poses fewer problems, making it possible for Edgeworth to delineate the foreign banker Montenero as if he were an English aristocrat. As one of the novel's major characters, Harrington senior, remarks, "Mr. Montenero, I observed, looked down upon Baldwin all the time with so much the air of a high-bred gentleman, that I began to think he could not be the Jew—Montenero." His comment is followed up by Baldwin's observation that "your Jew, Harrington, came up to me and with such a manner as I did not conceive a Jew could have—but he is a Spanish Jew—that makes all the difference, I suppose."[29] The novel's proliferation of different classes and nationalities of Jews—the poor English Jacob, the wealthy Spaniard Montenero, the self-consciously extravagant Hebrew scholar Israel Lyons, and then of course the ultimate simulacrum of a Jew, namely, the English Macklin playing Shakespeare's Shylock—reflects the author's uneasiness in dealing with the Jewish question on its own terms, as well as her failure to define Jewishness beyond the typologies in which her comprehension was trapped. Edgeworth's narrative revives issues brought up by the Jewish Naturalization Bill of 1753, which was proposed in order to help foreign-born Jews overcome trading hurdles by removing the difficulties they faced in seeking naturalization. But by conflating the conflict over the bill with the Gordon riots of 1780 against the proposed Catholic Relief Act, Edgeworth broadens the discussion of anti-Semitic stereotyping to encompass the extension of citizenship rights to religious minorities in general. And by further yoking anti-Semitism to francophobia, she explicitly introduces the idea that religious and national identities are fundamentally overlapping:

> The very day before Mr. Montenero was to leave town, without any conceivable reason, suddenly a cry was raised against the Jews: unfortunately Jews rhymed to shoes: these words were hitched into a rhyme, and the cry was "No Jews, no wooden shoes!" Thus without any natural, civil, religious or moral or political connexion, the poor Jews came in remainder to the ancient anti-Gallican antipathy felt by English feet and English fancies against the French wooden shoes.[30]

The novel's conclusion, which reveals that the daughter of the wealthy Jew Montenero is Christian and English even as it distances the father as Jewish and Spanish, rehearses the public debates over the legal status of the Jews since readmission. The difficulty of assimilating Jews in English society, even from a seemingly liberal point of view, has a narrative counterpart in the figurative conversion of Berenice to Christianity. Her "conversion" is not only a convenient device to smoothe the plot's ragged edges but also a concession to the limits of tolerance. The novel responds to the sensitive issue of Jews having to accept the sacrament shortly before their naturalization by preempting

such a potentially volatile situation altogether: the heroine Berenice is presented as already Christian and her father Montenero as irreversibly foreign.
Berenice is reassuringly preserved as English, and the threat of miscegenation
is indefinitely deferred and successfully kept outside the history of the English
nation.

Edgeworth describes the history of religious identity in relation to the nation
as always contradictory and conflictual. At its core the nation is profoundly
irrational (as seen in its racial bigotry), but at the level of official secularism the
nation is also capable of showing tolerance. The novel strains to resolve these
fundamental contradictions, but it can do so only by two means: first, by re-
verting to figurative conversion as a principle of narrative closure; and second,
by discharging its persistent bigotry on the socially alienated or disenfranchised classes, so that the myth of religious tolerance is still upheld as a principle of the social whole.[31] In *Harrington* the disaffected servant Fowler functions as the chief purveyor of sectarian prejudice. Her apparently infinite
capacity for anti-Semitism is undiminished by newly issued legal measures
against religious discrimination, yet her usefulness for the plot lies in her being
at once outside the (untarnished) class system and a necessary rallying point
for an English nationalism still driven by a majoritarian logic. Just as Dickens
later makes the subaltern classes of servants, unskilled workers, and women
the chief instruments of religious bigotry—and synonymous with the malevolence of the body politic—so too, in her novel about religious tolerance, Edgeworth confines the culture's ineradicable intolerance to the dispensable servant
classes. For instance, in an ironic reversal of the anti-Semitic novel where the
Jew is sent into exile from England, the maid Fowler (whose name is a deliberate pun on "foul") is banished to America at the end of the novel.[32] The novel's
depiction of England's linear progression toward civil emancipation is fractured by its own rationalizations of a lingering anti-Semitism in England,
which is rendered as class prejudice.

Both Edgeworth's and Dickens's novels cite the threat of continued unrest
and agitation by militant Protestants against Jewish and Catholic emancipation
as the chief cause for the reluctance of English civil authority to emancipate
religious minorities fully. One of the most memorable images of Dickens's
Barnaby Rudge is that of Dennis the hangman, whose identification with English legislative processes is so complete that he sees his profession as literally
allowing him to be the executor (in more senses than one) of Parliament's will:
"So I do [truly hate Papists]. . . . I'm a constitutional officer that works for my
living, and does my work creditable. . . . My work is sound, Protestant, constitutional, English work."[33] Recounting the hanging of Mary Jones, a poor
woman condemned for stealing a piece of cloth, he boasts:

> That being the law and the practice of England, is the glory of England. . . . If our
> grandsons should think of their grandfathers' times, and find these things altered,
> they'll say, "Those were days indeed, and we've been going down hill ever since."

. . . If these Papists gets into power, and begins to boil and roast instead of hang, what becomes of my work! If they touch my work that's a part of so many laws, what becomes of the laws in general, what becomes of the religion, what becomes of the country?"[34]

Dennis's complete identification with English law suffers from a time lag. The laws that he believes he is carrying out as hangman are themselves altered, and the anti-Catholicism that defines his vocation and gives it a weighty purpose is undone by the very state he serves—and strengthens—with every hanging. Catholic emancipation disorients Dennis precisely because it alienates his work from constitutional will. His comical egocentrism cannot absorb the changefulness of the state. Nor can it accept the fact that parliamentary laws do not embody the certainties of religious distinctions, which give Englishness and Protestantism their durable character. Threatened by a sense of his own superfluity, Dennis allays his anxieties by imagining that it is the state which is under threat, its will having been hijacked by antinational forces.

At the same time, Dickens's novel, like Edgeworth's, is also determined to present the English state's full commitment to promoting national consolidation beyond sectarian borders. That goal, however, is attainable only when the state acknowledges its obligation to protect the rights of all groups—with the tacit understanding, of course, that those rights do not conflict with the religious creed of the majority faith. In amalgamating the particular identity of Jews, Catholics, and other religious minorities into a generalized secular identity, the English state presented in these novels upholds national identity in its most diffuse form. Conceived thus, religious tolerance achieves its supreme expression as an act of incorporation, consolidation, and homogenization.

For this reason, the discourse of tolerance cannot abide either militant actions against the state or state actions against expressions of popular will. Dickens may be advocating religious tolerance, but he is also aware that incidents of popular anarchy based on religious bigotry cannot be reductively analyzed in terms of an irrational, easily manipulatable populace against a just, rational state. The mob's irrationality is the visible part of the sublimated religious bigotry of the nation, which Dickens seeks to present as the embodiment of reason. Yet Dickens rejects the state as a source of tolerant behavior and reverts to a romantic revival of pure belief as the only solution to sectarian violence. *Barnaby Rudge* epitomizes the historical dislocations between literature and legitimations of nation. In this work the state does not emerge as a hero for protecting Catholics against the mob. Instead, the timidity of figures like the Lord Mayor and the ineffectiveness of the city aldermen and magistrates expose the vast gap between civil and military authority, much to the frustration of the army, which regards the recourse to law as a major cause for the deferment of direct action. Impatient to quell mass rebellion by the use of military might, the English militia represents a nationalism that works in a direction contrary to a nationalism based on the doctrine of rights and equal protection under the law. Dickens's novel is unable to negotiate this split; consequently, he cannot present the state as the protagonist of his political drama because it is itself riven by two forms of action/inaction. Indeed, Steven Marcus interprets the novel's lower status in the Dickens canon as a result of readers' "discomfort" with its political nature, especially since Dickens "apparently came out for the wrong side" in the struggle for political power in England.[35]

Dickens's *Barnaby Rudge* repeats many of the issues raised by Sir George Savile's petition for the emancipation of Catholics back in 1778—an act that sparked off numerous anti-Catholic riots. Yet however serious Dickens's purpose may be in seeking a place for religious minorities in the English political system—even those, like Catholics, for whom he had no real sympathy—he is not able to invest enough faith in Englishness as a positive ideal to replace religious identification. On the contrary, Englishness is associated with the worst traits of the most evil character in the novel, Sir John Chester, whose Machiavellianism is a suitable complement to the sectarian passions of the mob:

> I thought I was tolerably accomplished as a man of the world. I flattered myself that I was pretty well versed in all those little arts and graces which distinguish men of the world from boors and peasants, and separate their character from those intensely vulgar sentiments which are called the national character. Apart from any natural prepossession in my own favour, I believed I was. Still, in every page of this enlightened writer [Lord Chesterfield], I find some captivating hypocrisy which has never occurred to me before, or some superlative piece of selfishness to which I was utterly a stranger. I should quite blush for myself before this stupendous creature, if, remembering his precepts, one might blush at anything. An amazing man! a nobleman indeed! any King or Queen may make a Lord, but only the Devil himself—and the Graces—can make a Chesterfield.[36]

No doubt lacking in subtlety, Sir John exemplifies a macabre hollowness that Dickens holds up as the horrifying outcome of a decaying political order. If the desired endpoint of religious emancipation is the creation of a new order of cultural citizens, less Christian than English, as Macaulay had anticipated, then Sir John Chester proved how pernicious that ideal really was. His Englishness is too inefficacious to offer a suitable alternative to religious identification. Hence, even as Dickens explored the possibilities of Catholic emancipation, he dreaded its eventual realization because of the cultural vacuum that the secular state signified, a vacuum that the mannered, machiavellian Englishness of a character like Sir John Chester (and his great forebear, Lord Chesterfield) only served to accentuate.

Dickens was no doubt alarmed to see the task of political protection moving from parliament to such regimented forces as the army or the police. But the very indecisiveness of the political process to put a stop to the carnage caused by the masses clearly indicated to him that religious tolerance could not be guaranteed by legislative fiat alone. In *Barnaby Rudge* there is a clash between what Simon During calls the "civil Imaginary" (the set of practices by which the order of the public world informs everyday life) and the decentering effect of a desired religious pluralism that dispenses with the monolithic will of the civil Imaginary.[37] The state figures in Dickens's novel as a body committed to the protection of the rights of religious minorities; but, though Dickens writes a novel ostensibly about religious tolerance, he feels no special empathy for the plight of Catholics. Nor, for that matter, does the chapel culture of dissent win his attention, either. For instance, the attempt at the end of *Barnaby Rudge* to assimilate the city of London into the natural order notably excludes Dissent: Only "the spires of city churches and the great cathedral dome" rise "up beyond the prison, into the blue sky, and clad in the colour of light summer clouds."[38] And yet the paradox is that if, as Valentine Cunningham argues, Victorian novels about cities are also inevitably about Dissenters,[39] Dickens's *Barnaby Rudge* reveals a fundamental disjunction between its author's penetrating exploration of the horrors of urban squalor and his disdain of the culture of Dissent that was often found in its midst.

Dickens transforms his novel into an abstract exposition of the threat to state authority by impassioned mobs, but his solution is neither a valorization of "the people" nor an affirmation of state authority. Rather, his point of reference lies somewhere else, as reflected in the title of the novel, which is named after a character who is peripheral to the novel's main developments. As a figure of the idiot savant, Barnaby Rudge is an innocent victim of both the mob and the state. Dickens's nostalgia for a romantic version of Protestantism is the final reference point for his solution to English sectarianism; law has no further appeal than the containment of civil tension.

If, as Simon During observes about a different group of texts, the novels of Walter Scott and Jane Austen are silent about the occasion of their writing and present a fictional world directly adjacent to the nation state, *Barnaby Rudge* on the other hand is more overtly didactic and aware of its address to sectarian politics. But rather than directly portraying Chartist agitation (which was its immediate contemporary event, referring to the series of petitions from 1838 to 1848 demanding extension of the franchise to England's lower-middle and working classes), the novel instead goes backward in time and depicts the Gordon riots, which took place in 1780 when Protestants objected to Catholic relief measures. Dickens furnishes a context for the novelistic recreation of the Gordon riots in the legal will of the English nation. Yet neither Dickens nor Edgeworth, for that matter, is able to offer a concept of Englishness defined in terms other than cultural. If culture is posited as a successor to discredited religion, how is it possible for a concept of Englishness to be an effective secular vehicle for establishing religious tolerance, when Englishness is itself polarized from religion? Dickens is too aware of the inherent contradictions in a project of religious tolerance founded on secular culture to look toward leadership in a secular elite. For the culture of the elite is too weak to carry the weight of fighting the inequalities of religious discriminations. Recognizing this limitation, Dickens accords more importance to marginalized characters like Barnaby Rudge, Mrs. Rudge, and Gabriel Varden than to other characters occupying responsible civic positions. Dennis Walder appropriately describes Dickens's "romantic" sense of a nondogmatic Christianity as a religion of the heart, a religion based upon profound feelings about man, nature, and God: "These feelings by definition transcend sectarian barriers, and offer a unifying rather than divisive faith."[40]

Dickens's reversion to a romanticized notion of Christian belief, however, does not obscure the fact that he clings to Protestantism as the touchstone for the evolution of English society. Unlike Edgeworth's tale, where the Jewish banker's daughter Berenice is discovered to be Christian after all, Dickens's story has no surprise conversions. The marriage of the Catholic heroine Emma Haredale to Edward Chester, a Protestant, has one thing in common with the couple's subsequent departure to the West Indies, where they spend the rest of their married lives: the two events are both narrative closures that assimilate Emma at once to Protestant and colonial culture. Marriage enables her incorporation into the mainstream culture in a way that legal emancipation does not. Presented as an alternative to legal emancipation, intermarriage functions ultimately to affirm the dominant culture and the majority religion.

The narrative paralysis of these two works by Edgeworth and Dickens is brought about by their authors' inability to resolve directly the question of incorporating Jews and Catholics into the English nation. The problematic closures in both novels lead one to speculate whether there is a generic link between novels of sectarian conflict and novels of conversion. We might well ask whether the narrative form of the latter picks up from the point where the former breaks down; whether novels about and by converts introduce alternative perspectives to achieve the resolution eluded by the sectarian novel; and whether conversion, though threatening to a society's demographic composition, offers imaginative possibilities for exploring questions of inclusion and exclusion more freely than is permitted by novels still working within the accepted religious categories, such as Edgeworth's and Dickens's. Arguably, the conversion narrative offers the ground for the literary exploration of how to integrate marginalized social groups (figuratively represented by converts) into the nation without effacing their claims to difference.

Indeed, converts function as strategic displacements of religious and ethnic groups, allowing writers to probe questions of selective incorporation and exclusion not easily approached by more direct means. It is no accident that novels about the conversion of Hindus and Muslims to Christianity had wide popular appeal in nineteenth-century England, not merely as wishful testimony to the efficacy of missionary ideology but more compellingly as exotic displacements of the pressing and often explosive issue of whether to admit Jews, Catholics, and Nonconformists into the English nation state. The emplotment of conversion often in terms of a narrative of romance and adventure further suggests a play of desire and imaginative freedom belying the urgency of its central dynamic—namely, the recovery of the imagined community of the nation, whose very idea slips into incoherence even as its established categories are unfastened by the opposed testimony of converts' will and belief.

An unusual narrative in which Hindu-Christian conversions are played out against the backdrop of European sectarianism is Sydney (Lady Morgan) Owenson's *Luxima the Prophetess* (1859), a novel that inspired the final cantos of Percy Bysshe Shelley's *The Revolt of Islam*. First published as *The Missionary* in 1811, the novel was reissued, after the Indian revolt of 1857, in a revised edition in which even the title was changed to reflect the new centrality of the female protagonist, Luxima.[41] Luxima's displacement of the missionary as the plot's main figure is Owenson's concession to the progressive irrelevance of missionaries in the confrontational atmosphere immediately preceding and following the 1857 rebellion. Marked by an experimental adventurousness unusual for romances of the same era, the novel collapses different time periods and locales, emplotting the conversion of a Brahmin priestess in a much larger story set in seventeenth-century Goa. The central historical event around which all other events in the novel converge is the inquisitorial persecution of Portuguese Franciscans by Spanish Jesuits and Dominicans. From a Jacobin, feminist perspective, Sydney Owenson produced a string of "national tales," primarily about Ireland but also including India, Greece, and Belgium, which were all characterized by an often wild juxtaposition of genres. Most often her plots were a cross between travel and romance, but her use of both genres reveals that she saw history deeply embedded in ideological systems. This is most dramatically shown in Owenson's exploration of romantic desire and its motivations.

To an extent, *Luxima* bears kinship with a certain tradition of romantic writing about India that includes conventional celebrations of English Protestantism pitted against both the arcane religions of the East and an obscurantist Roman Catholicism, both rendered in the most predictable and stereotypical terms.[42] However, though Nigel Leask is right to suggest that the novel is placed in a classical Orientalist tradition whose heavily overlaid European deism rewrites Hinduism into a familiar monotheistic religion,[43] *Luxima* is more than a derivative work taking its main inspiration from William Jones's idealizations of vedanta, or a tradition of philosophical commentaries on the Hindu religious texts, the Upanishads. In fact, the novel's setting provides the occasion for a devastating critique of the sectarian savagery at the heart of European history.

As a novel of conversion, *Luxima* begins as a conventional essay on repressive Hindu customs, including the notorious practice of sati, or widow burning. This initial emphasis falls in line with the missiological literature, in which the conversion of native females is presented as a crucial preliminary step to fighting the practice of sati and thereby securing the nation as a whole for the colonizers; for instance, M. Mainwaring's novel, *The Suttee; or The Hindoo Converts* (1830), falls unambiguously in the progressive "abolition of sati by Christianity" mold.[44] But in *Luxima*, sati is given a new twist, and convention takes off in unexpected directions as the heroine Luxima confronts her choices of either ascending her husband's funeral pyre or becoming a priestess. Her lament that it would have been better to die a sati, since her husband's death now closed off a life of active love for her, does not prevent her from pursuing the goal of a "profession" (in more senses than one, for she chooses to avow not Christianity, as the romance tradition would suggest, but a vocation typically identified with males). Her celebrated status as a Brahmin priestess makes her a desirable target for proselytizing attempts, and she receives (and reciprocates) the attentions of a Franciscan missionary, Hilarion, whose unrestrained passion for her subsequently causes her to be cut off from caste and declared civilly dead.

Owenson refuses to present Luxima's conversion as an inevitable acceptance of Christian tenets, nor even as a natural consequence of romantic attachment. On the contrary, her conversion is staged as the enactment of a doubt that resides stubbornly in the margins of the European religious tradition—a doubt that destabilizes the false certainties of religious absolutes. If Luxima resists the missionary while clinging to an ambiguous conception of Hinduism as "a religion which unites the most indifferent toleration to the most obstinate faith" (*L*, 105), Hilarion in turn, driven by "objectless longings and fears" (*L*, 152), admits the failure of his rhetoric and concedes to "an incoherence in her ideas, which was not to be reconciled, or replied to" (*L*, 108). His own alternating attraction to her physical beauty and repulsion from her idolatry produces a disordered conception of Christian conversion as a form of romantic possession. This troubling compulsion mimes the uncertainty of his convictions and undercuts the complacency of his proselytizing ambitions: "There is no love where there is no cause for solicitude; and the first moment when hope and fear slumber in the perfect consciousness of exclusive and unalienable possession, is perhaps the first moment when the calm of indifference dawns upon the declining ardor of passion" (*L*, 150).

Luxima has more than historical interest in its complex interweaving of religious identity with issues of free will, agency, subjectivity, and political consciousness. The novel's almost obsessive interest in its heroine's excommunication prevents readers from accepting its narrative line exclusively in terms of a straightforward, overdetermined spiritual movement to Christianity. Whether for purposes of plot development or the requirements of realist fiction, the novel presents the experience of spiritual change as an experience of social disruption, threatening to dislodge the convert as the subject of her own spiritual narrative. Nor is excommunication merely a meta-phor for alienation or a metaphysical abstraction, for the social isolation of Christian converts is carefully grounded in an elaborately drawn historical reality. In a deliberately anachronistic gesture, details taken from civil court records and judicial proceedings provide the defining strokes in the features of the novel's excommunicated characters who inhabit an otherwise purely liter-ary landscape.

Hilarion discovers that excommunication—the tyranny of custom and law—is an obstacle to the consummation of love, not only because it severs ties with community and nation but also because it obsessively nourishes a continuing attachment to whatever is forever lost. Excommunication translates as exile in Luxima's psychic imagination, and the divorce from com-munity becomes the loss of an entire nation. Pointing to what Hilarion describes as her "pagan" icons, she cries out, "I have nothing left now *but these!* nothing to remind me in the land of strangers, of my country and my people, save only these" (*L*, 203). The language of nationhood defines the religion of one's birth as equivalent to the ties of nature, and Luxima is com-pelled to ask whether her new faith commands her to break these ties. At every instance, when the missionary believes he is close to claiming Luxima both for himself and for Christ, he finds emblems of her persistent devotion to her former creed:

> He felt his enthusiasm in the cause weakened, by the apparent impossibility of its success; for he perceived that the religious prejudices of Hindustan were too inti-mately connected with the temporal prosperity of its inhabitants, with the estab-lished opinions, with the laws, and even with the climate of the country. . . . He almost looked upon the Mission, in which he had engaged, as hopeless; and he felt that the miracle of that conversion, by which he expected to evince the sacred truth of the cause in which he had embarked, could produce no other effect than a general abhorrence already paid the forfeit of all most precious to the human breast, for that partial proselytism to which her affections, rather than her reason, had induced her (*L*, 217).

What moves the missionary to accept Luxima's lapse into her old practices is his recognition that excommunication is a condition of self-alienation inherent in the nature of all custom and law, producing the psychic disjunc-tions that void all attempts at positive human relations. Paving the way to his detachment from European norms, Hilarion's own conversion is marked by his recognition that "the rites of excommunication were the same in both reli-gions, equally terrible in their denunciation, and equally inhuman in their re-sults" (*L*, 248). As victims of mistaken zeal, both Hilarion and Luxima learn to reject the false distinctions introduced by laws and institutions, which pro-duce the human suffering wrongly attributed to the "natural tendencies" of men and women (*L*, 288).

Recognizing the coercive power of law to create outsiderness in contrast to the tenderness of religious sensibility—a sensibility that, as Hilarion comes to realize, links Luxima's attachment to her Hindu icons with his own devotion to the rosary given him by his dying mother—the missionary is led to a profound consciousness of the bigotry and intolerance of his profession. As the Spanish inquisitors who later hunt him down suspect, his fiery passion has turned into "temperance in doctrine"; his attitude of "languor" and "tolerance" is denounced as being more characteristic of the people he is instructed to convert than of the true Christian spirit of proselytizing zeal (*L*, 262). In turn, the missionary denounces European culture for making its doctrines part of an oppressive system of control, with little or no connection to the spiritual lives of its practitioners. He inveighs against the hypocrisy of colonialism by reminding his accusers that "we bring them a spiritual creed, which commands them to forget the world, and we take from them temporal possessions, which prove how much *we live for it*."[45] Hilarion is condemned to die on the stake for heresy, a crime that has a double edge in its protest against both religious and colonial authority. By daring to say that faith must be freely chosen rather than authoritatively imposed—that it is "an act of private judgment or of free will, which no human artifice, no human authority, can alter or control" (*L*, 264)— the missionary rouses sympathetic Indians to perceive the political tyranny under which they labored and mobilize against their oppressors.

But it is the tragic spectacle of seeing their "celebrated and distinguished" priestess condemned to death that fully releases the suppressed anger of colonial Indians against "oppressions they had so long endured," and they rush forward in a frenzied but futile attack on the Spanish forces (*L*, 311). In the meantime, Luxima, who had been separated from her lover by a bizarre intrigue hatched by Spanish Jesuits, sees the smoke of the piles meant for Hilarion's execution. By this time mentally disoriented herself, she immediately confuses the spectacle of her lover's impending burning at the stake with the self-immolation "that Brahmin women present." The images, presented thus to her disordered mind, produce a strange illusion: "She believed the hour of her sacrifice and triumph was arrived, that she was on the point of being united in heaven to him whom she had alone loved on earth" (*L*, 312). This hallucinatory blurring of the scene of the missionary's intended execution with the scene of Luxima's own sati has to be read against an earlier exchange where the missionary admonishes her for wishing that she had died a ritual death at the time of her husband's passing. The missionary says to her: "If you have abandoned that religion, the ties it formed are broken, and with them should their memory decay" (*L*, 141). But memory does not only *not* decay for Luxima; it becomes the counterweight to the conversion experience. With images of Kamadev (the god of love) adorning her wrist, even as a cross dangled from her neck, so that she alternately resembled "a Christian Magdalene or a penitent Priestess of Brahma" (*L*, 195), Luxima the exile, doomed to a life of civil death, is the embodiment of a liminality created by her crossing over into another religious space, as she clings to past relics of her earlier, happier life in the community from which she is now cast off. Far from renouncing Hindu customs and turning her back on sati as an archaic practice, Luxima reverts to her former social identity. Her symbolic sati undoes the effects of her conversion to Christianity, and she dies saying, "Now I die as Brahmin women die, a Hindu in my feelings and my faith—dying for him I loved and believing as my fathers have believed" (L, 324).

To modern readers, this uncritical return to traditional practices that have a history of patriarchal oppression behind them is troubling. That Luxima's regression to an earlier mindset is prompted by the novel's rejection of European sectarianism makes the conclusion even more problematic. The novel's temporal and spatial blurring produces repetitions of central events in the lived experience of its characters, as we have just seen with regard to sati. But it does so in other instances too, as when the place of Hilarion's execution is remade into the site of Luxima's excommunication. If the double focus provides the occasion for a penetrating critique of religious absolutism as the source of both colonial and patriarchal oppression ("Man, the minister of error, was then, as now, cruel and unjust, substituting malevolence for mercy, and the horrors of a fanatical superstition for the blessed peace and loving kindness of true religion," L, 304), the critique, however, cannot get beyond the tyrannies of custom, law, and doctrine to point the way to "true religion," which remains undefined and deliberately vague. Owenson's novel is hobbled by its inability to carve out a space where religious sensibility might flourish as a product of the self-creating experience of conversion. Instead, the novel's reaction against sectarian excesses produces a regressive, backward-looking movement into known and familiar (albeit retrograde) practices. And so the novel concludes uneasily by laying itself to rest between these twin poles of coercive practice and doctrine, identified as integral to both western and eastern religions.

CONVERSION, "TRADITION," AND NATIONAL CONSOLIDATION

As a potentially destabilizing force in culture because of its radical displacements of meaning, conversion is variously employed as a trope in narratives to speculate on the possibilities of national identification, while at the same time allowing for religious difference. The potential ambiguity of tropes of dual affiliations—especially during moments of transition between exclusionary politics and legal emancipation—is often resolved in terms of positing syncretic rather than separatist identities. George Eliot's *Daniel Deronda* (1876) has as its central character a hybrid figure whose Englishness is dependent for its vitality on a redemptive mark of difference—the protagonist's Jewish origin. Likewise, as Mordecai Cohen remarks in appreciation of the Teutonic-looking Deronda, Jews as a febrile race can only be regenerated by a racial graft from hardy Anglo-Saxon stock. Deronda might well be considered the product of a historical moment when cosmopolitanism is too uncertainly poised between secular and religious definitions to be an appropriate ideal of modernity. Regarding Jewish emancipation, two related questions dominated as points of debate: "Where would Jews, first as individual disputants in discussion and ultimately as a community in agreement, come to draw the line between religious tradition and secular innovation?" and "How would they satisfy both themselves and the gentile majority in reconciling expectations of due conformity with the retention of a dignified distinctiveness?"[46]

The deliberate adoption of a religion defined as "minority" or "other"—whether it is a matter of becoming Jewish in a largely Christian society, Muslim in a predominantly Hindu society, or Episcopalian in a Greek Orthodox culture—obliges one to ask what is being reclaimed, recovered, or revived by such an act. To answer in terms of the preservation of tradition would be a fairly standard response, especially in contexts of almost certain persecution and savage suppression culminating in total annihilation of religious minorities. Mordecai Cohen in Eliot's novel appropriately evokes tradition to explain why Jews who had converted to Christianity in eras of persecution are returning to the fold several generations hence.

The moral center of the novel is defined by a stirring speech given by Mordecai in which he argues vigorously against cosmopolitanism because it destroys tradition, memory, and race. He delivers this speech even as his more worldly peers argue for a progressive nationalism based on pride of race rather than religion. In response to Pash's assimilationist Judaism and barely disguised Anglophilism (fitting Gladstone's model of the non-professing Jew), Mordecai twists English citizenship into a self-alienating concept designed to turn the Jews into deracinated exiles from Judaism: "Can a fresh-made garment of citizenship weave itself straightway into the flesh and change the slow deposit of eighteen centuries? What is the citizenship of him who walks among a people he has no hearty kindred and fellowship with, and has lost the sense of brotherhood with his own race?"[47] The language of alienated insiderness characterizing Mordecai's description of English citizenship is shown as disconnected from the body, defined as the bedrock of racial consciousness ("the slow deposit of eighteen centuries"). Such descriptions depend on the symbols of evolutionary development, which affirm species-and race-consolidation as having a natural logic that secular developments have subverted. Pash's brashly secular posture further provokes Mordecai to expatiate on the self-denying implications of calling oneself "a rational Jew," and he accuses Pash of

> los[ing] the heart of the Jew. Community was felt before it was called good. I praise no superstition, I praise the living fountains of enlarging belief. . . . I say that the effect of our separateness will not be completed and have its highest

transformation unless our race takes on again the character of a nationality. That is the fulfilment of the religious trust that moulded them into a people, whose life has made half the inspiration of the world.[48]

Embedded within these lines is a resistance to Jewish emancipation on the grounds of civil relief alone, especially relief offered under the aegis of a secular polity. Almost in confirmation of Gladstone's fear of the "professing Jew," Mordecai insists on going against the grain of his Jewish peers' desire for integration and rather seeks to salvage Jewish belief from the annihilative force of secularizing impulses. It is also significant that Mordecai conceives of nationality not as the convergence of plural identities but as the distinctive expression of a single race. At a time when English legislation was seeking to annul the distinguishing characteristics of racial and religious origins by subsuming all such characteristics within a national identity disembodied from race and religion, Mordecai calls for the preservation of these categories as markers of identity.

Mordecai's message to younger Jews emphasizes the recovery of tradition as a motive for conversion to practicing Judaism. This message, however, does not, illuminate the sources of his defiant assertion that "our race takes on again the character of a nationality." Mordecai proposes an innovative though controversial formulation: not legal principle nor political edict but belief as *racial consciousness* is the foundation of community. Mordecai's racial pride transforms what might have been a recounting of Jewish victimhood and near-annihilation into a passionate speech on Jewish superiority, extolling the Jewish sense of moral community as the ideal foundation of a nation fast losing its moorings. What we hear in these lines is not a separatist call for ethnic consolidation but a dispassionate statement of Hebraism as the very basis of modern Christianity. This assertion is given the weight of cultural authority by Eliot's contemporary, Matthew Arnold, who in *Culture and Anarchy* reconstructs English culture as the product of Teutonic and Hebraic elements, though it also has to be noted that Arnold was far less interested than Eliot's character in celebrating Judaism as proto-Christianity.[49] Mordecai, on the other hand, was primarily intent on arguing that the real hybridity and pluralism of English culture derives from the grafting of Hebraic belief onto Anglo-Saxon stock. By an extension of the same argument, Mordecai was able to argue that parliamentary relief, on the other hand, produces only a hollow hybridity: its pluralism is not the natural outcome of evolutionary principles but, rather, is contrived, the result of an artificial manipulation of the legislative process.

A new and powerful image of conversion emerges in these passages, which has less to do with retrieving tradition than with bringing about attitudinal changes in England toward its minority populations. Mordecai does not see the offer of citizenship as a panacea to the Jews' rootless existence in England. Rather, the rootlessness is symptomatic of the erosion of moral standards and cultural depth in English life, which no amount of legal measures can obscure. The novel's opening scene of Gwendolyn Harleth at the gambling table is a marvelous tableau of England's desperado plight. Mordecai's transfer of the condition of anomie suffered by Jews onto the English cultural landscape furnishes an altogether different set of meanings that contextualizes Deronda's symbolic conversion to Judaism. Deronda's reclamation of Judaism signifies an intent not merely to strengthen the bonds of a dispersed people. More importantly, he turns to the only community surviving intact in England that remained uncontaminated by the corruptions of a nation drifting aimlessly from its once strong moral center. The broader conversion George Eliot has in mind is intended to lead to a recognition by the Anglican community that England's attenuated moral fiber could only be revitalized by minority groups still strongly imbued with religious feeling. Daniel Deronda's embrace of the spirit of Judaism is the strongest measure of the disintegration of belief in English public life. From being despised minorities whose admission into the nation is a matter of fierce, vitriolic debate, Jews are re-presented as England's only hope against being consumed by total moral anarchy. In Eliot's idealized account, the restoration of real citizenship rights to Jews is as much an act of conversion of Anglican England to particular conceptions of future relationships with minority populations as it is a political act gesturing toward a nation based on the principle of plurality.[50]

Herein lies the specific literary contribution to the debates on religious minorities and English citizenship. The creative possibilities of national regeneration offered by what one might describe as *attitudinal conversion* are played out alongside the moves toward lifting civil disabilities against England's religious minorities. Even as civil emancipation presumes that the distinctions between "majority" and "minority" religious cultures can be leveled by a secular national identity, obviating the need to negotiate their relations in society, attitudinal conversion keeps alive the fact that these negotiations are not yet complete. Literary interventions of the sort made by George Eliot redefined the extension of citizenship rights to non-Anglicans as an opportunity for Anglicans to reconceive their relation not only to previously excluded groups. *Daniel Deronda* also makes an eloquent plea for a necessary reorientation by Anglicans to the religious traditions that had always remained polarized from the Church of England. Among those for whom such literary revisions had considerable salience were political figures who came to power at these moments of transition. If literature complements history by imaginatively reconstructing moral community from the foundations of political community established by parliamentary measures, it is instructive to examine the careers of major public personalities to ascertain the degree to which they are equally engaged with both modes of creating community, that is, the moral and the political.

No figure of nineteenth-century English politics and letters better exemplifies the complex literary manipulation of conversion's potential for self-imagining in relation to community and nation than Benjamin Disraeli. As a Jew baptized at birth, Disraeli long struggled with the weight of Christian assimilation, but he did not rest content with either acquiescing to or berating the self-denying implications of his father's decision to Christianize him. Rather, having risen to the highest post of prime minister, he used the ascendancy he had gained in English politics to reflect on the reorientation of relations between Christians and Jews in light of civil emancipation. Disraeli's advocacy of Baron Lionel de Rothschild's right to sit in parliament was complemented by novelistic interventions to induce changes in attitude to Jews among his largely Anglican audience. But instead of basing his appeal on grounds of tolerance, Disraeli believed that a reorientation of Christian-Jewish relations would ensue only when the common origins of Christians and Jews were recognized as, paradoxically, the source of England's rich hybridity. He wrote *Tancred: Or the New Crusade* (1847) originally as a fictional examination of the position of the Church of England, but instead, by describing the protagonist's discovery of moral and religious influences lying beyond the Anglican fold, the novel reveals that it is far more concerned with what Disraeli describes as "the position of the descendants of that race who had been the founders of Christianity," namely, the Jews.[51] The novel was published in a year— 1847—when the debates in the House of Commons on the Jewish Disabilities Bill pushed Disraeli toward abandoning his customary stance of minimal resistance, if not outright acquiescence, to Anglican priorities; for once, he defied his Conservative allies in order to uphold principle.[52] Rothschild's election as a member of parliament representing London was undermined by his refusal to take the parliamentary oath, which required that he swear "on the true faith of a Christian." As a result of his refusal, he was prevented from taking his seat. Rothschild's aborted entry into parliament exposed the lie to the Jews' recent victory in assuming most civil offices, which did not extend, however, to their right to sit in parliament; his case further laid bare the narrow limits within which British citizenship was defined for Jews.

Disraeli based his argument for the admission of Jews to parliament not on the expected liberal grounds of religious liberty and tolerance for diversity, derived from the broad brush strokes of John Locke's *A Letter Concerning Toleration*, but rather on specific religious grounds. The Jews, Disraeli contended, were the "authors" of the Christian religion, and therefore could not legitimately be excluded by Christians from government. He directly accused the opposition of anti-Semitism and went on to conclude that "as a Christian . . . I will not take upon me the awful responsibility of excluding from the legislature those who are of the religion in the bosom of which my Lord and Saviour was born."[53] Thus Disraeli strategically emphasized his own Christianity while simultaneously articulating the breakdown of boundaries between Christianity and Judaism (a theme he explored at length in *Tancred*).

Disraeli's defense of Rothschild's right as a Jew to sit in parliament exposes the dual life Disraeli lived out himself. Baptized as a child, he was fiercely defensive about his adopted Christian identity as alone enabling him to pursue a parliamentary career at a time when severe civil disabilities were imposed on Jews in England. Yet he spent his adult life recreating the contemporary fictional equivalent of marranos, fifteenth-century Spanish Jews who were forced to convert to Christianity to prevent forfeiture of their property as well as to avoid possible exile, but who often secretly practiced Judaism despite overt profession of Catholic precepts. Disraeli's most memorable character, Sidonia, who first appears in *Coningsby* (1844), is a Sephardic Jew who pursues the life of a cosmopolitan Englishman while living out another nationalism of sorts in his unwavering commitment to the principles of Judaism. A prototype for George Eliot's Mordecai Cohen, Sidonia is clearly a stand-in for Disraeli. But apart from the autobiographical interest, Sidonia, like Disraeli, is also a transitional figure who is attracted to religious difference but does not celebrate it outright, just as he feels a sense of national loyalty but does not entirely identify with England.

Indeed, Disraeli tranformed what might otherwise appear as ambiguity or hesitation into an attribute of uniqueness. That is to say, the combination of Jewish blood and Christian beliefs made the Sidonias of the world exceptionally qualified to have the necessary critical stance for enlightened citizenship:

> [Sidonia] brought to the study of [a] vast aggregate of knowledge a penetrative intellect that, matured by long meditation, and assisted by that absolute freedom from prejudice, which was the compensatory possession of a man without a country, permitted Sidonia to fathom, as it were by intuition, the depth of questions apparently the most difficult and profound . . . *independent of creed, independent of country, independent even of character.*[54]

Disraeli gave the marrano figure, such as he was himself, a dynamic capacity for movement in English society, a capacity that derived from the marrano's simultaneous profession of Judaism and Christianity. No doubt, Disraeli's own political rise glorified the myth of the social mobility of Jews in England, and autobiography strongly overdetermined his representation of the successful marrano. The relatively easy maneuverability of the marrano in English society is, in fact, a reminder that Christians and Jews did not have equal access to power. In the figure of the marrano, the question of religious convictions is subordinated to pragmatic considerations of survival and stratagem.

Yet Sidonia is also the fictional product of an idealized English society that Disraeli could only imagine but not inhabit. The supposed tolerance of English religious life gave the fictional Sidonias the opportunity they needed to participate fully in Judaism, and partially in British society. Sidonia is immensely wealthy and powerful but excluded from the political realm, as "his religion walled him out from the pursuits of a citizen."[55] During the course of his first meeting with the young English protagonist in *Coningsby*, Sidonia describes himself with a rhetorical flourish as "but a dreamer of dreams. . . . Action is not for me. I am of that faith that the Apostles professed before they followed their master."[56] He further justifies his propensity for imagining rather than acting by referring to England's laws against religious minorities: "Although I have been rash enough to buy several estates, my own opinion is, that, by the existing law of England, an Englishman of Hebrew faith cannot possess the soil."[57] Apart from being excluded from the political process, unconverted Jews were debarred for a long time from studying at Oxford and Cambridge. Still, despite his exclusion from British universities, Sidonia's privileged upbringing is made possible by the prodigious wealth of his family.

One of the most impressive scholarly works on Jewish identity and the English novel to appear in recent years is Michael Ragussis's *Figures of Conversion*. Detailing representations of Jewish identity in English culture not through the familiar inventory of anti-Semitic stereotypes but rather through the rhetoric of conversion, Ragussis offers an absorbing and learned account of how the Evangelical drive to convert the English nation resulted in repressions of Jewish identity through forcible assimilation. Forced conversions triggered off mechanisms of resistance in the Jewish population, even as many English Jews also permitted themselves to be absorbed into the general population.[58] Whereas Ragussis's chapters on Scott, Edgeworth, Eliot, and Trollope contain rich material on the literary revision of English conversionist zeal to annex Jewish identity, his chapter on Disraeli stands apart for several reasons. First, it alone gives the Jewish response both to emancipatory legislation and the repression of Jewish identity by Christian conversion (which Ragussis significantly regards as equivalent acts); and second, the chapter allows for a more complex reading of conversion not as an annihilative activity but rather a form of strategic movement in societies with long histories of religious persecution.

Yet without detracting from the undoubted brilliance of *Figures of Conversion*, I believe that Ragussis, in assigning a normative value to the idea of conversion as (forcible) assimilation, restricts himself to a model of victimization that prevents him from exploring the self-constituting character of conversion. By this I imply an idea of conversion that signifies its use not just for strategic (or instrumentalist) purposes, nor even as a turn toward one's own roots, but rather as the embrace of multiple positions. In other words, conversion offers the possibilities of imagining more than one religious affiliation in the composition of the new Englishman. Disraeli's sustained reflections on his twin connections to Christianity and Judaism indicate how fervently he believed that hybrid identities embodied the imagined future of the modern pluralistic nation. If Disraeli himself was a double convert—having first embraced Christianity, he increasingly turned to Jewish themes in what looked to be a religious conversion—he aimed for a similar double conversion in his contemporary readers, though in reverse order. The Anglo-Saxon born into

Christian beliefs is asked to reexamine his relation to the Jews whom he has kept out of the political process, just as he is also urged to reread his own Christianity from an estranged perspective.

Ragussis, on the other hand, while noting Disraeli's complex negotiation of the political culture of his adopted Christian identity, pursues an approach to his Jewish conversion as the reclamation of a suppressed identity. This approach recasts Disraeli as a nativist claiming Jewish identity as the basis also of Christian England's. To be sure, this argument is not entirely without merit, for there is sufficient evidence of ethnocentric pride in Disraeli. The Young England trilogy is replete with claims such as the one expressed by Sidonia, who declares in *Coningsby* that "the Hebrew child has entered adolescence only to learn that he was the Pariah of that ungrateful Europe that owes to him the best part of its laws, a fine portion of its literature, all its religion."[59]

Yet Ragussis's argument stops short of acknowledging Disraeli as one of the earliest and most important political figures who gave to conversion the function of scrambling the accepted categories of English nationalist politics, while simultaneously reconceiving the concept of citizenship in relation to the various possibilities generated by conversion. Indeed, wherever the word "conversion" appears in the context of Disraeli's writings, one is not entirely sure whether it means the adoption of Christianity or the return to Judaism. And that is precisely the point of a character like Sidonia, whose total immersion in the worldliness of English politics and commerce makes his expatiation on Jewish themes seem almost extraneous to his political insights and outside the main concerns of the novel. At times these discussions are so long-winded that Ragussis concludes they must serve as an oblique sign of Sidonia's actual disempowerment in English society.[60]

However, Sidonia's lengthy discourses on Jewish history are also the means by which he keeps his multiple affiliations alive. His wide-ranging conversations with young Coningsby are a reminder to his audience that he occupies more than one space in the circumscribed world of Anglican England. His is an ongoing conversion to the material and spiritual dimensions of identity, which shapes the outlines of the desired pluralism that would eventually give Jews a place in the English political process. That Disraeli does not believe civil relief can achieve real emancipation for Jews is apparent in his depiction of a restless, probing, and ceaselessly striving Sidonia, who continues to explore his location in English society as if legal emancipation had not occurred at all. Sidonia's dwelling on Judaism is less a form of nativist nostalgia or recuperation of tradition than a means by which he unravels the contradictions of a nation moving toward pluralism even as it presumes to be homogeneously composed.

Disraeli's subtle meditation on religious identity in changing political societies suggests another dimension of conversion that is not limited to its function in cultural criticism. Because conversion's alliance with cultural criticism is so apparent, especially when accepted as an activity rather than a state of mind, there is an obvious temptation to read conversion in general as originating in motives of critique. Undoubtedly, change of religion is not merely an oppositional activity, though it may begin as such. Furthermore, conversion expresses an altered consciousness deriving from the construction of norms within culture. This is a central point in William James's *The Varieties of Religious Experience*, as it is indeed in a great deal of writing about religious experience. For James the experience of awakened religious consciousness validates the believing self. Its significance for cultural development lies in the fact that the culture in which conversion occurs lends its own structural features to the content of religious experience. In turn, the heightened religious subjectivity makes visible the range of meanings embedded in cultural forms.

But the more interesting question is whether or not there is an internal critique of those norms even as they are being assimilated in the sudden "turning" signified by conversion experiences. In other words, regardless of whether conversion is an assimilative or an oppositional gesture, the specific circumstances, historical context, and political climate in which conversion occurs might suggest a more complicated trajectory. In somewhat paradoxical fashion, assimilation may be accompanied by critique of the very culture with which religious affiliation is sought. Equally, dissent may aim at reforming and rejuvenating the culture from which the convert has detached herself.

These are considerations that have as forceful an impact on colonial conversions as on the conversions occurring in England during and after legal emancipation of non-Anglicans. And if, as I have been suggesting, religious minorities in England often shared the position of colonial subjects, the strategies deployed by such figures as Disraeli to find a place for Jews in Anglican England—a place not circumscribed by legal edict—bear comparison with the strategies developed by colonial converts to create an alternative community to that provided by custom and law. Again, the key factor lies in the multiple affiliations opened up by conversion—the possibilities of occupying several positions in relation to both nation and religion. The blurring between the objects to which the convert assimilates and those he (or she) challenges—with a free crossover between assent and dissent—is precisely the source of the power of conversion. Thus, assimilation and dissent often crisscross with motives not immediately attached to their apparent function in conversion. The result is that converts may be engaged just as readily in a critique of their adopted culture and religion as in a project to reform the culture that they have renounced. In either case, conversion's instrumental significance cannot be denied, nor can its dynamic engagement with either or both cultures with which the convert is affiliated.

To my mind, the colonial figure who perfectly illustrates this last point is Narayan Viman Tilak, a Maharashtrian Brahmin convert to Christianity in late nineteenth-century western India. Although he assimilated norms of Christian belief and conduct, Tilak also sought to indigenize Christianity and make it compatible with Hinduism. His syncretic project contained an implicit critique of the alienating effects of British colonialism. Though his conversion may have suggested a rejection of Hinduism in favor of the colonizer's religion, his subsequent use of Christianity to enunciate an anticolonial vision of Indian nationalism was far more damaging to British imperialist ambitions than if he were to have remained a Hindu.

A major nationalist figure in the renaissance of Marathi literature, Tilak devoted his creative energies to articulating possible modes of relating to a revitalized India, and (paradoxically it would seem at first glance) conversion to Christianity appeared to him to be the most effective way of expressing that relation. Tilak conceived of Christianity as embodying a necessary vision of the future, with the power to purge Hinduism of its most hated caste features, yet at the same time adapted to India as a truly indigenous religion in its own right. The English missionary J. C. Winslow claimed that Tilak had confided to him that he was the founder of a new religion, and indeed Tilak's writings suggest that he had distanced himself equally from traditional forms of both Hinduism and Christianity.[61] Convinced that India's political enslavement was matched only by its own moral degradation through a coercive caste system enshrined in Hinduism, Tilak, like many other Christian converts, grew firmer in the belief that only a religious awakening would enable India to embark on a new era of reform and advancement.

But at the same time, Tilak wanted Indian Christians to be more truly Indian, claiming that the British missionary project had denationalized Christianity and made the West the exclusive reference point of Indian Christianity. In one of his poems he denounced the paternalistic attitude of missionaries in scathing terms: "We dance as puppets while you hold the strings;/How long shall this buffoonery endure?"[62] Tilak undertook to teach Marathi Christians to study older Marathi literature, especially the devotional poetry of Jnaneshwar, Namadev, and Tukaram. He insisted that he came to Jesus Christ "over the bridge of Tukaram's verse"[63] and continued to make it his goal to adapt Indian Christianity to the spirit of Indian cultural forms such as the bhajan, or Hindu devotional hymn. Interestingly, though deriving its force from the reformist impulse to which his Christian conversion gave him access, Tilak's nationalism was the means by which he also sought reconciliation with the former Brahmin community from which he had been excommunicated. His poetry is a combination of religious fervor, patriotic zeal, and antisectarian feeling; like his nationalism, his verse is conceived as much in a spirit of rapprochement as of critique:

> Thrice blessed is thy womb, my Motherland,
> Whence mighty rishis, saints, and sages spring!
> A Christian I, yet here none taunteth me,
> Nor buffeteth with angry questioning.

> I meet and greet them, and with love embrace:
> None saith, "Thou dost pollute us by thy sin!"
> My Guru they delight to venerate; they say,
> "He is our brother and our kin."[64]

Tilak's syncretic ambition was shared by converts from other regions of India, who also sought through conversion to recover a "national religion" that eliminated rather than preserved difference. The attempt to create a hybrid entity like "Hindu Christianity" was a keenly felt aspect of this synthesizing project. As the Bengali historian M. M. Ali has argued, the earliest symptoms of nationalist stirrings in Bengal, far from being a return to Hinduism and a revival of classical Sanskrit texts, were the setting up of Hindu Christian churches, which defiantly attempted to indigenize the Christianity introduced by English missionaries.[65] This observation implicitly endorses Robin Horton's widely discussed thesis that African conversions were not so much a tribute to missionary success as expressions of African nationalism, through which the colonial ruler's religion was given a strong indigenist bent.[66] In Horton's reading, conversion is a sign of acceptance of modernity, not of capitulation to colonial power, and the setting up of African churches introduced an Africanist discourse that not only indigenized Christianity but also brought what Horton calls a local-centered, "microcosmic" thinking in contact with ideas of nations and territories.

Horton's neat dichotomy between local and national community reproduces a premodern/modern split, which has inevitably come under attack by other critics, most notably by Terence Ranger, who argues that premodern African religions were never uniquely microcosmic but bridged ethnic and territorial boundaries.[67] But despite these reservations, Horton's thesis still has a certain usefulness in understanding Christian conversions in colonial societies as signifying responses to internal changes that were already under way, and as a form of domesticating (and to some extent neutralizing) alien religious and cultural beliefs. In post-Independence India, for instance, interfaith dialogue has merged into a much more eclectic practice of Christianity and spawned varieties of indigenous expression, such as "Bhakti Theology."[68]

The trajectory of this book brings together English nationalist ideology and colonial conversions within the same frame of discussion and asks in each chapter: if nationalist ideology in nineteenth-century England is questioned by conversion as a mode of asserting difference within a broad range of possible national identifications, what implications do the metropolitan challenges to this ideology have for the function, role, and significance of colonial conversions? Just as pressingly, how does the nature of colonial conversions redefine the shape, form, and object of metropolitan dissent? Turning back again to English dissent as counterpoint, can colonial conversions be regarded primarily as a natural fulfillment of missionary ambitions and a form of cultural assimilation to the English imperialist agenda? What specific relation might there be, for instance, between the English Tractarians' antistate appeal for the recovery of a pre-Reformation religious authority, symbolizing a unified culture, and the motive-force of colonial conversions? What ideas of "the nation" emerge from these conversions that suggest a larger connection with metropolitan realignments between state, religion, culture, and empire?

Clearly, to ask these questions is to shift the focus of conversion away from a discourse dominated and controlled by missionaries, who are invested with the sole agency to effect religious transformations. A missionary-centered focus prevails overwhelmingly in the existing anthropological and historical literature on conversion, which is primarily concerned with how conversions take place, whether or not they are successful, and what further kinds of changes are triggered in the culture by way of a chain reaction from the original "transformation."[69] The unidirectional flow of activity suggested by this model contradicts what is, after all, an exchange. Conceivably, a subject-centered discourse would do far greater justice to the transactions between missionaries and converts. If catechism is the ecclesiastical form of religious inculcation, dialogism would be its equivalent in literary terms. Indeed, some of the most penetrating analyses of colonial discourse have been missionary-native interactions, such as in studies by Homi Bhabha, Richard Fox Young, and Vicente Rafael.[70] Significantly, all three are studies of missionary failure, or at least of the frustration of missionary objectives, and whether one turns to colonial ambivalence (Bhabha) or apologetics and caste power (Young) or the subversive effects of translation (Rafael), there is sufficient evidence to locate the failure in the nature of multivocal discourse itself.

It will also be apparent that asking questions about English nationalist ideology and colonial conversions independently of each other is an incomplete exercise. Although we must begin somewhere in reconstructing cultural history, just as we must end somewhere as well, to assume that there is a fixed place of origin and an equally finite destination is to presuppose that both can be safely encompassed by the same frame of reference—a frame whose boundaries depend on unifying concepts of nation, religion, culture, and the like. The back-and-forth nature of the questions I enumerated earlier shows how difficult it is to confine our search for explanations and effects to one place or one time. The fact that significant trends in English culture and society, such as the moves toward disempowering ecclesiastical authority and secularizing civil society, are more than the product of internal developments points to a much more diffuse and therefore less manageable concept of history. England's involvement with the world beyond its own borders cannot be excluded from this history.

Indeed, the indeterminacy of culture's trajectory is a function of the crisscrossing of motive, intention, condition, and effect in different cultural spaces.

As soon as one set of questions about cultural formation is raised in the English metropolitan context, it provokes a related set in the colonial context, and back again in an indefinite chain sequence. The apparent unendingness and borderlessness of cultural developments describe the very process of history, whose fluidity, untidiness, and overlapping quality belie the ordering principles of national hagiography.

However, when English culture is narrowly viewed as self-generated, one specific outcome is that cultural identity as a value takes precedence over the historical discontinuities and asymetrical developments from which it emerged.[71] In this chapter I have sought to restore these discontinuities to a writing of the history of secularization, and have focused on the figure of the convert as dramatically making visible—by catalyzing into a state of almost subversive clarity—these disparate, heterogeneous formations. If the convert as religious dissenter shares unmistakable features with the convert as colonial subject, that point of contact initiates and sustains a scholarly reconstruction of the order of governance produced during the realignments between ecclesiastical and secular spheres. That the most subtle and unexpectedly productive challenges to this new order came from converts suggests conversion has a much more dynamic and creative meaning than is captured by the phrase "the conversion experience," which signifies spiritual self-transformation primarily rather than a knowledge-producing activity.

CHAPTER TWO

A Grammar of Dissent

"SECULAR" CRITICISM AND RELIGIOUS DISSENT

When John Henry Newman converted to Catholicism in 1845, his action galvanized his Anglican countrymen into the fearful recognition that their comfortable, secure positions in a largely Anglican culture were under threat. Their extreme reaction was all the more curious because, though Catholic conversions occurred often enough throughout the nineteenth century and even earlier, Newman's was a solitary gesture that showed no inclination to launch a mass conversion movement. Yet the prominent standing of Newman as an erstwhile Anglican thinker generated the fear that his conversion to Catholicism alone could undo the Anglican character of English society. Newman's numerous writings detailing the course of his conversion appeared to offer future initiates a perfect and compelling blueprint that would hasten their conversion to Catholicism. The more Newman talked about his conversion, in works ranging from such celebrated autobiographical memoirs as *Apologia Pro Vita Sua* (1864) to the quotidian sermons and lectures he delivered as Catholic divine, the greater the anxieties generated by his life story, which lodged in the Anglican imagination as certain evidence of the transformation of England's religious landscape.

Yet Newman's substantial impact was registered not merely in the confessional or epiphanic mode but as effectively in writing that belonged more sturdily in the realm of critical epistemology. Although Newman may have appeared to focus rather obsessively on his own conversion, his philosophical writings probed the possibilities of conversion as a critical practice. In particular, the idea of criticism that appealed most to him was one that mapped out a complex structure of assents to compelling beliefs. If this necessarily entailed an interest in the sources of knowledge, the result was that Newman was brought closer to defining the grounds on which assent is given. In so doing, he discovered that assent is often indistinguishable from dissent. That is to say, what appears to emanate from a religious discourse is as concerned with negotiating secular parameters as it is with establishing the claims of religious subjectivity.

Newman's epistemological project has contemporary interest because of its search for a mode of criticism capable of expressing belief without reducing it to either sentiment or dogma. In calling for a more direct, unmediated relation to experience, Newman's idea of belief as disembodied subjectivity, detached from an enclosed interpretive community that commands assent, converged with a notion of dissent as resistance to consensual thinking and institutional subordination. When translated into critical practice, such dissent aimed at disinvesting assents of their foundational assumptions.

In this respect, Newman's religious criticism ironically bears comparison with the attempt of modern (poststructuralist) criticism to interrogate the premises binding individuals to communities of interpretation, ranging from small, local institutions to large, abstract entities like the nation. Although Newman's interest in questioning institutional premises had far more to do with asserting the claims of religious belief than dissolving notions of unitary truth, his methodological approach bears scrutiny for comparative purposes. As an example of contemporary criticism, I have in mind Edward W. Said's important intervention on behalf of worldliness. This is a crucial concept in Said's work, which insistently reminds readers and critics of their obligation to recognize a text's groundedness in the conditions of history, experience, and material realities. "Secular criticism," Said's term to characterize intellectual work opposed to prevailing orthodoxies and mainstream ideologies, conceives of dissent from established principles as essentially a form of resistance to religious authority. No doubt, Said uses the word "secular" in a specialized sense to refer to worldly engagement with human rather than divine history. This use of the word has strategic value in developing his own theories of textual criticism, rather than accounting for the historical development of secularization. Still, despite Said's idiosyncratic usage, the deployment of "secular" as an epistemological concept restores a point of reference that I believe is central to the history of the term. The association of criticism with knowledge-producing activity obliges one to reexamine the roles of secular and religious discourses in both constructing and disputing systems of critical epistemology.[1]

Said points to Orientalism as an outstanding example of religious discourse in that "each serves as an agent of closure, shutting off human investigation, criticism, and effort in deference to the authority of the more-than-human, the supernatural, the other-worldly."[2] One of the most powerful associations Said makes in these formulations, which carry over forcefully into the final chapters of *Culture and Imperialism* (1993) and entirely inform *Representations of the Intellectual* (1994), compels a recognition of both culture and religion as systems of authority that operate in parallel ways to establish criteria for membership, command allegiance, and substitute shared values for individual critical consciousness. Indeed, skepticism and questioning, which are activities properly associated with intellectual work, are considered heresies in a religious order, and it is Said's particular objective to show how readily cultural criticism acquires a heretical cast, even in a supposedly secular climate, wherever revered cultural icons are challenged. His work suggests that the slide from criticism to heresy is a function of the prevailing hold of a cultural discourse that evokes the authority of religion to establish its own norms. Therefore, when Said urges the practice of "secular" criticism, he seeks to recover the oppositional quality of contemporary scholarship from the guild mentality that enjoins unreflecting obedience to abstract notions like "nation," "community," "culture," "citizen," and the like.

Said's strategic positioning of what he calls secular criticism within an interpretive community tightly governed by ruling orthodoxies is all the more striking because it replicates an historical move, not just from a religious to a secular culture, as might be supposed, but from an established to a dissenting ecclesiastical tradition. It is especially in the latter transition that, ironically, the full complexities of practicing secular criticism in the Saidian sense can be most sharply discerned, even though of course Said's analysis is not produced in the context of European religious history nor has it any particular interest in being applied to that history. The system of cultural authority that Said challenges as bearing religious overtones, even in a secular society, is a legacy of the historical moment of secularization, when the structures of official religion no longer supported the bases of political, social, and cultural power and the authority of the state gained ascendancy over civil apparatuses such as law and education. But it is not merely a question of one form of authority displacing another. If culture shares the guild features of the ecclesiastical order, this is largely because, as Matthew Arnold so persuasively argued over a century ago, culture takes over the moral purposes of religion in a civil society, and education becomes the instrument by which the moral mission of culture is propagated.

Even within the terms of Said's analysis, the difficulties of the intellectual vocation are embedded within a series of competing affiliations—between what Said describes as culture and system. However, even these bipolar terms can be extended further to refer to other contrastive pairs of affiliations, such as nation and religion, tradition and belief, or collective memory and personal knowledge or experience. Historically, these competing affiliations are constitutive of the inclusive discourses of the modern secular state. The dual allegiances that an individual may theoretically hold in a state self-constituted as liberal and tolerant produce the necessary tension that enables a certain type of critical activity in the first place. Such criticism occurs particularly as an engagement with the politics of identity, since one may be both a member of a minority group or religious sect *and* a member of the national collectivity. Said's larger point, as I understand it, is that what is often at stake in dissent is resisting the transformation of criticism into either an act of citizenship—a performative gesture of membership in a self-selecting guild—or an act of withdrawal into a self-enclosed space of particularism or separatism. Therefore, although Said seems to be polarizing terms like secular/religious, critic/cleric, human history/sacred time, worldly/mystical, he places dissent in a much more complex, adversarial relation not only to religious orthodoxy but also to state hegemony. This he does by his insistence that culture is a site for hegemonizing tendencies, open to cooptation by the state for its own purposes. With regard to both the colonial and the postcolonial state, Orientalism is, of course, the most egregious example of a religious discourse gone awry.

The historical role of dissent has been not only to question church orthodoxies but also unbuckle the consolidating ambitions of the secular state, within which former religious orthodoxies are subsumed. Simultaneously, at such a juncture, criticism comes dangerously close to slipping into a separatist, sectarian mode while resisting a citizenship function. This particular turn reveals a dramatic gap between private belief and the ideology of nationhood that can only be closed by an effective mediation between religious and national identity.

In societies where the concept of heresy still prevails as a religious concept, it is assumed that private belief has no place outside accepted parameters, its potential expression effectively usurped by public doctrine. On the other hand, in a disestablished society where "truth" is no longer a function of belief but of what is amenable to codification, proof, and administration, the potential of private judgment to act upon a world enveloped and defined by public doctrine is minimized, even marginalized. When identity is firmly situated within the public world of civil society, the subjectivity of private belief *legally* has little or no place. Historical secularization redraws the boundaries of the self that were once placed around religious doctrine or belief, but now repositions them around the affiliative terms of nationhood, citizenship, and the doctrine of rights. (I use the term "historical secularization" to refer to the disestablishment of church and state, in order to distinguish it from the more generic, descriptive label "secularism" signifying conditions pertaining to the practice of religion.) In secularization, one set of self-definitions drawn from an ecclesiastical domain gives way to another drawn from a temporal, legal sphere.

But if the historical choices for the determination of an individual's identity have been either religious authority or legislative reasoning, what is the place of private judgment in relation to public doctrine, be it about divinity or the nation? Or, as John Henry Newman presciently asked in his novel *Loss and Gain* (1848), can independence of judgment ever be reconciled with party affiliation and system building? When Newman writes, "There is that robust, masculine, noble independence in the English mind, which refuses to be tied down to artificial shapes," he is making an important observation about national character and masculine independence.[3] The fact that an independent mind is made over into an emblem of high English virtue tellingly suggests how deeply national identity is caught up in the contest between forms of external authority and personal knowledge. But that same English Protestant pride in independence and individual questioning does not extend its reach to ensure intellectual freedom, as the protagonist of Newman's novel, Charles

Reding, discovers when he confronts the closed, academically confining community of Oxford. Reding is admonished by his tutor Mr. Vincent against transgressing the borders marking off thought from opinion: "I have thought some of your remarks and questions at lecture were like a person pushing things too *far*, and wishing to form a *system*" (*LG*, 59; emphasis in original). The conversations between characters about party affiliation and Oxford life obsessively return to anxieties about community, nation, and identity, and it is clear that the root of the anxiety lies in the realities of exclusion and inclusion pervasive in their intellectual and social world.

The sources of critical consciousness—its positioning and relation to self-constitution, as opposed to affirmation of national interests alone—raise crucial theoretical questions about the nature of subjective belief. Most fundamentally, what distinguishes belief from critical consciousness, and, in turn, critical consciousness from conviction? If certitude is a function of normative value, what is the process by which criticism leads toward conviction but away from certitude? How is it possible for dissent to emerge from the very culture it contests, without being drawn into the culture's structure of assents?[4]

Awareness of the critical nature of dissent to succumb to the fatal alternatives of either citizenship or separatism shapes the career of the nineteenth century's most celebrated convert, John Henry Newman, and conducts him from pure theological exposition toward literary and philosophical criticism. His major philosophical treatise, *A Grammar of Assent* (1870) works through a number of carefully considered critical moves that retrace the stages of his own conversion, ultimately to posit Catholicism as a transreligious, transnational force. From this transnational perspective, Newman is able also to critique the very concept of the nation state, even as he simultaneously recovers a Catholicism of the popular masses that is truly national. Far from being separatist or sectarian, this view of Catholicism appears to Newman to perfect the idea of the English nation. The universalism underlying this formulation is won by translating the terms of assent to the existence of "One God," narrowly conceived in terms of Catholic dogma, into a grammar of dissent from all forms of rational, codified systems of thought that exist to induce membership into a national interpretive community.

Newman's universalism seeks to go *beyond* the nation, and in that sense aspires to bypass both citizenship and separatism. However, it turns out to be a universalism that works regressively, not only by reintroducing religious identity as a category both contained in and transcending national identity, but also by locating in the authority of Catholicism the foundational structure of true Englishness. In short, Newman's transnational solution, while enabling philosophical criticism to continue its engagement with the world while resisting both assimilative and rejectionist positions, cannot effectively disentangle belief from structures of authority, despite the privileging of popular imagination and intuition over rationality and elite modes of intellectual apprehension.

I should state at the outset that by drawing on Newman to complicate Said's notion of secular criticism I obviously do not mean to suggest a direct correspondence between Newman and Said or place them both within a common paradigm. Rather, my interest is in exploring how Newman's original defense of Anglicanism turns into a radical dissent from it, as it was also for other Tractarians. Newman's conversion encapsulates the contradictions of an historical moment when authority shifts from religion to the legal rationality of the state. The question that interests me is what the idea of "received notions" means in moments of historical change, such as during the move toward national union. Conceived in response to such historical change, Newman's transnationalism is riddled with contradictions, because by positing popular Roman Catholicism as a point *outside* established structures he believed he was disentangling authority from state power and separating real assents (involving independent judgment) from notional assents (based on received notions). Newman's conversion powerfully demonstrates the instability, the shifting ground, of concepts like "radical," "authority," and "existing power structures." When historicized, these concepts fully reveal their reorientation in dissent.

Central to the negotiation between religious and national identity is a viable concept of authority. In not only rendering discrete self-perceptions a mere formal subset of social classification but also leaving no place for private faith altogether, the displacement of ecclesiastical authority by the mid-nineteenth-century English state highlighted the failure of the Anglican establishment to provide spiritual leadership. The British census of 1851 collected data about church and Sunday School attendance which showed that half of England's worshiping population were non-Anglicans. This leads to speculations about the extent to which belief-as-dissent was increasingly articulated as an oppositional response to a standardized national identity, transcending religion and class.[5] Dissent is framed as a protest against the legislation of religious belief, and, paradoxically, against a new climate of religious freedom that effaced self-definitions in order to protect individual rights. If a considerable number of Tractarians were led to convert to Roman Catholicism following the decline of church authority, such mass conversions appeared to consolidate dissent as the religion of belief. Indeed, Robert Pattison advances the provocative argument that the Oxford Movement must be read in tandem with laissez-faire capitalism. In *The Great Dissent* (1991) he suggests that the repeal of the corn laws and Tractarianism are both part of the same cultural context of a deregulated economy. If, as Pattison suggests, moral relativism is the cultural counterpart of laissez-faire economics, then it was no longer possible for Tractarianism to withstand the "deregulated market of religious belief."[6] In salvaging belief from the eroded authority of the church, dissent acquired an aggressively separatist character that aimed to preserve religious difference in the face of homogenization. In the new emancipatory climate the pattern of conversions, especially to Roman Catholicism, affirmed the categorical rejection of national definitions and national institutions, even when the national spirit was expressed as tolerance and incorporation.

The most striking feature of the emergence of a culture of conversion-as-dissent is its contrast to a monolithic, exclusionary culture in which conversion functions as a sign of assimilation to the dominant group. Conversion in the latter sense is a gesture of acquiescence, a capitulation to the pragmatics of survival, where individuals either adopt the religion that will admit them to certain rights and privileges or accept the consequences of being rendered outcastes if they do not convert. Indeed, it would be fair to say that conversion in an era of religious tolerance functions as an expression of resistance to the centralizing tendencies of national formation. The blurring of differences between religious groups that marks the secularization process, by means of which discrete religious sects are transformed into comparable denominations of a trunk-like religious system, simultaneously produces a defiant reaction by certain groups to preserve difference even while they acknowledge the need for national identification. As a mode of preserving heterogeneity against the unifying impact of the state, conversion acquires an oppositional character that conflicts with its customary description as assimilative or adaptive.

Yet I shall also argue that the central paradox of conversion as an oppositional gesture is that the impression conveyed of individual identity and autonomy is a fiction produced by the state. As the source of the legal enfranchisement of religious minorities, the modern state is also the origin of a developing resistance to the pressures of a threatening homogenization. Not only is conversion as a mode of resistance enabled by the pluralistic possibilities of legal emancipation; in addition, the ideology of individualism celebrated in nineteenth-century conversion narratives unwittingly does far more to affirm the liberal, tolerant, and pluralistic foundations of the modern secular state than civil enfranchisement itself. The climate of religious tolerance highlights the operations of free will with which conversion becomes inextricably associated. John Reed points out that the nineteenth century preserved "a role for free will in history because the past thus could remain a romance developing into the present through the effective actions of men who were honed to moral superiority by that effort and those actions."[7] But there still persists a contradictory logic in the operations of free will, which, though "central to all human endeavor, . . . yet the highest function of that will is to subordinate itself to some higher power, institutional, moral, or theological."[8] As the next chapter will show, conversion testimonies unfold as a drama of subjectivity, even when they are set against an unlikely background such as the civil courts. The public assertion of belief in these court cases reveals an emerging individual identity confronting the taxonomic machinery of state apparatuses. This subjectivity is produced not as a function of epiphanic awakening but rather in the intersections of law, nation, and sectarian society.

At this juncture I want to return to my earlier point about the sobering possibilities of modern criticism being reduced to an act of either citizenship or separatism, in order to emphasize, once again, that the nature of religious dissent is no less subject to these twin perils. Furthermore, it is equally crucial to recognize that the ways dissent cuts a path between and beyond acts of either total participation or total withdrawal is as pertinent to the articulation of a radical brand of secular criticism as it is to the mediation of sectarian tensions. When these tensions are reductively represented as existing between the state and the people, or between secularism and popular religion, it becomes all the more important to understand the location of dissent in public life.[9]

On this last point, Hugh McLeod's work is particularly illuminating. McLeod explores the paradox that, though beliefs were necessarily private in the climate of religious disestablishment, sectarian allegiance in mid-nineteenth-century Britain was nonetheless highly public.[10] McLeod's important work on working-class religion helps one to reevaluate the effect that popular dissent had on secular authority, particularly as it is seen in the intertwining of religious belief and the ideology of the secular state. Indeed, McLeod goes so far as to suggest that, in nineteenth-century England, sectarian allegiance ranked next to class as the most important source of social identity. His observation takes issue with E. P. Thompson's contention in *The Making of the English Working Class* (1963) that Methodist conversions in the 1790s were intended to offer solace to the economically depressed working classes of industrial English towns—those whose numerous political defeats "created moods of temporary desperation, in which the religious revivalist could bring about mass conversions."[11] Instead, following Eric Hobsbawm's argument that working-class evangelicalism had many of the same causes as popular radicalism, McLeod offers an alternative view that suggests chapels were set up in impoverished towns, not as "compensations for the failure of radical politics, but as an integral part of the same movement of self-assertion by people from the working and lower middle classes."[12] Parenthetically, it should be stated that E. P. Thompson's posthumously published book, *Witness against the Beast: William Blake and the Moral Law* (1993), assigns a much more active role to alternative intellectual traditions in the shaping of eighteenth-century dissent from mainstream traditions. Thompson vividly describes the intellectual ferment of such sects as the Rosicrucians, Behmenists, Swedenborgians, and other millenarian and masonic cults in evocative terms, showing how members "argued amidst these groups, they fractured them, took a point from one and a point from another, conceived their own heresies, and all the time struggled to define their own sense of system."[13]

In taking the earlier Thompson work as his point of departure, Hugh McLeod is clearly not seeking to endorse sectarianism as a legitimate public ideology or a superior alternative to identification with the nation, or even to claim a separate and privileged status for popular belief. Rather, he appears to be arguing that sectarian identity has been a popular mode of dissent to claim a public space for the legitimate assertion of working-class aspirations, including the demand for the franchise. In McLeod's reading of working-class radicalism, dissent has far less to do with recovering the autonomy of popular religion than with making the state answerable to its deliberate exclusion of the self-definitions held by its citizens and subjects. Exclusion enforced by the legislative apparatus is all the more marked especially when people's self-perceptions conflict with the system of classification designed by the state. But the more important question still remains unchanged. How does religious dissent secure a critical position for itself from which it resists both the blandishments of a citizenship function and sectarian tendencies? For even in the case studies provided by McLeod, sectarianism is still an instrument for the attainment of working-class ends and the mode through which dissent is expressed.

A fictional illustration of McLeod's argument is the onslaught on parliament by the anti-Catholic masses in Charles Dickens's *Barnaby Rudge*, which I described in the previous chapter as a work marked by equal ambivalence toward the state and the masses. Here I want to extend my argument a bit further by noting that the cataclysmic revolt by the people introduces an extraordinarily subversive note into the novel, particularly because the work appears to espouse the cause of the tolerant state against the encroachments of militant Protestantism, even as it sympathizes with the working-class demand for equal representation in parliament.[14] The horrifying reality of a work like *Barnaby Rudge* is that Dickens confers an overpowering agency on sectarianism as the only effective means available to the English poor to press their demands for the franchise. Their bigoted cries of "No Popery!" slide indistinguishably into equally vehement calls of "No Property!"—an obvious reference to the property qualification for parliamentary representation. The search for an adequate critical position for the articulation of dissent, which eschews the extremes of total membership or total retreat, is obviously complicated by the history of English working-class radicalism, which employs separatist, sectarian strategies to seek accommodation within the public structures of English democracy. One of the most powerful images in Dickens's novel is that of the rampaging English mobs taking over the streets of London to converge on the most public of English national symbols—the Houses of Parliament—in a bid to reverse the exclusionary character of the English political process. For Dickens, this is a process gone awry, for even as it seeks to alleviate restrictions against religious minorities it cannot extend its tolerant arm to eradicate class distinctions. The simplified opposition between militant religious fundamentalism and the English secular state fails to establish the extent to which the public sphere continues to remain a contested terrain for the reclamation of belief.

"Belief" can now be more precisely defined against the backdrop of nineteenth-century social history as a reference not to doctrinal authority but to the aspirations, understandings, expectations, needs, imagination, and goals that constitute the self-definitions of people, the very content of which is denied or suppressed in the construction of their legal or social identity. The full measure of the state's tolerance is thus to be found in its acknowledgment of the validity of belief in the public sphere. John Henry Newman clearly saw that what was at stake in his conversion at an immediate level—and in philosophical criticism at a larger level—was the recovery of belief not as private epiphany but as worldly activity. In the popular demand for the franchise, viewed as the carrier of people's self-definitions, Newman found the most coherent expression of that belief. What is most striking is how ingeniously he grafted the agenda for electoral reform onto the call for a unified religious culture contesting the liberal tendencies of the day. When Newman saw that the potential anarchy of the masses' total enfranchisement could be offset by a return to a foundational authority—that of Catholicism—he overtly compromised the populist cause that he seemed to be espousing. At the base of his desire for a strengthened and fully enfranchised England lay the expectation of a fully restored ecclesiastical authority.

ANTI-STATISM AND CATHOLIC CONVERSION

Legal emancipation and enfranchisement thus open up a different perspective to analyze conversion narratives and histories, and provide the starting point for a productive discussion of John Henry Newman not limited to finer points of theology. Newman's conversion to Roman Catholicism must be read not solely as progressive spiritual awakening but as a passionate reaction against the absorption of religious sects and denominations into a diluted form of Anglicanism, stripped of its ecclesiastical influence. Newman's philosophical and critical system developed entirely on the principle of reversing earlier political positions. Such reversals underscored the ironical contours of a biography that was constantly being recreated in every retelling. Early in his career, Newman staunchly fought the English parliament's proposal to pass a Catholic emancipation bill. The repeal of the Conventicles and Five Mile Acts in 1812 had set in motion a series of developments relaxing the Anglican church's tight hold over religious culture. Newman reacted with alarm to these later developments because they signaled to his mind the introduction of a new mood of moral and cultural relativism. Whereas the Conventicles Act of 1664 had outlawed all non-Anglican religious assemblies, in order to prevent the congregation of seditious persons meeting under pretense of conscience, the Five Mile Act of 1665 imposed penalties on any nonconformist minister who refused to swear on oath that he would not seek any changes in the ecclesiastical policy.[15]

Another event occurred in 1812 that had an equally dramatic effect in years to come on what Newman saw as the culture's tendencies toward relativism.

A bill was passed without debate, which removed criminal penalties against those who denied the doctrine of the Trinity. A little over a decade later, in 1828, the repeal of the Test and Corporation Acts officially declared that those outside the Church of England could hold public office without being obliged to subscribe to the Church of England's articles. Alarmed that the ecclesiastical order had been weakened by these developments and doubtful that tolerance was the real aim of parliamentary reform, Newman saw the proposed emancipation bills as part of a progressive strategy to erode the authority of the Church of England. In his Tractarian phase, he tried to strengthen an Anglicanism that was losing political power and influence by alternatively proposing it as the inheritor of patristic orthodoxy and of the Catholic Church in England.

But influenced to some extent by Richard Whately's writings on disestablishment, Newman abruptly did a *volte-face* and submitted to the course of national developments in limiting the reach of the Anglican church.[16] By 1845, he saw that his Anglican position was hopelessly compromised, and he converted to Roman Catholicism partly out of a recognition that narrow sectarian interests were no longer politically tenable. Thereafter, Newman proposed the "stark alternative" of Roman Catholicism as the only bulwark against the infidelity toward which all other forms of Christianity tended.[17] If Newman's conversion was deeply motivated by a fundamental urge to restore unity of religious opinion, his movement in this direction was substantially assisted by his gradual acceptance of disestablishment of church and state in order, he claimed, to "fight the enemy on better ground and to more advantage."[18] That his own conversion to Catholicism went hand in hand with the moves toward the disestablishment of church-state relations establishes an inverse relation between religious relativism and the fierce assertion of religious identity. Newman's espousal of a religion that he had previously despised is one expression of these altered relations.

Newman was convinced that "crypto-infidelity"—his pejorative term to describe the dismantling of the established church—was hiding behind the screen of parliamentary and civic reform. Just as surely he believed that the reforming party's aim of removing civil disabilities against religious minorities obscured its resistance to what should have been an equally pressing parliamentary cause: the extension of the franchise to all social classes. Personally, he believed that "the most natural and becoming state of things" was for the "aristocratical power" to be the upholder of the Church; yet he could not deny "the plain fact" that "in most ages the latter has been based on a popular power."[19] Newman's position is exceedingly difficult to characterize, because while he was indefensibly reactionary in his support of establishment principles, he was at the same time devastatingly critical of the consolidated wealth of the clergy and the aristocracy and the class elitism they promoted. His savage critique of Lockean elitism in matters of thought put him on the side of a popular antirationalist cause, but it was counterbalanced by an uncompromising commitment to restoring those values of the Anglican church that had been eroded by post-Reformation corruption. His own rhetoric was too shifting to reveal his precise position, though it is clear the universal extension of the franchise became the rallying call around which, more covertly, he launched his campaign against religious and cultural relativism.

Newman's work simultaneously embraces contrary positions within a wide spectrum of possibilities. These positions range from an identification with aristocratic privilege to an espousal of popular radicalism. This breadth of identification was possible largely because Newman's unbuckling of the ideology of tolerance shifts alternatively between a class-based critique, in which he freely draws upon the language of egalitarianism and liberty, and an orthodox religious position, which seeks to unmask the anti-ecclesiastical impulses of the modern secular state. Looming over his work is the palpable fear that the emancipation of religious minorities would turn them into secular Englishmen, whose class position rather than their religious beliefs defined their participation in the nation. Stephen Thomas astutely observes that the success of Newman's polemic lay in his use of rhetorical analogies between the fourth-century heresies of the early church and the liberal forces of his own time. Newman was convinced that these liberal movements conspired to destroy Christian authority under the umbrella of utilitarian reform, and he described their intents thus:

> And so of the present perils, with which our branch of the Church is beset, as they bear a marked resemblance to those of the fourth century, so are the lessons, which we gain from that ancient time, especially cheering and edifying to Christians of the present day. Then as now, there was the prospect and partly the presence in the Church, of an Heretical Power enthralling it, exerting a varied influence and a usurped claim in the appointment of her functionaries, and interfering with the management of her internal affairs.[20]

Heresy, remarks Thomas, becomes for Newman rather "a function within a shifting set of strategies than the object of sustained reflection."[21] But the real ingeniousness of Newman's argument lay in redefining heresy not as an action against church and state as it was in an earlier, more unified era but rather as a directive *sponsored* by the state. Parliamentary reform represented the ultimate heresy in redirecting the goal of a fully emancipated society instead toward what Newman considered the lesser objective of tolerance toward religious minorities. By making religious difference not a matter of social organization but of false thinking, Newman shifted the burden of error back to the processes of religious emancipation and tolerance. For, in rearranging social relationships, religious emancipation establishes a new hierarchy that further fragments the possibilities of oneness offered by the return to an originary church. On the other hand, "right thinking" would eliminate religious difference more forcefully than the tolerant principles of the secular state. Newman's shrewd translation of the parliamentary discourse of civil enfranchisement into the language of heresy enabled him to restrict the idea of inclusiveness to principles of social equality, and so preclude religious or cultural relativism as admissible in the tolerant state's incorporative philosophy.

Although influenced by an increasing interest in "look[ing] to the people,"[22] Newman's own dissent from the established church nonetheless was based on an a priori reasoning that distinguished between centralization and democratization. In identifying himself with the people in order to restore the power of Christian belief to English society, Newman consciously separated the "nation" from the "state." He associated the "state" with pernicious bureaucratic, hierarchical, and taxonomic tendencies, and the "nation" with community-centered local experience. In October of 1834, he wrote a long letter to the *British Magazine* locating the greatness of English life in its promotion of private activity and thought outside the sphere of government, influencing even the spirit of private enterprise. After all, the East India empire, he argued, was the result of independent mercantile efforts, not a government enterprise.[23] The implications of the analogies Newman draws between imperial activity and the exercise of people's will are vast indeed, since his suggestion is that both lie outside governmental control. As we shall see shortly, it is in these extraconstitutional sources rather than governmental initiatives that Newman locates the energy for social and cultural transformation. The space of the "private" is expansive enough to include popular will, belief, *and* colonial ambition. What emerges as a fairly consistent rhetorical strategy in Newman's work is the advancement of an aggressive conservatism upholding both Catholicism and Englishness by recourse to an anti-elitist, populist agenda.

But Newman's lack of a sustained center of political reflection led him to make all sorts of miscalculations about the sources of social change. Though he reluctantly acknowledged that centralization, despite its destruction of local influences, occurred simultaneously with the projected ameliorative measures of the 1832 Reform Bill (which, in the abstract, he approved), he refused to see these moves as emanating from state imperatives. Rather, the democratization that the Reform Bill stood for appeared to him to represent the autonomous power of the popular will, which aimed "to supersede the necessity of a government, and to make the House of Commons, and so the people, their own rulers."[24] The failure of the Reform Bill to extend the franchise to the working classes appeared to Newman to be nothing short of a dangerous derailing of the people's will, and in both his fictional and nonfictional writings he warned of the catastrophic turmoil that the thwarted legislation would bring in its wake.

Newman's novel *Loss and Gain* (1848) makes a trenchant critique of the English state's alienation from the masses of people who remain unaffected by the legislative reforms leading up to and following the 1832 Reform Bill.

The novel is compulsively drawn to noting the fact that the lower-middle and working classes had already begun to mobilize in popular movements culminating in the Chartist petitions to government first in 1838, then in 1842, and finally in 1848 (the year, incidentally, in which the novel was published). In a passage that erupts unexpectedly out of an otherwise placid conversation among several Oxford students about contemporary religious controversies, Newman has Carlton, one of his more politically observant characters, remark that

> agitation is getting to be recognised as the legitimate instrument by which the masses make their desires known, and secure the accomplishment of them. Just as a bill passes in parliament, after certain readings, discussions, speeches, votings, and the like, so the process by which an act of the popular law becomes law is a long agitation, issuing in petitions, previous to and concurrent with the parliamentary process (*LG*, 121).

The context for this remark is the students' debate over the relationship between law and party action, and the degree to which spheres of influence are formed as "extra-constitutional or extralegal" agencies of action. The issue of influence as a "principle supplemental to the law, and as a support to the law, yet not created or defined by the law" (*LG*, 118) suggests the operation of two parallel systems—legal and extralegal—that replicate the divide between parliamentary democracy and popular will, and between secular prescription and belief. The conjoining of these themes in Newman's reading of the English political process is best illustrated by a conversation between characters that immediately precedes the passage cited above. In the interests of preserving the complex negotiation of the franchise issue by the novel's characters and in order not to miss their many nuances, I will quote the conversation at some length:

> "Thus constitutions are gradually moulded and perfected," said Carlton, "by extra-constitutional bodies, either coming under the protection of law, or else being superseded by the law's providing for their objects. In the middle ages the Church was a vast extra-constitutional body. The German and Anglo-Norman sovereigns sought to bring its operation *under* the law; modern parliaments have superseded its operation *by law*. Then the State wished to gain the right of investitures; now the State marries, registers, manages the poor, exercises ecclesiastical jurisdiction, instead of the Church."
>
> "This will make ostracism parallel to the Reformation or the Revolution," said Sheffield; "there is a battle of influence against influence, and one gets rid of the other; law or constitution does not come into question, but the will of the people or of the court ejects, whether the too-gifted individual, or the monarch, or the religion. What was not under the law could not be dealt with, had no claim to be dealt with, by the law."

"A thought has sometimes struck me," said Reding, "which falls in with what you have been saying. In the last half-century there has been a gradual formation of the popular party in the State, which now tends to be acknowledged as constitutional, or is already so acknowledged. My father could never endure newspapers—I mean the system of newspapers; he said it was a new power in the State. . . . The great body of the people are very imperfectly represented in parliament; the Commons are not their voice, but the voice of great interests. Consequently the press comes in—to do that which the constitution does not do—to form the people into a vast mutual-protection association. And this is done by the same right that Deioces had to collect people about him; it does not interfere with the existing territory of the law, but builds where the constitution has not made provision. It *tends*, then, ultimately to be recognised by the constitution" (*LG*, 119–20; emphasis in original).

If it is the case that official secularism can make no space for the disenfranchised classes, who are thus denied a place in history, Newman sees in the space of the extraconstitutional the possibilities of legitimately mobilizing the people to supersede the institutional imperatives of both state and church. In Newman's reading, law becomes the discursive source of what is construed as reality. Legality is disassociated from meanings that attach it to the allowable limits of the law. On the contrary, what is not recognized by law is presumed not even to exist—as if excommunication were in force—so that such things as people's will or belief have no palpable reality as long as the law refuses to acknowledge them. It is because of such mutually exclusive spheres of existence that Newman believes revolution becomes possible, since without recourse to either law or constitutional process the will of the people can be expressed in no other way than civil revolt, as the frustrations of the failed Chartist agitation proved.

Reding's comment about the press as a surrogate for the constitution, organizing people in ways that would have otherwise been the preserve of constitutional process, recalls Benedict Anderson's argument that print capitalism has transformed notions of self and community.[25] For Anderson such transformations are the means by which the imagined community of the nation comes into being. But for Newman popular media such as the press constitute an alternative space running parallel to the terrain staked out by legislative process. The world of the marginal and the private, to which the masses are relegated as firmly as is belief, may be unaffected by the constitutional workings of the public sphere. But the artificial distinction between public and private provides an unexpected occasion for relocating the sources of social change not in law but in popular will. Newman returns his readers to the world of experience (or action) by insisting that belief and will assert themselves as the constitutive bases of relationship to the external world. Furthermore, the balance between belief and social structure functions mutually to regulate the political process (a balance that he defines as a "grammar" in *A Grammar of Assent*).

The failed promise of the Reform Bill leaves Newman no choice but to conceive of the functioning of modern societies as two parallel processes. If parliamentary law has become the expression of vested class interests, then agitation has the force of legal enactment of popular "desires." This word is so suggestive of both repellent anarchy and inviting pleasure that the narrative of *Loss and Gain* virtually comes to a standstill. Vincent's entry provides a casual interruption to Carlton's climactic historical account of how "the first instance of this was about fifty or sixty years ago, when . . . Hallo!" The novel never resumes the broken thought, but the extraordinary position of Carlton's observations within a narrative framed by convulsive religious controversies and sectarian tensions suggests that the key to evaluating English sectarianism lies in its relation to the electoral franchise. The narrative repression that we see in this instance is repeated even more insidiously in Newman's other writings, and still more in Newman criticism, where the question of parliamentary reform in relation to the franchise disappears altogether and Newman's dissent is read as directed primarily against the erosion of Anglican authority.

Newman's enthusiasm for a recentering of English politics in the people led him to see a disestablished and popular Roman Catholicism as a powerful instrument for recovering the unified religious culture of the primitive church, lost since the time of the early church fathers. His syncretic vision, compounded by a nostalgia for an originary community disrupted by the equally sectarian forces of papism and protestantism, expressed a deep revulsion from government in favor of the people. Newman's sentiments are expressed in *Loss and Gain* through Mrs. Bolton, who avers that emancipation had introduced sectarian feeling into England, whereas earlier under the "syncretic" rule of English Protestantism there was unity and harmony (*LG*, 46). However, Newman's sense of a preexisting unity was blind to the state as the source of a series of orchestrated political and legal moves that gestured toward emancipation of religious minorities, but ultimately with the objective of forging a coherent English national identity. In his zeal to recover a lost, pre-Reformation unity, Newman failed to see that his own developing romance with popular radicalism and cultural universalism was not as undermining of the state as he thought it was.

This suggests that the hidden meaning of religious tolerance could well lie in its cultivating a sense of a common, or even national, identity, engendered by the mythos of the people as the real nation before the nation. Newman's nostalgic yearning for a unified religious culture, no longer subject to sectarian struggle, is at the same time an expression of the will to national unity emanating from the state. The syncretism celebrated by the state is the ideological expression of what is assumed to be innate.[26] Newman's radical espousal of Roman Catholicism may have given voice to populist dissent from establishment politics, but such dissent is also a precondition for the process of centralization that follows the disempowerment of ecclesiastical authority. Ironically, it turns out that, for reasons having to do with his own earlier pronounced Tory stand against Catholic emancipation, Newman had rejected this same process. Morever, he denied that it had the potential to construct a syncretic identity out of the materials of emancipatory civil legislation. Such legislation, in effacing class interests, obscured for Newman the English parliament's continued investment in the absorption of religious minorities, and he persisted in reading every parliamentary attempt to relax restrictions against excluded religious groups as an onslaught on truth itself.

RELIGION AND CULTURAL IDENTITY

Could Newman be both assertively Catholic *and* English, as he claimed, without undermining the historical progression toward a secular, national identity that resisted invoking religious difference as one of its constituent elements? To Newman the pressure to achieve compatibility between two contrary affiliations appeared more easily resolved in a critical epistemology of belief-as-dissent than in praxis. To be sure, his conversion to Catholicism was an act of political dissent that turned to religious belief over national affiliation in the construction of selfhood, simultaneously with the political recovery of the popular will. Yet the sustained and unresolvable tension between Catholicism and Englishness inevitably diluted the efficacy of his dissent from Anglicanism and rendered it compatible with assent to prevailing secular norms. His own conversion was thus considerably compromised in the service of English nationhood. In his struggle to achieve balance between two opposing affiliations, not only are Newman's Englishness and imperial ambitions for English Catholicism made transparent but his espousal of popular radicalism is unraveled. A theory of belief that he affixes to popular will collapses under the burden of the hybrid identities that he simultaneously moves toward *and* rejects. His political stake in taking up the issue of the electoral franchise and opposing religious emancipation is nowhere more firmly undermined than by his philosophical contradictions. These serve to disable both the radical intents of his conversion and the dynamic model of belief and will upon which it is premised. A critique of the interwoven strands of nationalist and imperialist interests and popular radicalism that compose Newman's conversion must, therefore, begin with an analytical consideration of his ideas about belief.

More than either his novel *Loss and Gain* (1848) or his celebrated memoir *Apologia Pro Vita Sua* (1864), Newman's *A Grammar of Assent* (1870) attempts to resolve the ambiguity of a cultural identity split between religion and nation by forging a middle ground that one could call "the worldliness of belief."[27] *A Grammar of Assent* could easily be retitled "A Grammar of Dissent" in its detachment of Catholic belief from established structures and institutional practices, including the discourses of education, metaphysics, literary criticism, and law.[28] The clear aim of this literary and philosophical work is to turn Newman's own conversion into praxis. In effect, the dynamic intent of the work is to show the action of belief on the world, and its means of doing so is by tracing the development of "real assent," as distinguished from notional assent to abstract propositions presenting themselves as reality. Praxis for Newman entails developing a dynamic *critical* practice that negotiates between consensual interpretations and private judgment. Belief-as-dissent refers *back* to history and to the world by moving *beyond* the text, and beyond provisional understandings of experience based on abstract propositions. Newman acknowledged the impact of history and the mutations of ideas and cultures on belief systems, maintaining that "doctrines and views which relate to man are not placed in a void, but in the crowded world, and make way for themselves by interpenetration, and develope [*sic*] by absorption."[29] At times, when Newman wrote about the material reality of history, he did so in terms that saw history as a rationalization of events that went by the name of belief systems, as when he observed that "in Parliamentary conflicts, men first come to their conclusions by the external pressure of events or the force of principles, they do not know how; then they have to speak, and they look about for some arguments."[30] Some critics have sought to rationalize Newman's assertion that doctrines are historical and material by noting he was translating "Aristotelian physics into the language of Anglican theology."[31]

Newman sets down as a condition for belief a disembodied subject severed from an interpretive community, especially a community hobbled by a structure of notional assents that engages the individual at only a mechanistic level. Notional assents, Newman maintains, are based on "appeals to what cannot be thought through and explained, except by consensus and appeals to authority" (*GA*, 290). Assenting to an abstract proposition entails that the knowing subject accept, without further question, the cumulative history of assents that the proposition contains. To move to another level of assent—what Newman calls "real assent"—is only possible by examining the grounds of the notional. The effect of that activity is a breaking up of the accretive history of past responses delineating the marked boundaries of an interpretive community, be it secular or religious, national or local. Newman's worldly project is thus a reinsertion of belief into history by a disruptive technique of questioning all previous assents.

Newman does not claim that assent to a proposition makes it true. Indeed, he believes that assents are made in far too many dubious ways and remain too fraught in error to warrant the claims to truth. Nor does he argue that only assents based on unassailable reasoning should be held as true. In *A Grammar of Assent* Newman seeks to provide a description of the subjective state of holding a belief. Newman's test for the truth of a proposition rests on the way we hold the belief, rather than on the reasons for our holding it. Newman terms such belief a *certitude*, which is often accompanied by a subjective feeling that he describes thus: "When a man says he is certain, he means he is conscious to himself of having this specific feeling. It is a feeling of satisfaction and self-congratulation, of intellectual security, arising out of a sense of success, attainment, possession, finality" (*GA*, 166). This feeling of self-repose does not come easily; Newman insists that certitudes are rare, and those who claim they are certain about the "truth" of a proposition usually have only a conviction of its probability.

Complex assents, convictions, and certitudes are acts of self-consciousness in Newman's theory. They all involve bringing to awareness both the content of a simple assent and that of the inferences supporting the proposition to which one has assented. But because these are all acts of self-consciousness, we do not become aware of the content of belief, and instead we become aware of the manner in which we hold it. This would include, of course, whether or not we are secure, reposeful, and sure in our belief. Certitude is thus presented as infinite self-affirmation.

The structure of cumulative assents comprising the norms of an interpretive community is given a much more solid, material basis in Newman's thought than is allowed by some critics. Alan Crowley, for instance, suggests that Newman's subject is "the provisionality of all linguistic formulations" and that *A Grammar of Assent* is essentially a questioning of the sufficiency of language itself.[32] Although Crowley is certainly correct to argue that *Grammar* is not a self-contained closure of philosophical definition, his reduction of the content of assent to language limits him to reading Newman's dissent as having utility only in dismantling hollow propositions, not in reassembling them into acts of will. Rather, I would argue that Newman invests language with such density, materiality, and sensuousness as to suggest that language becomes the vehicle for arriving at history. Furthermore, it is also the means by which the individual moves from notional to real assent.

Although Newman vehemently attacked Locke for advancing an epistemology that presents science and reason as a neutral ground superior to a fully centered self grounded in faith, his critique does not consist of simply reversing the privileged order of these terms. Nor does he wish to consider belief as a formal subset of science and suggest that the proofs offered by science are what faith intuits all along. What he aims to do, rather, is to reimagine a critical stance that enables individual self-definition and individual freedom. This is a stance that refuses the duplicity of pretensions to objectivity made by the neutral culture of science and to value-free, disinterested judgment made by an equally neutral cultural relativism. The freedom to believe remains paramount: individuals freely choose their beliefs or freely give up their capacity to believe. The critical position Newman stakes out for himself preserves the role of dogma and authority in the reproduction of systems of belief, but—and this is where Newman is a puzzle to readers who regard him as an upholder of religious orthodoxy—it also creates spaces in which these beliefs are all the time redefined individually as they are apprehended.

It is already clear by this description that the terms in which Newman presents his theory of assent gradually turn backwards on themselves, so that what appears to be about assent is really descriptive of *dissent*. For instance, it would appear that Newman suggests assent requires a steadily increasing acceptance of the community's norms and values. But he draws an even finer distinction between simple and complex assents to give the word "assent" a much more complicated trajectory that scrambles its relation to a text or a proposition. Simple assent is unreflective and not necessarily even conscious that it is assenting to propositions. A complex assent, on the other hand, "has the strength of explicitness and deliberation, that it is not a mere prejudice, and its strength the strength of prejudice. It is an assent, not only to a given proposition, but to the claim of that proposition on our assent as true; it is an assent to an assent, or what is commonly called a conviction" (*GA*, 162). The distinction between prejudice and conviction is that prejudice is simple, willful assertion, whereas conviction involves a deliberate, rigorous, reasoned investigation of one's grounds before reconfirmation of the assent. Newman does qualify this statement to say there is a residual possibility of error in conviction. However, the category of doubt is not Newman's primary concern, nor are doubt, skepticism, or disbelief ever made synonymous with dissent. It is for this reason that Newman can focus on the intertwined nature of belief and dissent as philosophically compatible terms. If dissent is the refusal to give assent to some propositions because of commitment to other propositions, this does not imply that the dissenter has no belief. Rather, it affirms that the creation or clarification of a system of belief by interpretation signifies one's refusal to accept other predetermined beliefs.

By distinguishing between not only notional and real assents but also simple and complex assents, Newman already drives a wedge between communal understanding on the one hand and private judgment on the other. For notional assent is given to abstract propositions on the grounds of hearsay, credence, opinion, prejudice, or plain trust, whereas real assent is assent to the experience of objects and is unmediated by axioms or first propositions. Charles Reding's insistence, in *Loss and Gain*, that the development of belief should not be construed as disobedience to authority finds its test case in Willis, whose shaky conversion to Catholicism is described not as a real assent to the

complex structure of Catholic feeling but as a reactive gesture against intellectual authority. The hollowness of Willis's convictions is reflected in his eventual backsliding.

Newman sets up the terms of his argument to suggest that the notional assents of a secular, interpretive community can never lead to certitude precisely
because they do not begin from a position of individual liberty. Furthermore,
Newman's sustained distinction between notional and real assent not only dis-
criminates between collective and national definitions on the one hand and
private, personal knowledge on the other but also between learned systems and
intuitive, imaginative belief. Newman claims that "I have wished to trace the
process by which the mind arrives, not only at a notional, but at an imaginative
or real assent to the doctrine that there is One God" (*GA*, 108). But even while
making this assertion, Newman distances himself from theology, which he
insists deals exclusively with notional apprehension. He further allies his project with the revival of religion. His characterization of religion as "imaginative" allows him to establish a case for the legitimacy of aspirations, goals, and
thoughts expressed by the uneducated masses, as opposed to those held by
learned thinkers. Newman's resistance to philosophical analysis derives from
his feeling that he was writing to explain the assents and certainties of the
ordinary man, not the educated philosopher or scientist. His emphasis on the
power of imagination rather than reason is foundational to his hope of attaining
a universalism where there will be a complete eradication of classes. Strong
assent, he averred, is given to the reality that impresses itself on the imagination; by the same token, feeble assent is drawn "to the notion of it as enter-
tained by the intellect" (*GA*, 155).

Newman's romantic individualism links the child with true belief; hence
conversion to Catholicism is virtually the recovery of a lost childhood. In *Loss
and Gain* the protagonist Charles Reding's growth into conviction and firm
belief begins soon after his father's death, which he describes as a moment of
spiritual rebirth: "It was such as to throw him back in memory on his earliest
years, as if he were really beginning life again. But there was more than the
happiness of childhood in his heart; he seemed to feel a rock under his feet"
(*LG*, 296). John Coulson has drawn links between the Oxford Movement and
English Romanticism;[33] but although these links open up numerous insights
into the nature of a theological imagination, Coulson stops short of establishing "the people" as those marked by class who find no political place in England's representative system of government. Newman's interest in the conditions of childhood is not driven by a wishful return to the past, but it is
instead an attempt to understand childhood as a prototype for the imaginative
life of a nation, which he saw being corroded by a system of knowledge affirming the power and interests of a select few.

Because cultural relativism is the very obverse of universalism (which Newman alternatively translates as transnationalism), his argument sets up as irrefutable the notion that cultural relativism keeps class distinctions in place. The

stress on the imagination, which commits Newman to a theory of the materiality and immediacy of image and sense-objects, perceived "as we might map a country which we had never seen" (*GA*, 95), suggests that he was less interested in propounding orthodox Catholic doctrine than in showing how the *ordinary* person gains an image of divinity and gives a real assent to the existence of divinity. "In its notional assents as well as in its inferences, the mind contemplates its own creations instead of things; in real, it is directed toward things, represented by the impressions which they have left on the imagination" (*GA*, 76). If reason creates a confined circle that defines the parameters of English nationhood, then imagination expands that circle to allow for an identity that transcends nation. The Catholic church becomes for Newman a focal point for the dissolution of all class differences and embodies a transnationalism in the service of which his antistatism is employed.

The distinction between real and notional assents allows Newman to do several things. Primarily, it enables him to note that there are some systems founded on such principles as nation, community, and *civitas* that permit no more than a notional assent. To these he opposes those systems like Catholicism—his exemplary universalist system—that have the capacity to evoke a real assent, because they transcend the arbitrary delineations cast around them. Just as importantly, the distinction also enables him to critique the more formal, doctrinaire aspects of Catholicism and call for a form of Catholicism that is pre-Anglican in its spirit. A measure of Newman's self-consciousness in combatting what he must have surely known was a regressive move—he was, after all, trying to justify the coexistence of a populist agenda with a call for a return to church authority—is his repeated effort to demonstrate that, in an era of mass democracy, religious authority and individual liberty are not necessarily opposed terms. Furthermore, to represent them as such is to give a false view of the promotion of the free, private self in a secular culture.

Like many Evangelical missionaries who opposed the legalistic apparatus of British colonial rule, Newman denounced the fallacy of believing that truth can be autonomously ascertained by judicial reasoning. Newman made no effort to conceal his alarm that Anglicanism was tending toward the status of secular law, a set of prescriptions by which the nation was to be governed rather than a set of living principles or ideas providing the defining strokes of cultural identity. He submitted the 1850 Gorham judgment of the Privy Council to stringent criticism for treating church doctrine and secular law in analogous ways, and archly refused to justify his faith on legalistic lines: "I confess to much suspicion of legal proceedings and legal arguments, when used in questions whether of history or of philosophy. Why am I to begin with taking up a position not my own, and unclothing my mind of that large outfit of existing thoughts, principles, likings, desires, and hopes which make me what I am?" (*GA*, 329). Newman's resistance to legal arguments coincides with his protest against more exclusive definitions of the self emerging from centralized forms of administration. In *A Grammar of Assent* the rise of secular institutions (such as national education and the civil courts) are seen as inimical to self-definitions such as those based on faith, which cannot be expressed within institutionally validated parameters.

The replacement of dogma by reason had a different significance for Newman than for Benthamite utilitarians, and he lashed out at a form of reason that chained individuals to institutions and to impersonal, systemic authority. This conviction places Newman at a considerable remove from the utilitarian logic that increasingly shaped English political institutions. To Newman, the critique of rational utility was proof of his solidarity with anti-elitist popular radicalism, so much so that he was able to persuade himself that his call for ecclesiastical authority provided the *only* condition for the true enfranchisement of the masses.

Newman's primary concern was to salvage the subject from the structures of law and reason that increasingly issued the terms of self-definition (and in which, he was convinced, atheism was firmly embedded). But his ultimate goal had little to do with releasing the subject into a free and unadulterated space of autonomous judgment, devoid of all authority. For he remained convinced that the inadequacies of logic and inference led one into an unhealthy state of skepticism. Despite what cultural relativists might say, Newman could not accept skepticism as a critical stance ensuring freedom: "They who have no religious earnestness are at the mercy, day by day, of some new argument or fact, which may overtake them, in favour of one conclusion or the other" (*GA*, 330). The inevitability of submission to some form of authority remains unchallenged by Newman, though he was continually plagued by how that authority was to be defined. The question acquired enormous importance because of Newman's own interest in determining how and under what authority the human subject could be enabled to find the most creative means of self-definition.[34]

It was clear to Newman in 1845, five years before the Gorham judgment had robbed ecclesiastical authority of much of its power to excommunicate, that the Anglican church was too hopelessly mired in its own troubles to provide a creative solution. But he did also recognize that one of the ironic effects of the privatization of belief was that individual faith, by definition, lay beyond the interpretive net of state power. Indeed, this condition provided rousing possibilities for the articulation of dissent. The freedom opened up by a position lying outside the legislative functions of the state pushed Newman to explore the role of personal knowledge in the constitution of the world. This turn toward recentering belief in the subjectivity of knowledge-production is not surprising; as a number of critics have pointed out, such shifts often occur in periods of crisis and cultural change.[35] When Newman asked in *A Grammar of Assent*, "Can I attain to any more vivid assent to the Being of a God, than that which is given merely to notions of the Intellect? Can I enter with a personal knowledge into the circle of truths which make up that great thought?" (*GA*, 95), the disturbing possibility that "personal knowledge" may be merely another description of subject-centered reason is considerably deflected by his own insistence on framing the question of belief outside the space of legal action.

THE FAILURE OF NEWMAN'S BELIEF

But for all the subtleties and ambitions of *A Grammar of Assent*, what promises to be a work that attempts to guide cultural criticism toward the realm of action—the action of belief-as-dissent—turns into a mere protocol of possible critical strategies, at best an elaborate description of mental phenomena. The work stands out in the Newman corpus for its delineation of a dynamic critical practice aimed at disempowering notional assent to foundational premises, yet it really never manages to enter the realm of action or engage with the materiality of historical change. Paradoxically, Newman's theory of belief was grounded in historical change: he insists throughout that beliefs do not exist as eternal verities but are developed by individuals through their immersion in the world. Yet the possibilities of the theory remain unrealized in his account of how beliefs are then projected back into the world. In part this failure is due to his resistance to making matter wholly dependent on mind.

In *A Grammar of Assent* an epistemology of critical practice replaces rather than complements the historical project of realizing the worldliness of belief, which his work originally promised. An ethics of withdrawal, which Newman names "a state of repose," or "a tranquil enjoyment of certitude" (*GA*, 166), marks the ultimately nonactivist nature of his dissent. So pronounced is his withdrawal that if, today, Newman has become a mere "parenthesis in Victorian studies,"[36] that inexplicable tendency toward stasis must be held responsible for his relative lack of success in influencing the modern world. Newman abandons the concept of thought as materiality, just as he relinquishes the dynamism of mental processes in reconstituting and influencing human conduct and perceptions. As he contemplates the virtues of silence, the gains of personal knowledge become no more than private acquisitions:

> In such instances of certitude, the previous labour of coming to a conclusion and the repose of mind attendant on an assent to its truth, often counteracts whatever of lively sensation the fact thus concluded is in itself adapted to excite. . . . Hence it is that literary or scientific men, who may have investigated some difficult point of history, philosophy, or physics, and have come to their own settled conclusion about it, having had a perfect right to form one, are far more disposed to be silent as to their convictions, and to let others alone, than partisans on either side of the question, who take it up with less thought and seriousness (*GA*, 177).

In these lines Newman argues against the very logic of proselytism, which dictates that, having been won over to a proposition by an arduous process of dissent, one will try to spread its truth among others. In fact, Newman insists on equating proselytism with a lack of commitment to convictions, which he believed tolerance breeds because of its too ready openness to contrary views (*GA*, 165). Its unthinking relativism, he argued, encourages people to thrust their half-baked views on others, which would not be the case if people rested securely in the certainty of their convictions. "Intellectual anxiety," he concludes, underlies the need to disseminate far and wide the half-truths that pass off as deep conviction (*GA*, 167). Statements of this kind revert to the idea of conversion as an intensely private experience, which, when fully grasped, leads to the withdrawal of the individual from a larger collectivity. Newman's own investment in the worldliness of belief is considerably eroded by this unexpected shift of perspective, signaling his retreat into a rhetoric of self-fashioning.

However, Newman's narcotic view of repose does not extend to the dogmatic, proselytizing role he has already preassigned Catholicism, which is invested with such aggressive authority as to discountenance all dissent.

> Suppose certain Bishops and priests at this day began to teach that Islamism or Buddhism was a direct and immediate revelation from God, she [the Catholic Church] would be bound to use the authority which God has given her to declare that such a proposition will not stand with Christianity, and that those who hold it are none of hers; and she would be bound to impose such a declaration on that very knot of persons who had committed themselves to the novel proposition, in order that, if they would not recant, they might be separated from her communion, as they were separate from her faith (*GA*, 100).

What is remarkable about this passage is how swiftly Newman has detached personal knowledge from the formalized, rigid system of Catholicism, which is given as timeless and immutable and totally unresponsive to the exigencies of history, circumstance, or experience. The dynamism of belief has no place here, and Newman's categorical imperiousness reinvests orthodox Catholicism with absolute power to set the terms of inclusion and exclusion. His complete rejection of an accommodating Catholicism is in stark contrast to his otherwise historical engagement with "great events happening at home and abroad, which brought out into form and passionate expression the various beliefs which had so gradually been winning their way into my mind" (*Apo.*, 146).

The stasis of development reached by Newman's critical practice replicates the undifferentiated experience of conversion represented in Newman's work. In reducing conversion to a form of change that is *not* real change, Newman neutralizes the radical characterization of dissent and renders it into a discovery of what is already present: a universal, transnational Catholicism that is both the method and the endpoint of all world religions. The Catholicism that Newman affirms, both through his fictional hero Charles Reding and through his narrative voice in *Apologia Pro Vita Sua* and *A Grammar of Assent*, is a much more diluted version of the ultramontanism (a movement advocating papal supremacy) that was then fashionable in Roman Catholicism but with which Newman was by and large uncomfortable. Indeed, Newman's Catholicism is much closer to the faith of pre-Reformation England.

Embedded in the universalist affirmation of Catholicism is a return to origins that prescribes a specific agenda for the English nation. England is resituated globally not as the renegade nation that broke away from Rome but as the imperial center of what Newman posits as the only true world religion. Newman's vision for English Catholicism readily accommodated England's political venture into the accumulation of colonial territories. In a description that precedes by a few decades theosophy's evolutionary account of an emerging world federation (the subject of Chapter Six, below), Newman preferred what he termed an historical reading of the simultaneous developments of Catholicism and English imperial ascendancy:

> As time goes on, and as colonization and conquest work their changes, we see a great association of nations formed, of which the Roman empire is the maturity and the most intelligible expression; an association, however, not political, but mental, based on the same intellectual ideas, and advancing by common intellectual methods. And this association or social commonwealth, with whatever reverses, changes, and momentary dissolutions, continues down to this day; not, indeed, precisely on the same territory . . . but extended itself to Germany, Scandinavia, and the British Isles.[37]

And continuing his description of these developments in terms that anticipate T. S. Eliot's hopes for a resurgent Christian culture, Newman writes: "Certain analogies . . . hold between Civilization and Christianity. As Civilization does not cover the whole earth, neither does Christianity; but there is nothing else like the one, and nothing else like the other" (*Idea*, 192).

It is not surprising that Eliot's *The Idea of a Christian Society* (1939) borrows so much of its argumentative style (including the structure of its title) from Newman, though as it has also been pointed out, "Eliot was seduced from the path of perfect fidelity to Newman's ideal by the allures of culture, and he ended by making that compromise with liberalism that Newman had anathematized."[38] Eliot's tract is written as a diatribe against what, in his own newfound Anglican consciousness, he called a foreign-inspired paganism that celebrated eastern religions in order to refute Christian doctrine. "Paganism" is Eliot's acerbic term for the blasphemy of the English state which turned believing Christians into minorities in their own land. Insistently transforming paganism into an umbrella term for the negative conditions that had made Anglican England alien onto itself, this rhetoric persists in different but related ways in the convulsive debates about the place of religion in modern secular states. In its reaction against the banishment of religion to the periphery of society, Eliot's move reproduces what Stephen Thomas has described as Newman's diatribe against the state as the source of modern heresy. Eliot's attempt to recover belief as a component of civil society would make blasphemy, in turn, an offense that can only be committed within a community of belief.

Newman viewed the Catholic Englishman, far from being "a member of a most un-English communion" (*Apo.*, 120), as more English than is an Anglican by virtue of his connectedness with his national and religious origins. Newman's fiercely defensive assertion that "I had rather be an Englishman . . . than belong to any race under heaven" (*Apo.*, 112) was not simply chauvinistic bravado but rather reflected the extent to which belief was marginalized in nineteenth-century England. The irony, of course, is that his more accommodating Catholic position led him to be regarded as "the most dangerous man in England" by both Anglicans and Catholics.[39] Alan Hill aptly remarks that the success of Newman's *Loss and Gain* "turned on showing that the converts were not bizarre adherents of some foreign creed, but more truly 'English' than their opponents," who in turn accused them of insincerity and backsliding.[40] The attempt to restore a local domestic hierarchy of bishops to the Catholic church in England, controlled since the seventeenth century by Vicars Apostolic under the direct authority of Rome, was part of the effort by the English Catholic community to demonstrate their Englishness, their relative independence from Rome, and hence their loyalty to the English Crown. Yet, when the restoration of the hierarchy finally came, it proved to be "not a symbol of independence from Roman and papal control, but rather the seal upon the process by which English Catholicism steadily came to be dominated by the continental tradition of Roman devotion, loyalty to the papacy, and centralized clerical control."[41]

Of course, Newman's painstaking exertion to prove his patriotic credentials may have a great deal to do with the suspicion with which his own conversion was received by his peers, most of whom believed that he had either been duped by foreign agents or always been a latent Catholic and therefore antinationalist.[42] The devotional symbolism adopted by converts to Catholicism (such as the rosary, monastic dress, and public procession) was strikingly alien not only to the English Protestant tradition but also to the English Catholic tradition, which alike denounced these symbols as un-English. Far more challenging was Newman's task of warding off charges of effeminacy and celibacy, with which Catholicism was notoriously identified. Quick to respond, he asserted his heterosexual English manliness by proclaiming his allegiance to those most English of virtues—scientific objectivity, rationality, and evolutionary progress.[43] This demonstration was obligatory in light of the characterization of Catholicism as "the sublimation of a homosexual impulse."[44]

Newman attempted to deal with the anxieties generated by anti-Catholic suspicion by assimilating the contradictions of dual affiliations and hostile identities into a simultaneous whole. A contrived condition of hybridity, how-ever, proved to be more unsettling than choosing one or the other identity, as this three-way conversation between Charles Reding, Campbell, and Bateman in *Loss and Gain* reveals:

> "Well," he [Bateman] said, "Campbell, you are more lenient to the age than to me; you yield to the age when it sets a figured bass to a Gregorian tone; but you laugh at me for setting a coat upon a cassock."
>
> "It's no honour to be the author of a mongrel type," said Campbell.
>
> "A mongrel type?" said Bateman, "rather it is a transition state."
>
> "What are you passing to?" said Charles.
>
> "Talking of transitions," said Campbell abruptly, "do you know that your man Willis—I don't know his college, he turned Romanist—is living in my parish, and I have hopes he is making a transition back again" (*LG*, 199).

Apart from the not so subtle deflection of unsettling questions, even one as absurdly disingenuous as Charles's "What are you passing to?" as well as the repression of critical engagement that is a regular feature of the novel, the distinction made between the "mongrel type" and "transition" proposes two different models of conversion. The first one stresses the simultaneous em-brace of conflicting identities. But this model is rejected in favor of another that preserves recognizable boundaries around nation, religion, and identity. The rejection of plural identities has both political and literary consequences. Politically, it confirms Newman's rejection of a possibly creative response to legal emancipation—and its taxonomic logic—in the fusion of disparate and conflictual identities. He thus disavows his own inclinations toward a hybrid-ity resistant to management by legal definition. In literary terms, Newman's refusal of plurality reinstalls the novel of conversion as a narrative of linear progression along discrete points, rather than the action of will upon a hetero-geneous and fluid material world. Had Newman embraced plurality, the impact on narrative form would be reflected in a recursive, repetitive, nonlinear struc-ture. In *Loss and Gain* this structure already circumscribes the world of every-day student conversation and intellectual debate, but it is not sustainable be-yond it. "Mongrelitude" cannot be accommodated by a theory of change as transition, a safe passage between two dissimilar but continuous positions. In Newman's ultimately conservative reading, the mongrel is rendered as the obverse of the convert.

Given the fact that change of any kind is regarded as subversive and threat-ening, it is understandable that Newman would have sought to convince his suspicious English readership that he had not changed at all. But that raises a far more unsettling question about the representation of his conversion: If it is true that he had not undergone significant change, how then can he persuade his readership of the need for reform of both the English church and the En-glish political process so that they are both made truly accommodating? Is he caught on the horns of a dilemma where his eagerness to be accepted as English *and* Catholic makes him finally reduce reform (which must involve change after all) to a lesser priority? The accent on continuity is basically incompatible with the primacy of historical change, which is so crucial to Newman's painstakingly developed notions of assent and belief. For Newman to declare that he has merely rediscovered what was always present might make sense at a level of personal experience, but that knowledge does not automatically transfer to the restructuring of institutions. This failure marks a severe limit to Newman's dynamic model of criticism, disengaging his conversion from the critical activity with which it is so closely allied.

The hybrid identities or modes of difference that Newman sees as crucial to the historical progress of secularization—to be both English and Catholic, "Caliban and polite," as he puts it—are not discarded as irreconcilable opposites but embraced as syncretic possibility. But that same syncretic ambition erases the relativity of the terms "assent" and "dissent" (after all, an assent to a proposition is a dissent from another, and vice versa), and there is only the confirmation, or what Newman calls the *certitude*, of what is already known. Caught between the conflicting demands of secular national identity and local religious differences, Newman turns his back on conversion as a dynamic principle of change—the action of belief upon the world. Instead, he embraces conversion as an act of self-confirmation and discovery of what is already latently present as religious teleology. The radical revisionist possibility of conversion is reversed, as achieving a point of compatibility between Catholicism and Englishness replaces the earlier challenge to the desirability of nationhood posed by his conversion. For after all, when assent is reinscribed as political dissent, it changes the terms of reference, and England does not have to be bound by concepts of nationhood or nationalism. Nor, for that matter, does being "English" necessarily have to be the goal of reconstructing religious identity.

Part Two

COLONIAL INTERVENTIONS

CHAPTER THREE

Rights of Passage: Converts' Testimonies

A THEORY OF RIGHTS

Conversion and Civil Law

This chapter is concerned with the subject of civil law—including the laws of marriage, divorce, property, succession, adoption, and maintenance—and its role in establishing the solidarities of community and the foundations of religious nationalism.[1] It is readily apparent that forces such as those of modernity, colonialism, and feminism impinge on these laws and produce conflicts that significantly challenge the terms by which national identity is shaped. I propose examining conversion as an act akin to the forces of modernity in its appeal to personal (rather than collective) choice, will, and action; to the forces of colonialism in its introduction of other epistemologies, ideologies, and cultural frameworks; and to the forces of feminism in its representation of a subjectivity at variance with what is legislated not only in code books of social morality but also in civil and ritual practices. Combining the effects of all three, conversion posits a severe challenge to the demarcation of identities set by the laws that govern everyday life and practice. Changes of religious belief reconstitute the shape of the nation just as forcefully as do systems of personal and customary laws, which lay the groundwork for organizing different communities along sectional lines.

Some sense of this is conveyed by a group of English missionaries in India, defending liberty of conscience and the rights of converts to both spiritual and material entitlement. These missionaries regarded the exercise of English law in the colonies as a just complement to the national reconstructive work performed by conversion. Urging British administrators in 1876 to reconsider their cautious and deferential approach to local customs, members of the Madras Missionary Conference asserted in their letter that "though, by reason of the distinct laws affecting every relation of life, [Hindus, Muslims, and Christians] co-exist as separate and very distinct communities,—*they are yet regarded as one nation*, enjoying under British rule equal political rights, and having perfect equality before the tribunals."[2] If India's religious diversity is manifested in the sheer proliferation of customary, personal, and statutory laws, then English law provides the uniformity required for steering religious differences into enlightened nationhood. As a transgression of religious barriers, conversion participates in this transformative act. In the British missionaries' plea for protecting the rights of native converts, an equivalence is established between the unifying impact of English law and the dissolution of boundaries performed by conversion. In this move, the construction of a national community transcending sectarian lines is seen as the natural outcome of both English law and conversion. More broadly considered, the equivalence lends support to the view that the emancipatory legislation proposed in England since the eighteenth century functions within a frame of centralization and unification that also includes the extension of English law to the colonies.

This unifying tendency, however, does not necessarily mean that conversion is identical to assimilation, nor is conversion always a coercive ideology that erases existing traditions, though the effect produced may suggest that it is. As proposed in the previous chapter, conversion in an age of tolerance connotes the emergence of pluralistic possibilities—and more fluid movements in society—than evident in situations of religious absolutism. Conversion establishes the principle of the nation as egalitarian, just, open, protective, and constitutional, and at the same time committed to a leveling of religious differences. From all these attributes, conversion narratives liberally derive an ideology of individualism and free will that renders the religion to which one converts less important than the possibility of change itself.

Interpretations of Hindu law by British judges focused on precisely such an individualistic ethic contained in conversion. In an 1870 case of the Madras High Court, Justice Holloway defined Christian conversions as a revolt by individuals against "Hindu law [which] is characterized by the entire sinking of the individual, by the contemplation of the world as a unity in multiplicity, having no place whatever for individual rights, by regarding the individual himself as a mere link in the chain."[3] Indeed, the guaranteeing of fundamental rights, including the right to freedom of conscience, elevates abstract principle to the level of individual subjectivity. The compulsions of belief are absorbed in a discourse of rights that contains the contradictions of preserving religious difference, while denying it, by transforming difference into a legal, or constitutional, issue.

If converts do not see their actions as contributing to the consolidation of the nation, that explains why their perceptions enter so rarely into the official record. And if, as the missionaries' analogies suggest, converts are the ground for the articulation of English concepts of "nation," "community," "rights," and "equality," recovering converts' testimonies becomes crucial in establishing what precisely has been repressed in the records, the extent to which their subjectivities are appropriated by a rights-based discourse, and the degree to which alternative visions of "nation" and "community" are proposed by their conversions. I suggest that, considered thus, conversion is not limited to the function of either preserving or erasing identity but, in far more complex ways, is associated with a deconstructive activity central to modernity itself.

One of the key paradoxes explored in this chapter is how conversion and English law, although both interested in bringing the order of modernity to forms of social organization, diverge dramatically in the means, motives, and objectives. If conversion destabilizes the restrictive, political functions of social organization, English law works to strengthen them into forms of control. From the colonizer's perspective, the potential legal conflicts created by the conversion of Muslims and Hindus to Christianity provided an opportunity for management, not necessarily by direct intervention but by the reworking of English law into the structure of an already codified set of customary, personal, and statutory laws. Although this maneuver appears to bring colonized societies into the uniformity required for conceiving themselves as a modern nation, the substance of the rulings suggests that modernity is relocated not in the capacity for change but in the authority of institutions to establish criteria for membership. That this conception of modernity is made compatible with both indigenous and metropolitan patriarchal structures marks the radical break between the transformative potential of conversion and the more accommodating effects of English law.

Impasses of Identity

"The convert must be maintained in his legal rights, but the greatest prudence and forbearance should be practised in the mode of dealing with the excited religious feelings of the people."[4] This statement, made in 1853 in what was to remain a formulaic description of the challenge posed by Indian converts adopting Christianity, Islam, or any other religion, alluded to a situation that had become increasingly commonplace by the mid-nineteenth century: the refusal by converts to accept the pronouncement of civil death and their determination to claim their rights "under the law." Which law, under what circumstances that law was valid, and the laws it superseded or challenged: all these were sticking points of a crossover of identity that was not—indeed, could not—be confined to issues of personal choice. The subject of the above comment was an unnamed convert to Christianity who returned to Coorg, the southern province he had formerly inhabited, in order to take possession of the lands of which he was the proprietor. But on his return he was turned out of his property and driven away by both his family and the people of the neighborhood. The reason: excommunication and the forfeiture of both community and entitlement upon conversion. The situation is already unusual in that the convert refuses to accept the punitive condition of civil death (in this instance, literally a form of exile from his land) and appeals to the British authorities for restitution of his property. He could take recourse in the Caste Disabilities Removal Act, which had been passed in 1850 to protect the rights of converts against forfeiture of property rights. The curious irony, of course, is that even three years after the act was passed and made applicable to all of British India, there should have been such equivocation on the part of colonial rulers toward "maintain[ing] [the convert] in his legal rights," counterbalanced as it was by "forbearance" of his community's religious sentiment.

Although colonial Indians were relatively complacent about the effects of missionary activities (the numbers of Christian conversions never coming close to the efforts and labors expended by missionaries), the event that triggered widespread panic about mass conversions had less to do with missionaries than with the publication, in 1845, of the draft of what was to be the immediate precursor of the Caste Disabilities Removal Act—the Lex Loci Act. One among many complex moves toward the drafting of a uniform civil code for India, the Lexi Loci Act was proposed in the hope of blending the Indian and English legal systems while resisting any further codification of Muslim or Hindu personal law. The colonial thrust toward modernity coexisted uneasily with administrators' determined resolve to leave untouched the classical laws of the country. The colonial project was itself undermined by its own constitutive contradictions, since many of these laws were no more intrinsic to Indian society than the proposed meld of English and Indian systems. The laws had, after all, been carefully cultivated through translations undertaken by prominent British Orientalist scholars, including William Jones, Nathaniel Halhed, Henry Colebrooke, and William Grady. The application of laws derived from Sanskrit classical texts leveled the community of Hindus to include all those who were not Muslims or Christians, and it absorbed under the category of "Hindu" both outcastes and members of religions as diverse as Buddhism, Jainism, Sikhism, Judaism, and Zorastrianism.

The very phrasing of legislative reform unavoidably opened up what Arthur Dicey, in the Victorian context, described as issues involving the conflict of laws, which characterize international situations of discrepancy between the laws of the country of origin and the laws prevailing in the place of residence.[5] Which law should prevail in deciding cases of divorce, succession, adoption, and so forth—the law of the community to which one belongs or the law of the land? In French overseas territories, the general rule was to regard French law as superior to any indigenous law, and when conflicts arose between the French law and the indigenous law, the former was obliged to prevail. In British overseas territories, however, the relationship between indigenous and English law was less clear-cut, and "there was no one general principle which [could] provide a convenient solution."[6] In a speech before the Legislative Council in 1872, James Fitzjames Stephen maintained that "native laws should not be changed by direct legislation, except in extreme cases, though they may and ought to be moulded by the Courts of Justice, so as to suit the changing circumstances of society."[7] The contradiction lies in the fact that although "direct legislation" is forbidden, a certain adaptability to changes set in motion by colonial governance is encouraged.

The proposed law of the land (referred to in the colonial records with a touch of hyperbole as the "Emancipation Act") sought to revive an inactive clause in the 1832 Bengal Regulations.[8] This clause aimed to protect the inheritance rights of converts from what British administrators considered some of the most punitive features of Hindu and Muslim personal law, including the forfeiture of rights to ancestral property by individuals who converted to another religion.[9] Enveloped in controversy and argument from the start, as evident in its stalled enactment, this piece of legislation—and the heated debate over it—highlighted the uncertain status of converts in Hindu society. Among the most vehement protests to the 1845 draft was a memorial to Lord Dalhousie by a group of Bengali Hindus, whose combined solidarity against the proposed measures helped to prevent the act from becoming law. For a short while, the clause in the 1832 Bengal Regulations protecting converts' inheritance rights became a dead letter again. But in 1850 the act was revived and finally passed into law as Act XXI, which henceforth became known as the Caste Disabilities Removal Act. A memorial of protest, similar to the earlier one in 1845, was again presented to the British governor-general to urge him to revoke the act; this time, however, the administration was not moved, and the law was firmly put in place.[10] The act expressly restored to converts only their rights to property; it did not return them to the position they had formerly occupied in caste society. The distinction was to prove an important one in continuing to place the convert outside the fold.

Hindu and Muslim religious bodies justified depriving converts of their rights to property by resorting to what legal scholars today term a legal fiction, that is, the fiction of civil death. This construction views the convert as deracinated and, as an outcaste, no longer recognized by scriptural law as a functioning member of his or her former community. Given the explanatory appeal of caste as a category of analysis in official British discourse, it is not surprising that British legislation showed more than unusual interest in interpreting changes of religion in terms of the loss of caste by converts and the sentence of civil death imposed by Hindu law. On the question of conjugal rights, the resulting uncertainty in the status of converts married earlier under a different personal law exercised no less fascination. For instance, how binding was the marriage of a Christian convert if the unconverted husband or wife testified, "as a free agent," that he or she did not wish to live with his or her spouse upon loss of caste? Could the declaration of "civil death" be sufficient to dissolution of a Hindu marriage, as it seemed to be regarding forfeiture of property under Hindu law?

These questions were not merely of relevance to the administration of the colonies but also to the management of domestic social issues in England. The challenge of removing the caste disabilities of converts intersected with women's social movements in England, which demanded the lifting of property disabilities imposed on women. The condition of civil death pertained to both women and converts, with married women forfeiting rights to property on marriage until the passage of the Married Women's Property Act in 1870, just as Hindu and Muslim converts forfeited rights to property until the appearance of the Caste Disabilities Removal Act in 1850. The outcome of one situation implicitly affected the other, and it is therefore not surprising that the conversion of Indians should have been a subject of interest not only to British administrators and judge but also to the English popular imagination in general and to English women in particular (witness the number of novels about conversion by and for English women).[11]

The legal challenge of ensuring converts' rights met with a complex and contradictory British response. A paradoxical but persistent pattern of rulings emerges from a random survey of cases filed in civil courts by converts petitioning for restitution of their rights, wherever these were sought to be revoked by Hindu or Muslim personal law. British judicial decisions had of necessity to respond to the fiction of civil death as the central problem in applying liberal principles on English lines. Although seeming to protect the rights of converts, judicial rulings dissociated Christian converts from a broad-based community of Christians to which converts may have believed they were admitted, and recast their religious identity in the form of the religion they had renounced. The rationale for this move was the judgment that customs and usages (often deferred to in civil suits as a last resort) were slower to change than beliefs. The way out of the impasse created by the offending clause in the Lex Loci Act was to declare that, however divergent their doctrinal inclinations from the original faith, converts to Christianity could still remain Hindus for purposes of law, especially if their habits and manners remained essentially undifferentiated from so-called Hindu customs. The basis of this discursive move is fairly obvious. If Christian converts were really Hindus, they could not be treated as civilly dead and their civil rights could not justifiably be revoked under Hindu law.

But although this tactic may have served the immediate end of ensuring that converts were not discriminated against by Hindu or Muslim personal law, in the long run the British rewriting of conversion from a spiritual to a material act complicated the self-definitions of converts and reduced existing heterogeneous and fluid populations of India to two fixed categories—Hindu and Muslim. In the name of protecting the civil rights of Christian converts, British legislation characteristically endorsed a homogeneous—essentially Hindu—social identity, rejecting both the assertions of converts about real differences in their past and present religious convictions and a parallel move by communities to enforce those differences on the grounds that loss of caste was irreversible.

Legislation that was ostensibly designed to protect converts' inheritance rights often led to an even greater infringement of rights, especially in the case of female converts. Seeking redress against the trammels of either Hindu or

Muslim personal law, women often found their pleas unheeded. In a gesture of placid indifference, the British government washed its hands of involvement in the internal workings of indigenous caste society. From an administrative point of view, what was at stake was neither amelioration of the socially alienating features of conversion nor alleviation of the exilic condition of civil death to which converts were doomed. Rather, the focus fell on an abstract concept of inalienable rights vested in such things as inheritance and succession to private property (but not extending to marriage and divorce). The defense of that concept was so impassioned that it created the illusion that its true subject was the personal and historical experience of exclusion suffered by those who had renounced one religion for another. But rulings that confirmed Christian converts as Hindus (or Muslims, as the case might be) for purposes of law were by and large indifferent to the conditions of liminal existence that converts were forced to cope with. "Native Christians" (and here I am using the official term to describe Christian converts) were left floating in a nebulous space, neither Hindus nor Christians in their social existence.

For converts, the experience of colonial history is thus one of contradictory and disingenuous moves. While they were treated as dead by their former religious community, the lease of life they were given by civil courts was founded on an equally unreal fiction, a perverse denial of their adopted religious identity. Although British officials claimed that they took legal measures to protect the rights of converts, the fact that they chose to do so by reaffiliating converts to the religion they had repudiated further alienated native converts from both the old and the adopted religions. Moreover, the increasing numbers of cases that involved converts or their families as plaintiffs forced British judges to make a series of rulings and establish a set of principles that might serve as precedents in future cases.[12] These reveal that changes of religion of any kind (which, under other circumstances, might be taken as positive signs of a society's fluid, adaptable nature) posed insuperable problems for colonial administrators, who were more inclined to deal with stable, fixed categories. The reams of correspondence on the intricate issues involved, which flowed back and forth between local and district-level judges and officers and further between legal officers in India and counsel in England, are rimmed with anxiety about the unsettling effect of Christian conversions, particularly those of youth and women. Rulings in favor of an undifferentiated social identity, conflating Hindu and Christian, Christian and Muslim, were conservative and apprehensive reactions to change, inasmuch as they were also defenses of what British officials categorically adjudged to be certain inalienable rights.

The court decisions reveal with astonishing clarity how not only Hindus and Muslims but also their colonial rulers regarded conversion as a disruptive act, complicating the smooth functioning of compartmentalized laws in Indian society. These laws were historically differentiated to reflect the customs and practices particularly of its two major communities, Hindus and Muslims. The prerogative of the courts to determine the laws by which a convert was to be governed brought conversion—which theologians and historians of religion might view as an act of religious conscience and will—squarely within the province of the British legislative and judicial system. Because of the patently material dimensions of religious change, it is not surprising that the official British position on conversion should so strongly stress its political rather than religious aspects, affecting such decisions as whether, for example, to allow Christian missionaries to continue their activities in India, even in seemingly innocuous enterprises like education or social service for the poor.

The political concerns extended to a devaluation of the status of belief and religious conviction itself. The least important consideration in judicial rulings was how converts perceived and experienced their new religion. The degree of converts' commitment to and investment in their adopted faith, the strength of their belief in its doctrines and teachings, had no place in the discussions. The insistence on formal rituals like baptism as evidence of religious change and the refusal to accept profession of faith, as missionaries urged, made no room for accounts of converts' spiritual autobiographies in official records. Indeed, the devaluation of belief followed from a cynical assessment of conversion as no more than ample testimony to the efficacy of Christian ideology. In the cases I have selected for discussion, the British judges characteristically dismissed the converts' repeated assertions of Christian sentiments as having less to do with belief or conviction than with the power and forcefulness of missionary instruction. Therefore, if a convert chose to embrace Christianity or any other religion, such a choice could not be taken as proof of personal commitment to the beliefs contained in that religion, but more likely represented the successful realization of proselytizing intentions for which missionary institutions were set up in the first place.

Belief, Meaning, and Community

In the conflicting messages that converts received about their religious identity—how were they to reconcile themselves to their legal status as "Hindus" or "Muslims" when they had adopted Christianity?—native Christians had little recourse to anything like a language of religious experience, or a language of subjectivity that would offer them the means to express their relation either to doctrine or community. Indeed, with rules of law establishing the terms for self-definition, to the point that it could be said the identity of Christian converts was legislated rather than self-determined or self-determining, the very concept of "a language of religious experience" is necessarily reduced to an abstraction. Among other things, such a concept presupposes an unencumbered self metonymically standing in for (but not displacing) community. In the humanist script that traditional conversion narratives follow, the lines between self and community, consciousness and culture, vanish in the ideological figuration of religious experience as an experience of change *that is not change*. This paradoxical effect signals at the same time the teleological fulfillment of a culture's innate aspirations for itself. In part a legacy of Augustinian mysticism, the metonymic self emerges in conversion narratives as an indispensable fictional trope for resolving the conflicting demands of community and individual will. If community is bent on preserving the boundaries it has established for individual action, belief, and behavior, it clashes with the subjective will of the individual, for whom the arbitrary constraints of barriers are paradoxically the necessary conditions for giving form, if not content, to belief.

The ideology of self-sufficiency and self-transcendence promoted by such a tradition of thought is fundamentally incompatible with the historical elision of converts' self-definitions. The conflict is particularly marked wherever there exists a structure of laws invested with final determining power over what forms of religious experience constitute the basis of religious identity. The pressure of such social and political constraints upon the presumed autonomy of religious experience is precisely what is absent in a work like William James' *Varieties of Religious Experience*. I make this observation not to dismiss James's extraordinarily powerful and moving argument, but rather to situate it historically in relation to narratives of conversion ranging from the biographical-literary to the juridical and official. These texts are all framed by situations of discrepant social transactions. If the conversion narrative is associated more familiarly with the confessional, experiential mode of spiritual autobiography, the governing tropes by which the "spiritual" becomes a self-constituting category of experience remove the debilitating consequences of restrictive social contexts and legal structures on the construction of religious identity. Religious experience is thus understood and described, as it is by William James, as one of the potentially great turning points in cultural development, whose main stabilizing features lie in the recovery of authenticity, integrity, unity, and selfhood. Or, as James describes the experience:

> To be converted, to be regenerated, to receive grace, to experience religion, to gain an assurance, are so many phrases which denote the process, gradual or sudden, by which a self hitherto divided, and consciously wrong and inferior, becomes unified and consciously superior and happy, in consequence of its firmer hold upon religious realities. This at least is what conversion signifies in general terms, whether or not we believe that a direct divine operation is needed to bring such a moral change about.[13]

This is, of course, far from saying that the conversion narrative is inherently constituted in a purely spiritual domain, or that political and social contexts are always removed from the confessional mode of presenting religious experience. Indeed, an important question raised by the colonial negotiation of the conversion experience is the degree to which the idea of personalized religious experience even within the Christian tradition has always required the authorization of institutions such as law. Augustine's *On Christian Doctrine* dispels the myth of autonomous religious experience as readily as do the British legal judgments that I cite later in this essay. This work also suggests perhaps more clearly than does his *Confessions* the connotations of political strife in spiritual transformation. What interests me is the fictionalization of religious experience as self-engendered and separable from the authority of law and other institutions. My discussion of William James is framed by this interest, and is not intended to polarize western religious experience from other cultural or historical traditions, or same-religion conversion experiences from those involving conversion to a different religion.

In William James's work the use of "turning" as a literary trope of transformation from lower to higher mental states—from dullness to vibrancy, division to wholeness, delusion to enlightenment, and perhaps the most celebratory of all movements, from imprisonment to freedom—dispenses with the need to engage with history, more specifically with the contradictory aims of societal norms. Whether the crisis of conversion is caused by a real, verifiable event or is merely based on a suggestive fiction is of less consequence to James than the very real movement it initiates into a new phase of creative self-reconstruction. Conversion is thus presented as more than a change in the state of one's belief. It is for the Jamesian individual what archeological tools are for the historian, a literary instrument for plotting out life-stories and resituating oneself in relation to forgotten signposts of individual identity covered over by the dust of neglect, indifference, repression, and mental enslavement, be it coerced or self-induced. Conceptualized as a democratic, emancipatory critique of the self, the conversion narrative for James is interchangeable with cultural narratives of progressive modernization, of which the story of American democracy is its most exemplary instance. The emancipated selfhood that emerges from the conversion experience ensures some measure of congruence and continuity between the American religious experience and the secular goals of American democracy. The trope of "turning" embedded in conversion turns on metaphors of enslavement and posits conditions of political freedom as the end point of religious awakening.

By casting the leap into freedom in the language of Platonism, the full measure of which is brought out in idealist notions of "selfhood," "authenticity," "wholeness," and "unity," James provides some clues as to why conversion narratives, spiritual autobiographies, and religious confessions have held such an unyielding, privileged place in Western cultural history, overshadowing a view of conversion narratives as products of tension between civil society, religion, and political authority. Among the most glaring occlusions in the Jamesian account is a history in which altered relations between church and state produce changes in the law, including the abolition of the ecclesiastical courts entrusted with trying blasphemy and heresy cases. Such changes accommodate and create an understanding of religious subjectivity removed from its political moorings. In James's scenario the unshackling of bonds by the regenerated individual is never compromised by a state of intolerable alienation to which he or she might well be subject as one who has detached himself or herself from some larger group. On the contrary, the state of division in which the unregenerate spend their lives is what James regarded as especially alienating and illusive, a thwarting of any effective attempt at community as it might be conceived in an ideal political society. The moment of spiritual regeneration, of receiving grace, is the moment of achieved community for the transformed self, now triumphantly freed from the illusion that it is wholly encompassed by social laws that need the fiction of boundaries to exert their true force.[14]

The appeal of the conversion topos rests on the fact that it makes the experience of conversion the central, self-authenticating moment in cultural development. Conversion for James competes with but never actually challenges the power of law and other social and political institutions to confer their own brand of legitimacy on individual identity, and legislate the forms in which identity is socially serviceable and politically meaningful. For James, the ever-present possibilities for self-regeneration and transformation offered by religious experience are resources peculiarly available to a uniform culture, which James assumes American democracy to be. From this premise he deduces that religious experience has some degree of autonomy from the authority of state machinery to set itself up as supreme legislator of individual identity.

The "self-appropriation of interiority" by which theologians and psychologists of religion explain the heightened self-differentiation in conversion experiences is not a purely inward or subject-centered process.[15] Rather, it is an activity of objectification aligning the subjective state with structures of thought, laws, and beliefs that remain at a latent level of consciousness until they are activated by a transformed subjectivity. To suggest that the advance of culture influences (and is influenced by) an ever-differentiated consciousness is to say that the culture in which the conversion experience occurs lends its own structural features to the content of the new religious consciousness. In turn, the developing religious sensibility gains unmediated access to the full range of meanings of cultural forms and institutions, whose interpretability it has in some way now activated.

The socially alienating quality of conversion is thus diminished in proportion to the self-differentiation that ensues, by which culture, including its various realms of meaning, becomes available as an object of appropriation to the convert, duly transformed. If the relation between culture and conversion is not construed as oppositional in James's narrative of religious experience, it has a great deal to do with the terms in which the religious experience itself translates into social understanding and enters social practice. As willed consciousness of religion, conversion, in the Jamesian meaning of "sudden turning" to a religious faith that has been abandoned, forgotten, or unknown, draws much of its force from a unitary theory of civil society. James's confidence in the transformative power of religious experience stems from his conviction that however worldly certain Western secular institutions such as law might be, no institution that is part of Christian culture can remain untouched by its pervasive influence. If both law and religion (as understood in Christian society) are said to be joined in a common purpose to achieve an undivided community of regenerate persons, it is easy to see why the recovery of an authentic self becomes a necessary fiction for sustaining the symmetry between civil society and Christian religious experience.

The subjectivity of religious feeling that emerges so powerfully in James's work partly evolved in response to conceptions of law that placed human beings as responsible agents acting in a natural environment and a human community.[16] However divergent their particular forms of expression, and however numerous the differences on points of doctrine, method, and application, law and religion in an abstract, general sense share a common concern with ensuring and affirming a particular sort of individual identity. It is by such affirmation that the culture is to be defined and progressively refined. This identity is not just understood as a set of specific characterological attributes (such as industriousness, thrift, social responsibility, and so on) but, more importantly, is perceived in terms of a general outlook or consciousness that is as inseparable from lawful action as it is from moral or religious behavior.

With regard to civil law, however, the situation is obviously more complicated, not least because of the greater variability in laws pertaining to such things as conjugal rights, marriage, divorce, succession to property, inheritance rights, and guardianship and adoption, where community-based usage rather than abstract principle has tended to be a more reliable touchstone. As long as the composition and identity of the community remain consistent, small variations in civil customs do not constitute a major threat to the integrity of that society. But real disruptions may occur when a member undergoes intense religious transformations, since change of religion or religious sensibility may cause that person to regard as transgressive what the community accepts as normative. Frequently cited examples are those that relate to conflicts over the status of polygamous and monogamous marriages, and to disputes between the brother and the wife of a deceased person over who is the rightful heir to property, and so on. Conversely, the community may come to regard the convert's change of religion, or altered subjectivity, as in itself a transgressive act, because the pattern of usages current in that society may be disturbed by the demands of (an alien) principle.

In any event, it is in the area of civil law that there is the most intransigence to changes of religious identity, even within a society that is characterized by greater continuity with a dominant religion. Because civil laws are so closely tied to usage, just as much as to the identity of the groups with which those practices are associated, it is more difficult to speak of a stable structure of beliefs, attitudes, and thought that is readily available for appropriation by a converted subjectivity. The one factor that minimizes but never totally elimi-nates the opposition between civil law and the effects of religious conversion is the degree of unity between civil society and religion, that is, the extent to which the dominant culture is permeated by the character of the religion laid claim to by new adherents.

The underlying tension between the transgressive and the assimilative as-pects of conversion erupts most obviously and most dramatically in situations of asymmetry between civil society and religion, where the adopted identity of the convert is at variance with the cultural meanings sanctioned by that society. The radical displacements of meaning brought about by religious change are unquestionably major political disruptions and treated as such in the discourse of the dominant community. By vitally affecting the numerical strength of one group or the other and rendering the relation between "majority" and "minor-ity" and "dominant" and "subordinate" groups forever uncertain, unstable, and unpredictable, the material impact of conversion on patterns of demography undermines—and renders illusory—what the dominant community would like to regard as the self-perpetuating strength of its cultural norms. Where there is such disparity, dominant communities prefer to use the term "proselytism" rather than "conversion" to indicate the forcible nature of religious change. The term also carries with it a baggage of associations that identify religious change as an effect of manipulation, propagandistic activity, loss of individual self-control and will power, and sustained political mobilization. The use of the term "proselytism" further denies subjectivity, agency, or choice to the subject and replaces individuals with masses as the unit of analysis.

Needless to say, the colonial context exacerbates these tensions, not least because of competing claims to the status of "dominant community" based on numerical as well as political criteria. It might be expected that every act of transgression against the native community(ies) is an act of assimilation into another—an act that is encouraged and indeed even promoted by colonial au-thorities. But where the cultural and religious identity of a colonized civil society is itself at stake, to regard individual acts of conversion as incontrovert-ible evidence of transgression for the sake of separation from a predominant religious culture ignores the structure of civil laws operative in that society, rendering problematic the simple movement between religious communities. It may be true that, politically, British colonial power in nineteenth-century India represented an ultimate point of authoritative and legal reference. But when indigenous elite groups, occupying positions of power and privilege in that society, still continued to function according to their own laws, customs, and usages in civil matters, as was the case in colonial India, assimilation into the colonizer's religion often meant legal excommunication from Hinduism or Islam for converts from either religion.[17]

The power of these laws to enforce complete forfeiture of rights on converts (often confirmed by the British courts, despite legislation supposedly to the contrary) casts dubious light on the extent to which conversion-as-assimilation was truly desired by the colonizers. Contrary to what Robert Lingat describes as "arbitrary and incoherent decisions" taken by British judges, who selectively appropriated Sanskritic texts in order to extricate themselves from written law and substitute in its place their own sense of equity, there is a much greater sense of a systematic development of legal principle.[18] When placed in the context of the structure of laws enacted under British colonialism, Christian conversion is less identifiable with an assimilative practice, designed to induce colonial subjects into a community affiliated with the governing class, than with permanent dislocation and exile from a sense of community at large. The issue here is the legal standing of the Christian convert. If he (or she) still remains part of the subject race for legal purposes, what does this say about subjecthood in relation to religious conscience? Does race intervene as a factor to mitigate willed changes of belief?

It is apparent that, under these constraints, religious change is severely strained and qualified. Because of civil laws governing such things as inheritance rights, conjugal rights, and succession to property, religious conversion in the political context of British colonialism is reduced to being an expression of the individual's shifting allegiances to community, not of self-transformation or spiritual illumination. The laws that regulate the daily activities of individuals from birth to death are not easily shed with a change of religion: these laws track converts into their new identity, their new selfhood, to mock their self-willed renunciation of the old faith and the adoption of the new. Jamesian formulations of the recapturing of authenticity—the shattering of metaphysical illusions that the great conversionary moment is expected to bring about—have long been the mainstay of missionary ideology. But they vanish in the constructed identity legislated by the colonial law courts, even as the epiphany of transcendence putatively marking the inner experience of conversion becomes a meaningless fantasy. Indeed, it is more true to say that the private, subjective changes that occur in colonial societies are progressively regulated by the laws that manage and define self, even when that self moves away from a natal community and religion.

It should be apparent, therefore, that my use of William James is not intended to set up opposing models of conversion in the post-Enlightenment West on one hand and in colonial societies on the other, with Western culture offering a paradigmatic liberal model whose normativity is perverted in colonial transactions. On the contrary, the colonial context does not so much distort the norms of liberal discourse as expose its insufficiencies and interrogate its founding categories. The inability of liberal discourse to address the colonial context explicitly suggests that colonialism has a much more active role than mere historical background for the evolution of liberal doctrine. Where liberal discourse does address colonialism, it finds that it can do so only by privileging legislated identity over individual and private self. For British colonialism sets in motion a contingent disavowal of the liberal notion of individual subjectivity as belonging to the privatized realm of meaning.

CASES AND TESTIMONIES

Reclaiming the Renouncer

What is the minimum condition for removing someone permanently from a religious community? For some religions such as Hinduism, neither agnosticism nor blasphemy alone can remove a person from the community in which he or she is born; however, complete adherence to a foreign religion automatically signals excommunication for that individual.[19] A plausible inference drawn from this singular condition is that community outweighs personal belief: regardless of the extent to which beliefs may undergo transformations or remain subject to individual caprice and variations of mood or disposition, membership in community is not severed even for a blaspheming agnostic. The other, far-reaching inference, following from the first, is that a change of religion is less a change of beliefs than a change of community. The antagonism between the individual and the community inherent in this description would seem to overtake the compulsions of private conviction. Precisely this impression is fostered both by British colonial authority and the dominant community from which the apostate Hindu escapes.

Cases brought before British authorities by Hindu parents seeking to reclaim their apostate children provide one of the most readily accessible representations of both the social antagonisms between community and individual and the attendant derogation of private belief. One of the most thoroughly documented conversion cases in the British records is the petition filed in 1844 by the parents of Ananda Row, an eighteen-year-old Brahmin youth of Mangalore who, his family alleged, had been "abducted" by his missionary-teachers and forcibly converted to Christianity. What brought a "reluctant" British administration into this case was the part played by the local English magistrate who, according to the parents of the boy, had abetted the missionaries by turning a blind eye on their activities. The sole redress that the family sought, they repeatedly asserted in a phrase that would have sounded ominous were it not for the pathetic transparency of the euphemism, was to have the boy returned home so that "he could be brought to reason."[20] The magistrate rebutted in his turn that, as a result of his refusal to intervene, the family had staged an ambush on the mission house to reclaim Ananda Row, and when that failed, (again according to the magistrate's testimony) they had concocted a macabre plot to implicate Christians in the desecration of a nearby mosque, so that in the ensuing melee the family would be able to whisk the boy away, undetected.

This 1844 case gains in importance if one considers that it marks precisely that point of transition between a policy of deliberate nonintervention and the enactment of legal measures to protect converts like Ananda against the imposition of caste disabilities. The detailed attention it received back in England, evident in the fact that nearly seventy years later the case inspired a hugely popular novel, Fanny Penny's *The Outcaste* (1911), partly throws light on why the Lex Loci Act surfaced so soon after the Ananda Row imbroglio and culminated eventually in the Caste Disabilities Removal Act of 1850. What were the particular challenges posed by Ananda Row's plight to the timely intervention by English law? Did the parents have a right not only to reclaim their son and undo his conversion to Christianity but also involve the British government in enforcing their parental will? Or were British administrators obliged to resist the punitive measures contemplated by Ananda's family on principles that would have surely brought them in conflict with principles central to Hinduism?

I want to take up these questions by examining the form and structure of the official correspondence on Ananda's conversion, a bricolage of governmental minutes and letters and depositions from Ananda's parents, wife, neighbors, teachers, and other figures of the community (but *not* from Ananda himself).[21] This structured set of documents can be more accurately understood as a palimpsest, a word connoting, as its dictionary definition gives it, "writing-material the original writing on which has been effaced to make room for a second" (Oxford Dictionary), though the traces of the first writing may still be faintly visible. How, in this assemblage of official notes and documents, might one recover the voice, conscience, and experience of its ostensible subject, of what we might metaphorically describe as the "original writing"—the subjectivity of the convert Ananda Row? Wherein do its traces lie, if at all, and to what—and how—does it give way?

First, the most striking feature of this composite text is the note of deliberate tentativeness that structures its formal arrangement. For instance, opinions and judgments from other presidencies are constantly being solicited, while the resolution of the immediate problem—Ananda Row's conversion—is endlessly deferred. This produces a Chinese-box effect, with histories encapsulated within histories, and past social relations between Muslims and Hindus established as paradigms for evaluating contemporary relations between Christians and Hindus. The impact of such a construction is the removal of colonial agency in promoting Christian conversions, such conversions being regarded as chance events in an already well-regulated society. At least this is certainly an intended effect of the highlighted conflict between local British officers and their superiors on issues relating to government interference in matters of free will, self-determination, and personal autonomy. The local officials whom Ananda Row's family petitioned for redress refused to get involved in the case, partly out of support for the missionaries who had given shelter to the youth. The district officers' argument that individuals have to be "left to [themselves] with regard to their religious principles" and that British officials had no authority to "enable [Ananda Row's] relations to enforce any control over him in these respects,"[22] assumed that matters of religious conscience were well beyond the purview of the administrative machinery of government, which had little power to regulate in the private area of personal choice.

This view, however, conflicted substantially with that of their superiors in the London office, who also urged noninterference, but on quite different grounds. The Court of Directors refused to countenance appeals made by the local officers to the "will," "religious conscience," and "conviction" of Indian youth, deeming these considerations wholly irrelevant to the main concern of secular administration. Their view that Hindu or Muslim parents were entitled to reclaim their "apostate" children by whatever means they wished blurred the lines between noninterference and acquiescence far more insidiously than the version of noninterference practiced by local officers.

Such instances of radical disagreement on the extent of desirable involvement in parent-child disputes replay the debates on women's reform in Bengal, particularly the issues of widow burning and widow remarriage. As Lata Mani's work shows, if the British government desisted for a long time from actually outlawing sati, instead setting up distinctions between voluntary and coerced self-immolations as instances of "good" satis (in which case British noninterference was the preferred course) and "bad" satis (justifying British intervention), it was primarily because it sought to leave a space in which the British reformist impulse could be adjusted to the strictures of traditional Hindu society.[23] As with the earlier history of sati, in the case of young Hindu converts the government's position was to refrain from giving any appearance of wishing to disturb the upper-caste Hindu family structure. To intervene in disputes between parents and children, as between husband and wife, was to transgress the tacitly accepted demarcation between private and public domains. The government made clear its wish to preserve inviolate indigenous forms of parental authority, no matter how differently these relations were construed in England and no matter how far English law was able to extend itself in England wherever that authority conflicted with the "free will" of youths. Ananda's case is doomed to irresolution because of the nonintervention of both sides.

However, as again with sati, the stated British policy of noninterference in cases of voluntary conversions obscured the main issues considerably. At the higher administrative levels, the decision to intervene or not in disputes between parents and children did not emerge from empirical observations of what could clearly be construed as voluntary or involuntary conversions, but was based on redefining will and agency in terms that decided beforehand what constituted a voluntary conversion. For instance, age was a major determinant in assessing whether conversions were voluntary or involuntary, since minors were presumed to be ill-fitted to exercise choice. In Ananda Row's case, it was his young age that predisposed the British government to heed the parents' charge that their son had been mentally coerced to adopt Christianity. But the view from the top was not necessarily shared by the local British officers, whose indifference to the parents' pleas for government intervention was supplemented by their own pious appeals to "will," "conscience," and "conviction." In a case that remained curiously unresolved (at least from the viewpoint of the Hindu parents) because the British refused to intervene, resolution was presented in the form of a London order to transfer the recalcitrant local magistrate who allegedly precipitated the trouble to a remote province of British India.

The deferral of resolution, by now a marked feature of the Ananda Row papers, is further supplemented by the conflict between missionaries and higher-level administrators. The tensions between them show up the internal divergences in British responses even more glaringly. Not surprisingly, many missionaries protested against the antiprogressive, self-serving deference shown by British officials to the authority of Hindu parents. To give one example of the later forms that this protest took, some missionaries made an ambitious but ultimately futile effort to amend the Native Christian Marriage Act of 1864 to lower the legal age at which native converts could marry without their parents' or guardians' consent. The age of marriage proposed by the missionaries was fourteen. The original act set the legal age for marriage at twenty-one. But as one missionary, the Reverend Thomas Boaz, pointed out, the act was made to apply generally to all Christians, including Europeans and East Indians, as well as native Christians, whereas native Christians "have until the passing of this Act always been dealt with by the Government of India as Hindus and have been ruled and judged by Hindu law."[24] If, under Hindu law, the legal age for marriage was sixteen years "for all purposes," then the new marriage act placed the legal age for native Christians five years beyond that recognized by Hindu law, and three years beyond that sanctioned by the Company's regulations for the inheritance of property. The act put native converts in an anomalous position, for as the Rev. Boaz pointedly argued, Indians tended to marry earlier in life than Europeans did.

To maintain the same age of consent as the one prevailing in England was to work against the cause of conversion, since young Christian converts—who were civilly dead under Hindu law—could not expect to secure their Hindu (or Muslim) parents' consent to their marriage and were essentially discouraged from converting if they wished to marry. In seeking an amendment to the marriage act, the Rev. Boaz emphasized that "the legal age for marriage ought not to be regulated by the practice of western nations, but from the habits, feelings, and practices of the people of India."[25] The motivation for seeking this differentiation of native Christians from European Christians was, of course, to remove barriers to conversion which were sure to prevail if young Indian converts still had to secure the consent of their parents to marry.

Thus, the missionaries, no less than British administrators, participated in the dissociation of Indian Christians from a larger community of Christians and continued to identify the customs, practices, and usages of native converts with those of Hindus. In this case the government declined to amend the legislation, but the fact that it was unyielding about lowering the legal age for converts to marry threw a pall of gloom over minors, whose parents' authority was undoubtedly strengthened by the act's provisions. Despite the evidence of maturity, intelligence, conviction, and self-conscious judgment displayed by young converts, acknowledged even by judges in numerous cases, chronological age rather than maturity or discretion was used as the basis for determining whether young people were free to exercise their options. The effect of bringing English law to bear on the prevalent customs and practices of Indian Christians was an attempt to standardize the community of Christians, but it simultaneously worked against a recognition of the individual will and religious conscience of its members.

In the framework of a past history of Islamic conversions in India, Christian conversion takes on an unusually charged political significance, reflected in the markedly different and complex ways that converts to the two religions are described in this textual ensemble around Ananda Row. The potential celebration of Christianity that might accompany the disparagement of Islam is held in check by a distancing from converts who undertake to ruffle the even patterns of a society's functioning. Castigating Islam as an historical agent of violent and ruthless change, the tone of the correspondence commiserates with Muslim converts from Hinduism for their loss of rights and isolation from their former community, treating their plight with almost heavy-handed concern.[26] On the other hand, not Christianity but *Christian converts* are blamed as the cause of the Hindu community's disruption, disorientation in the rules of caste, and reckless challenges to parental authority. Ananda Row may have reached the age of eighteen, "when the law recognizes his right to act for himself"[27] and his family no longer had the right to control his actions, but the stubborn conclusion of administrative opinion remains that his rights as an individual to exercise reason and free will are usurped by the absolute primacy accorded to community.

Placed in a continuum that included Islamic conversion at one end, Christian conversion evoked a familiar picture of religious fanaticism and violence, a picture so threatening to British rule that it prompted a call to enact legislation to regulate conversion. The background of Islamic proselytism—and the perceived threat of communal violence induced by Hindu resistance to Muslim "fanaticism"—enters into the discursive representations of Christian conversions as signifiers of disruptive violence. Such representations partly explain the reactive edge of ensuing legislative enactments, which appeared determined to protect and preserve Hindu society. The raked-up history of medieval India, when deployed in the context of debating how best to resolve the Ananda Row dilemma, functions to bring the British government's position in concurrence with the Hindu family's. Past Islamic history acts as a backdrop to the decisive pronouncement that conversion has "ruined the caste of the boy" and produced estrangement of family connections, domestic misery, disturbance of the peace, and dangerous communal tension among Muslims, Christians, and Hindus.[28]

The thrust of the Ananda Row papers reveals a deep anxiety to preserve intact the main structures of traditional Hindu society, even if that meant ignoring the right to self-determination by Indian youth who were of an age to act for themselves. Yet the correspondence also shows a reluctance by administrators to impose civil disabilities on converts, as requested by their families. Such legislation is interpreted as being "at variance with a just regard to the rights of civil and personal liberty, with the principles sanctioned by the British Parliament, and with the express precedents of past legislation in India."[29] This statement points to a major irreconcilable contradiction in the British position: the challenge was to maintain the status quo in the Hindu community, even if that meant denying the self-willed actions of would-be rebels and apostates, while at the same time defend the civil rights of converts to property and life wherever those rights were revoked by Hindu society. The more interesting question to ask at this stage is how the conflict of goals is resolved—in what manner and on what terms.

My contention is that the contradiction not only remains unresolved but gets effaced by making the convert the ground, rather than the subject or even object (the British records are neither of or about converts), on which the whole question of rights is worked out.[30] In other words, if the British task was to accommodate the "rights of civil and personal liberty" to the preservation of the Hindu community without diminishing either, the convert's subjectivity—an account of his or her own spiritual and material needs—is necessarily suppressed in the process of upholding the principles of constitutional liberty so valued by English political doctrine.

In hindsight (since we know that, in the years immediately following Ananda Row's conversion, a string of relevant legislation was passed to address issues left unresolved in that case), what now clearly presents itself as a central paradox is that the regulation of Christian conversion demanded by the Ananda Row case should have taken the form of civil legislation to protect converts from the forfeiture of rights to property and life. Rather than banning conversion or treating it as a crime, the solution to divisions within indigenous communities caused by conversion is to treat the convert as still a member of the community in which he or she was born, and therefore entitled to all its rights. Although not a ban on conversion, such a discursive move effectively minimizes, and even negates to some extent, the radical force of the will to renounce one religious identity for another. It is indeed telling that nothing was more effective in regulating Christian conversion as an actual change of religious belief than the legislation enacted to protect converts against civil disabilities imposed by Hinduism or Islam. It was so effective that even ordinarily astute scholars could comment, as does J. Duncan Derrett, that "it does not seem practicable to enquire too closely into the genuineness of a conversion, once it is established as a fact."[31]

It is of no small significance that the Ananda Row papers, which run over two hundred pages in the board's collections, has not a single account of Ananda's conversion from his point of view, though there are letters and depositions from his parents, wife, teachers, friends, and practically everyone else in his immediate community. Of these by far the most remarkable is the letter by Ananda's young wife, who pleads that if her husband's conversion were not reversed and he failed to return home, she would henceforth be considered a widow by her community and forced to suffer another version of civil death as alienating and horrifying as the one endured by her young husband:[32]

> I am now only fifteen years old, in our caste the females are married but once, and should they loose [sic] their husbands in any way they cannot marry again as the women of other persuasions do. Should I not meet with relief, against the grievances which my misfortune has brought upon me, at this my early age, my life shall be of no worth, and it will be better for me to give it up. I therefore most earnestly crave that your Hon. Council on consideration of my age and sex, will see me a fit object of indulgence, and will deign to give orders to give over my husband to my charge, and thereby relieve me from my grievances and save my life.[33]

The conflicts raised by the wife are key to Ananda's disappearance from the papers: can the administrators to whom she appeals turn a blind eye to his conversion without subsequently opening the door to Hindu society to consign his wife to widowhood? The phrase introduced by Gayatri Chakravorty Spivak in another context, "chain of displacements," might be appropriately invoked to apply to this case, where the husband's civil death produces another death (threateningly more than merely symbolic): death through widowhood for the Hindu woman.[34] The widow's redemption from the heavy penalties imposed by Hindu orthodoxy is simultaneously the subject of another set of parallel reforms initiated by the British government, which aimed to protect widows against forfeiture of their rights to their late husbands' estates. In *this* chain of displacements, whether the wife converts along with Ananda or not, her civil death is absolute and irreversible, unless Ananda himself returns to the Hindu fold. "Relief" for Ananda's wife means undoing his conversion. "Relief" for Ananda, on the other hand, means acknowledging his conversion. Whose situation takes precedence, Ananda's or his wife's?

Again, apart from the abrupt transfer of the magistrate, the absence of resolution in the entire case indicates that neither individual secured the relief they sought. And indeed the pattern of administrative behavior is consistent with the judicial system's perceived obligation not to change the law to provide relief for a particular individual but rather to focus its attention on ascertaining the law of the land. But even to consider meeting the wife's request and returning Ananda to her charge required nullifying his conversion, or at least reducing it to a type of manageable social behavior.

Social management is precisely what is achieved by the papers' establishing the structure of influences producing Ananda's conversion in the first place, and once established, slowly dismantling it, beginning with the missionary school he attended. A teacher's testimony reveals that Ananda Row and at least two other boys in the school read the Bible alongside the Hindu shastras and began to feel "painful conflicts that must harass the thoughts of those who begin to feel the insecurity of their own religion, and yet see the difficulty of embracing another."[35] The teacher's description of his pupil's already irresolute, alienated state of mind enters into the official record through another interpretation as well—that of John Bunyan's *The Pilgrim's Progress*. This literary comparison focuses on whether Ananda's will is strong enough to withstand not so much the trials of religious doubt as the harassments of his family:

> All the dangers and difficulties that would beset his faith if he renounced Hinduism for Christianity were . . . set before him; at the same time the vital importance of the decision he was then about to make was not withheld from him. His resolution seemed for a moment to fail him and he took leave of his friends, but it was only momentarily, for in a few minutes he returned, saying, "I have sent back the peon to say I will not return to my people; here I am and here I will remain."[36]

This construction of events is the closest we get to hearing a narrative of Ananda's conversion, yet no account given by the convert himself finds inclusion. All subsequent responses to his conversion—ours as well as his contemporaries'—are, therefore, mediated by surrogate testimonies. These testimonies, however, while standing in for Ananda's voice, also usurp certain claims that get swiftly undone by the voice of administrative reason. For instance, the claim that Ananda came to Christian feeling "naturally" by a reading of the Bible is dismissed as disingenuous by the public functionary who receives the teacher's testimony; the school, he rebuts, was set up for a European society, run by Protestant missionaries, and designed for the express purpose of converting young Indians. By the same token, however, he also pointed out that since attendance at missionary schools was entirely voluntary, the obligation to undo any instruction that was perceived as false lay in the hands of the parents, not the British government. If learning, reading, thinking, and deliberating are given as such unstable, manipulatable, and even reversible activities, the actual changes occurring in these young people are robbed of their materiality and substance. The need to represent change is appropriated to some larger, more abstract purpose.

The Ananda Row papers demonstrate the calculated mediation of religious conversion from its potential aspect as catalyst of social and cultural change to a more conservative function as preserver of the status quo, regardless of the changes in the content of the convert's religious beliefs. The areas of selective emphases and inclusions in the papers document the privileging of a legislated religious (translated as *social*) identity over private or subjective religious experience. Needless to say, terms like "religious identity" or "subjective experience" are no less open to critical scrutiny for their suggestions of a fixed referential meaning than the split between public and private realms of experience that they come to signify. The hierarchic reordering of religious identifications with community and caste is achieved in at least two closely related ways: first, positing the unstable and indefinable category of "private religious experience" as a separable, essentialized, and even inconsequential reality falling outside historical affiliations of caste or community; and second, isolating belief as wholly extraneous, indeed even irrelevant, to determining Ananda's membership in community.

In proportion to the marginalization of religious conversion as an active agent of cultural change, religious identity is fixed both conceptually and historically as a construct of the institutional discourses of law, among other social systems. If belief is a disengageable aspect of community or caste affiliation and made separate and antithetical to socially determined identities, the erasure of the convert's subjectivity is the logical outcome of this process. For even as liberal discourse upholds a notion of individual subjectivity as the emergence of the free, private self under bourgeois capitalism, the colonial context denies that such a notion can be accommodated by the logic of institutionalized social practices. Indeed, the suppression of Ananda Row's self-definitions in the official British records runs parallel to the relegation of religious experience to the realm of religious ideology—to the self-delusions of errant individuals presuming a naive transcendence of the inclusive hold of community.

When the focus falls on converts and their civil rights, we begin to see that the contradictions inherent in the premises of English liberalism are sustained only by disqualifying the converts' subjectivities for official consideration. Clearly, abstract concepts of rights lend themselves more readily to political expression *outside* the self-representations of the convert whose rights are presumably being defended. This move toward abstraction is all the more pro-

nounced especially when legal protection of rights requires converts to be considered as members of the community they have renounced, not of the one they
have chosen to embrace. Heeding what converts have to say about themselves
also exposes the attempted erasure of their self-defined identity through civil
legislation. It is, therefore, not surprising that in the colonial records converts
become abstractions for the articulation of a notion of rights based on English
liberal doctrine, designed to ensure "civil and personal liberty."[37]

Escape from Community

The discursive representation of aberrant youth is reinforced in an astonishing
case that appears in the 1876 government records concerning Huchi, a young
female convert in Mysore who was baptized as Helen Gertrude.[38] Unlike the
Ananda Row case, Huchi's testimony is included in full detail in the collected
court records, yet its repeated undermining by the dramatic structure of interrogation and judicial pronouncement disqualifies her subjectivity as decisively
as the noninclusion of Ananda's testimony negates his. The case reveals, as
none other does in quite the same way, the startling contradictions in the legal
reforms initiated by the British in colonial India. First, it dramatically illustrates how, although British law commissions and judicial deliberations were
shot through with a reformist impulse, the objects of reform in actual case
rulings often tended to be "errant" youth, especially females, who ventured to
rebel against Hindu patriarchy. The Huchi case dramatically illustrates how a
liberal rhetoric of self-determination and free will is, at the same time, qualified by deference to a Hindu scriptural tradition that the English in India had
codified and made the basis for judicial pronouncements. William Grady's
Hindu Law is drawn upon more consistently than any other legal text to adjudicate Huchi's petition for dissolution of her marriage.

Second, the case reveals two conflicting definitions of free will and self-
determinism, with judges increasingly loading the terms in the direction of
legalism and constitutionalism, whereas the female convert sought to re-create
herself in an area broadly defined as the "spiritual"—a term, however, that
does not necessarily connote a predetermined credal belief. This last point is
important if we are to see that what emerges from Huchi's court depositions
and testimony is a definitional concept of agency and free will that is not
specifically tied down to any doctrinal content. The relation between converts'
subjectivity and their spiritual needs is better understood not in the Jamesian
sense of the merging of self-consciousness in a determinate religious philosophy but in terms of the resistance of converts to the legislated identities thrust
on them by the law courts—a resistance that takes on the character of a spiritual struggle. If the conversion experience for young converts like Huchi can
be described as the creation of a space for subjective self-definition, that inten-

tion is constantly contested by the operative categories of a scripturally derived, codified Hindu personal law, adapted by the British in India to new legislative enactments regulating the shape of religious identities.

Huchi's story begins with her education at the London Mission School where, by her own account, she was deeply influenced by Christian teachings, as a result of which she requested several times to be baptized by the missionaries. At the time, the missionaries declined to comply with her request, fearful that baptizing a minor would expose them to the wrath of the Dewanga (weaver caste) community to which she belonged. Not only by her own testimony but also by that of her parents and relatives, Huchi had repeatedly declared that she had "joined" the Christians and had become herself a Christian, even though she had not yet gone through formal baptism.[39]

> I used to say prayers and read the Bible at home. As I loved the Bible I read it, not to obtain marks or prizes in school. I spoke to my parents about the Christian religion. I told them that the Christian religion was a true one. I spoke to them two or three times. I used to speak to my school-master also about the Christian religion. I attended the London Mission Chapel when I was reading in school to hear the words of God. I used to attend the chapel once a week on Sunday mornings. I used to attend the prayer meetings in the houses of Christians and in churches. I used to say my prayers in school occasionally. I listened to the prayers said in school. I simply listened to the prayers. I used to repeat the prayers. I don't believe in the gods of my parents. I ceased to have faith in these gods from the time I wished to become a Christian.[40]

Alarmed by her repeated declarations of renouncing Hinduism, Huchi's parents withdrew her from school and tried to arrange a marriage for her without further delay. However, the men they sought as potential grooms refused to marry their daughter because of her unyielding stance about turning Christian and severing her ties to Hinduism. Eventually an aunt of Huchi's removed the girl to her home in another Mysore village and arranged for the betrothal of her son Appiah to Huchi. At the time of her hastily arranged marriage, Huchi was thirteen and a half years old, while Appiah was eighteen.

> I was very ill at the time of marriage. I was suffering from fever. I had the fever on for eight days before marriage—very strong fever. I was suffering from fever and headache. Chickamma [her mother-in-law] got a doctor to treat me and to give me medicines. I had fever on me on the day of marriage also. I did not take part in the marriage. I was in great sorrow as I did not wish to marry and as the marriage was celebrated against my wish. As I was very ill at the time I had no recollection of the ceremonies; nor could I in my illness form any opinion of them. I don't recollect what ceremonies I underwent at the time of marriage.[41]

Her husband Appiah, for his part, claimed that Huchi "was as joyous as I was during marriage."[42] Huchi's blurred memory of the marriage rituals, crippled further by the hallucinatory fever that she so repeatedly and painfully evokes, further clouds her reconstruction of the emotional texture of her life in the first six months of her marriage, when she was forced to live in her husband's house. The marriage itself, she insisted, remained unconsummated.

> I never slept with Appiah. I used to sleep separately, with Chickamma's daughters. Appiah used to sleep in the same house. We all used to sleep in one and the same *huzara* (hall). Appiah used to sleep on one side, I on another side of the same hall. I never recognized Appiah as my husband. I was not on speaking terms with Appiah. I never spoke to him. He never spoke to me. No ceremony called *Sobana Prastha* was ever performed between me and Appiah.[43]

The estranged relation with her husband continued for another six months until, receiving a note from her former schoolteacher Louisa Anstey, Huchi was persuaded to escape and take refuge with her. Huchi then ran off to the church, where she received baptism. Under Anstey's tutelage, the *tali*, or betrothal symbol tied around the bride's neck, was returned to her in-laws as a sign that the marriage with Appiah was dissolved, and a marriage was arranged between Huchi and Lutchmiah, another Christian convert. The removal of the bridal *tali* produced a deep emotional effect on Huchi, as if an albatross were being lifted from her neck:

> About two or three weeks after I came to the Mission House I took the *tali* off my neck and kept it with me. As I did not wish that the *tali* should be on my neck, I took it off as it was tied round my neck at the time of my marriage. As I was sick at the time of marriage, and was afraid they would beat me if I took off the *tali*, I did not take it off my neck. Up to the time I returned to the Mission House I did not take the *tali* off, because I was afraid they would beat me. When I came to the Mission House I had itch on me. I felt weak because I was very sorry in mind.[44]

The fear of being beaten by her husband or her in-laws induced Huchi to be silent about her baptism, and when the police were sent to retrieve her from Anstey's house, her fear spilled over into fierce disavowal: "I then denied I was baptized because I was afraid Chickamma would beat me. . . . At the time I denied the baptism I had a love for the Christian religion. I cherished the love in my own mind."[45] Even the police inspector remarked that her demeanor belied her reticence: "She appeared to be depressed and quite downcast and not lively. She did not look like a wife who lived happily and contentedly."[46]

As Huchi's religious sensibility turned inward in proportion to her terror of physical abuse (her mother-in-law warned her, "If you leave the house and go to the Mission School and admit the baptism you will be beaten to death whenever you may be caught"), she returned to her mother's home and, that same day, momentarily enjoyed the mirthful occasion of the Hindu festival Dussera. But overnight, "while I was in the crowd witnessing the *tamasha* (merriment)

I escaped from the crowd and went to the Mission House."[47] At that moment of return to communal celebration of a much-loved Hindu festival, Huchi's denial of Christianity and her feigned acquiescence to her family's demands gave over to the compulsions of silenced desire. She laid claim to an alternate set of affiliations displacing older, more repressive ones: her adoption of a new religion merges with her accepting new parents (Louisa Anstey and the Reverend Campbell) and a new husband (Lutchmiah). The congruence of religious feeling, (af)filiative need, and sexuality constitutes the outer frame of her conversion, which was at once a rejection of Hindu doctrine and a repudiation of the social and sexual conventions that coerced her into acting against the grain of her sensibilities.

Her decision to marry Lutchmiah, a Christian convert, was partly at the missionaries' urging, but the intended marriage was by no means to a man unfamiliar to her. At the same time, in a pattern that runs through much of her testimony, Huchi's acknowledgment that "I know Lutchmiah. He came from Madras to marry me,"[48] was both assertive and withholding, for if her admission was intended to show that this was a consensual not coerced marriage, she seemed to be aware that its hint of a prior intimacy would have weakened her case against Appiah on grounds of religious incompatibility. At any rate, just when the marriage between Huchi and Lutchmiah was to be performed, Appiah dramatically reappeared, claiming that Huchi's first marriage to him was still binding. His forcible reclamation of her was supplemented by an ominous warning that, upon her return, she would have to reconcile herself to living with him not as his wife but as his prostitute, because her renunciation of Hinduism had left him no choice but to treat her as an outcaste. His confused, rambling, distorted, and inconsistent testimony must be heard in his own words:

> I was not the cause of [Huchi's] leaving me. I gave her all that she wanted. Why she left me I cannot say. . . . If I had known that she became a Christian I would not have performed *Sobana Prastha*; nor would I have taken meals cooked by her. I would not have had sexual intercourse with her if I had known she was a Christian. [Huchi denied the marriage was ever consummated.] I would have treated her as an outcaste. Now as plaintiff is a Christian I would not admit her into my house. I would not eat the food prepared by her; but I would sleep with her, treating her as a prostitute (*Soolai*). I wish to have her for this purpose. I would not recognize her as my wife. As she has lost her caste I would treat her as *Soolai* and not as a wife. But I still consider the marriage subsists.[49]

Appiah's claims to conjugal rights as sex-rights were repudiated by Huchi, whose refusal to return to her husband culminated in the filing of a suit to have her marriage dissolved. The role of the missionaries in this process is key, for they instructed her to petition not for divorce but for *dissolution* of the marriage (an important distinction), on the grounds that, as a Christian, she had been married against her will to a non-Christian and that her parents' authoritative action exposed her to the ignominy of excommunication by her husband and the rest of her caste society.

Sandwiched between the testimonies of the key players—Huchi, Appiah, Chickamma, Louisa Anstey, Huchi's parents—and the rendering of the final verdict, which resoundingly went in the husband Appiah's favor, a great deal of activity went on to solicit legal opinion and seek precedents from other related cases. It is to this activity that I shall now turn. Drawing heavily on William Grady's *Hindu Law* for support,[50] the judge in the Huchi case declared that dissolution of the marriage was possible only if Appiah had either committed adultery or deserted his wife, but the judge maintained that Huchi's conversion to Christianity by itself could not be taken as sufficient grounds for dissolving the husband's conjugal rights conferred by Hindu law. From the court's standpoint, Huchi was married under Hindu law and remained a Hindu, regardless of whether she was baptized or not. And especially because she had not received baptism at the time of her marriage, she had no choice but to be subject to Hindu law, her self-declarations of Christian belief evidently annulled by the absence of formal rituals attesting to the same fact. For purposes of the law, Huchi could not claim recognition of her Christian identity until her husband consented to dissolve the marriage.

Though technically Appiah could have ended the marriage on the ground that Huchi was civilly dead, having forfeited her caste by "joining" the Christians and communing with them, the fact that he did not do so left Huchi in his virtually unchallenged control.[51] The power to decide whether the marriage was to continue or not rested with Appiah, not Huchi, despite the outcaste status that Huchi was consigned to live with by converting to Christianity. British reform legislation had effectively excluded change of religion as in itself a ground for dissolution of marriage, presumably to thwart abuse of that provision (for example, of people changing faiths only to get out of bad marriages), yet the evidence shows that such laws consolidated the power of Hindu patriarchies, the right to continue or discontinue a marriage resting exclusively with the unconverted husband.[52]

In thus confirming that the marriage between Appiah and Huchi was legal and still binding, the final court judgment rejected Huchi's claim that in sentiment and in conviction she was a Christian and not an assenting party to the marriage performed according to Hindu rites. It also declared that Huchi's remarriage was not allowable ("practicable" was the word used in the court ruling) under the Native Converts' Marriage Dissolution Act of 1866, though apostasy from Hinduism caused her to be regarded as civilly dead. Huchi's petition was based on an appeal to invoke the provisions of the Caste Disabilities Removal Act of 1850, which protected converts against forfeiture of their rights upon conversion. This act, however, turned out to be quite irrelevant in this case, since Huchi as a Christian convert wanted to detach herself from her former community, whereas the 1850 act was intended to mitigate the sever-ance of community and restore to converts the civil rights they had *before* conversion. In short, the act aimed to ensure continuity with community rather than disruption. Contrary to the impression generated by the string of legisla-tive acts in the 1850s and 1860s aimed at protecting converts' rights, converts were no better off in having their new religious identity acknowledged in law. Indeed, the Caste Disabilities Removal Act was framed in such a way as to ensure the inheritance rights of converts *as if they had not converted at all* and still remained Hindus in terms of the law. Similarly, the Native Converts' Marriage Dissolution Act of 1866 allowed a marriage to be dissolved if the *unconverted* spouse refused to cohabit with his or her partner following con-version. The act was not intended to help converts seek release from a marriage on the grounds of religious incompatibility if their unconverted spouse refused to assent to its termination. The fact is that there was no law to apply to the peculiar circumstances of Huchi's case. Protection of her rights as a convert meant acknowledging her right to sever ties contracted by a community she had already repudiated through her conversion.[53]

The case was further complicated by a multiplicity of conflicting agendas. Huchi wanted the marriage dissolved on the grounds of her own personal conviction and faith in another religion—a religion her husband was not willing to share; Appiah, on the other hand, claimed it was his exclusive prerogative to end the marriage; the missionaries were opposed to forced marriages and urged the introduction of legislation to allow women to choose their own spouses; and the courts were intent on upholding the authority and status of parents in the Hindu hierarchy. Regarding Huchi's objective, there was little ambiguity: she was single-mindedly determined to have her marriage to Appiah dissolved and her chosen identity as a Christian recognized in law. When asked, "Supposing Appiah becomes a Christian, would you like to live with him and recognize him as your husband?" she responded, "If Appiah becomes a Christian, and lives like a true Christian, I have no objection to recognize him as my husband and to live with him. If Appiah wishes to remain a Hindu professing the Hindu religion, I have no mind to live with him, even though he allows me to remain a Christian and to attend the Mission Chapel."[54] The missionaries were supportive of Huchi on all points, but they equivocated on the crucial issue of her divorce from Appiah. Indeed, they were far less interested in responding to Huchi's immediate needs, her resistance to her parents' attempted effacement and derogation of her spiritual wants and physical desires, than in disclosing the "appalling bondage" in which women in India were held by recondite Hindu custom. For in Huchi's case, not only did her parents succeed in forcing her into a binding marriage against her will but they did so in full knowledge of the fact that, having espoused Christianity, their daughter was bound to be treated as polluted and civilly dead by her husband.

The courts, on the other hand, were more interested in addressing other issues, foremost among them the following: first, whether Huchi had converted to Christianity of her own accord and free will and whether she was "then and now" a free agent, capable of acting and judging for herself; second, whether her marriage was performed against her will and consent; and third, since she was a minor at the time, whether the marriage was valid according to Hindu law, irrespective of her consent (which was really a nonissue since she was a minor).[55]

In the lower court's judgement of 1873, it was ruled that since Huchi was not yet sixteen, she could not legally be considered a free agent capable of deciding for herself either in religion or in marriage, although the presiding judge did confess that Huchi during her direct examination "exhibited sufficient intelligence and discretion to judge for herself; but I regret that the law does not permit her to use that discretion in opposition to the wishes of her parents or her husband."[56] The judge further went on to say that Huchi's reluctance to marry was one thing, but such hesitancy could not be taken to imply either total rejection of the marriage or actual coercion by other parties: "The marriage having taken place, the question of discretion is at an end, for the maxim applies that a fact cannot be altered by a hundred texts."[57] One lone judge voiced a dissenting view that "the discretion of the child, its competency to form a correct judgement and not an arbitrary point of time, is the true criterion. There is no age at which a child may not be said to be of a weak, of a foolish, or of a precocious intellect . . . there is no such age in fact—and there is none in law."[58] But his was a solitary view, and political expediency dictated contrariwise, for "to make discretion rather than age in every case the criterion by which a minor's claim to liberty of conscience and protection of the law shall be tested would probably prove impolitic."[59]

The Huchi case preceded by a decade the much more publicized and better known case of Dadaji v. Rakhmabai, which was a suit filed by a husband for restitution of conjugal rights.[60] More recently, it has been resuscitated for commentary and analysis by Uma Chakravarti and Sudhir Chandra.[61] In March 1884, Dadaji moved the Bombay High Court to order Rakhmabai to live with him; she was around eleven at the time of her marriage to the then nineteen-year-old Dadaji. The marriage was never consummated, and Rakhmabai continued to live apart from her husband. After eleven years of this apparently suspended marriage, Dadaji demanded that she live with him, only to be firmly rebuffed by her. The case went to court, but the first judgment on September 21, 1885, concluded that the suit was not tenable. Interestingly, the judge who made that ruling, Justice Pinhey, denied that the restitution of conjugal rights had any foundation in Hindu law and was, in fact, a transplant from England: "What had been imported was a practice that stood discredited and inoperative in England."[62] The belatedness of the English import in India is evident in the fact that, in England, after 1884 (incidentally, the year Dadaji v. Rakhmabai came up in the courts) a wife legally could not be imprisoned for refusing conjugal rights, and after 1891 husbands were no longer allowed to confine their wives in the matrimonial home to obtain their conjugal rights. When Dadaji's denied petition came up again in the courts, Justice Farran reversed the earlier decision and, in March 1887, ordered Rakhmabai to go and live with Dadaji within one month of the court order, or else be subject to imprisonment for six months. Justice Pinhey's worst fears of an imported practice continuing belatedly in colonial India were chillingly vindicated.

Framed primarily by the issues of coerced marriage and the determination of the age of consent, the Rakhmabai case addressed only a portion of the concerns of the Huchi case, yet its position within the reform legislation of the late nineteenth century and its relation to age of consent issues in England made it a *cause célèbre*. The fears generated by the consent issue were exacerbated by the implied devaluation of the nonconsensual marriage and, by definition, of the Hindu marriage. There was a great deal at stake in Rakhmabai's refusal to live with her husband, for if the courts upheld her refusal, the apprehension was that every unconsummated marriage could be struck down as null and void, and Hindu sacraments placed under siege. Rakhmabai's case was controversial for several reasons: it involved the case of infant marriages; it was unconsummated; and, as Uma Chakravarti points out, it appeared at a time when public opinion was consolidating around Hindu nationalism. The right to repudiate an early marriage, especially when there was neither consummation nor formal cohabitation, threatened to destroy the idea of marriage as a sacrament, which none of the male Hindu reformers was willing to do. Nor were they keen to raise the age of consent for females. When Justice Farran ultimately ruled against Rakhmabai and ordered that she return to her husband—just as a decade earlier, Huchi was remanded to her husband's custody—he helped allay the terrible anxieties that women like Huchi and Rakhmabai had released in Hindu society. On the other hand, if the verdicts had gone in Huchi's and Rakhmabai's favor, it would have so jeopardized the sanctity of Hindu marriages, turning marriage from a sacrament to a contract issue, that it appears highly unlikely the judges would have ever ruled in this direction.

The outcomes of both Huchi's and Rakhmabai's cases were of interest not only in India but also in England, especially at a time when English parliamentary legislation to raise the age of consent was being considered to shield children from sexual abuse.[63] The notion that marriage is a sacrament obviously not being a purely Hindu matter, the increasingly volatile debate over marriage as a sexual contract highlighted the extent to which civil law had become a terrain on which shifts in patriarchal authority were being negotiated. In her book *The Sexual Contract*, Carole Pateman observes that "civil law does lawfully what men might have had to do forcibly: that is, overpower women."[64] In viewing the marriage contract as a retention of patriarchal-political right, rather than an expression of consensual agreement, as Uma Chakravarti does, Pateman plays down the age of consent issue, even as she also advances to the forefront of discussion the false distinction between the spheres of nature and civil society connoted by the word "contract," a distinction that she regards as instrumental in perpetuating the subjection of women under the rubric of a civil pact.

Huchi's defeated petition may have been overshadowed by the much better known Rakhmabai case, but the former is subtler and far more complex. Its main participant being not only a female but also a Christian convert, the key issues of the earlier case go far beyond the prescribed debate over prepubertal marriages or the age of consent—a debate, I might add, that has continued to define the boundaries of present scholarly discussions of gender and colonial law. Some of the issues that get played out in greater detail in the Huchi case include the relations between maturity and chronological age, belief and the structure of civil law, modernity and religious sensibility, and female subjectivity and patriarchal authority. The ruling on Appiah's restitution of conjugal rights, conjoined with the denial of Huchi's Christian identity, made it clear that women's bodies *and* their religious sensibilities represent the "nature" that must be controlled and transcended if social order is to be created and sustained. If, as seems the case, Huchi's feminine desire is expressed through religious feeling, both are subjected to the control of patriarchal right, as much as her relation to belief is mediated through male reason and judgment. The opinion issued by the Legislative Department, which reduces the multiple dimensions of Huchi's petition to a narrowly defined, shrill sexual complaint, made that very clear:

> The Government of India can hardly take any notice of Huchi's *ex parte* statements about her husband's present treatment of her, or future intentions in regard to her. She complains that he wishes to have sexual intercourse with her: but this desire is justified by ordinary marital right. . . . There does not appear to be anything special in Huchi's circumstances entitling her to expect a privilege not conferred on other women who dislike living with their husbands. . . . A variety of reasons for asking the Government of India to declare the marriage dissolved are set forth . . . these reasons are quite irrelevant, unless the whole theory of marriage is to be reconsidered from the speculative point of view of a disgusted party to the contract.[65]

In requiring Huchi to return to her husband, the final ruling not only disqualifies the relevance of the age of consent issue, as it does a decade later with Rakhmabai and, indeed, other related cases involving coerced marriages too. More importantly, the ruling also negates the constitutive bases of Huchi's subjectivity in religious dissent. If resistance to the conjugal demands of her husband leads Huchi to seek protection by the colonial state, as well as to appeal for the extension of the laws of British India to Mysore (then a "native state"), the provisional support she receives through the legal process blocks off the articulation of her religious sensibility as constitutively female, since the protection provided by the state will extend only as far as ensuring that no civil disabilities, such as alienation from property, are imposed on her following loss of caste. With such a restricted definition of civil disabilities, Huchi is reduced to an abstraction, her gendered appeal to the colonial state receiving attention only to the extent that it is assimilable to a larger colonial project: namely, the reform agenda of legislating against infringement of inalienable rights on caste grounds. No piece of writing on the Huchi case expresses that compulsion to abstraction more succinctly than this dispatch from the Legislative Department: "If the law is against her, I don't see how we can sacrifice the 'Law' to the 'Lady.' "[66]

It is clear from the debates among the judges and administrators that the relation between age and discretion was not easily settled by empirical observation. In trying to establish specific ages at which the capacity for rational choice was manifested, the judges refused to countenance the possibility that free will and self-determinism are not circumscribed by chronological age. Instead, without denying agency or giving up on notions of free will and self-determinism, they reestablished these as appearing at specifiable stages in one's development, and therefore linear, chronological, commensurable, and amenable to legal definition. The redefinition of agency along these linear, legalistic lines provides the dramatic tension in the Huchi proceedings, where Huchi's attempt to present herself as a mature, thoughtful, and self-aware young woman at the age of thirteen is rendered irrelevant in establishing her credentials as an independent agent capable of acting on her own behalf. The brilliance of the British discursive strategy of substituting chronological age for discretion as the basis of agency lay in the fact that at no point could the ruling judges be accused of saying that Huchi had no right to act on her own. If they had said this, she would have been an unnaturally suppressed subject so contrary to the ideals of English liberal rhetoric. Rather, the judges shifted their rhetoric to declare that her actions would be recognizable in law only if they conformed to the pattern of grading established by "natural" human development (that is, when she would be in a position to act as a free human being). In placing autonomy within a temporal scheme, the final rulings were successfully able to accommodate regulation of errant Indian youth to English principles of self-determination.

Free to be neither Christian nor Hindu, Huchi was thus caught in an impossible double bind, the religion that she now declared her own not allowing her to remarry as long as her Hindu husband still claimed her as his wife (or rather his prostitute), and the religion that she had renounced refusing to accept her as a member of that community. On the question of releasing Huchi from this intolerable condition of liminality, the British government maintained a position of outright hostility that belied its avowed espousal of converts' rights. Where questions of marriage and divorce were concerned, the alacrity with which Hindu law was deferred to (despite it being, in the words of one British judge, "difficult, if not impossible, to reconcile the principles of that law with the principles of the law of England, and those whose sentiments are formed under the one system must naturally disapprove of the results of the other")[67] was as startling as the unwavering determination with which the British opposed civil disabilities imposed on converts by the punitive action of Hindu law. Yet the common feature of both responses to conversion—of preserving Hindu structure *and* guarding against violation of rights—is the recasting of Christian converts as Hindus, despite the self-declarations of converts to the contrary.

The derogation of Huchi's Christian belief was further accentuated by the outside counsel of three London advocates, James Fitzjames Stephen, Charles Bowen, and Henry Manisty.[68] These three radically altered the emphasis of the case by categorically stating that, in order to change the personal law by which one was governed, an actual change of habits of life was necessary, and that a mere change of religious belief, coupled with a *wish* to change habits of life, especially when such a wish was frustrated by parental authority, was not sufficient to change the personal law. The question they proposed for determining religious identity was not "what are your beliefs" but "how do you live your life," not private belief but social behavior and habits. In her passionate testimony Huchi elaborated in extensive detail how she had deliberately and openly changed her habits of life so as to accord with her change of religious belief. But the three London advocates were not convinced, decrying what they saw as the obvious plan of a girl of "such tender age" to use change of religion as a way of putting "an end to her father's right to have the custody of her, and to dispose of her in marriage by a form of compulsion not in itself illegal." They also added the following remark which stands by itself in its uncompromising patriarchal-colonialist sentiment: "Huchi's parents have succeeded in forcing her against her will into a binding marriage; but if the marriage is void, it will follow that changes in the religious opinion of children of tender years have the legal effect of taking away a right which Hindus value above all others—the right of disposing of their daughters in marriage."[69] In the conflict of rights—the child's and the parents'—the Hindu parents' rights decidedly held sway in British legal opinion.

James Fitzjames Stephen's unyielding position on the necessity of restoring Huchi to her husband must be set against the history of his own involvement with India. Replacing Henry Maine as legal member of the Viceroy's Council in 1869, Stephen approached his work in India with an almost experimental glee, as if he were a "schoolboy let loose into a pastry cook's shop with unlimited credit. The dainties provided, in the way of legislative business, are attractive in kind and boundless in quantity."[70] Within a short space of three years, he shepherded into existence three legal provisions in India: the

Evidence Act, the Contract Act, and a revised Code of Criminal Procedure, each more doggedly European than the other in developing juristic notions of individual rights for a culture in which customary laws were organized around the beliefs of communities. In the exercise of good, sensible English laws, Stephen imagined the possibilities of a "moral conquest" more palpable than physical conquest—a possibility that he described in terms of a "new religion." Even more than Macaulay, Stephen fervently believed in the eventual displacement of Hindu and Muslim customary and personal laws by English law (or what he called the "gospel of the English"), and in India he saw the perfect test case for legislation that was, as yet, too sluggisly implemented back in England.[71]

From his years in India, too, emerged the political and moral positions that he adumbrated in *Liberty, Equality, Fraternity* (1872) with Hobbesian determination. Establishing a close and irrevocable connection between morality and religious conviction, Stephen advanced a view of the state that anachronistically evoked a pre-disestablishment character, a view in which religion was clearly central to the state's functioning. But the man who denigrated Huchi's Christian conversion himself moved from an initial acceptance of the primary tenets of Anglicanism to eventual unbelief. The deep distrust of religious sentiment that drove him to celebrate rational utility—and caused him to see John Henry Newman as one of the most fearsome enemies to the progress of scientific rationalism—also led him to be deeply suspicious of belief as an alternative system of thought, invulnerable to skepticism and disdain. Indeed, Stephen had far less discomfort in dealing with mysticism of the sort he identified with Thomas Carlyle, because it appeared to him more harmless and disabling. Given his own loss of faith in the historical truth of Christianity, it is not difficult to understand why his tone in the correspondence on Huchi is so consistently disparaging.

The Huchi case demonstrates the subtle and not so subtle shifts of blame for social disruptions on youth, especially women, whose developing religious consciousness is seen as contributing to the destabilization of Hindu patriarchy. Huchi's resistance to the will of her Hindu parents and her Hindu husband is translated, in the British records, as the errant action of an excitable and immature girl indulging in the illusion of a newfound religious sensibility. If Huchi is marginalized and ostracized by both colonial authority and Hindu patriarchy, and her self-consciousness as a woman (not a child) and a Christian convert consistently denied, it would seem, as Gayatri Chakravorty Spivak argues, that there is no space from which the female subject can speak, or rather be heard, "the dubious place of the free will of the constituted sexed subject as female" having been successfully effaced by the symmetrical alignment of the legal systems of colonized and colonizer.[72]

The exercise of English law in Indian civil cases, which still regarded Christian converts as Hindus under the law, could not but rewrite conversion as a principle of self-willed change into an agent of cultural continuity. The crossing over between discrepant social spaces is neutralized by the reduction of disparate belief systems into an essential sameness of form. I have presented the cases of Ananda Row and Huchi as exemplary social texts of British colonialism, whose interpretation depends on an analysis of the status, function, and nature of personal conviction in the determination of identity in legal discourse. What is on trial in both these cases is not so much the family's right to recover their child, as in the Ananda Row case, or the husband's right to reclaim his young wife, as in the Huchi case, as the religious sensibility of these young adults. This is evident in the small sample of questions posed by the British administrators and judges. What should count as evidence of maturity and discretion? How real is the assent of these converts to the new religion? Are their conversions merely a protest against a restrictive caste society? For both these young converts, to prove that their conversions had grown out of a developing sense of selfhood and conviction requires a new form of narration altogether—a narration that bears only minimal resemblance to spiritual autobiography.

Some sense of this search for an alternative narrative style is gained in Huchi's testimony. Her stumbling, repetitive, and interrupted efforts at telling her story of religious feeling are far from betokening tentativeness, reticence, and hesitation. The form of her narrative might well suggest this, particularly given the state of silence into which her husband's and her in-laws' threats had pushed her. Nor does her testimony confirm that she had self-serving motivations, as the judges' queries imply. Rather, a new form of subjectivity emerges from the courts' denial of her individual, private self, transcending the simple polarity of legislative will and free, autonomous selfhood. In suppressing or marginalizing converts' self-definitions, a rights-based discourse may have trivialized spiritual experience as inconsequential to how communities are defined, but it merely succeeded in banishing religious experience to the realm of uncolonized space. It further cleared the possibilities for turning religious experience into a site for articulating new forms of resistance. Agency is now defined in terms outside those provided by liberal humanism, which describes the emergence of the bourgeois idea of the private self as autonomous from the coercive machinery of legislative definitions.

In the situations I have been describing, on the other hand, resistance to the law takes the form of a spiritual struggle located outside doctrinal content. The emergence of spiritual agency as resistance to legal definitions suggests an alternative form of conversion, subjectivity, and will that cannot be subsumed within liberal humanism. If the liberal norms of conversion accept religious change as subjective transformation—marking a moment of epiphany, or "turning"—this understanding is undermined by another knowledge produced by colonial conversions. Conversion unsettles the discourse of rights, foundational both to the British nation state and the British empire, even as such legal discourses are produced precisely at the moment when colonial rule establishes itself over its subjects in specifiable ways. Although liberal thought may have had its own trajectory within the confines of English intellectual history, the emergence of the colonial context irrevocably displaces and disturbs its prevailing categories. Converts' testimonies play a substantial role in seriously qualifying the liberal notion of individual subjectivity. Though the ambivalence produced by the disavowal of the free, private self is contained by invoking legislative reason, the need for order, and so forth, it cannot but render problematic the notion of conversion as a private, subjective experience.

Consolidating Community

Undoubtedly one of the most legally complex cases involving the rights of converts is the Abraham v. Abraham suit (1863), which centered on the question of which law of inheritance and succession—Hindu personal law or English law—should govern native Christians.[73] More than any other case, Abraham v. Abraham provoked argument and debate in British Indian courts about the relations between civil law and conversion, religious change and community identity, belief and social custom. Abraham v. Abraham began as a conflict over property between the brother and the widow of a native Christian, Matthew Abraham. Francis Abraham claimed half his deceased brother's property on the grounds that, though Christians, the Abrahams were descendants of converts who were formerly Hindus and still retained aspects of Hindu social organization in their everyday practices, the undivided joint family being one of them. Arguing that conversion—even several generations removed—did not efface social continuity with Hindu practices, Francis appealed to Hindu law as having more applicability in this case than English law. Matthew's widow Charlotte (who came of a class known as "East Indians," a term connoting descent from a British father and an Indian mother and often disparagingly referred to as a "half-caste" community) claimed, on the other hand, that through marriage Matthew had completely adapted to an East Indian life-style and bore no traces of any social or religious identity other than a Christian one. Her argument that native Christians came under the authority of English law, by virtue of the fact that they practiced the religion of English peoples, equated religion with nation and conversion with assimilation.

The judicial determination of the case depended on a reconstruction of the Abrahams' history to establish at least three facts: first, whether Matthew Abraham was a practicing Christian both in belief and social observances and followed the usages and habits of Englishmen after his marriage to Charlotte; second, whether the property in Matthew's possession was accrued exclusively through his own efforts or through the combined efforts of other mem-

bers of his family, especially his father and his brother; and third, whether
succession to property was to be determined by the Hindu law of parcenership, as Francis Abraham claimed, or the English law of heirship, as
Matthew's widow Charlotte demanded. In piecing together the family's genealogy, the judges had little doubt that the two brothers were brought up as
Christians, having been educated in Protestant schools and exposed to Christian teachings at home as well. As far as the father's material circumstances
were concerned, little could be established other than the fact that the father
died in 1820 without leaving any property, though five years before his death
he did help his elder son Matthew secure his first job at an arsenal in Bombay.
The same year his father died, Matthew married an East Indian woman whose
father was English and mother Portuguese. In colonial classification, the distinction between "native Christians" and "East Indians" was a salient one and
implied totally different communities, even though both were ostensibly
Christian.[74] In colonialist parlance, native Christians were understood to be
either first-generation converts or those who descended from Christian converts, such as the Abraham brothers, whereas East Indians could trace at least
one of their parents or ancestors to a European Christian and were closer racially to "British residents" (the top term in the hierarchy of Christians, native
Christians being the lowest). Marriage to an East Indian was construed as a
step upward: after his marriage Matthew, according to his widow's testimony,
made the crossover from one community to another by conforming entirely to
his wife's social practices and adopting the language, dress, and habits of English persons.

Incidentally, the vexed issue of distinguishing native Christians from British Christians surfaced often in disputes over burial grounds. The records
are replete with forceful requests by native Christians to be buried in government cemeteries. But although the government permitted those who did
not use the liturgy of the Church of England—even Nonconformists—to bury
their dead in the unconsecrated ground of cemeteries, British officials issued
a distinct ruling prohibiting burial of native Christian converts in government
cemeteries. The reason given was that the same principle about refusing
grants-in-aid to native Christian churches should apply with respect to the
use of government cemeteries. As the governor of Bengal's minute ordered,
"The ecclesiastical establishment of government exists only for its European
civil and military servants. If we agree to provide and keep in repair cemeteries
for native private citizens merely because they were Christians, we should be
unable to justify a refusal to a similar application on behalf of Hindus and
Muslims."[75]

The reconstructed history of Matthew Abraham's life showed that, by about
1823, he had accumulated enough capital to build a distillery in his home town
of Bellary in south India. Four years later he placed his brother Francis, then
fourteen, as a writer and attendant in the shop attached to the distillery. In 1832

Francis and a third person, Mr. Richardson, were admitted as partners under a deed of partnership, which entailed that each derived an equal entitlement to the profits. In addition to running the distillery, Matthew also managed to secure a contract (the Akbarry contract) with the British government for supplying liquor to troops in the cantonment in Bellary. Matthew did not take any partner for that venture, but hired his brother Francis as a clerk or manager to run the business when Matthew was away. In time Francis married and, like his brother, also took an East Indian wife.

In 1837 the partnership between Matthew, Francis, and Richardson was dissolved. Not long afterward, in 1842, Matthew died intestate. At the time of his death both his sons, aged twenty and nineteen, were away in England (the younger one died shortly after Matthew's death). Matthew's brother Francis continued to run the business and took over the contract with the distillery. The initial suit against Francis was filed when Matthew's widow and surviving son were prevented from receiving any share in the profits beyond a small maintenance sum, Francis claiming for himself both full profits and ownership of the distillery. When requested by Matthew's widow to hand over the accounts to her, he refused, claiming that as coparcener he alone, and not Matthew's widow or his sons, was entitled to inherit Matthew's business. Charlotte Abraham and her son filed a suit in the civil court of Bellary to reclaim Matthew's property, including the distillery business and Akbarry contract with the government, all of which (they declared) exceeded 300,000 rupees in amount. In addition, they demanded a full account of the profits that were due Matthew from the shop that Francis was appointed to manage, with the promise that if Francis handed over the books, he would be provided with a just allowance for managing the distillery.

Among the various responses Francis made to Charlotte's plaintiff motion (including a refusal to give Charlotte anything more than minimal maintenance support), the most complicated and unusual one was the argument that, though the two Abraham brothers were Christians and married to East Indians who followed English customs, Matthew and Francis were nonetheless descendants of natives of Hindu origin and hereditary members of an undivided family. Francis claimed that the property left behind by Matthew was the undivided property of the Abrahams, and that, in conformity to Hindu social practice, Francis as the sole surviving brother was now the true head of the family. By emphasizing residual Hindu social observances even in the lives of native Christians, Francis ingeniously shifted the ground in his favor from the question of heirship to that of parcenership. And the civil court of appeal, the Sadr Diwani Adalat, concurred after consulting Hindu pandits, who opined that Matthew Abraham's property ought to be divided according to the custom of the Hindu joint family. The Sadr Diwani Adalat, in fact, held that the brothers represented two branches of a family governed by Hindu law with regard to property rights and with equal shares. Ruling that "change of dress and manners could not alter the law of inheritance, or any local law or usage," the court maintained that where rights to property were concerned, Hindu law was the rule observed by native Christians from generation to generation.[76] On 12 March, 1855, the case came up before the civil judge of Bellary, who ruled in favor of Francis and ordered Charlotte to pay the costs of litigation.

When Charlotte Abraham appealed and the case was referred again to the Sadr Diwani Adalat and later the Privy Council, she scored what she thought was an early victory, since the members of the Judicial Committee, which included John Taylor Coleridge and Lord Kingsdown, refuted the lower court's presupposition of parcenership in settling Francis's claim.[77] And they were not as dismissive of Charlotte's claim that, as an East Indian, she came directly under English law, ruling that the evidence of other East Indians about their general usages ought to have been admitted by the lower court. And, finally, the Privy Council conceded that the question of which law was to govern native Christians continued to be a thorny issue, since they clearly were not Hindus or Muslims and could not legitimately come under Hindu or Muslim law.[78]

But this was the extent of the Privy Council's disagreement with the Sadr Diwani Adalat. In the main the Privy Council upheld the view that Francis had a right to succeed to his brother's property, though for quite different reasons than the one the lower court had endorsed (that is, that Matthew and Francis Abraham constituted an undivided family). It is true the Privy Council maintained that conversion *in theory* changed the focal point of succession from parcenership (the lateral sharing of property within an undivided family) to heirship (or vertical devolution of property). Since a member of a Hindu family who converted to Christianity was instantly severed from the family and considered civilly dead, the ties which bound the family together as a legal unit were not only loosened but dissolved, and the obligations connected with the ties were presumably dissolved with them too. The partition from the Hindu family structure produced by the declaration of civil death—created and recognized by Hindu law—would by definition effectively put an end to parcenership. Therefore, reasoned the Privy Council, from the moment of the original conversion of Hindus to Christianity, Hindu law would normally cease to have any obligatory force upon converts and their descendants—a point that is asserted with minimal equivocation by the lords on the Judicial Committee.

But theory did not amount to fact—or so it would seem if one were to go by the Privy Council's subsequent judgment. To Charlotte Abraham's argument that, as an East Indian Christian whose late husband also conformed entirely to East Indian customs and usages, both she and her husband had a right to claim English law, the Privy Council declared that though the East Indians most closely resembled the British residents in their religion, customs, and manners, they could not claim exemption from the jurisdiction of Hindu law nor enjoy the privilege of English law which the British in India did ("such is the limited sense of the terms of the jurisdiction of the charters of the supreme court").[79] The case unfolds as a succession of conundrums. The Privy Council accommodated Francis's claim that the case fell under the jurisdiction of Hindu law and declared that converts had the option of either accepting or rejecting the old personal law, even though they might have renounced the old religion.[80] The Council even went one step further by declaring that the general customs and laws of the religion to which converts presently belonged were not obligatory on them.

In fact, the changeability of human beings and the instability of beliefs are invoked as an argument to support a view of native Christians as still relationally placed vis-à-vis the religious community they leave behind. If a family of converts either retained or abandoned the customs of their unconverted predecessors, their choice need not be construed as invariable and inflexible. Both they and their descendants could conceivably change; as Lord Kingsdown phrased it, "human beings are naturally variable, dependent on the changeful inclinations, feelings, and obligations of successive generations of men. . . . *Though race and blood are independent of volition, usage is not.*"[81] Significantly, the idea that Hindu law might still have an obligatory force on Christian converts was introduced neither by the plaintiff nor the respondent, but solely by the courts. Both Charlotte and Francis, in their different ways, appealed to the customs and usages of *families*, not of Hindu society. Their respective legal claims avoided generalized appeals to religious community or religious laws and were instead based on the day-to-day practices of the smallest possible unit of community, the family.

Charlotte Abraham's strongest argument against Francis's claim to coparcenership maintained that Matthew's property was acquired entirely through his own efforts and not from his ancestors (in which case Hindu law might have been applicable). The fact that Matthew Abraham's father died without leaving him any property weighed heavily on the Privy Council's accounting of Matthew's assets and turned out to be the most difficult point for Francis to contest. In examining the evidence, the Privy Council was satisfied that the property in Matthew's possession at the time of his death was acquired by his own "unaided exertions" and without the use of any common stock. Therefore, no rule about its use that Hindu ancestors may have voluntarily imposed upon themselves—such as the one that only those who continued to be Hindus could inherit ancestral wealth—was applicable to a descendant amassing his own wealth. And indeed after the Indian Succession Act of 1865, which soon followed the Abraham case, it was no longer possible for converts from Hinduism to *elect* to be governed by Hindu law if they so chose.

It is therefore all the more surprising that the Privy Council should have concluded that *had the family possessed property*, they most probably would have enjoyed it in common, according to Hindu custom. The basis for this unexpected pronouncement was not empirical observation of the Abraham family's behavior and customs, but *the class of family* the Abrahams represented—"a class of native Christians which *commonly* retains native usages and customs."[82] Francis's argument that the land of one's birth rather than the habits and customs one followed should determine the laws by which one is governed seemed to have made a sizable impression on the judges hearing the case. They too increasingly spoke in behalf of native origin—country of birth—as a definitive factor in determining laws of inheritance, correspondingly minimizing the potentially disruptive force of individual and religious change. Lord Kingsdown's final judgment, which was handed down on June 13, 1863, came close to concurring with Francis's argument that "[the Abrahams'] religion was an accident, and that in fact they were Hindus" who were subject to Hindu law and no other law.[83] Kingsdown phrased it differently, less emphatically perhaps, but clearly he made the same argument: "The profession of Christianity releases the convert from the trammels of the Hindu law, but it does not of necessity involve any change of the rights or relations of the convert, in matters with which Christianity has no concern, such as his rights and interests in, and his powers over, property."[84] In short, it was ruled, on the basis of "justice, equity, and good conscience,"[85] that Francis Abraham had a right to inherit half his brother's property, not because he was Matthew's coparcener or the property was ancestral, but because of the shadowy legal status of native Christians in India, who could be affiliated to neither European Christians nor Hindus. Clearly, Matthew's profession of Christianity was virtually irrelevant in the final decision, which was arrived at as if he were a Hindu.

When Kingsdown justified his ruling by arguing that property had a different set of meanings in India, which Christian conversion was powerless to change, his argument rested on two distinctions that were mistakenly applied to the Abraham case, which is manifestly *not* a case about a first-time Christian convert breaking away from the Hindu fold. First, succession to property in Hindu law is construed as a sensibility, not a right: ancestors are injured by apostasy, a wrong that Hindu law tries to redress by devolving property on the next male heir capable of performing duties that attach to it. Going as far back as the 1845 petition submitted by Bengali Brahmins to Dalhousie to protest antidisabilities legislation, one of the enduring arguments marking off Hinduism from other religions maintained that the property of the ancestor only descended to the male heir who still had the religious capacity to perform ancestral rites. Religious obligations and rights are linked in a reciprocal relation: if individuals cannot perform religious duties toward ancestors, they enjoy no rights. Second, property is treated not as a material object but a sacred trust. Although the first point is alien to English law, Kingsdown interpreted the second to have some bearing on the way the Abraham case could be adjudicated. The notion of trustee is both Protestant and masculine: It explains why the brother in the Abraham v. Abraham case is accepted more readily as a trustee of the deceased Matthew's property than the widow, who struck the judge as too incompetent to administer it properly. It would appear that Kingsdown, in favoring Francis, was enunciating a principle not dissimilar from Hindu law—that the right to inherit property is a trust, if not entirely a sacred one.

Misapplied or not, the distinctions between Hindu and Christian attitudes to property proved to be nominal in selective instances, as in the latter point, and indeed they help to illuminate the Privy Council's ruling in favor of Francis. Though Charlotte did not come away empty-handed, since Francis was ordered by the court to pay her and Matthew's son adequate maintenance support, the general tone of the Privy Council's deliberations was persistently condescending toward her. The aspect of Francis's testimony that most fascinated the judges is his narration of the various business strategies he worked out (full of "Protestant thrift and management," marveled the judges) to build up the distillery begun by his brother Matthew.[86] In what must be seen as an extraordinary coup de grace, Charlotte Abraham is severely admonished by the Privy Council for her lack of business sense and general irresponsibility: if Francis had not taken over the distillery when he did, she is told, it would have surely collapsed! That a civil suit, filed to contest a native Christian's claim to succession of his brother's property under Hindu law, should have concluded with a stern reprimand to the widow to offer her gratitude to the "Protestant thrift and management" of her brother-in-law (who presented himself as a Hindu under the law) reveals the extent to which religious categories were reassembled for administrative purposes, while lived forms of experience were made meaningless by the imperatives of English legislative action.

CHAPTER FOUR

Silencing Heresy

FEMINIST STRUGGLE AND RELIGIOUS DISSENT

Pandita Ramabai (1858–1922), Christian convert and renowned social re-former, lived a life that was a prototype of feminist aspiration to succeeding generations of Indian women, but to her own generation her career appeared confusing, inconsistent, and even contradictory. As a scholar of Hinduism who had profound quarrels with its philosophical premises, particularly with regard to women, and later as a Christian convert who rebelled against Christian dogma, Ramabai seemed always to be outside the system of which she was ostensibly a part. The travails of her early life reinforce this impression.

Born in 1858 to an upper-caste Chitpavan Brahmin family of Maharashtra, she survived a series of deaths in her immediate family, including the deaths of her parents, sister, brother, and husband, with a resilience steeled by her determination to turn misfortune into salvation for herself and other similarly afflicted women. (Years later, in 1921, she was to lose her only child Mano-rama, whose death would soon be followed by her own in 1922.) A peripatetic Sanskrit scholar for much of her early life, Ramabai's years of pilgrimage through the length and breadth of India mirrored the tragic rootlessness of her orphaned status, culminating eventually in her happy though brief intercaste marriage, then early widowhood, and finally espousal of women's causes—especially the plight of child widows—as her own personal mission. If, over the years, her life has tended to inspire hyperboles, such as A. B. Shah's ex-travagant description of her as "the greatest woman produced by modern India and one of the greatest Indians in all history," such high praise is undoubtedly prompted by her achievement as an exceptionally learned woman and outspo-ken champion of women's rights and social reform.[1]

One of the few women of her time whose voice found its way into male-controlled public discourse, Ramabai quickly shot to fame as a passionate and enthusiastic spokeswoman for the amelioration of women's status in Hindu society. Publicly honored by the Sanskrit scholars of Calcutta as a "Pandita," or learned woman, she is nonetheless better known for influential works like *Morals for Women* (1882) and *The High Caste Hindu Woman* (1888), which are devastating critiques of Hindu patriarchy and the circumscribed lives to which upper-caste women were doomed. These diatribes earned her the wrath of orthodox sections of the Hindu public and the admiration of modernizing elites and social reformers. Both works express Ramabai's extreme disillusionment with the religion of her birth, particularly the false views of sublime philosophy that, to some extent, western Orientalism had helped promote. She importuned women in the west to resist the seductive subtleties of Hindu philosophy and resolutely look beyond them to unmask the thralldom in which Hindu women were held.

> I beg of my Western sisters not to be satisfied with the looking on the outside beauties of the grand philosophies, and not to be charmed with the long and interesting discourses of our educated men, but to open the trapdoors of the great monuments of the ancient Hindu intellect, and enter into the dark cellars where they will see the real working of the philosophies which they admire so much. There are thousands of priests and men, learned in the sacred lore, who are the spiritual rulers and guides of our people. They neglect and oppress the widows and devour widows' houses. . . . Thousands upon thousands of young widows and innocent children are suffering untold misery and dying helpless every year throughout the land, but not a philosopher or Mahatma has come out boldly to champion their cause and to help them. . . . Let not my Western sisters be charmed with the books and poems they read. There are many hard and bitter facts we have to accept and feel. All is not poetry with us. The prose we have to read in our lives is very hard. It cannot be understood by our learned brothers and comfortable sisters of the West.[2]

Refusing to be intimidated by accusations that such remarks merely confirmed the colonialist and missionary criticism of Hinduism's moral bankruptcy, Ramabai directed her ire against the guardians of a priestly tradition who obscured what she called the "prose" of Hinduism's social hierarchy by turning it into a "poetry" of refined moral sensibility.[3] Her disgust with Hinduism over its treatment of women made it impossible for her to accept religion as an exclusively philosophical system. This was an attitude to religion that would stay with her even when she had formally renounced Hinduism; even Christian missionaries never fully appreciated how repugnant she found a purely philosophical approach to religion. Thinking they had a better chance in winning her over by appealing to her logic and intellect, they turned to a view of Christianity as philosophy rather than historical revelation. In the long run, this approach bore consequences detrimental to their own interests.

Nor could Ramabai ever see religious devotion as purely personal salvation or search for solace in light of the ideological deployment of such a notion of religion for rationalizing women's subordination. *The High Caste Hindu Woman*, for instance, meticulously takes apart the various philosophical underpinnings of Hinduism and shows how they have succeeded in maintaining the low status of women in Indian society, such as propagating "the popular belief among high-caste women that their husbands will die if they should read or should hold a pen in their fingers."[4]

The path to Ramabai's rupture with Hinduism, however, was by no means a straightforward one, nor did her conversion to Christianity immediately follow her disillusionment with Hinduism. Attracted briefly while in Calcutta to reformist organizations like the Brahmo Samaj and the Prarthana Samaj, which had a practical agenda but were still focused on ridding Hinduism of outdated superstitions and rituals, Ramabai found that she could make her most enduring contributions not to debate and disputation but, rather, to the social welfare of women. That brought her back to her own native Maharashtra, where she revived a number of contacts with people active in establishing institutions for the benefit of women. She even appeared before the Hunter Education Commission in 1882 to offer detailed recommendations for the improvement of female education. The momentum for reform certainly grew after her arrival in Maharashtra, but not quickly enough. Her plans to start a home and school for child widows and child wives in Poona received little support, and she was driven by a desire to go abroad to seek wider assistance from sympathetic organizations in the west.

While in Poona, she came in contact with Sister Geraldine, who had come to India from an English missionary order at Wantage, the Community of St. Mary the Virgin. There were other missionaries from the same order in Poona who saw, in Ramabai, an eager and alert young woman intent on learning as much as she could about Christianity. Ironically, in these first few encounters with the missionaries, Ramabai's openness to Christian teaching came about primarily because she was interested in learning English in order to promote the education of women. With the missionaries' encouragement, Ramabai left for England on April 20, 1883 with her young daughter Manorama and, on her arrival there, was received by the sisters of the Wantage order, who welcomed her into St. Mary's Home. Within five months of her arrival in England, Ramabai received baptism along with her daughter.

The simplicity of this chronology, however, does not come near to revealing the complex relationship Ramabai had to both Christianity and the missionaries in England. Some sense of this is already apparent in her initial interest in Christianity for pragmatic reasons, but the complexity extended to profound conflicts with Protestantism's position in England and the doubts that it engendered in her about the promise of Christian liberty offered by the scriptures, a promise that she found vitiated by the hierarchical government in which it was deeply mired. After all, it was the gender hierarchy of Hinduism that alienated her from the religion of her birth. Though Ramabai claimed she had no intention of converting to Christianity or any other religion at the time she went abroad, she had already begun to turn her back on Hinduism, decrying its cruel and heartless attitude to women. Yet when she joined the Wantage sisters and accepted their baptism, she discovered that the Christianity they propagated gave her little room to develop the sensibilities and spiritual inclinations that drove her flight from Hinduism.

Critical representations of Ramabai's feminism have tended to obscure the depth and intensity of her own spiritual struggle, either glossing over it as an incidental aspect of her feminism or as the instrumental medium through which she expressed her critique of Hindu patriarchy. Her anguished search for a personal God who is also a source of justice and love rarely finds a place in accounts of her battles with the Maharashtrian elite society. These accounts also invariably omit her protracted effort to define a conception of divinity that satisfied her craving for interpretive freedom. Ramabai's spirituality is accorded relevance only to the extent that it illuminates her protest against brahmanical ritualism and codification of women's social roles.

Receiving even less critical attention is the fact that Ramabai's developing religious sensibility enabled her also to critique the philosophical contradictions of British colonialism. Ramabai's search for a moral and theological framework of social critique did not merely serve her immediate purposes in disputing the gender disparities of brahmanism, but also provided her a point of entry into a devastating analysis of British colonialism. Her growing distance from the Trinity and other focal points of Anglican doctrine was compounded by her perception that other religious groups like Jews, Nonconformists, Wesleyans, Congregationalists, and Methodists were left outside the Anglican fold as decisively as were colonial subjects. That she was able to attain this insight through a questioning of the theological inconsistencies in British Christianity—even as she affirmed her own faith in Christianity independently of the pressures of the English church—places her critique of colonialism uniquely in the framework of both Indian nationalism and English religious dissent.

It would be a mistake to regard Ramabai's Christian conversion as motivated entirely by assimilationist motives or to suggest that she was essentially rejecting her own cultural background in an act of identification with Western traditions of thought. Her learned readings in the religious literature of those who colonized her country helped her to see the divide between two possible meanings of religion as the source of cultural and national identity on one hand and, on the other, as universal moral value. She reached startling insights about the distinctions between these meanings in a long and fractious correspondence with Sister Geraldine, her chief mentor in England. At one point, warned by the missionary that she was in danger of forfeiting divine grace through her arrogant questioning, Ramabai retorted that "the door of the Universal Church of God is not shut against me, and I believe the Universal, the Holy Catholic Church is not confined within the walls of the Anglican Church." Her response disaggregates religion from political, national institutions,[5] even as it also seeks out a subjective location for belief beyond the circumscribed world of Anglican doctrine. And though her use of the term "Catholic Church" might lead one to conclude she was still narrowly focused on interpreting religion in institutional terms, the context of the passage as well as the repetition of the

word "Universal" suggest that she had a metaphorical and expansive understanding of Catholicism as an analytical concept signifying unity, as opposed
to the divisions that produced institutions historically ranged against each
other. This is further apparent in her attempt to detach religion from all forms
of territorial associations, whereby "Catholic" and "universal" become interchangeable terms: "Baptism and the solemn oath which we take before GOD
do not belong exclusively to one person or to one church with particular belief
or customs. They are Catholic, i.e, universal."[6]

In her own critical practice, by which we must understand both her writing
and her conversion, Ramabai further drove a wedge between these two ways
of conceiving religion and, by converting, asserted a moral scale of values
independent of the cultural systems of both her native and adopted religions.
The warning issued to Ramabai by the missionary sisters "against making . . .
a self-chosen religion" reminds one that conversion is not necessarily a mode
of assimilation to a predetermined reality, identity, or system of thought.[7]
Rather, conversion is a dynamic process that *creates* the ideal system to which
the convert aspires. The self-styled construction of such a system is precisely
what renders it heretical, and conversion's instrumentality in producing heresy
marks it off dramatically from assimilationist goals.

In the absence of a perspective that accepts religious dissent as resistance
not only to dogmatic interpretations but also the political structures that support them, Ramabai's conversion to Christianity is invariably written off as the
source of a divided consciousness that alienated her from the nationalist stirrings of her fellow Indians. If Ramabai was considered a disloyal Indian by her
Hindu peers because she converted, that impression has not been substantially
countered by subsequent critical commentaries, which focus on her conversion
as the axis along which she realigned herself with a colonialist agenda for
women's reform. First, one will have to be deeply skeptical about the primary
source for such a charge, which happens in this case to be missionary records.
These reveal that Ramabai was clearly being trained, in true filtration style, to
take up the task begun by missionaries in redeeming Hindu widows from their
situation of destitution and social disgrace. Yet for this reason it is important
to fragment and disperse the monumentality of the missionary archives in
order to locate the dissonant voice of the subject herself. Does Ramabai see
herself participating in a colonial reconstructionist scheme? Does her conversion signal her acceptance of missionary objectives for Indian women? Or
does she place her conversion in the service of other objectives that, although
focused on ameliorating women's position, did not necessarily partake of the
missionaries' agenda for reform?

Although Ramabai's spiritual battles may have appeared to culminate in her
conversion to Christianity in 1883, they never ceased, even with her apparent
discovery of a more satisfying religious ethic. Her religious conversion was
less a turning point than an intermediate stage in her pursuit of a moral goal
that she believed Hinduism obscured by its denial of parity to women. Rama-

bai's search for religion encompassed a framework for her social activism that went far beyond the moral imperatives of contesting patriarchal oppression. In her restless striving for an ideal of human perfection she refused to accept that such an ideal could emerge either through institutional measures or from a system of philosophical thought based exclusively on human rationalism. Unlike other Hindu social reformers, such as Keshab Chander Sen in Bengal or M. G. Ranade in Maharashtra, she did not believe that Hinduism's egregious record in ensuring basic rights for women and other oppressed groups could be rectified by a materialistic ethic, professed by such reformist organizations as the Brahmo Samaj and the Prarthana Samaj. On the contrary, Ramabai rejected purely rational approaches to religious reform. Though she was initially drawn to these groups in her early gropings for religious alternatives to orthodox Hinduism, she was convinced they could not adequately illuminate pathways to basic philosophical dilemmas regarding such things as the apperception of supreme godhead. Since it was still necessary to deal with human authority as a mediating factor in perceiving divinity under these systems, Ramabai was persuaded that such dilemmas could only be resolved by private exertions of conscience and independent judgment. Her studious discrimination between the planes of the human and the divine meticulously separated obedience to the word of God (which she implicitly believed offered the path to salvation and liberty) from obedience to the law (which she considered to be the source of human enslavement). Her search for religion was essentially a search for viable ways of defining and realizing liberty far outside the boundaries of priestly intervention.

Ramabai's explicit quest for unconstrained spiritual freedom brings her squarely within an antinomian tradition of dissent particular to English history. For her careful distinction between two forms of obedience—to God and to the law—rehearses the antinomian rejection of "Moral Law" as a product of institutional and priestly repression. Antinomian literature describes such repression as having the effect of removing the believer further and further from God's divine mercy and love; consequently, restoration to a position prior to one's estrangement from God means a repudiation of all forms of legal authority. As E. P. Thompson points out in his brilliant study of Blake and Muggletonianism, the term "antinomian" itself means *against the law*, and is broad enough to include a range of oppositions to prescriptive dogmas. Primarily, antinomian doctrine takes its inspiration from Paul's letters to the Romans and to the Galatians. Apart from the fact that the Pauline emphasis on justification by faith resists a purely regulated form of worship involving ceremonial observances and rituals, its distinguishing attribute is its contestation of the imperatives of Mosaic Law. In its injunction to believers to obey moral commandments and follow the letter rather than the spirit of the law, Mosaic Law turns these commandments into what Thompson calls "the necessary rules of government imposed upon a faithless and unregenerate people."[8] Ramabai's admonition to her missionary mentors in England to respect her as a student "not of letter alone but also of the spirit of religion" reproduces the language of Paul and salvages religious belief as personal testimony from the crude pit of religious ideology, which Ramabai came to see as a product of the instrumental rationality of the colonial English state.

Ramabai's disillusionment with the reduction of religious belief to a form of cultural and national identity is further aggravated by Sister Geraldine's comparison of the Christian kingdom to the English nation. By bringing the two within the same frame of reference, Geraldine establishes a bureaucratic worldliness in Christianity matching the complex requirements of the modern state:

> A corporate body . . . [such as] a nation, a municipality, a regiment, school or anything you like to name . . . must have its rulers, officers and discipline. If any member, or members, refuse to submit to its officers or otherwise set discipline at nought, they would be free to give up the rights and privileges of membership and go elsewhere. Now the Church is an invisible Kingdom with a visible and delegated Government. Christ is its King, and the Government which He has ordained for His Kingdom is that of Apostles or Bishops. We as members of Christ's Kingdom are not free to choose any other form of religious Government than this. If therefore any set up a self-chosen organisation or depart from His teaching, it is they who cut themselves off from the Church our Lord has founded and refuse to be governed in the way which He has appointed, and not the church which separates itself from them.[9]

The most interesting remark in this passage, of course, is the one that relates excommunication to civil disenfranchisement. In Sister Geraldine's presentation of the argument, what naturalizes the withholding of citizenship rights to non-Anglican groups, just as much as to colonial subjects, is their willing estrangement from the undivided community of God because of their refusal to submit to church authority. Heresy is an offense not pardonable by any but God; therefore, if non-Anglicans fail to be included in the body politic, the fault is theirs alone for stubbornly persisting in their misguided pride and false judgment. In Geraldine's stern reworking of church-state relations, the issue of obligatory citizenship rights is made irrelevant by a religious discourse that attaches criteria of sworn national allegiance to the practice of religious belief.

The antinomian rejection of "Moral Law" laid the foundations for an antistatism that was to persist in English history. It also confirmed that challenges to English political life would invariably come from dissenting religious groups like the Anabaptists of the sixteenth century, to whom Pandita Ramabai is at one point disapprovingly compared by Sister Geraldine. The Anabaptists, declares Geraldine, "taught polygamy and an entire freedom from all subjection to the civil as well as the ecclesiastical law."[10] This allusion to an antistatist movement of English history—one that was not even contemporaneous but went back at least three centuries—suggests that Ramabai's rejection of authority is much greater than resistance to colonial subjection. Indeed, it is a rejection of the entire structure and content of civil and ecclesiastical law, which leaves no space for the articulation of belief outside doctrinal content or institutional constraints. Ramabai's repeated insistence on belief as inalienable choice openly repudiates the usurpation of her subjectivity by law or creed: "When people decide anything for me, I call it interfering with my liberty, and am not willing to let them do it. I have a conscience, and mind, and a judgment of my own. I must be allowed to think for myself."[11]

Ramabai's outsider position enables her to say this. Coming to an established religion from the outside allows her and other converts to interpret the new religion with a freedom not necessarily available to those already within the fold. She complains to Sister Geraldine that "you have never gone through the same experience of choosing another religion for yourself, which was totally foreign to you, as I have. You, wise and experienced and old as you are, you cannot interpenetrate my poor feelings."[12] Ramabai articulates a viewpoint that is not often heard in missionary literature: the convert's conflicted sense of cultural and spiritual change is compounded by the inability of missionaries to understand the reorientation of the convert's subjective reality. From the perspective of the missionaries, the challenges posed by choice are interpreted as willful refashioning of reality. If Ramabai is typically seen as crossing a fine line between conversion and heresy and moving toward a "diluted Christianity without Christ"—her spirited independence convinces her detractors that conversion, in her case, *is* heresy.

Ramabai's refusal to accept the command of law, coupled with her embrace of God as the only uncreated deity and Christ as a messenger but not surrogate of God, brought her into sharp conflict with her English mentors. The sisters, like many an Anglican divine who lambasted antinomianism as a smug recapitulation of the Calvinist heresy promising unmerited grace to the elect, warned Ramabai that she was reposing far too much confidence in her salvation without exerting any effort toward winning it through service and obedience to authority. Quoting Ruskin on unlimited liberty as being no different from licentiousness, Sister Geraldine turned the statement into its obverse to suggest that true liberty really implied obedience to law. Shortly after Ramabai's conversion, noting that she had grown more distant from her friends and community, Sister Geraldine and other missionaries concluded that her alienation was a mark of her developing pride. But Ramabai's own words suggest that the narrowly defined Christianity in which she had been trapped caused her to feel estranged from the spiritual longings she had been experiencing. The sisters' use of alienation as a metaphor for pernicious rootlessness and lack of meaningful community is transformed by Ramabai into a metaphor for the loss of intimate communion with God brought about by institutional regulation.

Ramabai's disagreement with Sister Geraldine regarding the existence of the Church before the Bible, however, is more than a young convert's refusal to accept a new religion on other people's terms.[13] Ramabai's often intemperate language appears to personalize her conflict with her mentor and sponsor, but the idiosyncratic tone of her responses is belied by her own careful, close reading of English religious history. But this kind of meticulous attention to church history is vehemently denied by Sister Geraldine, who interprets as pride what Ramabai puts forth as legitimate intellectual inquiry. Bishop Westcott, when informed of Ramabai's vexing recalcitrance, counsels Sister Geraldine that "those dealing with her should seek to get her to believe rather than define."[14]

The clash of perspectives between teacher and pupil is further exacerbated by the heady novitiate's refusal to allow a description of her turbulent state of mind as intransigent self-absorption; rather, by painting her situation as involving a loss of self, she castigated obedience to law as the source of a tragic self-estrangement. If Ramabai is accused of being smug, she turns the charge of complacency into a point of doctrine that distinguishes between divine election and personal belief—that is, between an offer of salvation on predestined grounds, as supported by Calvinism which Ramabai roundly rejects as disparaging of individual effort, and Pauline mysticism whose promise of salvation requires the believer to seek out personal truth in Christ's word. Ramabai thus overturns the charge that she is proud by denying Calvinist predeterminism and, instead, emphasizes the depth of her struggle for spiritual salvation as itself a process of Christian understanding.

On the other hand, the Anglican sisters, perceiving Ramabai's stance as dangerously presumptive in challenging the foundations of both Anglican doctrine and English law, remind her ominously that "you have by your Baptism looked into this Law of Liberty."[15] Their stress falls pointedly on the word *this*, which narrows down liberty to a prescriptive law sanctioned by church authority alone. Refusing to accept the regulated logic of such admonitions, which reduced liberty to an obligatory contradiction that included constraint as part of its self-definition, Ramabai heaped contempt on the missionaries' qualified notion of liberty as typifying "the will of those who have authority to speak as expressing His will."

> It seems to me that you are advising me under the WE to accept always the will of those who have authority, etc. This however I cannot accept. I have a conscience, and mind and a judgment of my own. I must myself think and do everything which GOD has given me the power of doing. . . . I am, it is true, a member of the Church of Christ, but am not bound to accept every word that falls down from the lips of priests or bishops. If it pleases you to call my word liberty as lawlessness you may do so, but as far as I know myself, I am not lawless. Obedience to the law and to the Word of God is quite different from perfect obedience to priests only.[16]

Ramabai's meticulous dismantling of her mentors' logic sets up private interpretation not as an exalted alternative to institutional authority but rather a means of recapturing a lost affinity to God. Her God is less a product of human rationality (as the Brahmo Samajists believed) than a source of self-empowering reason. What ought to have been a point of little dispute between Ramabai and the missionaries, however, turned into a major disagreement because she used her God-given reason to construct her own religious system in which the Christian God is then placed (arbitrarily, according to the shocked sisters). Furthermore, her new system empties deity of established gender attributes as the first step toward an egalitarian order ensuring liberty. This is in contrast to the hierarchical religious scheme upheld by the missionaries, who acknowledge that "in Christ she had learned that there was perfect liberty, and though there was necessarily a church order and subordination, yet in the Spirit, there was in Christ neither male nor female. It seemed going back to what she had been delivered from."[17]

Yet, despite the obviously heretical components of Ramabai's Christianity, few critics are willing to see her conversion—or what Geraldine haughtily dismissed as her "self-chosen religion"—as the site from which she chose to fight both British colonialism and Hindu patriarchy. Ram Bapat, for instance, who has written with considerable perspicacity about Pandita Ramabai's negotiation of the dialectics of faith and reason, sees her Christian conversion as a transitional moment in her fight against Hindu orthodoxy. He views her conversion as a crucial turning point in her resistance to the tradition that shaped her early life and established the foundations of her own deep learning in Sanskrit texts. In Bapat's reading Ramabai's point of reference for converting to Christianity remains Hinduism, despite her apparent attraction to the tenets of monotheism and the claims of mystical faith. He thus views her conversion as a reactive gesture against the retrograde features of Hinduism and patriarchal society, rather than as an act of will directing the self toward an exploration of the spiritual realm. If, however, the latter proposition is considered more seriously, it leads to the consideration that Ramabai's spiritual restlessness has less to do with Hindu religious reform than seeking out existential conditions of freedom from temporal bondage—conditions leading to the creation of a selfhood released from social restrictions. It is to this trajectory that we shall now turn our attention.

RAMABAI'S EARLY UPBRINGING

Ramabai's conversion to Christianity could not have been predicted from her early religious behavior. Critics make much of her repeated insistence that she never intended to convert to Christianity, especially to a religion that she initially described as composed of meaningless and empty rituals. Perceiving no substantial difference between Christian and Hindu ceremonial worship, she writes sarcastically of the Christians she encountered in India, "We did not see any image to which they paid homage but it seemed as though they were paying homage to the chairs before which they knelt."[18] Christianity's own mysticism and ritualism appeared to be no more than a westernized form of Hinduism. Ramabai's view that Christianity lacked a lively tradition of disputation on doctrine and dogma drew her initially to the Brahmo Samajists, who, as avowed social reformers, were dynamically engaged with debates on the nature of divine substance and theistic ideality. Certainly the instruction in Hindu religious texts that she received from her father did not prepare her for the questioning that later led her to reject Hinduism. Her father, Anant Shastri Dongre, believed it was imperative for women to read sacred texts, but he scrupulously excluded the Vedas as one of the required texts in Ramabai's Sanskrit education. As Meera Kosambi points out, it was not until Ramabai had encountered the monotheistic system of the Brahmo Samaj that she began to consider alternatives to the tradition-bound practices of Hinduism.[19] Yet not even the new attractions of a monotheistic faith can explain why Christianity should have so compelled her attention, particularly when there was every likelihood that, by converting, she would jeopardize her respected standing amongst her Hindu peers as a reformer and thinker.

The answer to this vexed question requires one to take a brief biographical detour, particularly in the circumstances of Ramabai's growing distance from a sense of affiliation to community, which her spiritual mentors in England noted as culminating in crisis around the time of her conversion: "She was less free with her early friends, less confidential [sic]. She seemed somewhat less cordially disposed towards us, and to have a sense of distrust."[20] Ramabai's utter isolation following the loss of all members of her family was certainly a factor contributing to her gradual detachment from community feeling. In the years following her parents' deaths, Ramabai traveled extensively across India with her sole surviving sibling, her older brother. Together, as pilgrims, they wandered from temple to temple, impressing people with their deep knowledge of Sanskrit texts and holding their own in learned conversations with pandits. Educated in the classical religious texts by her father, who was officially censured by a village council for exposing his wife and his daughters to the sacred texts, Ramabai was brought up in an atmosphere that was essentially oriented to the Dharmashastric Vedic tradition of Hinduism, the scriptural tradition of moral codes and precepts.

However, though providing the primary textual bases for legal and social identity, this tradition of moral precepts is only one of the many presentations of Hinduism, yet Ramabai remained fairly oblivious to popular expressions of other religious forms. Her subsequent disenchantment with Hinduism was entirely on the basis of the scriptural texts in which she received instruction from her parents, among which are the *Bhagavatapurana*, the *Bhagavad Gita*, the *Kaumudi*, the *Amarokosha* and other works in the oral tradition.[21] Thus, in spite of the fact that there were varying sets of religious scriptures, practices, and beliefs among Hindus, Ramabai held on to the conviction that "no woman as a woman can get liberation" in the Hindu tradition, since she assumed that all the Hindu traditions treated the knowledge of the Veda, Vedanta, and Brahma as a necessary condition for religious salvation.[22] Her learning, though deep and wide, was limited largely to Sanskrit Bhagavata literature, and her impressions of the possibilities of female emancipation were confined to what this literature offered. Until she moved to Calcutta, where she acquired a new set of acquaintances in the reform-oriented Brahmo Samaj, Ramabai had not studied the Vedas, the Upanishads, the six systems of thought other than the *nyaya* (or analytical) system, nor the Dharmashastras. Nor was she familiar with the literatures even of the Varkari, the Lingayat or the northern Sant sampradays which offered the promise of salvation to the lower caste of shudras, women, outcastes, and sinners, in total defiance of the Vedic scriptures and the Smritis (traditional texts). Thus, as Bapat argues, "in spite of her bitter, pertinent, and acute attacks on the fundamentals of the modernizing Hindu elitist world-views, she continued to operate within the confines of the same privileged discourse which was set up, first, by Western students of Hinduism, and then appropriated by the nationalist elites in India to meet their colonial or class interests and which valorized the Vedas and Smritis as the authoritative texts governing a monolithic Hindu order."[23]

Ramabai's assessment of her early instruction helps explain her later antagonism to the reform of Hinduism along purely secular lines. Ramabai writes in her autobiographical tract, *My Testimony*, about the strictly religious emphasis of her classical training:

> My parents did not like us children to come in contact with the outside world. They wanted us to be strictly religious, and adhere to the old faith. Learning any other language except Sanskrit was out of [the] question. Secular education of any kind was looked upon as leading people to worldliness which would prevent them from getting into the way of *moksha* [salvation]. To learn the English language and to come into contact with *mlecchas* [non-Hindus, or foreigners] was forbidden on the pain of losing caste and all hope of future happiness. So all that we could and did learn was the Sanskrit grammar and dictionaries with the Puranic and modern literature in that language. Most of this, including the grammar and dictionaries which are written in verse form, had to be committed to memory.[24]

Ram Bapat reads this passage as unassailable evidence of Ramabai's restrictive outlook within what he calls a "high caste, high form of Hinduism." And to some extent this is true. Anant Shastri's rejection of Shankara's monist philosophy of Advaitism and acceptance of Vaishnava doctrines did not necessarily mean that he welcomed dissenting traditions of low-caste protest, nor did it indicate his openness to other interpretations of Hinduism. As Bapat rightly points out, "his revolt was rather expressive of the age-old contradictions and confrontations within the high caste, high form of Hinduism, rather than that of the emancipatory, egalitarian, popular Bhakti ethos emerging from below."[25] Yet Bapat's evaluation of the "patrician" aloofness of Anant Shastri's Vaishnavism assumes too quickly that bhakti, as an expression of religious dissent, is synonymous with anticasteism and low-caste protest, whereas in fact the mystical leanings of bhakti are perfectly consonant with the rigid orthodoxies of hierarchical brahmanism. Indeed, the accent on mystical unity in the *bhakti* tradition of worship does not preclude either the appropriation of bhakti by caste Hinduism or its accommodation by the requirements of upper-caste privilege.

In 1883 Pandita Ramabai, by then already a widow with a small child, set out for England. At the time of her departure she had already acquired a formidable reputation not only as a woman of profound classical learning but also a social reformer of great perseverance and courage. But Ramabai had to pay a heavy price for her reformist activity: her espousal of widows' causes and her mobilization of (an essentially conservative) social conscience against child marriage earned her the wrath of Maharashtrian Brahmin society. Though it would not be accurate to say that she was driven out of India, nonetheless conditions in her home state of Maharashtra were too hostile for her to continue her relief efforts unhampered. Determined to study medicine, in order that her moral impulses for reform would be amply buttressed by a professional degree, Ramabai eagerly took up an offer made by the Community of St. Mary the Virgin at Wantage, which promised to finance her higher studies. She paid her passage to England by publishing a book in Marathi, *Stree Dharma Niti*, translated into English as *Morals for Women*, which earned her both money and fame—far more than she or anyone else anticipated.

However, Ramabai's professional plans to study medicine abroad were quashed by her acute hearing problems, and she was instead channeled into a course of studies in English and natural science. The sisters of the Wantage community who sponsored her stay in England arranged for her to teach Marathi and Sanskrit at the Cheltenham Ladies College. In return for her own education in Western learning, Ramabai was expected to offer missionaries setting out for Poona the training in vernacular languages they needed for their proselytizing work. Here undisputedly was the case of the imported native informant, a prototype for upcoming generations of Indians traveling to England and America for higher studies, absorbing Western knowledge in exchange for "native" languages. The exact terms of the exchange were to play a significant part much later, when Ramabai defied the accepted conventions and insisted on teaching missionaries more than the obligatory native languages. Far more shocking was her request that she also be allowed to teach English—and that, too, to young men, no less.

The Community of St. Mary the Virgin was a small order of missionary sisters that had branches in western India, the largest and most important of which was in Poona. We have little information about the circumstances of their operation in England, though brief allusions in the letters indicate that they were in frequent communication with the Society for the Propagation of the Gospel, to whom they often sent novices and initiates from their own, much smaller order. Again, from the correspondence one has an impression that the order was challenged severely by the personal trials of missionaries: of failing health, inadequate resources, and the psychological demoralization caused by recalcitrant converts. At least one of the missionary sisters freely confessed that she suffered a nervous breakdown while working in the Indian missions. The frantic, almost hysterical tone of the correspondence between the missionaries—and between them and Pandita Ramabai—is partially explained by the stress these missionaries experienced in their effort to gain the most useful (that is, the most socially respectable) converts to continue mission work in India. Hence, the extraordinary investment in a high-caste learned woman like Pandita Ramabai, whose conversion was a prize acquisition and one not to be lost easily. Hence also the almost fastidious deference to her volatility and a willingness to mollify her at all costs, even when it clearly meant compromising the sisters' own Anglican principles.

Ramabai's ostensible motive in going to England for studies was to break what she called "the bondage of social prejudice"—restrictions that were so great within India that "higher principles of action" could only be pursued elsewhere.[26] But as her correspondence with the Wantage sisters shows, even as she disparaged the many strictures of Hindu patriarchy, she was no less critical of the orthodoxies governing the missionaries' conduct. Her letters reveal her alienation not only from Hindu society but also from the institutional culture of the religion to which she had converted. The letters further provide powerful insights into the lonely world of the convert, struggling to resist cooptation by both Hindu and Christian culture, even as she strove to recreate herself within a restrictive space offering little or no room for private maneuver. Sister Geraldine, Ramabai's chief mentor, was clearly aware that Ramabai was refashioning Christianity to her own requirements, far beyond what her sponsors desired for this young woman whom they aimed eventually to embrace within their fold: "I fear she is willingly accepting a religion which has no claim to the name of Christianity, as she thinks it will commend itself more to the intelligence of her countrywomen than the revealed Truth, which latter will require for them a higher standard of moral and spiritual perfection than they would be willing to accept."[27]

Because the correspondence between Ramabai and the missionaries elucidates Ramabai's construction of a belief system more systematically and coherently than any of her other better-known works, including her celebrated book *The High Caste Hindu Woman*, the primary text I shall focus on is A. B. Shah's edition of *The Letters and Correspondence of Pandita Ramabai*, a comprehensive collection of the correspondence between Ramabai and her missionary sponsors exchanged almost entirely during the time Ramabai spent in England. Unlike many missionary-convert interactions that form the basis for most scholarly analysis, this work registers the impressions of a new Christian convert writing from her location not in the colonies but in England. Ramabai's residence in England at the time she debated the missionaries gave her a closer perspective on English ecclesiastical history and its impact on the English state. Her letters powerfully reveal the fissures and dissensions within Anglican England, just as they also shed light on well-entrenched divisions in church history, which were by and large glossed over by the Anglican self-presentation of unity and strength required for efficacious missionary instruction. Ramabai's puncturing of the false certainties and presumed stability of mainstream Anglican orthodoxies paradoxically gave her an uncanny sense of release from the social constraints that bound her as a Hindu. Partly sensing this, the sisters with whom she was in communication found their own proselytizing ambitions uncomfortably compromised. For it was evident that, although to her English mentors' approving eyes Ramabai was loosening her ties with Hinduism and turning a suspicious and skeptical eye upon her native religion, yet her repudiation of Hinduism was accompanied at the same time by an intellectual resistance to accepting a version of Christianity handed down as scriptural authority. Chided by the sisters for her "arrogant" independence, Ramabai angrily retorts that "I have just with great efforts freed myself from the yoke of the Indian priestly tribe, so I am not at present willing to place myself under similar yoke by accepting everything which comes from the priests as authorised command of the Most High."[28]

Ironically, Ramabai's departure from Hinduism is brought on by an independence the missionaries now wish to curb. Though the Wantage sisters initially believed that Ramabai's orphaned status and unencumbered situation would help them to transform her into whatever shape and form they desired, they found her rootlessness to be the source of an obstinate refusal to accept institutional will and authority. Their view that she offered "fair promise of good at the outset of her career, but in consequence of having no restrictions is unprofitable to the world" disparaged her unattached status as the source of a pernicious intellectual ("heretical") independence. Their insistence on familial ties as the basis of temporal authority established dependence on a community or a family as a measure of one's usefulness, thus also confirming the family as a primary source of traditional, dependable, and sustaining values. Unfettered liberty is the antithesis of a communitarian vision that Sister Geraldine locates at the heart of Christian enterprise, as she remarks in a pointed aside: "The most unhappy person of my acquaintance, and one who has made shipwreck of her life is one who in independent circumstances and without family ties can do pretty much as she pleases."[29]

If the single woman as a danger to society persists in the resolutely Victorian consciousness of Sister Geraldine, it was Ramabai's special insight that the persistently negative perceptions of women who chose to remain outside the family structure provided a rationale for the passing of retrograde British legislation, both in England and India. Referring to the infamous Rakhmabai decision of 1887 passed by the British Indian courts, which ordered a young woman Rakhmabai to return to her husband against her wishes (see Chapter Three, above), Ramabai remarked with great bitterness, "A Hindu woman— *unless she be a widow and destitute of friends and relatives*—cannot follow even the dictates of her own conscience."[30] Clearly Ramabai did not see widowhood as a condition of deprivation but rather understood that the absence of social ties also loosened obligatory ties to prevailing orthodoxies.

However, Ramabai's orphaned and widowed situation made her extremely culpable in the eyes of the missionaries. For her capacity of private judgment, which made her such a prime candidate for conversion, contributed at the same time to a questioning of all received notions and undercut the conceptions of priestly authority favored by the Anglican order to which the Wantage missionaries belonged. In the absence of parents, husband, kinsfolk, or community, Ramabai appeared to have the mobility that was the substance of heterodoxy. With the family as the undisputed touchstone of stable, orthodox values, the missionary order proceeded to turn into heretics single, unattached women like Ramabai, whose lack of ties to family or community made her extremely susceptible to the "pride" of interpretative freedom. Not only did Ramabai's rejection of moral commandments puncture the family-based, community-oriented patriarchal authority of Mosaic Law, which the missionaries' beliefs affirmed, but such rejection was enabled by a slackening of all connections with a filiative order of things.

In other words, disruption of an affiliative model of the family becomes the source of a new and powerful assertion of antinomianism, in which unmediated faith in God challenges the moral prerogatives of obedience to law. The communitarian vision informing the missionaries' perspective required a web of alliances between women, family, and community for the efficacious administration of religious law. The selflessness of community service is the norm of Christian liberty. Because this so clearly contradicted Ramabai's own sense of liberty as self-inspired devotion, her assertions cast a cloud of suspicion over the reasons for her conversion if, as seemed to be the case, she did not intend to serve Christianity in the same spirit as did the Wantage sisters. An early exchange between Ramabai and Sister Geraldine reveals that they had been talking at cross-purposes for a tragically long time, with Geraldine lauding Ramabai's conversion as having been inspired by the "holy unselfish life" led by the missionaries. Ramabai breaks her silence on this representation of her conversion by finally responding to Canon William Butler:

This is her opinion. I held my silence when I heard this, thinking that it was not of much consequence to discuss upon such points of question but now I see that the misunderstanding is growing too formidable not to be corrected.

I was indeed impressed with the holy life of the Sisters, and their sublime unselfishness, and am so impressed to this moment, but I must say for the sake of truth that their life was not the cause of my accepting the faith of Christ. It was Father Goreh's letter that proved that the faith which I professed (I mean the Brahmo faith) was not taught by our Veda as I had thought, but it was the Christian faith which was brought before me by my friends disguised under the name of Brahmo religion. Well, I thought if Christ is the source of this sublime faith, why should not I confess Him openly to be my Lord and my Divine teacher?[31]

Phrased in these terms, "heresy" is at once a condition of Christian conversion as well as of its subversion. The form and content of *The Letters and Correspondence of Pandita Ramabai* have particular salience in relation to the dual, contradictory function of heresy. Originally compiled by Sister Geraldine of the Community of St. Mary the Virgin as vital source material for writing the history of conversion in India, the epistolary exchange between Ramabai and other sisters of the order was preserved in the hopes that it would contribute one day to the writing of her biography.[32] But Sister Geraldine's proposed biography was not necessarily intended in the spirit of hagiography, nor was it meant to record the inspiring story of a great Indian woman who had witnessed and received God's truth and then returned to India to translate Christian truth into social service. Indeed, most missionary accounts of Christian conversions among natives are written as celebrations of achievement— that is, the acquisition of one more soul for the proselytizing enterprise. Pandita Ramabai's story was an exception to the principle of missionary biographies, for Sister Geraldine had a much more cautionary tale in mind when she decided to preserve Ramabai's often volatile letters. She believed her subject, Pandita Ramabai, had historical importance as an imperfect, erring sinner whose quarrels with certain doctrinal aspects of Christianity constituted an allegorical tale of warning to true believers.

If Ramabai is relegated to the ranks of a heretic by the very people who seek her conversion, their refusal to accept her conversion as a final event condemns as heretical the spiritual questioning they would have otherwise welcomed as a definitive step toward conversion. Thus, as long as Ramabai continued to probe into the varieties of Christian belief found in English sects, her receiving of Christian grace was deferred indefinitely and she remained disqualified from being accepted as a true Christian convert. From the missionaries' perspective, conversion is the affirmation of a given set of propositions. For Pandita Ramabai, on the other hand, conversion is a form of self-fashioning, the right to "have a voice in choosing my own religion."[33] Ramabai keeps drawing attention to her "own free will: by it we are to decide for ourselves what we are to do, and fulfill our intended work."[34] When Ramabai claims the right of free will and choice, she conjoins a theological point with a political and cultural one. She is making the argument, contrary to the missionaries' wish or liking, that Indians have to make their own country, and that the free will, independent conscience, and judgment demonstrated in their religious choices strengthen the kind of moral society Indians must make for themselves. Ramabai recognizes that the missionaries' attempt to restrict her thinking about religious questions is also a form of colonial control, and it is a central feature of her own critique that she makes independent conscience a matter of national reconstruction.

The narrative organization of *Letters and Correspondence* suggests that not only did Ramabai's questioning epitomize willful pride but, more importantly, it also elucidates why she failed to achieve real conversion and hence justified the missionaries' refusal to acknowledge her baptism. Sister Geraldine writes:

> I have found the most interesting and edifying biographies to be those where the faults of the person under review are not withheld. Shadows shew up the light and help to give true proportion. Secondary lives which are brought onto the stage are often brought into high light and become an inspiration by a truthful narration. A life with all the faults suppressed is dazzling, but tends to depress. Where the opposite plan is followed, that life simply told is bracing and heartening.[35]

The extraordinary point of this passage is that the containment of Ramabai's heresy is possible only by presenting her conversion as a failure. Such an objective goes completely against the customary rationale of missionary writing, which was driven by a compulsion to record successes not only in order to commemorate the certain spread of Christianity but also to satisfy those who were subsidizing missionary efforts abroad. But in this particular case, the recounting of Ramabai's life story as a rough passage through a variety of theological quarrels and controversial arguments—none of which, by the way, was satisfactorily resolved—is seen to offer a more valuable lesson if her conversion is understood as *never having occurred at all*. Ramabai's conversion, presented by the missionaries as incomplete, irresolute, and endlessly deferred, takes place on so many different sites, so many different levels of meaning, that the multiplicity of its occurrence—the distended repetition of her conversion as performative gesture—is taken as definitive proof by missionaries of its lack of credibility. The conflict between Geraldine and Ramabai was most pronounced on the issue of baptism. When Geraldine insisted that Ramabai could not assume her baptism implied full conversion to Christianity, in the absence of her complete acceptance of church tenets, Ramabai was forced to reenact her conversion by other intellectual means, which took her through a cycle of religious introspection, dialogue, and disputation.

THE UNITARIAN HERESY, OR SECTARIAN OPTIONS

Pandita Ramabai's correspondence with the missionaries is noteworthy in another respect. The religious controversies and intellectual debates of the nineteenth century are rehearsed not in the Oxford classroom as in John Henry Newman's *Loss and Gain*, but in an often heated exchange between English

missionaries and their Indian Christian initiate—an exchange that is consciously framed by the reality of colonial relationships. Two historical positions—that of colonial subject and religious dissenter—dramatically collapse
into a single one in the missionaries' representation of Ramabai's questioning.
The blurring of Ramabai's colonized status with the position of those coming
out of a dissenting religious tradition in England produces a description of
colonial acculturation as a process not significantly different from the containment of English religious dissent. Ramabai's refusal to accept the main tenets
of the Anglican church put her firmly in the subject position of England's
hated Dissenters. Her rejection of the Thirty-Nine Articles, coupled with an
insistence on her own five articles of faith, aligns her unmistakably with several dissenting groups falling outside the Anglican fold. In asserting her faith
on the grounds of direct scriptural interpretation unmediated by institutional
authority, Ramabai affiliates herself to a tradition of protest that claims the
autonomy of religious subjectivity from church intervention:

> I shall tell you my Articles of Faith which I am so far able to draw from the
> Scripture, as my limited knowledge of the Word of God enables [me to do]. I have
> of late, as you know, after realising the sublime truths of Christ's teaching, be-
> come one of the least of his disciples, and believe in Him as the Messiah of God,
> and therefore am bound to receive every word which falls from His lips as the
> command of God which comes to me through His meditation. I am baptized
> according to His direction in the name of the Father, of the Son and of the Holy
> Ghost; and, therefore, I call myself a Christian, though I do not know if after
> hearing my creed my fellow Christians would call me so.[36]

In this last line, Ramabai enters the unambiguous ground of heresy by calling her faith "my creed" and setting aside the doctrinal creeds considered piv-
otal to Anglican worship. Though she may declare herself a Christian, she does
so in defiantly subjective terms, marking the distance between herself and a
community of Anglican believers by her claims to the sanctity of private interpretation. Rewriting the Thirty-Nine Articles of the English church into her
own five articles of faith, Ramabai denied the terms of membership by which
alone, at one time, she would have been accepted as a subject of both England
and Christianity. As instruments of enforcing allegiance to the Church of England, the Thirty-Nine Articles also historically established the terms of inclusion in the English nation. This fact did not escape Ramabai, who read as
emotional blackmail the sisters' condition that she had to subscribe to the
Thirty-Nine Articles if she were to remain attached to St. Mary's Home in
Wantage. The drama being played out between Ramabai and the sisters turned
Wantage into a microcosm of England itself.

Ramabai's increasing attraction to Unitarianism accompanied her inquiry
into sectarian differences. Her Unitarian sympathies came from a range of
popular religious literature that missionaries denounced as distortions of

Christian doctrine. Their indictment of mass-based pamphlet literature as sources of heretical thinking is suggestive of the deep sectarian divide in English society, just as Ramabai's intellectual resistance to religious authority allies her, as a colonial subject, with the English masses' disaffection from a rule that represented only landed and clerical interests. Indeed, Unitarian heresy becomes, for Ramabai, the means of contesting colonial authority. Her reaction against Trinitarianism stems from her perception that it is the very foundation of Englishness; axiomatically, anti-Trinitarianism lends itself to strong expressions of anti-colonialism.

The major obstacle in Ramabai's acceptance of the missionaries' faith was that pillar of Trinitarianism, the Athanasian Creed. No issue caused greater bitterness between the missionaries and Ramabai than the doctrine of the Trinity, and when Ramabai virtually ordered the sisters not to teach her daughter "anything about the mysterious Trinity, and about the deity of our Saviour, until you quite convince me that these doctrines *are* according to the Bible,"[37] she pushed them to the point where they were no longer willing to humor her claims to individual interpretation ("She is altogether off the lines," complained an exasperated Geraldine).[38] In reality Rambai's primary objection against praying to Christ, and to the Holy Ghost, as a person separate from the godhead had less to do with a close, sustained reading of anti-Trinitarian literature than with a deep-seated reluctance to accept Christ as a metonym for the godhead in its entirety, a reluctance that she attributed to her own dissatisfaction with a religion like Hinduism where godhead is dispersed among different icons. When she asserts that "I am not commanded by Christ (in the New Testament) to address my prayers either to Himself or to the Holy Ghost alone,"[39] her statement has shock value because not only does it deny that Christ partakes of the divinity of God but it also implies that the claim to being the son of God is a declaration of faith that can be made by others in totally nonblasphemous ways, as long as God is recognized as the only true divinity. In other words, the importance of Christ lies in his being the messenger of hope, divine mercy, and salvation, rather than in any specific identification with God or in having attributes that are interchangeable with God's.

To a large extent there was a certain literalness in Ramabai's understanding of the Trinity, since she appeared to believe it referred to three separate aspects of divinity, whereas the crucial historical issue that failed to engage her in any sustained way was whether Christ the Son was of similar substance (*homoiousios*) as God the Father, or of the same substance (*homoousios*). This was, of course, the fundamental conflict that had led, in 325 A.D., to the adoption of the Athanasian Creed by Constantine to resolve the dispute. Not only did the creed assert that Christ is identical with God and, together with the Holy Ghost, constitutes the Trinity, but it emphasized that the Trinity comprises three aspects of a single, *uncreated* unity, with God the Father being the one underived or unbegotten principle. Because the godhead is uncreated,

Christ the Son is not considered to have been begotten in human fashion but rather is an image of the godhead. "To be begotten," therefore, simply means completely to share in the entire nature of God the Father.

To insist otherwise, as did the fourth-century bishop of Antioch, Arius, who asserted that "the Son is an unrelated and an independent being totally separated from, and different from the substance or nature of the Father,"[40] was to invite public condemnation as a heretic, and Ramabai was sufficiently well acquainted with church history to know the dangers of recapitulating the Arian heresy even in nineteenth-century England. With a religious history still haunted by the hangings and public prosecutions of anti-Trinitarians, England was not yet a place for the open expression of Unitarian feeling. The Athanasian Creed pronounced Arianism a heresy and condemned those who were guilty of professing it. As late as 1695 a Scottish student Thomas Aikenhead was hanged for declaring the Trinity an absurdity and Christianity an illusion. Such events occurred despite the fact that a leading religious figure like Archbishop John Tillotson (1630–1694) complained about the Athanasian Creed (albeit privately): "I wish we were well rid of it."[41] Nor were institutions of higher learning exempt. William Whiston (1667–1752), who succeeded Isaac Newton to the chair of mathematics at Cambridge, lost his professorship because of his Arianism.

Even efforts at compromise aroused parliamentary disapproval, and those who tried to accommodate Arianism to Anglican doctrine suffered the consequences. David Lawton provides an absorbing history of some of these developments which culminated in the radical Unitarianism of such figures as the great scientist Joseph Priestley and William Frend. Frend was dismissed from Cambridge for his disavowal of the Athanasian Creed and for putatively authoring an influential pamphlet, *An address to the members of the Church of England and to Protestant Trinitarians in general, exhorting them to turn from the false worship of three persons to the worship of One True God* (1788). Lawton's conclusion that "enforcement of orthodoxy against Unitarianism extended into the highest ranks of Church and University—and continued to do so into the nineteenth century" reveals that there was virtually no space in public life to discuss Unitarianism without repeating an offense against both English Christianity and the English state.[42] For the close identification of Trinitarianism with English nationhood was certainly not lost sight of even by an intrepid inquirer like Pandita Ramabai, who in her sporadic attacks on Anglican church doctrine quickly discovered that impugning the Trinity was tantamount to inveighing against the English Crown itself.

Ramabai's attraction to a Unitarian conception of divinity sprang from what she perceived as its clearcut demarcation of the divine from the human. In the absence of such necessary distinctions in its own religious system, Hinduism was reduced to a mindless pantheism, and Ramabai turned to Unitarianism because it offered an ideal expression of a religious faith in which the divine could be steadily contemplated as a pure entity. When Ramabai is faulted for saying human beings are not perfect, she defends herself by saying that perfection implies an absence of distinction between humans and God: the virtue of Unitarianism, in her opinion, was that it preserved this distinction. The Wantage missionaries were correct to conclude that Ramabai's dissatisfaction with pantheistic expressions of worship drew her compulsively to the Brahmo Samaj, a reformist branch of Hinduism that resisted the facile blurring of human and divine features.

But as in so many other instances, where Ramabai's "heresy" produced an ambivalence in the missionaries' attitudes to her intellectual probings, the sisters were simultaneously aware that Ramabai's resistance to Trinitarianism had a positive aspect, because her rejection of godhead in three figures reinforced her rejection of the polytheism of Hinduism and its blurring of human and divine. A letter by Dorothea Beale, principal of Cheltenham Ladies College, to Canon William Butler reflects the missionaries' ambivalence: "She will never perhaps think exactly as we do, but if she did, she would not so well be a teacher for India. I am now beginning to see why she does not so readily accept sacramental teaching as we do. She is afraid of its being confused by native thought with their own pantheism. She sees dangers, which would not occur to us."[43]

Though Ramabai may not have engaged directly with the historical debate on the substance of godhead, she did engage quite conspicuously with two related issues: the possibilities of perfection and the Incarnation. Her seemingly innocuous discussions with Sister Geraldine about the impossibility of human perfection led her to make some of her strongest statements about Christ as an independent being totally distinct from the substance of God the Father, and thus to reveal her own developing position as a Unitarian. Ramabai's argument may be summarized as follows: proceeding from the dictionary definition of perfection as "not defective, completed, unblemished, possessing every moral excellence," she maintained that if human beings are describable in these terms, they would have foregone the progressive condition of souls and become not merely transfixed in time but God himself, since only God can be outside time. Since this is theologically impossible, the maximum state to which human beings can aspire is to be *like* God but not *as* God. Therefore, the real translation of Christ's "Be ye perfect," is to strive for perfection and approximate God, but remain substantially distinct from God and therefore imperfect. Trying to be perfect *like* God and *becoming perfect* are thus two totally separate arguments, the first signifying a paradox of necessary imperfection and the second a theological cul-de-sac:

> If we understand "Be ye perfect," etc., literally and in its fullest sense, then "As the Father" also must be taken literally and full which I know according to Christian teaching cannot be. For if we were to become *like* or *as* or equally perfect with

the Father, we should undoubtedly be so many supreme Gods, as the Vedantists say. There would not be any difference between us and the Father in perfection. Such a thing is an impossibility to me at least. I do not at the same time say that we shall not be perfect like the Father in a certain degree, but I object to saying that we shall be as perfect (not defective) as the Father is.[44]

Ramabai had less to say about the Incarnation, but her chief difficulty lay in reconciling immaculate conception with the doctrine of the Trinity: three beings are either separate from each other or they are one, but they cannot be both. Similarly, one is either born the way that human beings are, or one is uncreated; one cannot have both a human birth and be uncreated at the same time. To her mind, the entire idea of God emptying himself of omnipotence and omniscience in order to undergo human birth as Christ and suffer human travails is simply incompatible with the perfection and oneness of godhead.

The subject of the Incarnation roused Ramabai to new heights of theological argumentativeness. Whereas she was incredulous about the Trinity because the concept of three deities made Christianity no different from Hinduism, discussions of the Incarnation left her much more defensive about Hinduism. One might even say she was perverse in her defence, since her reason for wishing to leave Hinduism was precisely its free mixing of human and divine attributes. Earlier, she had expressed great doubts in believing that the boundless and pure essence of godhead could ever be limited or mixed with the impurities of the lower human nature, though it may be everywhere and remain boundless and pure in every limited thing.[45] Her dissatisfaction with Hinduism sprang from its erratic combinations of divine and human elements. But Christianity fared no better in her analysis, and she mercilessly lampooned some of its more salient contradictions. For instance, if the traditional Christian objection to Hinduism lay in the latter's conception of God as alternatively incarnate (that is, many persons) *and* One, Christianity itself could not claim to be exempt from the same tendency. "If Christian teachers laugh at the Hindoos because they want to reconcile these two opposite natures, on what ground, may I ask, they can establish their doctrine ... that Jesus Christ although omnipotent and omniscient emptied himself for a time of his qualities[?]"[46] Needless to say, her conclusion that no religion could base its theology on the Incarnation did not win much favor with the missionary sisters.

To Ramabai, the intermixture of human and divine was not merely a problem of substance; it had as much to do with the capacity to distinguish good from evil. In fact, Ramabai disparaged discussions of the Trinity in terms of substance alone by showing how foolish Hinduism had been made to appear because substance overtakes morality, as when incarnation is described as air filling up different rooms, "so the three persons being one fill three persons, yet they are one [like air], and that at last these different vessels or bodies will be broken up and the whole essence of God will be again united."[47] If Hinduism was pilloried for treating deity as substance, neither could Trinitarianism be exempt from the same charge, and Ramabai mercilessly applied what appeared to the sisters as cold logic to dismantle their arguments.

Similarly, if human birth is irreconcilable with unchanging essence, so too is the narration of national history with the scheme of spiritual redemption. Indisputably, no point of doctrine in Christianity has created more problems for narrative than the Incarnation, which symbolizes the uneven, discontinuous relationship between human history and scriptural revelation. When Ramabai asks, "How could Christ be called the offspring of David if He had not a human father," her question not only voices skepticism about the coexistence of opposites in the figure of Christ, but it also interrogates the construction of universal religion as a counterpart to national hagiography.[48] Ramabai's insistence on the exceptionalism of human birth also emphasizes the particularism of national history, and resists all attempts to accept the birth of Christ as simultaneously signaling the rise of a new nation.

Despite the missionaries' obvious outrage at Ramabai's persistent questions, it is partly out of a sense that she would be useful to her people only when she was able to discuss Christianity dispassionately as one among many other religious systems that led Dorothy Beale to advise Sister Geraldine that

> she must study Christianity as a philosophy. She cannot receive it merely as an historical revelation, it must also commend itself to her conscience. *We* say (who are brought up as Christians),—"Such things *were* and they reveal to us such and such truths." She *can* only say, "Such and such things are metaphysical necessities, therefore I am ready to receive evidence." And it was thus that St. Paul often spoke to the Greek-thinking converts. "It was *necessary*, is common in his mouth; and so our Lord spoke to His disciples.[49]

The sisters rationalize Ramabai's resistance to the Trinity as in fact a healthy sign of her determination to distinguish all aspects of Hinduism from her faith. Yet, although the missionaries recognized that Ramabai's Unitarianism was logically the only way she could justify leaving Hinduism, the fact remained that it brought her simultaneously to the brink of heresy. The sisters were caught in a position where they wished Ramabai at once to think and *not* think like themselves.

Ramabai's objections to praying in the name of Jesus Christ were not only on the grounds that Trinitarian worship blurred the divide between human and divine. Her reluctance must also be linked to her acute awareness that the ascription of full deity to Christ meant the exclusion of Jews from the community of Christ. Her opposition to the exclusionary character of Trinitarianism mounted with Sister Geraldine's declaration that "the Apostles distinguished the faithful from Infidels and Jews in that the former called on the name of the Lord Jesus Christ."[50] "In the name of Christ" functions, for Ramabai, as a cue for a politics of exclusion that England had come to symbolize. Although Ramabai's own probings into the fabric of English social life led her to recognize the plurality of England—that there existed, besides Anglican believers, a whole host of other religious communities including Jews, Dissenters, Methodists, Wesleyans, and Nonconformists—she was also made fully aware that such central pillars of the Anglican church as the Athanasian Creed and swearing by the Thirty-Nine Articles historically denied an inclusive role to these other groups. Under the cloak of heresy, non-Anglican groups had for long been deprived of citizenship rights.

Early in Sister Geraldine's text we are told that Ramabai was "dangerously inflated by her getting hold of points of controversy from her non-Conformist friends and dragging them clumsily and offensively into her letters."[51] These friends are not named, but elsewhere Geraldine reveals that Ramabai's reading includes a great deal of "popular religious literature" from which she derived ideas deemed to be distortions of Christian doctrine, though it was also the case that some of these ideas were no more palatable to Ramabai than they were to the missionaries. At other times, the sisters would not even countenance the fact that Ramabai's inquiry extended into some of the leading heresies of English history, and they obstinately concluded that her questions must come "from a *native* source."[52] This directly contradicts their earlier perception that she had derived "heretical" ideas from English popular pamphlet literature. Significantly, Ramabai's reading indicates her interest in a comparative perspective between and within religions, particularly in those books that compare "Heathen philosophy" with Christianity. We learn, for instance, that she had bought *History of Different Sects in India* "by an Indian gentleman" and also Max Müller's "Biographical Essay."[53]

Ramabai's intellectual interest in, if not close identification with, a mass-based religious ideology contained in English popular pamphlet literature curiously links her spiritual probings with the religious dissensions of English working-class radicalism. We do not know the full extent of Ramabai's acquaintance with English Nonconformity, especially in its lower-class expression, but her marked interest in the forms of religious controversy that were most specifically coming from the English working classes is not easily reconcilable with standard interpretations of Ramabai as an elitist, upper-caste Brahmin woman who had little interest in or contact with lower-class movements in India.[54] How then does one explain the uneven pattern of her class consciousness? Was her inability to connect with movements across class and caste in India—with nonelite women, shudras, and other low-caste groups—a product of her own Sanskritic, Dharmashastric background, a background that she was never able to surmount despite her Christian conversion? By the same token, did her conversion to Christianity open up a transnational space of identification that was impossible within the more narrowly defined caste structure of India? Could Ramabai, a high-caste Brahmin woman, indeed find unlikely points of contact with English working-class radicalism through her conversion?

A starting point for answering these questions is the course of English sectarianism as a whole and its relation to Ramabai's discovery of English Nonconformity. The decline of the established churches by the middle of the nineteenth century saw a new polarization developing in English religious life. On the one hand, there was renewed interest in established religion among the upper classes, particularly among conservatives who sought to remobilize the well-entrenched system of established churches to preserve a paternalistic, hierarchical society. On the other hand, the conservatism that favored maintaining the status quo was countered by movements for political reform, which saw in the proliferation of new religious sects and ideologies the opportunity for conveying new ideas of political change. The dissenting churches were among the most significant institutions in nineteenth-century British society, partly because they revived the hopes of those who believed the collapse of the French monarchy and the weakened power of the papacy augured a new era of equality and social justice.

Theological controversy may have deepened the divide within the established church, but it also opened up a much more heterogeneous set of religious ideas. For instance, the 1790s saw a great acceleration in the growth of Nonconformist religion. In a society where theological controversy provoked widespread engagement, the range of religious options to choose from was reflected in a bewildering array of descriptive labels, which signified hairsplittingly different doctrines and believers such as Calvinist, Arminian, Socinian, Anabaptist, Baptist, Paedobaptist, and the like. These tags of religious identification were seen by many in England as reflecting fundamental choices, and the definitions played an important part in the way the key players saw themselves and others. As a number of historians of English religion have pointed out, the structure of English society was such that sectarian identity influenced most areas of life; even those least interested in religion found that there were occasions when such an identity was forced upon them.[55]

If it was customary in nineteenth-century English discourse to place colonial subjects in the same frame of reference that included England's working classes, it is equally the case that resistance to the rule of empire by colonized peoples evoked comparisons to another oppositional group internal to England: the heterogeneous group of religious dissenters, atheists, and sectaries. The effect of such comparisons was to revive memories of an odious history of rank divisiveness in England's past. The bloody battles between Catholics and Protestants, and the subsequent fracturing of these two main groups and the proliferation of various subsects, remained too vividly etched in the English national consciousness for the questionings of a young native convert like Pandita Ramabai to go unnoticed. For her spiritual probings had the effect of recalling England's highly divisive past and threatening the return of the suppressed memory of fissures in English religious history. The sisters' grave apprehensions about Ramabai's questioning are due in part to the fact that she was beginning to learn about sectarian differences in English history, for these differences provide the various subject-positions from which Ramabai launches her critique of Anglicanism. At various points in their often virulent correspondence the Wantage sisters describe Ramabai successively as a Wesleyan, a Nonconformist, an Anabaptist, and an English Dissenter. Interpellated in these terms, Ramabai is identified with sectarian tendencies in England and charged with the crime of repeating, through her questioning, the violent schisms that tore England apart in earlier times.

Not only did the English missionaries seek to present a unified version of Christianity but they also fiercely resisted Ramabai's inquiry into sectarian differences—an inquiry that culminated in her realization that she had a choice in the precise form of the Christianity she embraced. Ironically, Ramabai's recognition of the splintered, sectarian history of English Christianity brought her to the insight that the existence of religious differences creates the option of choosing a particular idea of religion in which to believe. Ramabai commented disparagingly that "missionaries who want to convert the Hindoos to their own religion would do well to take care not to call themselves the only inheritors of truth, and all others 'the so-called false philosophers,' for the Hindoos as a rule will not be content to look or hear only one side."[56] Such a sense of choice radically transformed her prospective identity as a convert into that of a heretic.

This leads one to surmise that Ramabai's modernity derives less from her repudiation of Hindu tradition than from her embrace of an ideology of free will and choice. Ramabai's understanding of religious choice as a byproduct of English sectarianism suggests a line of thought that allows one to rethink the conventional polarization between tradition and modernity. As the details of Ramabai's conversion emerge more precisely, we learn that the proliferation of sects in English religious history impressed itself on her imagination in intellectually enabling ways. As Ramabai engaged in an animated exchange with her English sponsors, she began to see that there existed a fractured Christianity which the missionaries, for their part, were trying to present as an undivided religion identical with Anglican England. Hence, their unusual description of the Anglican church as Catholic Christianity, "the holy, apostolic Christianity," which Ramabai learned was a misnomer only long after she had parted company with the missionaries. Remarked an amused but also bemused Ramabai in 1886, "The Roman Catholics say the Protestant interpretation (including the English Church) of the word 'Catholic' is purely imaginary"; she then taunted Geraldine by sarcastically pointing out that "she had no right to call the Dissenters heretics, because she herself belonged to a Church which is but a Dissenting sect of the Roman Catholic."[57]

Recent scholars have drawn attention to the crucial role of choice in distinguishing conditions of modernity from those of premodernity. Christopher Queen describes the exercise of individual choice based on reason, careful deliberation, and historical consciousness as defining characteristics of modernity. If modernity comprises a complex range of ideas, philosophies, and systems, the ability to process them calls for not only reason to make the requisite discriminations between them but also the skill to evaluate the quality of their respective demands on one's attention. Such evaluation is itself a form of choice, but the important point is that choice is possible only when the heterogeneity of belief-systems is made visible. Such acts of conscious selection account for new types of conversion narratives, which reflect the individual subject's greater access to a range of traditions, ideas, and doctrines.[58] In this context, the more empowering aspects of English sectarianism for a young convert like Ramabai take on new meaning, for religious choice is as much a part of the logic of modernity as an increasingly differentiated individual subjectivity. If Ramabai is repeatedly accused of indiscriminately exercising reason in areas where faith took precedence, in her defense it would have to be said that the varieties of Christianity practiced historically in England required that she respond not with faith but with reason—that is, with the mental acuity to respond to minute distinctions between creeds, as well as the judgment to assess their relative importance within their respective branches of Christianity.

As Ramabai progressively moves toward defining her idea of religion from the sectarian options offered by English Christianity, her own status as a convert undergoes radical change. Sister Geraldine's description of English dissent emphasizes the dilution of religious truth as a product of rank sectarianism. In her earnest yet anxious correspondence with Ramabai she attempts to persuade the impressionable young Indian convert that the Anglican church represents a healthy syncretism, in sharp contrast to the dogmatism of individual sects:

Since [Wesleyanism] sprang into existence it had split up into 80 different sects drifting farther away from the Truth [which] shewed that their original separation from the Church was in itself a wrong act. This led to a conversation on dissent generally . . . *that all dissent was the undue stretching-out of one doctrine so as to hide or overshadow the other doctrines of the Christian Faith.* I said that in the Church's teaching, a perfect harmony was kept between all the dogmas of the Christian Faith; each had its due value given and helped to form a perfect texture; whereas in dissent an undue importance being given to one doctrine, the symmetry of the whole was marred.[59]

Geraldine's account of Anglicanism is nothing short of an aesthetic description of religious utility. If dissent signifies the attenuation of truth by competing hegemonies, which assert the dominance of one doctrine above all others, then Anglican orthodoxy represents that essential syncretism by which all creeds are kept in perfect aesthetic balance. Anglicanism does so not by manifesting a plurality of difference but by merging into oneness. Not entirely dissimilar to the Arnoldian idea of culture as a containment of disparate forces by filtering the "best that is thought and known," Geraldine's aestheticized religious ideal explains why sectarianism is as disruptive to the perfect balance represented by Anglican England as working-class anarchy is to English culture.

SILENCE AND HERESY

"The silence of a thousand years has been broken, and the reader of this unpretending little volume catches the first utterances of the unfamiliar voice. Throbbing with woe, they are revealed in the following pages to intelligent, educated, happy American women."[60] These are the words of Rachel Bodley, dean of the Women's Medical College in Philadelphia, as she introduced Pandita Ramabai to the western world. These resonant words open Bodley's preface to Pandita Ramabai's hugely successful book, *The High-Caste Hindu Woman* (1888), and establish the terms for the evaluation of Indian women's emancipation as emergence into "utterance."

If Ramabai is known at all in the west, it is precisely because she heralded a new, yet unknown voice whose calm, dispassionate presentation of a patriarchal religion from a female point of view ruptured the Orientalist celebration of Eastern philosophy as a repository of sublime mysteries. Rachel Bodley's account locates the hitherto suppressed narrative of the Hindu woman within a continuum of silence that it was Ramabai's particular achievement to disrupt. If Ramabai is remembered as a Hindu social reformer of great note, her outspokenness about the conditions of women's oppression stands out above all other characterizations of her social activism. Her access to public forums such as the print media and the lecture platform allowed her to make the necessary interventions that gained a "hearing" for her "voice." Thus, according to Bodley's rhetorical stance, it stands to reason that if silence is oppression, then speech is liberation.

Yet the fearless Ramabai also confessed that she "was obliged to keep silence," especially on the subject of church doctrine.[61] This is a strange admission, given that *The Letters and Correspondence of Pandita Ramabai* leaves no doubt in any reader's mind that Ramabai was not one to suppress her skepticism about received notions of religious faith, nor refuse engagement in the most forthright manner with ideas that she found unacceptable. Indeed, thus far I have been arguing just the reverse: that Ramabai declined to accept Christian faith as a given, especially on other people's terms, and was willing to carry on her quarrels with received notions right up to the highest authorities in the Anglican Church.

Why then did she resolve on numerous occasions to "hold my tongue . . . and not say one single word" but "read the Bible by myself, and follow the teaching of Christ?"[62] Is her withdrawal into silence a surrender to the impossibility of free intellectual debate on questions of religious worship? Or rather does her preferred choice of following Christ's teachings reflect a growing Pauline inclination to replace scriptural exegesis with the practice of private faith? But does that then suggest Ramabai's retreat into spiritual isolation, producing a rhetoric of self-fashioning of the sort that characterizes John Henry Newman's final conversion as an intensely private experience, contrary to the worldliness of his engagement with belief? As we observed earlier about Newman's conversion, his antipathy to large-scale dissemination of convictions arrived at through a laborious process of intellectual dissent grew out of a sense that the compulsion to proselytize masked an intellectual anxiety about the durability of hard-won convictions. Hence his willingness to slip into silence, or what he calls a "state of repose . . . a tranquil enjoyment of certitude."[63] Does Ramabai's retreat into silence signify a comparable withdrawal into the self-enclosed world of private experience?

First, the pattern of Ramabai's silences reveals a curious feature. She claims that she ceases to argue further on doctrinal issues whenever she feels the futility of doing so, especially when she is misunderstood by the missionaries or accused of being difficult and proud: "I see I cannot make you understand what I mean, nor can you make me believe in all your doctrines exactly as you believe in them."[64] Ramabai is told in no uncertain terms that her heresy must remain unspoken, or otherwise it will result in the sisters' severing of their relation to her ("I feel my duties as your teacher are now at an end," cautions Sister Geraldine ominously).[65] Yet while Ramabai recedes into silence on crucial theological points, she continues her resistance to missionaries on other fronts. Disarmed by the charge of sinful pride in her theological quarrels with the missionaries, who equate her speech with willfulness and thus effectively muffle her probings into religious questions, Ramabai's alternative method of expressing her disagreement with official interpretation is to "talk back" to the sisters, angrily challenging them in their control of her and in the matter of her daughter's religious upbringing. As an expression of colonial insubordination, the petulance and shrillness of her retorts displace blasphemy as an offense against religious doctrine and sentiment. Even when she is evidently impugning prevailing creeds, her "heresy" takes the form of a stern tongue-lashing:

> Am I to submit to this kind of teaching? Am I to submit to the teaching of the clergy like Canon Butler, who denies that I have a voice in choosing my own

religion, or to you who say that my conscience is no conscience at all and who say that outside your Church no truth can be bound, and if I tolerate with all the bodies of Christian people, I cannot be truthful? . . . You or rather some of the clergy of your church think that they could make many converts to their faith in India by telling them the Anglican Church only teaches the true religion, but I think it otherwise.[66]

This passage nicely illustrates the thin line separating heresy—as an offense against orthodox doctrine—from rank verbal assault ranging from sheer impertinence to outright insubordination. The most striking quality of Ramabai's alternating silence and speech is her uncanny ability to mix intellectual interrogation with insolence, as she strategically blurs the boundaries between the two and shifts the focus of her transgression from heresy to effrontery. In the above passage, for instance, it is significant that nowhere does she attack points of doctrine; there is no engagement with ideas—only retort, condescension, and retaliation. Similarly, ordering Sister Geraldine to desist from teaching her daughter Manorama the rudiments of Trinitarian belief, including the Athanasian Creed and the Thirty-Nine Articles, Ramabai's rebuke is more noticeable for its sharply reprimanding tone than for an analytical objection to Trinitarianism. If Ramabai is disarmed by the charge of pride, she in turns immobilizes the missionaries by the grating vehemence of her response.

Because the severity of Ramabai's tone conveys the uneven quality of a relationship presumed to be built on pedagogical trust but now exposed as paternalistic in fact, the missionaries are unable to reduce her recalcitrant posture to pride alone. Indeed, Ramabai's tone creates a context for her challenge of church doctrine—a context that includes the colonial conversion of subject peoples, the imposition of a religious creed which is interchangeable with imperialist hegemony, and the whole structure of unequal relationships that these presuppose. Her "heresy" is transformed from a repudiation of specific points of doctrine into a sharp questioning of the rationale of colonial expropriation, culminating in an unequivocal denunciation of the arbitrary imposition of one people's will on others.

The missionaries' attempt to control Ramabai by curbing her speech is consistent with what Gyan Prakash has described as a general colonial attempt to normalize what cannot be named or recognized—in this case, her intellectual independence and spiritual integrity.[67] Ramabai was fully aware of the terror and fear that filled the missionaries in the face of her transgression's unnameability. That is why she could scornfully rebuke them for making "the word 'pride' almost meaningless by applying it to everything that you see in me."[68] And there was a certain truth in her accusation, for vastly conflicting kinds of verbal behavior—be it a lack of communication or persistent questioning—were all attributed to the same cause; pride assumed an explanatory power that far exceeded the behavior that it putatively described. Apparently for missionaries and colonial officers alike, it was much easier to deal with their native subjects' outright rebellion and even "heathenish" superstition than with Indians' rewriting of Christianity to suit their own purposes. What were administrators and missionaries to do when subjects claimed belief as entitling them to independent judgment? As an unmanageable part of colonial rule, belief was resistant to the space that was sought for it in programs of governance and reform. Indeed, colonial manipulations were actually far more successful in creating a space for English culture than in regulating belief. The successful introduction of English literature is a case in point.[69]

Yet it is also the case that Ramabai oftens turns to silence as a form of resistance to doctrinal coercion. Silence in such instances is preparatory to the private interpretation that made her so subversive in missionaries' eyes. The missionaries in their turn read this as evidence of her "alienation from her friends"—in other words, as conclusive proof of her ever-present, errant pride distancing her further and further from divine mercy. And so the circle of accusation continues. Given that it was unlikely Ramabai would easily change her mind about central doctrinal points, how could she be brought to a situation where she would refrain from uttering views that the church declared to be heresies, yet at the same time not withdraw into a silence that had equally heretical outcomes?

Indeed, the missionaries' dilemma centered around the complex, even contradictory function of silence. In her refusal to speak, Ramabai was as transgressive as when she committed herself to speech. For as Dorothea Beale, principal of Cheltenham Ladies College where Ramabai was a student and instructor, confides in a private letter to Sister Geraldine, "If she does not find someone to whom she can speak freely, she will be silent, and might easily pass into Unitarianism."[70] The relation between silence and heresy is clearly more complex than can be understood by descriptions of heresy hunting as a matter of policing by silencing alone. As the last quoted remark makes clear, complete suppression of speech is no more effective in stemming the tide toward heterodoxy than the threat of punishment or ostracism from community. Though curbs may be effectively placed on speech to prevent unacceptable utterances, the ferment from which those utterances are produced remains unchecked. Therefore, speech must be allowed, but only in such ways that its influence will be confined to a carefully circumscribed space and not extend beyond it.

It is of no small significance that the limited space offered to Ramabai for voicing her religious doubts is that of an enlightened but enclosed community of women. The sisters' repeated declaration that Ramabai could not speak to a man about certain religious subjects—"there are some subjects that she could only discuss with a woman"—offers the construction of a feminist community as a counterpoint to existing barriers in social interaction between men and women.[71] Sister Geraldine's assurance that "to a woman she can speak on the Incarnation as she could not to a man" discovers in the confessor relationship not only a practice for maintaining institutional authority but also a convention for forging sisterly bonds.[72] The conditions for the possibility of speech have a gendered aspect that merges with the boundaries of acceptable theological doctrine. For, of course, the missionaries' refashioning of community is not aimed at establishing sisterhood but, instead, at containing heresy. The feminist bonding offered by the Wantage order leaves intact the structure of patriarchal authority derived from church tradition, even as it encourages the new convert to enact her heresies on a stage especially constructed for her via feminism. The difference, of course, is that on this particular stage Ramabai's heresies will be restrained and rendered harmless, even though they are articulated freely as sisterly communication.

Yet here too the missionaries failed to meet their objectives entirely. Though the sisters assumed that the inhibitions a woman might be expected to feel about discussing the virgin birth would be naturally applicable to Ramabai, a Hindu widow, they were not prepared for her obstinate refusal to avoid questions about immaculate conception, nor did they have a ready answer to her blunt remark that "as far as we know of the history of mankind told in the Scripture, and from other sources, as well as by our experience, we know that no man except the first couple was ever born without the natural course."[73] Amid these scattered remarks is a refusal by Ramabai to accept a community of women as her sole interlocutors in theological debate.

Nowhere is this refusal more apparent than in her translation of "conversion" into the sphere of gender relations. Of her many actions that so chagrined her mentors, none was as aggravating as her insistence on teaching English to both men and women. Other teachers attached to the Wantage order were known to instruct men at the Working Men's College, so her request was not an unusual one. Yet the alarm bells that it set off exposed the Orientalist assumptions about Hindu women that still guided missionary policy. In her caustic response to Sister Geraldine's disapproving letters, Ramabai reminds her that in the course of their numerous pilgrimages she and her brother habitually addressed communities of male scholars, as a result of which she earned the title of Saraswati, or goddess of learning.

> It surprises me very much to think that neither my father nor my husband objected [to] my mother's or my teaching young men while some English people are doing so. You can call some of my countrywomen "hedged" but you cannot apply this adjective to Marathi Brahmin women. You have yourself seen that Marathi ladies are neither hedged nor kept behind thick curtains. . . . Can I confine my work only to women in India and have nothing to do with men?[74]

When reprimanded that it was indelicate of her—a Hindu widow—to teach men or visit "gentlemen friends," especially given her own orthodox background, Ramabai rebuts with one of the most sustained anti-Orientalist diatribes in nineteenth-century letters. Simultaneously, she punctures almost all the cherished notions of women's reform held by English missionaries and claims a more privileged status as a Hindu woman by virtue of exposure to indigenous reform movements (like the Brahmo Samaj). Is this backsliding or sheer perversity? That question worries the missionaries, and Ramabai's determination to set her own agenda for women's reform coalesces into the "heretical" construction of a belief system antithetical to the missionaries' objectives: "Unless I begin to have a regular and pure intercourse with men, I shall in vain hope and try to help my countrywomen."[75] For the feminist community proposed by Sister Geraldine is akin to the secluded *purdahnasheen*, zenana-style arrangement from which Ramabai and other Indian women had determined to emerge. By the time Geraldine perceives that the source of Ramabai's vehemence is a retrograde feature of caste society missionaries had long sought to remedy, Geraldine realizes she has no choice but to permit the transgressions that her attempt at forging sisterly bonds sought to contain.

> I see now why she makes this a matter of principle. I think we must remember that God seems to have anointed her with power to throw down the pernicious caste restrictions and those barriers which wrongly separate men and women. In this she has worked with all whom God set over her—father, mother, brother, husband. She would feel herself disloyal to their memory, who approved of her (a young girl) speaking in mixed assemblies if she gave in to any rules which said a woman should not teach boys. . . . It seems to me a matter in which we ought not to bind her conscience.[76]

Producing inevitable conflict and ambivalence in the Wantage sisters' dealings with Ramabai is their representation of England as at once a desirable symbol of modernity and a source of corruption. Although the learning contained in western knowledge has the power to dispel Hindu superstition, the sisters fear that it also fosters a superciliousness taking the form of either self-estrangement or a false sense of independence.[77] Either way, separation from earlier patterns of understanding and behavior complements the alienation brought about by Ramabai's loosening of ties to family and community. If the missionaries object to the self-sufficiency of Ramabai's posture, they cannot help concluding that English education contributed in no small way to it. Ramabai recognizes the inherent contradiction in such a representation and, in her counterattack, forces the missionaries to peer into the mirror of modernity as the source of human depravity, displacing biblical explanations of depravity as the result of original sin. When challenged by the sisters who trace Ramabai's and other colonized Indians' arrogance to the detrimental effects of western education, Ramabai turns the customary missionary explanations of human pride and sinfulness adroitly against them: "I believe it is not learning or wisdom that makes people either proud or idle. It is their own nature that makes them so."[78] Ironically, Sister Geraldine's ponderous words on Ramabai's proud nature return to haunt the nervous missionary, and it is Ramabai who, in deflecting them back toward her, has the decisive word on the subject.

CHAPTER FIVE

Ethnographic Plots

RELIGIOUS EXPANSION IN COLONIAL HISTORIOGRAPHY

Facts have a dubious place in the memory of a nation. When, in times of conflict, monuments are destroyed or whole communities converted to a conqueror's religion, these events take on an empirical power shaping the description of future relations between groups of people. Historiography's role is key, particularly when written from an apparently dispassionate outsider perspective. If, as Peter van der Veer argues, the inimical relations between Hindus and Muslims constitute "one of the most important master-narratives of colonial orientalism in India," it is not only because such narratives legitimate British rule as one of enlightened disinterestedness but also because they marshal "facts" that can be deployed to construct different plotlines.[1] The destruction of Hindu temples by Muslim rulers and the forcible conversion of Hindus at the point of a sword represent one type of fact that underwrites a master narrative of violent change, as recorded for example in James Mill's *The History of British India* (1817). Opposed to it is another kind of fact, which is also documented in British historiography in works such as Thomas W. Arnold's *The Preaching of Islam* (1896): the patronage of Hindu shrines by Muslim saints and Muslim tomb-worship by Hindus, and the sharing of titles and names as well as certain social practices and customs by Hindus and Muslims. If both Mill's and Arnold's narratives claim to be equally accurate descriptions of Hindu-Muslim relations, then tolerance and intolerance would have to be defined as the respective absence or presence of violence and forcible change from outside.

But in the official sociology of India drawn up in the last quarter of the nineteenth century, when the first British census reports were commissioned on an all-India basis to ascertain patterns of religious growth and decline, among other things, religious change through outside intervention is no longer the central issue. Islamic conversion is represented as having less to do with either the coercive or the charismatic character of Islam than with economic necessity or social ostracism from Hinduism. What models of tolerance or intolerance are then suggested in this reading of Muslim expansion, where conversion to Islam is the result neither of a gradual mystical insight that incorporates aspects of Hindu worship nor a violent rupture of existing beliefs, but rather arises from the exclusionary character of caste Hinduism?

Indeed, in this description the agency of intolerant action would seem to have shifted from Islam to Hinduism, which, by casting out its members, enables Islam to offer the possibilities for social betterment to these same excluded groups.

However, the meanings of exclusion and incorporation are as volatile as those of tolerance and intolerance, for the conversion to Islam precipitated by low-caste status in Hinduism also gives rise to movements of *reconversion* to Hinduism. In principle, reconversion attempts to reverse the principle of exclusion, as well as challenge the appeal of rival religious systems by reabsorbing those who had earlier been cast off or had not been fully assimilated.[2] Yet, belying their incorporative philosophy and reformist tendencies, reconversion movements often exhibit a morbid defensiveness, expressing themselves through group solidarity and an enforced collective identity. Exemplifying this tendency is the Arya Samaj, a reform movement in late nineteenth-century India that grew out of the impulse to rehabilitate Hinduism and restore it to center place after the assaults made on it by Christianity. Indeed, in redefining the boundaries of the Hindu community, the reformist rhetoric of these movements locked reconversion firmly into the discourse of Hindu nationalism.

The art historian Vidya Dehejia poses similar questions (albeit in a different context) about the wisdom of defining incorporation as a benevolent gesture and, conversely, exclusion as an annihilative move. In a provocative essay on Tamil religious art, she points to the appropriation of Vaishnavite features in Shaivite art as possible evidence of sectarian tension.[3] As rival sects of brahmanical Hinduism, Shaivism and Vaishnavism have long struggled to claim the terms of defining godhead, worship, ritual, and community. If there is doctrinal conflict in conceptions pertaining to divinity—conceptions such as whether evil is immanent or the creation of rival forces—it is unimaginable that the outcome of the conflict would be in terms other than the denial and even effacement of the legitimacy of one set of claims by the opposing party. Yet in illuminating the patterns of appropriation and borrowing that define sectarian struggle, Dehejia contests the assumption that rivalry or contention between two religious communities inevitably will lead to the total destruction of features of the rival religious system. Just as questionable to her is whether the establishment of a separate identity necessarily requires negation of the competing system.

Arguing the contrary, Dehejia's argument raises fundamental questions about the identification of tolerance with syncretism and intolerance with absolutism and exclusivity.[4] How, for example, do we respond to reconversion movements which, in a broadly reformist way, attempt to include groups that were formerly excluded? Does the gesture of reclamation and incorporation made by such movements efface their earlier marginalization of these same groups? In responding to these questions, we may wish to recall emerging patterns of religious tolerance in England: we noted earlier, in Chapter One, that the relaxation of penalties against non-Anglican groups occurred simultaneously with parliamentary initiatives to absorb religious minorities as useful citizens of the state. While not identical to the English pattern, Hindu reconversion nonetheless shares features with tolerance as a practice of incorporation, especially to offset the inescapable loss of numbers that ritual expulsion necessarily entailed.

But what if the groups being wooed do not want to return to the fold? Are they then denying their true origins and willfully attaching themselves to a community to which they are united not by the ties of birth but by social affiliation? Though it is impossible to do more than speculate about the links between movements of reconversion to Hinduism in colonial India and the conferral of citizenship rights on non-Anglicans in metropolitan England, what is fairly clear is that the two developments are both embedded in the formative processes of national identity at a time when expulsion or excommunication no longer had the power to confirm the authority of an exclusive group. Obviously, voluntary departure from the fold posed an even greater threat to the ability of dominant groups to assert their power.

With the complex meanings of appropriation and exclusion as a backdrop, it should be possible to re-read official British discourse about conversion in order to ask how it emplots the relationship between rival religious communities. At what point are the "facts" of forcible and violent change, as presented in works like James Mill's *History of British India* (1817), and the "facts" of peaceful assimilation to Islam, as described in Thomas Arnold's *The Preaching of Islam* (1896), no longer clearly demarcated as self-evident examples of Islamic intolerance in the first instance and tolerance in the second? Why does establishing the motives for conversion matter so much in order to describe the relationship between communities? Or is the real center of interest not why people converted but who they were before they converted—in other words, not motives but origins? If Mill's and Arnold's texts simplify the history of religious expansion by maintaining that the true test of a society's tolerance is its capacity to absorb difference, a third narrative emerges in official discourse in which difference becomes the contested object of reclamation rather than of absorption. In short, the stage beyond the dialectical opposition between Mill and Arnold is one where incorporation and exclusion resist being unproblematically located in ideas of religious syncretism and religious absolutism, respectively.

The point in British discourse at which narratives of tolerance and intolerance acquire a shifting center of reference—at times it is Islam and at other times Hinduism—is determined by the writing of India's official sociology in the third quarter of the nineteenth century, when the first census reports, settlement reports, and district gazetteers were commissioned. The enumeration of India's populations marks the period when the boundaries of religious communities are redrawn in relation to empirically derived explanations about the expansion of the Muslim population in nineteenth-century India. As Peter Hardy notes, although Muslim groups are identified as separate from the Hindu community and therefore also a separate political entity, a large majority of Muslims are also recognized for the first time in British discourse as originally having been Hindus who had converted for reasons other than direct force or spiritual illumination.[5] More visibly than in the past, the discourse of nationalism is processed through a discourse of origins. For instance, questions confronting British administrators included deciding how the numbers of Muslims in India were to be categorized: as descendants of those who originally came from Arab lands and were subsequently indigenized (that is, "hereditary" Muslims), or as descendants of native Hindus who had converted. Were Hindus who had converted to Islam to be considered less Muslim (that is, more Hindu) than other Muslims of Arab descent groups? Is there already thus a split Muslim identity based on differential lines of descent and lateral movement?

Obviously, these questions are important not only in the immediate context of present-day Hindu-Muslim relations but also because in a broader sense they probe the construction of racial purity and hybridity against the backdrop of migration, conversion, and intermarriage. This chapter approaches these questions of origins and racial composition through that institutional instrument most directly focused on the determination of identity—census taking—and in particular census taking as an established feature of British colonial administration. The all-India census reports issued between 1872 and 1901 made the first systematic attempt to categorize the religious identities of Indian peoples (including converts) according to criteria of racial origin, customs, and laws. In the course of such categorization various oppositions were constructed out of the material of enumeration—oppositions such as foreign/indigenous, national/local, pure/hybrid, lineal descent (or hereditary)/convert. In assessing the strength of the Muslim population in India between 1872 and 1901, the census threw the bulk of its weight on the side of the second term in each of these oppositions to draw a picture of the Indian Muslim, not as an autonomous "other" but as a version of the Hindu at an earlier historical moment before the advent of Arab, Afghan, and Turkish groups—and before possibly forcible conversion of Hindus to Islam.[6]

I will suggest that the "contrived" assimilation of Muslim Indians to Hindu India is not simply a nineteenth-century Indian nationalist strategy of fighting colonial oppression, as it is portrayed by recent Hindu revivalists, but just as much a feature of late nineteenth-century British discourse. I might add, incidentally, that the discourse of origins also marks the historiography of England in its attempt to negotiate the divide between the Norman and Anglo-Saxon strains in British history. For instance, in a move reminiscent of the British census of India, Edward A. Freeman, whose *History of the Norman Conquest of England* (1873–1879) argued that the basis of English national identity is racial, denied the otherness of the Normans by minimizing their foreignness. I raise this point obviously not in order to suggest that Normans and Muslims are interchangeable in a scheme of racial organization, but to argue that British historiography in the metropole and British sociology in the colonies converge on one crucial point: the creation of a mythology that makes the racial basis of the modern nation state continuous and pure. This compulsion is easier to explain with regard to England than India. If it is understandable that English nationalist historiography benefits from the translation of conquering races into groups already indigenous to England, what investment does colonial sociology have in the racial continuity of India?

For one thing, the British assertion about the local origins of Indian Muslims challenged the separatist impulse among Muslims as an exaggerated claim that was belied by the facts accumulated by British ethnographic data, census reports, and commissioned surveys. The data indeed placed the Muslims closer in racial features, behavior, habits, and customs to other native inhabitants of India, including Hindus. The "Muslim" represented in the British census reports is marked by an ambivalent identity—neither truly Muslim nor truly Hindu, riven by social class differences that, in their turn, displace the possibilities of a unity of religious belief or identity. The critical issue in the historiography of Hindu-Muslim relations is not that British policy conceived of Hindus and Muslims as separate communities. Rather, the theory of common origins from which other social and religious identities were willingly or forcibly adopted, produced a crippling situation that disallowed either total (homogeneous) unity of Hindus and Muslims or total (heterogeneous) division between them.

I should point out at the outset that I am not reading these reports to suggest a continuity between British colonial discourse and the rhetoric of modern communalism, or to argue that the roots of contemporary communal problems lie in late nineteenth-century information-gathering techniques. Rather, I am arguing that acts of classification, such as the census, create an overarching narrative plot in which race, caste, and religion override the self-definitions of the groups being enumerated. Furthermore, such instruments establish the categories of knowledge that, in becoming part of the contrived memory of the population, present complex problems in the construction of future relationships between these groups. The shift from elite to mass politics in Indian nationalism gave a new importance to the masses of Muslim converts who were denied an origin outside India. As a descriptive catalog of India's ethnic composition, the British census establishes fixities of racial and religious categories, even as it insinuates the possibilities of overlapping and common origins rather than real historical difference. The function of the census to introduce categories of difference and then deny them must be seen to have a complex effect on the structure of perceptions about Hindu-Muslim relations, if not on those relations themselves. My interest, therefore, is in examining the mediating role of British ethnography in the production of a field of remembered identities, both Hindu and Muslim, which subsequently feeds into the discourses of religious nationalism.

In his 1992 revised edition of *Imagined Communities*, Benedict Anderson appends a chapter on the census that acknowledges the crucial role of data collection in constructing what he calls the "grammar" of nationalism.[7] Though Anderson's focus is on Southeast Asia, his observations are broad and general enough to permit their application to other contexts. The most striking aspect of his reading relates to the notion that census gathering is itself a form of imagining. Although I would emphatically distance myself from his view that colonial subjects are imagined even before they come into historical existence through the census, I do not doubt that administrative reason is a much less apt term than imagination to describe the creation of ethnicities bearing little or no connection with the self-characterizations of groups. Driven by the "power of the grid," an alternative name for the imagination, the colonial census creates a scenario that names its characters and assigns them roles in an unfolding ethnohistorical drama.[8]

But though Anderson's interest is in the census as an exercise of the imagination, he has little to say about the plots it develops and less about their narrative resolution. I would argue that the colonial census's distinctive point of departure from indigenous census reports does not lie in quantification, as Anderson suggests, nor even in its exhaustive cataloguing of peoples (including women and children, who were usually ignored in the precolonial census). I believe the British census's significance lies rather in its meticulous construction of narrative plots, in the working out of which race, caste, and religion become visible as analytical categories. This is, of course, not the same as saying that these categories function as the principles of classification guiding census gathering. Indeed, I am suggesting something quite different, and wish to show that these categories follow from rather than precede the resolution of the census's various plots. The qualification I want to add aims at elucidating the imagining process in the census as central to how relations between religious communities are conceptualized. The plots list key players in terms that would be familiar to readers of literary narratives; they describe the livelihood, location, and life stories of their subjects with the sort of detail that readers would have expected of the nineteenth-century English novel. The elaborate descriptions are brought into focus by the trope of conversion, which weaves the different plots together to provide an historical narrative of communities sundered by religious change.

CENSUS TAKERS AND THE ORIGINS
OF MUSLIMS

The first systematic assessment of India's Muslim population was made in the British census reports of 1872. H. Beverly, the superintendent of the census, made the potentially explosive assertion that the large presence of Muslims in Bengal was due not so much to the introduction of foreign blood into the country as to the conversion of the former inhabitants, for whom a rigid system of caste discipline made Hinduism intolerable.[9] Many Bengali Muslims took exception to this conclusion, and Khondkar Fazli Rabi wrote *The Origins of the Musalmans of Bengal* (1895) to prove that the truth was indeed quite the opposite: he was at pains to point out, for example, that many leading Muslim families could trace their origins to foreign roots—families such as the Saiads, who refrained from intermarriage with families of more "dubious" ancestry. Piqued by what he took to be Beverly's social condescension, Rabi wrote, "It can safely, and without any fear of contradiction, be asserted that the ancestors of the present Musalmans of this country were certainly those Musalmans who came here from foreign parts during the rule of the former sovereigns, and that the present generation of Musalmans are the offspring of that dominant race who remained masters of the land for 562 years."[10]

Other Muslim historians, however, were less extreme in their claims, and, though committed to the theory of the foreign origin of Indian Muslims, reluctantly admitted that local converts bulked largely in the total. But at the same time the figures quoted were conservative for the most part. Abu A. Ghaznavi, who was asked by the British to respond to Fazli Rabi's claim, calculated that roughly 20 percent of the Muslims living in Bengal were lineal descendants of foreign settlers, 50 percent had a mixture of foreign blood, and the remaining 30 percent, he claimed, were probably descended from Hindus and other converts.[11]

The 1901 Census, however, dismissed these figures as too disproportionate and placed the percentage of converts from Hinduism much higher. The idea of the original "Hinduness" of Muslim inhabitants extended to the argument that the early Muslim invaders in Bengal were not even Arabs but Pathans. Yet the fact that gets recorded in the census is that the Muslims who called themselves "Shekh" outnumbered those who professed to be Pathans in a ratio of fifty to one, and furthermore, that many of these "Shekhs" had only recently begun to claim this name and were formerly known as Ashraf in south Bengal and as Nasya in north Bengal.[12] Two different commentaries are thus juxtaposed in a contained narrative of conflicting memories: the descriptive record of Muslim self-definitions placing Indian Muslims as Arab-descended is framed by a commentary that negates those self-perceptions and posits an alternative explanation of Muslim origins in the fractured space of Hindu communities.

Explanation further takes on a racialist turn through the ethnographic contributions of Herbert Risley, who was brought into the census-taking operations at a crucial stage of description. The ethnographic scale of measurement, or "cephalic index," that he devised conclusively "proved" the Hindu origins of Indian Muslims, despite the latter's claims to foreign ancestry that their names and titles presumably asserted. By taking measurements of the proportion of the breadth of the head to its length, as well as of the breadth of the nose to its length, Risley placed Muslims closer in racial features to the lower castes of Chandals and Pods than to Semitic peoples.[13] Here is a clear instance of how the discourse of class, blending indistinguishably with the discourse of race, appropriated the category of religion as uniting both discourses, where it was indeed possible to state that "although the followers of the Koran form the largest proportion of the inhabitants [of Rangpur district], there is little reason to suppose that many of them are intruders. They seem in general, *from their countenances*, to be descendants of the original inhabitants."[14]

The split between "original" Muslims, defined as those who comprised the higher classes, and local Muslim converts from Hinduism, who were consistently identified with the lower classes, did two things. First, it accentuated differences not between Hindus and Muslims but rather between Muslims and Muslims on the point of foreign or native descent. Muslims converted from Hinduism were regarded more ambiguously as Muslim and more relationally placed vis-à-vis Hindus. Second, the dichotomy of foreign vs. locally descended Muslims replaced unity of Muslim identity—which the profession of Islam presumably implied—with differences based on social class. Both factors figure importantly in the reconversion movements led by Hindu groups as early as the nineteenth century, and which continue to function today in certain regions of India (especially in those areas where mass conversions have taken place, such as in the southern town of Meenakshipuram).

The reconversion movements (which often include rituals of purification, or *shuddhi*) are a relatively unusual phenomenon in that they seek to reverse the total excommunication from Hinduism that apostasy to any other religion generally demanded. Furthermore, reconversion is premised on the activation of remembered identities long since lost or abandoned. The readmission to Hinduism of converts to Islam required, often as a test, that they displayed types of behavior that no Muslim would ever be identified with, such as eating pork. (Many Muslims who had converted from Hinduism had still not adopted the taboo against pork eating, so that for such converts it was possible to exhibit those behaviors that made them acceptable to caste Hindus.)[15] The emphasis in reconversion rituals on practices, habits, and usages as markers of religious identity bears a strong resemblance to a similar emphasis in the British census reports that gave greater weight to customs and practices over the self-declarations of religious identity as a means of classifying religious groups in India. If apostates could be reclaimed back into the fold despite their earlier rejection of Hinduism in favor of another religion, such reclamation was made possible by a political discourse of religious identity whereby a Hindu remained a Hindu by virtue of retaining certain social customs. What the census report does, in other words, is to establish a set of scientifically derived representations that enables the Hindu community to claim Muslims as its own by virtue of criteria drawn from racial categories. These categories give rise to the notion that Hindus and Muslims have a cultural continuity that conversion is powerless to undo.

In its preoccupation with the question of Muslim origins, the census revealed its own bias toward downplaying the foreign element in the composition of Indian Muslims, only one-sixth of whom were placed as Arab-or Pathan-descended Muslims. The rest were listed as local converts from Hinduism who still preserved habits and usages from the religion they had supposedly repudiated. The census report consistently accentuates the "Hinduness" of Muslim converts in proportion to minimizing the self-definitions of those whom it sought to enumerate. The census taker often assumed the prerogative of listing them under the group to which *he* thought they belonged, even though extensive inquiry was adopted as a means of eliciting more detailed information from Muslims and other religious groups on where they placed themselves. In almost every category—age, religion, caste, marital status, and so forth—questions generated a bewildering range of responses that often led the census taker to make the determination himself. An infuriating inexactitude of response emerges as one of the central frustrations of census taking. For instance, when asked about age, many an inhabitant of Indian villages was known to respond with a blithe *bis-chalis* (twenty or forty). Such vagueness (which Benedict Anderson terms "politically transvestite," because it is ambiguous, indefinite, and fluid in its multiple identifications) encouraged the census takers to transfer the authority of self-classification from their subjects to themselves.[16]

On the matter of religious classification, the census takers had clear instructions that they were to accept each person's statement about their religious affiliation, no matter how vague or imprecise it might be, but in practice this rule was systematically overlooked. Instead, the census takers took it upon themselves to decide whether an individual was Hindu or Muslim, which in practical terms often meant determining whether a Muslim could trace his roots to foreign ancestors or whether he was descended from local converts from Hinduism. Apart from a physical observation of racial features, the basis for such determinations was often the set of customs and usages practiced by individuals. As for personal declarations of religious identity or religious belief, these were routinely subordinated to the census taker's classification. As seen in Chapter Three, above, this was also true with regard to Christian converts who were often judged as Hindus, not Christians, in cases filed in the British Indian courts for restitution of rights forfeited by converts under Hindu law. The basis for judicial decisions was the degree to which converts' behavior, habits, and manners conformed to those of Hindus, such as preserving the joint family system.

Classification was made even more problematic in the case of Muslims who appeared to follow Hindu customs to some extent and had half-Hindu names, yet called themselves by an upper-class Muslim title. Some were formerly high-caste Hindus who, on conversion to Islam, were allowed to assume upper-class Muslim titles such as "Shekh" even though they continued to adhere in part to Hindu customs, and in a few rare cases even to intermarry with those Muslims who were of foreign descent. On the contrary, the lower castes, who were often converts, had to be content with the title "Nau-Muslim," or "New Muslim." It was only in the case of converts who came from functional groups that Hindu names and titles were still retained, such as Kali Shekh, Kalachand Shekh, and so forth. As a Muslim convert of low social position rose in station, he was likely to assume more high-sounding designations that combined Hindu and Muslim names. For instance, almost in a crude sort of parody, the gradual upgrading of a low-caste convert like Meher Chand is seen in the progressive combination of names and titles that he acquires through conversion to Islam: first the name of Meher Ullah, then Meheruddin, next Meheruddin Muhammed, then Munshi Muhammed Meheruddin, Munshi Muhammed Meheruddin Ahmad, then finally Maulavi Munshi Muhammed Meheruddin Ahmad.

Perhaps the most damaging assessment made by the census report, at least in terms of the repercussions that it had on future constructions of Muslims as "outsiders," was that although the majority of Indian Muslims were identified as local converts or descendants of converts from Hinduism, the conclusion established by the British census takers was that Indian Muslims saw themselves as "other"-defined, their point of reference for personal identity lying *outside* India in a quasi pan-Islamic unity:

> All Mohammedans look on Arabic as their sacred language and they interlard their conversation with any Persian or Arabic words they can pick up from their Mullahs or from their religious books. The grammar remains Bengali and it is only some of the vocables which are changed. The better educated converts often deliberately abandon their native language. The Garpeda Bhunjas of Balasore furnish an illustration of this. They are descended from a Brahman and the females are still so far imbued with Hindu prejudices that they abstain from beef. But they have completely given up the use of Oriya and now speak Hindustani even in the family circle.[17]

In this accent on the practice of difference by those who were indeed drawn away from Hinduism at one point in their history, the British census gave

Hindu nationalists of a later generation a language of "foreignness" and "otherness" to describe Muslims who had no proper claims to a unique foreign identity, and who yet were said to have made such claims in a gesture of denial of their (in many cases) Hindu origins.

In other words, a complex construction of Muslim religious and ethnic identity is produced by the British census that plays on both the assertion and the denial of difference. The very function of the census is to show, through enumeration, that the assertion of difference—the idea of Muslims as "outsiders"—was propagated by Indian Muslims themselves. And once this is established as a specifically Muslim claim, that declaration of difference is promptly denied by the categories adopted in British census taking, which sought to demonstrate that the bulk of the Muslim population came from local converts. Although Indian Muslims were anxious to link their ancestry to Arab roots, British commentators seemed bent on proving their mixed heritage—that the majority of Muslims in India at the time of the first major census in 1872 were indeed converts and not descendants of Arab settlers and conquerors.

ROMANCE OR COERCION?

One of the most fascinating sections of the 1901 census is an appendix that lists individual cases of conversion in various districts of east and north Bengal. In this listing (see Appendix), the cause of the vast majority of conversions is established as neither proselytism nor doctrinal conviction but, rather, romance. The elaborate narrative sketch that follows each case reads like a romantic novel in its stress on Hindus converting to Islam primarily to marry men or women with whom they had fallen in love.[18] As in any romance novel worth its name, each story is carefully annotated with the names of principal characters, central episodes, conflict, and climactic resolution. The tabulation outlines a prototypical plot for each case, a plot that includes locale, place of exchange (the workplace in most instances), event (falling in love), resolution (marriage), and outcome (conversion). The disjunction between the resolution and the outcome encapsulates the failed possibilities of love and marriage in repairing the communal divide, even as it also points to the antinational obstacles to marriage as potentially a union of different races and religions.

However uncanny the overlap between census documentation and romance novels, the comparison with the conventional romance plot stops at the point of narrative structure, which slips into the realist mode despite the compulsions of the romantic imagination. Though romance is presented as the main motive for conversion, the play of human desires and feelings has no place here. Obviously, the census report is not intended to be anything other than an instrument of data collection. Yet the enumerated instances of mixed marriages between Hindus and Muslims become examples of exile, excommunication, and existential isolation, as marital union is achieved only by the conversion of one partner to the religion of the other. Not only does conversion erase racial identity but it also nullifies the community that grounds racial identity. The potential function of interreligious love to offer a model of cultural syncretism is not able to hold its own against the irreversible loss of community caused by romantic attachments. In narratological terms, the loss of community displaces romantic union as the predominant plot in the census.

Ordinarily, romantic attachments bridging religious faiths might reasonably be considered a positive counterpoint to the exclusionary practices of a self-contained religious culture. After all, desire as an instrument of national unification has given a certain potency to the English romance novel especially from Walter Scott onwards. One has only to recall the plots of novels whose triumphant resolution in intermarriage culminates simultaneously in an English nation state made stronger by the cementing of affective ties. Walter Scott's *Ivanhoe* (1819), for instance, celebrates the marriage of the Saxon Rowena and the Normanized Ivanhoe as the union of the races. As Michael Ragussis points out in his subtle analysis of the novel, Rowena figures in the racial politics of medieval England as the object of two competing marriage plots, both of which subordinate her personal identity to her racial identity.[19] One plot would have a Norman husband, DeBracy, foisted on her, dramatically disrupting her lineage and effacing her Saxon descent. The second plot, on the other hand, places her in the middle of the battle to restore the Saxon dynasty: Cedric's design to have her marry Athelstane is an attempt to preserve the purity of Saxon bloodlines.

When Rowena instead marries Ivanhoe, their union signifies more than the "fulfillment of her own personal desire," though it is that also.[20] Their intermarriage represents an alternative plot to the other two plots, which in the first instance aims for the absorption of Rowena's Saxon ancestry by the Norman race, and in the second, moves toward the reclamation of Rowena by her Saxon forebears. Resulting neither in conversion nor retreat into nativism, Rowena and Ivanhoe's union is an intermarriage of the races, a successful solution to the historical problem Scott noted right at the outset of the novel as peculiarly marring England's cultural identity: "Four generations had not sufficed to blend the hostile blood of the Normans and the Anglo-Saxons, or to unite, by common language and mutual interests, two hostile races."[21] Contrary to representations of English history as racially uniform, such as manifested later in Edward A. Freeman's influential *History of the Norman Conquest of England*, which described the Normans less as foreign invaders than as local kinsmen, Scott believed that England's greatness lay in its being the product of racial and cultural mixture. *Ivanhoe* is perhaps his most successful novel celebrating the mixed racial heritage of the English nation. By concluding his novel with the marriage of Rowena and Ivanhoe, Scott refused simple, reductive readings of English history as either "the simple preservation of the Saxon past in the face of the Norman invasion, [or] as the simple conversion of the Saxons into Normans."[22] Not only does Rowena and Ivanhoe's marriage promise a new racial strain to invigorate English culture; the fusion of the two strains of Saxon and Norman through their union also augurs the working out of age-old enmities between the Normans and the Saxons. Yet as Ragussis reminds us, even the happy marriage of Ivanhoe and Rowena is dislodged from being the true climax of the novel, for the fate of the Jewish heroine Rebecca reveals that the position of another race in England—that of the Jews—still remains as fraught as ever.

The marriage plot of *Ivanhoe* represents the full potentialities of a racially mixed nation that comes into being by permitting different races to retain their essential identities while merging with one another. Robert Young perceptively notes that the fusion of two sexual principles constitutes the basis of cultural production, and in *Ivanhoe* one certainly sees the programmatic fulfillment of that principle. Scott expressed the differences between Normans and Saxons as cultural differences, affecting such things as language, literature, and custom. If racial differences are expressed in cultural terms, the heterosexual mixing of the races is not merely a biological event but also a cultural one. Thus, "culture is produced by the same process of sexual relations between the male and female races that produce the degenerative force of endlessly miscegenated offspring."[23] But rather than contemplating the decay of civilization, Scott envisioned its invigoration through intermarriage. By making romantic desire the trope of choice for the unification of England, Scott presents love as endowed with the power to take the nation beyond a divisive ethnicity and the grasp of possessive, punitive communities.

Scott's romance plot stands in stark contrast to the ethnographic plot in the British census of India. Despite the visible prominence of individuals from different religious backgrounds falling in love with each other, the predominant impression conveyed by the report is that the motivations for conversion have little to do with love and even less with the desire to merge with the beloved. Rather, forfeiture of communal membership haunts the actions of individual players and compels them to convert in a final act of desperation. A note of grimness pervades the plot synopses in the census, as the obstacles to marriage can only be resolved by conversion, which in turn produces isolation and separation from community. Though twenty-one of the forty reported cases list romance as the motive for conversion, the inner details of each case suggest that caste is the main player, not love. If we follow the thrust of the census report's latent argument, it is not the impulse of desire that drives Hindus to embrace the religion of their Muslim spouses but rather the fact that Hindus lose membership in their former community because of their romantic attachments. In other words, the real cause of conversion still continues to be a condition that is built into Hinduism: namely, its ability to turn caste members into outcastes through mere contact with non-Hindus. The primary association with Muslims is through romantic intrigues, but other forms of association include the sharing of food and coming under the care of Muslims during illness (the other two causes of conversion to Islam listed in the appendix).

Of the inherent appeal of Islam, only six of the forty cases listed suggest that doctrinal inclination has anything to do with conversion. All these instances add up to show the extent to which a vast number of Hindus became Muslims not because they chose to or in order to attain the objects of their desire or even for reasons of expediency, but because the door had been permanently shut on them by Hinduism. The point of reference in these conversion histories thus resolutely remains a feature salient to caste Hinduism.

Indeed, the deceptively simple tabulation of conversion cases contains even within its bare outlines a far more suggestive scenario involving love, intrigue, and high drama. The imbrication of caste, class, gender, and occupation is apparent too in these conversion histories, with most of the converts listed here (both men and women) being artisans and laborers. A literal reading of their occupational background would lead one to believe that their low-caste status induced these individuals to improve their lives by converting. But the fact that so many of those listed as day laborers are women reminds one that the economic circumstances of these individuals made the customary demarcation of gendered spaces untenable, allowing men and and women to have greater (sexual) access to each other in places of work. Hence, romantic involvement is itself enabled by the mobility of women who have, by necessity, broken out of the traditional space of the home. The remapping of gender boundaries has a considerable role in initiating these romantic plots; yet the culmination of these plots in conversion redraws new boundaries around religious identity. Although romance may thus work against the strict demarcation of public and private spaces, the coercive power of community ostracism transforms conversion into the obverse of romance.

Historians of colonial India describe the ranking of actual castes as a by-product of census documentation. That is to say, the accumulation of knowledge about social groups elicited through demographic procedures constructs the social categories by which groups are organized, which then establish the categories in a hierarchy of functions. In the hands of an ethnographer like Herbert Risley, who wielded anthropometric instruments as if they were weapons of war, the caste system fed into theories of racial purity and social hierarchy. Bernard S. Cohn has powerfully shown how the British system of objectification through census taking hinged on caste and religion as crucial sociological keys to understanding Indian society and Indian people. Cohn maintains that "ideas about caste—its origins and functions—played much the same role in shaping policy in the latter half of the nineteenth century that ideas about the village community and the nature of property played in the first half of the nineteenth century."[24]

But if one examines the pattern of romantic plots, as well their resolution in conversions signaling major ruptures with community, it becomes apparent that the idea of caste is produced within the space of such ruptures. This is very different from saying that the documentation process produces caste hierarchy and establishes the inflexible categories of religious identification. Rather, I am suggesting that it is through the working out of the romantic plot in the census—and the generic shift from romance to realism—that caste is established as a key player. The issue, therefore, is less one of inventing caste (as some scholars seem to believe) than in making caste visible in narratological terms.[25]

The situations described in the report vary in the amount of detail, but read together they constitute an impressive catalogue of representative motives for conversion, all of which combine to suggest a range of plots from which entire novels could be constructed (and indeed there are enough novels about conversion to suggest that these ethnographic plots were consistently played out in literary fiction).[26] One case describes a widow Dasi Goalini who, two years after her husband's death, converts to Islam after falling in love with a Muslim, Soleman [sic], from another village. Another case, on the other hand, alludes to a situation of domestic discord as the cause of a married woman Abhoya Dasi's conversion to Islam. The report appears to suggest that seduction precedes these conversions; words like "enticed," "paramour," and "elope" certainly reinforce this impression. One is reminded that, in certain iconographic traditions, sexual attraction between people of different religions is staged as a kind of conversion.[27] To draw again from the romance tradition, when seduction is posed as a function of economic and social power, the embrace of another religion is a form of yielding to the seducer's desire. But in the census table, despite the overtones of seduction in some cases, the question posed for Hindu women is not so much whether they are right to yield to Muslim desire, nor even whether they are justified in giving up their religion for emancipation from oppressive conditions. It is rather that desire triggers the mechanisms for caste to reassert itself through excommunication. The barriers between religious communities are made even more implacable as a result of romantic desire, which appears in the British census as an entirely divisive force.

The presentation of case histories is itself marked by an unusual reflexity and self-consciousness. One of its most conspicuous features is the scrupulous annotation of the religious and racial authorship of each section of the returns as Hindu, Muslim, or British. It is to be expected that the sections written by Muslim informants would stress that Hindus converted to Islam voluntarily and as a result of the deep impression made by Koranic teachings, communicated not just by preachers but by enthusiastic lovers as well. It is also to be expected that the descriptions written by Hindus would minimize the role of individual conviction and attribute conversion to force, and by extension love to seduction. The persistent divisions between Hindus and Muslims on the interpretation of conversion—Muslims claiming that the bulk of Islamic conversions were voluntary and Hindus claiming that they were forced—are reproduced in the interpretations of love and marriage between members of the two communities. Whereas the Muslim authors stress the conventionally romantic aspects of Hindu-Muslim liaisons and the attractions of Islamic faith as being intrinsic to romantic love, the Hindu authors of the report's various sections dismiss love as a motive existing independently of proselytizing zeal and just as strongly deny that love signifies certain emotional and spiritual needs.

The sections attributed to British authorship articulate a position that appears to work in a space between the two positions on romance and conversion taken by Muslim and Hindu authors, representing the two extremes of volition and coercion. But the British position turns strategically on a stance of measured uncertainty and ambivalence. Is falling in love the result of free will or manipulated desire? That central question is raised but never answered, because falling in love is shifted from the category of *effect* (that is, the result of conviction, sexual passion, emotional or spiritual needs, desire to establish autonomy in human relationships, and so on) to that of *cause* (that is, of excommunication, civil death, and eventually conversion). The focus again returns to the caste features of Hinduism.

Just as persistently, the focus lingers on the notion that an undivided community preceded the disruptions wrought by mixed marriages, which also posed threats to a stable religious identity. This movement parallels the shift in emphasis from the individual to the community. The shift is apparent in the very mode of the census-taking operations, including the types of questions asked and physical observations made. Community increasingly subsumes the subjectivity of converts and reduces their actions to the helpless *reactions* of those who have been shut out from a secure and proper place in Hindu society. The conversion of Hindus to Islam in the context of romance is thus represented as a result of excommunication from Hinduism, not as willed change or the exercise of unfettered choice whose unfortunate outcome incidentally happens to be exile and excommunication.

In the long run, this representation has important consequences for British historiography, for it sets up the larger argument that India can never have true nationalism because it is divided by caste. This must certainly be an intended effect of the cataloguing of conversions originating in romance. If English nationalist ideology was served by the romance novels of Walter Scott, which probed ways of negotiating the racial divide and posited intermarriage as the principle of national unification, colonial ideology fragmented the unifying tendencies of romance and accentuated its divisiveness. Colonial India's failure to be a true nation united "by common language and mutual interests," as Scott describes nationhood in *Ivanhoe*, is exemplified by the failure of the romantic plot, which exposes the overwhelming power of caste divisions and the impossibility of national unity. In ethnicizing romantic love and reducing it to the status of religious communities, the British census established the terms for an assessment of Indian nationalism as flawed at its very core.

ORIGINS AND THE RIGHT TO SELF-GOVERNANCE

What should we make of the pattern discernible in the census reports suggesting a keen British interest in proving the Hindu origins of the Muslim population of India? In considering several hypotheses, we may find it profitable to examine Peter Hardy's provocative argument that deciding whether Muslims were either foreign settlers or local converts was vital to resolving the British debate about whether to confer the right of self-governance on Indians. If, as Hardy speculates, Muslims in British India were descendants of foreign settlers with a culture foreign to India, the British could claim justification for not treating the population they ruled as a united people capable of sustaining self-governing institutions of a kind that required, for their successful functioning, a modicum of shared moral values. But since the thrust of the census reports seemed not to favor the theory that Muslims were foreigners but rather that they were converts from Hinduism, a different type of reasoning seems to be behind the conclusions put forth by the census reports. Hardy does indeed consider the possibility that the presence of a large number of voluntary converts among Muslims could have suggested to the British political establishment that the Hindu community had an inherent instability, marked by innate fissures within its membership. This would have given sufficient grounds for the British suspicion that India could not be dealt with as a homogeneous political community.

But I would like to advance two slightly different arguments: one, the emphasis on class differences between so-called hereditary Muslims and Muslim converts is part of a well-documented tendency in British commentaries to explain Indian society in terms of the caste system. Hindus converting to Islam presumably repudiated not merely a religion or world-view but caste itself. But their imperfect assimilation into Muslim society and the pursuit of titles and rank by low-caste converts are interpreted by the British not as a genuine desire for upward social mobility, as recent Muslim historians suggest,[28] but as evidence of the continuing influence of Hindu social ideas and the perpetuation of an invisible caste system even in the new Islamic order.[29] Indeed, the dislike of educated Muslims for the theory that most of the local converts in east and north Bengal were from the lower castes is doggedly read by the British as reflecting a persistent caste mentality. That is to say, if Indian Muslims wanted to be recognized as descendants of foreign settlers, they must have been motivated largely by a desire to conceal their low-class Hindu origins. Edward Gait, the census commissioner of the 1901 report, goes so far as to make this rather disdainful remark: "The Moghals are converts, just as much as are the Chandals [low-caste tribe of Bengal]. It is only a question of time and place. The Christian religion prides itself as much on converts from one race as on those from another, and except for the influence of Hindu ideas, it is not clear why Muslims should not do so too."[30] We can infer from this sort of analysis that the British determination to prove the local origins of Indian Muslims assumes that any future political scheme for India would have to consider—even to the point of reproducing to some extent—the systems of social stratification by which Indian society had come to be defined in colonial discourse.

The other argument I would make, however, might seem to be a contradiction of the first. At the same time that the census reports showed a tacit recognition (and even acceptance) of social stratification, there was also an eagerness to show the forces of change that had been set in motion in traditional Hindu society: even outcastes like the Kochs of Bengal were converting to Islam because they had a "disposition to change."[31] That the conversions revealed the existence of a volatile and dynamic society, constantly in flux, appeared to confirm some of the positive consequences of outside intervention, be it by the Mughals or the British. And so the almost inordinate British preoccupation with proving that the large majority of Muslims in Bengal were originally Hindus ran parallel to the British zeal in demonstrating the validity of catalyzing India into social and cultural change. Thus, the dual aspects of time—as both static and changing—serve to define a conception of Indian history as at once closed to change and open to modernization.

But the effect of this dual, contradictory move was to complicate further the ambivalent identity of Indian Muslims, who are represented as having both rejected (either voluntarily or involuntarily) the religion they once professed (even several generations removed) and retained aspects of it in their social orientation. There are therefore two kinds of often conflicting memories that inhabit the Hindu past: one, the memory of having once been an undivided community that had been violently torn asunder by foreign invasions, depredations, and cultural violence, of which forcible conversion is the most radical and divisive; and two, the memory of betrayal, repudiation, and willful reaffiliation to another community that the Muslim self-definition as "foreign-descended" appeared to suggest to Hindus. In both cases the Indian Muslim could not readily be identified as either outsider or insider. The sense of betrayal is further accentuated by the mythologies surrounding forcible conversion that were often propagated—or so claimed the British census reports—by Muslims themselves. One typical story recorded in the census report tells of a time when the Muslim population in Bengal was still scattered and it was customary for each Muslim dweller to hang an earthen pot (*badana*) from his thatched roof as a sign of his religious affiliation. The census report recounts a story about a learned maulvi, or clerical scholar, who, after a few years' absence, went to a Hindu village to visit a disciple dwelling there. Unable to locate the latter's earthen pot, he was told on inquiry that his Muslim disciple had renounced Islam and joined a tribal group. The maulvi on his return to the city reported this incident to the nawab (nobleman), who in a fit of rage ordered his troops to surround the village and compel every person there to become Muslim. As part of Muslim folklore, this extravagant story is narrated at one level as an example of Muslim assimilationist zeal and dogmatic pride. But when retold in the context of the census report, it has the effect of mythologizing the increase of the Muslim population in Bengal and removing history and ideology from the construction of a hybrid Indian identity.[32]

In increasingly alarming ways, Hindu revivalists have sought to reinscribe that history and ideology through the reconfigurative instrument of memory and through rituals like reconversion, which in many respects function as the handmaiden of memory. The whipped-up hysteria surrounding forcible conversion as one of Muslim India's most bitter legacies is not just expressive of Hindu antagonism to Muslims and to the history of violent rule in the past that their presence connotes for Hindus. The hysteria is also part of a well-developed, concerted effort to remind Muslims of their original identity as Hindus, inasmuch as it is at the same time a sinister reminder to them that Muslim claims to difference and otherness are falsely founded and therefore untenable.[33] Within this extreme logic, if there is anything worse than marauding Arab and Afghan invaders plundering Hindu temples and destroying Hindu religious life and culture, it is the fact that those who were once Hindus and subsequently converted (even if only because they occupied a low or outcaste position in Hindu society) now dare to deny their "true" heritage and make claims to a separate religious (and also political) identity.

What makes the intolerance of Hindus invisible, especially to Hindus themselves, is a rhetorical strategy that can be seen in the British census reports and which Hindu nationalists have subsequently adapted for their own purposes. This strategy consists of contrasting the fluid, mercurial status of Muslims with the fixed, essentialized status of Hindus as the original, real inhabitants. Muslims are either foreigners or converts, but they are never presented as having a direct, unmediated relationship to India. Though the census introduces the category of "Animists" to suggest a pre-Aryan presence in India, the incorporation of the culture of animists to that of the early Aryans is presented as a process outside conversion and religious expansion. Although Aryan incorporation of animist features in such things as Aryan stone images is unchallenged as an example of syncretic adaptation, a similar process of incorporation-as-assimilation (for example, Hindu stone pillars used as steps in mosques) is considered a defilement of Hindu culture by Muslim conquerors. The fact that the former is considered an example of tolerance and the latter of intolerance has a great deal to do with the distinctions drawn between an originary culture and a culture described as derivative and foreign. Although the census account of the conversion of low-caste Hindus to Islam would seem to have shifted the agency of intolerance from Islam to Hinduism, the simultaneous representation of Hinduism as the "original" religion of India removes Hinduism from a history of expansion and religious conversion as active as that of, say, Islam. To conceptualize Hindu-Muslim relations as a relationship of native to convert (as the British census did) or native to foreigner is to introduce notions of incorporation and exclusion that become ideologically charged in the struggle to affirm origins. Sadly, history vanishes, leaving only distorted memory in its place.

NEGOTIATING RELIGIOUS CONFLICT

Hindu right-wing organizations, including the Bharatiya Janata Party (BJP) and the Vishwa Hindu Parishad (VHP), claim that their destruction of the Babri Masjid in Ayodhya on December 6, 1992, has now made the temple-mosque controversy a nonissue. Nothing could be further from the truth. But that is not because the demolition of the mosque had been preceded by viable alternative ways of resolving the crisis. If there was a strange commingling of modernist and mythic elements in the political symbolism of the movement to install the Hindu deity Ram at his presumed birthplace, the very oddness of such an admixture would have seemed to make it open to swift dismantling. But the reaction against Hindu revivalism has not been particularly successful in enabling a higher level of discourse to develop. For the counterresponse either asserts an equally positivist claim (that is, that the Babri Masjid was built on an empty plot of land, Islamic settlements predate Hindu presence in Ayodhya, Islam forbids the construction of a mosque over a "pagan" temple, and so forth), or it takes the form of postmodern skepticism against *all* truth claims (that is, there was no temple, there was no Ram, there was no Mughal "invasion" or forcible conversions or iconoclasm, for the history of Ayodhya, like all given histories, is subject to doubt and can never be known).

In either case religious belief—Hindu or Islamic—remains unplaced and unaccounted for. No matter what the evidence might be for or against the existence of a Ram temple before the Babri Masjid came to be built, the weight of the evidence (or lack of it) has not seemed to affect the authoritativeness with which belief in Ram is accepted by Hindu devotees. Letters to various national dailies during the period of the Ayodhya crisis suggest that the immediate priority of building the temple had receded into the background ("God lives in the heart, not in temples" is the line one encounters most often), but not so the firmness and solidity of belief in the deity Ram. Wrote one writer to the editor of the Madras-based *The Hindu*, "I am prepared to accept the declaration of historians that Ram probably never existed, but that will not stop my believing in him nonetheless."[34] If this can be taken to be a typical response, then the very debate over Ayodhya—the historicity of the Hindu god Ram, the presence of a mosque on the site of a Hindu temple, and the instances of iconoclasm that accompanied Islamic conversions—is narrowly concentrated on the verification of facts that in reality have little or nothing to do with the actual problem. The pressing problem is how modern secularism can accommodate and absorb the reality of religion and the power of religious conviction experienced by believers, while at the same time protect the rights of those who believe differently.

Among recent critics, Ashis Nandy makes a significant contribution in demonstrating that the colonial state is one of the primary historical causes for prioritizing national identifications at the expense of local affiliations and displacing heterogeneous religious beliefs by the secular authority of the law. But although he is certainly correct to suggest that secularism has so polarized religious belief as to reduce the latter to religious ideology, his analysis suffers from the very tendency he critiques, for he fetishizes the popular faith of the masses in much the same way that secularism, in his view, fetishizes the state. Furthermore, though Nandy tries to provide a corrective to the dismissal of religion as belief, he provides too neat a scheme whereby secularism in its ideal manifestation must be essentially syncretic, "non-monolithic and operationally plural," whereas, he argues, all other forms of secularism that require national identification are inherently flawed because they can treat religion as nothing other than ideology.[35]

Ashis Nandy is probably right to challenge the secular identification of religious tolerance with the separation of private and public spheres and with economic and legal rationality. His attempt to demonstrate the ideological underpinnings of such identifications has produced one of the most uncompromising antistate critiques in the discourse of contemporary politics. But in dissenting from the state's refusal to concede the autonomy of popular belief, Nandy comes perilously close to endorsing a sectarian stance that privileges "the people" and treats people's beliefs as uncontaminated by ideology or elite manipulation. His undiluted faith in the continuing vitality of religion as a "living reality" in the lives of people, independent of the state's secular character, reasserts the split between private and public spheres and treats people's beliefs and state ideology as essentially noninteractive and mutually exclusive. Nandy's idea of religion revives a romanticized image of "the people" as the true repository of belief, unknown and unrecognized by the state.

But despite this critique of Nandy's position, it is impossible to ignore either the vehemence of his stand against secular ideologies or his impassioned search for more viable ways of conceiving religion's place in modern society. Indeed, his contention that Indian secularism has exhausted itself and failed to offer a potent alternative to the rising tide of violence in Indian politics and religion has been construed by some of his critics as a reactionary, antisecularist argument. What I take Nandy to mean, however, is that Indian secularism has taken the form of the very thing it opposes in principle—religious intoler-ance—and allowed for further divisions between religious ideology and every-day practices of religious belief.

If, as Nandy contends, one of the trends in recent South Asian history is the splitting of religion into faith and ideology—faith defined as a way of life, a "tradition which is definitionally non-monolithic and operationally plural," and ideology as organized religion that is identifiable with a set body of texts—the modern Indian state has chosen to define its secular character more *in reaction against* religious ideology than *in relation to* religious belief. As an illustration of how this tendency translates into policy, one can point to the state's control of religion when it spills over into public space. The regulation of excesses of religious ideology threatening the national interest has become an acquired function of the modern state, which is authorized to act as the ultimate arbiter for religious disputes. The reality of individual belief cannot be dealt with as an autonomous reality by the machinery of state, because the secular nation recognizes only the social component of religion—its hierarchic structures and organizational features. Hence, the state cannot engage with the individual; it can respond only to the material and symbolic orderings of reli-gion as a social institution. The urgent challenge to Hindu revivalism made by secular historians reveals the latter's own difficulties in dealing with religion as a heterogeneous belief system irreducible to mere ideology.

Are the possibilities of religious communication thus foreclosed in the mod-ern secular state, especially if part of the imported baggage of the state is an ingrained skepticism toward personal conviction? Perhaps, as David Krieger suggests in a recent essay, if ideology and faith as polarized terms are replaced by a notion of "cultural metanarratives" at work in nonmonolithic, pluralistic societies, it would be easier to conceptualize—and revitalize—possibilities for the attainment of a pragmatics of discourse where the *meaning* rather than the validity of truth claims is foregrounded.[36] This would be, in other words, a discourse that presses to the very limits the contestations of religious ideol-ogy—to the point where it can be broken down to illuminate areas of personal belief. In Krieger's conceptualization of the problem of communication, every form of knowing can be construed at a level of discourse higher than argumen-tation, or what he calls the level of a discourse of limits. Such a discourse accepts the possibility of unknowability and preserves an agonistic concept of truth in a pluralistic context, "where discontinuity upon the level of limit-discourse is an inescapable fact."[37]

An instance of such discontinuity is the shading of ideology into faith, which is effected by what Krieger calls a "methodological conversion." Krie-ger draws heavily on religious conversion as a metaphor for a theory of knowl-edge to suggest the conceptual means by which the gaps between different cultural metanarratives might be bridged. The cognitive rejection of one narra-tive through the conative acceptance of another is a conceptual analogue to the displacement of religious ideology by faith. "Such a conception is necessary," Krieger writes, "to deal with the problem of how global thinking—the general validity of knowledge, the universality of norms and a more than merely local solidarity with fellow humans and with nature—is possible in a radically pluralistic world and a postmodern context."[38]

Strictly at the level of argumentation, an impasse can be overcome only when the ideological premises of the parties to a dispute are comparable. If they are not, even the same sets of facts, including those that are entirely noncontroversial, can yield totally different conclusions, as is all too apparent in the Ayodhya debate where Hindu and Muslim activists derived completely contrary conclusions from virtually the same evidence. That these facts have a different meaning within the different paradigms involved in the dispute—mythological and historical—is further complicated by there being no metalanguage to negotiate the conflicting paradigms. The only possible form of negotiation is one that entails a transition, or a *conversion*, from one paradigm to another. Indeed, the process of transition between world-views emerges, in contexts of pluralism, as the only credible form of negotiation. If discourse beyond the level of argumentation is to materialize, it cannot be grounded in a unitary world-view or religion but rather in the ability to move *between* world-views.

If a higher level of discourse is to be made possible, certain pragmatic conditions for communication would necessarily have to be in place. For one thing, the clash of metanarratives cannot be resolved in terms of the pursuit of knowledge, which is how it had been approached in the Ayodhya debate right up until the time of the mosque's destruction. "True" knowledge is conferred an authority that is belied by the resulting intransigence of both parties in the dispute. The search for knowledge is unavoidably bound up with a struggle for social and political power. For Muslim believers and secular Indians alike, the general fear of losing power to Hindu revivalists has certainly raised the stakes for proving the nonexistence of a Hindu temple at the mosque site. To all parties concerned, unraveling the truth about Ayodhya has become tantamount to a struggle for hegemonic dominance.

In their challenge to conceptions of conversion as forcible and radical change, recent advances in the scholarship stress the relational features of conversion, though not always critically or with a view to examining the grounds of relationality. An historiography based on notions of transition rather than change is interested in recovering a pragmatics of intersubjective communication. The work of scholars like Robin Horton, Susan Bayly, Deryck Schreuder, and Geoffrey Oddie has aimed to supplant the contestational features of conversion with a version that stresses its adaptive tendencies. For instance, in her work on Muslims and Christians in South Indian society, *Saints, Goddesses and Kings*, Susan Bayly challenges as misleading the view that conversion is a radical movement from one religion to another, resulting in the total repudiation of one for the other.[39] Rather, she emphasizes the fluidity of the original religion which allowed for the "conversion" of its individuals to other religions. Bayly, echoing Robin Horton, contends that conversion is not transgressive or disruptive of the norms of a society as generally maintained. Applying Horton's theories of African conversion to the Indian context, Bayly argues that conversion is not simply a shift of individual conviction or communal affiliation. If low-caste Hindus have embraced other religions in the past, it is not because they believed in the egalitarian message offered by the new religions but rather because they invested an alien religious system with new divine power associated with the old. But in maintaining that transference and continuity are more salient features than disruption or repudiation in conversion histories, Bayly minimizes the force of change and moves closer toward replacing relationality with identity, and modernity with tradition.

At the end of a provocative and learned essay on perceptions of Islamic conversions by vastly different groups in South Asia—medieval historians (both Hindu and Muslim), European commentators, and modern scholars— Peter Hardy speculates

> whether the hypotheses of modern commentators and scholars are themselves essays in conversion, albeit not wholly conscious or deliberate ones: the conversion of agents of the East India Company or of the Crown to particular conceptions of their interests and their duties in India; the conversion of South Asian Muslims to particular conceptions of their future relationships with each other and with non-Muslims; or, to look into an area of inquiry not here entered, namely that of Hindus' interpretations of conversion to Islam, the conversion of Hindus to particular conceptions of their future relationships with Muslims.[40]

The power of conversion as an epistemological concept is that it reclaims religious belief from the realm of intuitive (nonrational) action to the realm of conscious knowing and relational activity. Scholars and political parties alike have a great deal at stake in ensuring that future discussions, however tentative they may be, examine that unexplored area pointed to by Hardy. This would require that they address not only Hindu interpretations of Islamic conversion but, more importantly, the reorientation (or *conversion*) of Hindus to ways of relating with the Muslim community in India. Conceived in these relational terms, conversion is defined not as a renunciation of an aspect of oneself (as it is in the personal or confessional narrative form), but as an intersubjective, transitional, and transactional mode of negotiation between two otherwise irreconcilable world-views.

CHAPTER SIX

Conversion, Theosophy, and Race Theory

CONVERSION AND THE WRITING OF BIOGRAPHY

Sketching the varieties of character and disposition that compose what he calls the "divided self," William James describes certain individuals as "heterogeneous" in that, unlike those with an inner tendency directing them toward harmony and balance, these other individuals live out the inconsistencies of their often whimsical temperaments, frequently with startling effects. He names Annie Besant as one such characteristic figure, whose extreme social shyness gave little indication, least of all to herself, that she held vast reserves of public presence. From all contemporary accounts, her dramatic platform personality gave her advocacy of causes ranging from birth control to labor union strikes a spirited, passionate quality not strikingly evident in her private interactions with people. James quotes a candid passage in Besant's autobiography in which she freely confesses the sharp contrast between her private and public selves: "Combative on the platform in defense of any cause I cared for, I shrink from quarrel or disapproval in the house, and am a coward at heart in private while a good fighter in public. . . . An unkind look or word has availed to make me shrink into myself as a snail into its shell, while, on the platform, opposition makes me speak my best."[1]

Citing this passage as a perfect illustration of her divided self, William James omits to say that Annie Besant's frank remarks about her shyness are sandwiched between descriptions of her desultory marriage to the clergyman Frank Besant and her confession that she "slid into marriage blindly and stupidly, fearing to give pain."[2] Besant's resigned acquiescence to a life of disappointing conjugality is offset by her refashioning of her persona as a public speaker; the lecture platform is redesigned as the site for the molding of a public personality whose private face disappears behind the elusive façade of integrated wholeness conveyed by the lectern. The gap between Annie Besant's inward reticence and her public assertiveness would seem to suggest it is in the social-political sphere that her beliefs find the most complete expression, her political consciousness usurping her subjectivity of personal needs and wants.

Yet the issue is not so much about a contrived public image masking the divided self, as William James portrays it, but rather the deliberate channeling of energies considered to be properly limited to the private world onto a much wider public canvas. It is of no small significance that Annie Besant's sense of power as a speaker dawns on her as she surveys the empty pews in the church where her husband customarily delivered his sermons. Her play at surrogate preaching, however, is more than a fanciful curiosity about her husband's chosen vocation. Rather, it is a powerful displacement of the orthodoxies he represents:

> A queer whim took me that I would like to know how "it felt" to preach, and vague fancies stirred in me that I could speak if I had the chance. I saw no platform in the distance, nor had any idea of possible speaking in the future dawned upon me. But the longing to find an outlet in words came upon me, and I felt as though I had something to say and was able to say it. So locked alone in the great, silent church, whither I had gone to practise some organ exercises, I ascended the pulpit steps and delivered my first lecture on the Inspiration of the Bible. . . . As the sentences flowed unbidden from my lips and my own tones echoed back to me from the pillars of the ancient church, I knew of a verity that the gift of speech was mine, and that if ever—and then it seemed so impossible!—if ever the chance came to me of public work, this power of melodious utterance should at least win hearing for any message I had to bring.[3]

The power of speech is so intimately connected to the immediacy of public presence that it draws a line between the life of detached domesticity to which Besant is consigned as a married woman and the world of public engagement preemptively made available by her breaking across the barriers of silence.

In part, such truncation is produced by Besant's own autobiographical mode, which treats verbal utterance as transgression, not merely in a symbolic sense but also in the sense that it has a material reality enabling her to make the crucial move from domestic to public life. In this respect, speech emulates the transformative reach of conversion, for it performs the identical function of reanimating a hitherto neutral, suspended situation into a state of dynamic activity. Especially striking in the passage just quoted is Besant's reinscribing of her own interpretation of the Bible derived from "heretical" and Broad Church literature onto the ecclesiastical space inhabited and controlled by her clergyman husband. For his stout adherence to Church of England doctrine not only occluded the possibilities of Besant's public avowal of heterodox principles but also compromised the character of her marriage and reduced her eagerly anticipated companionate status to one of irredeemable silence.

Viewed from the perspective of Victorian norms, Annie Besant's crossing of obdurate boundaries appears to split the lives that she led, her chosen vocation of public speaker and social activist bearing no relation to the life of settled domesticity that she was expected to live. And indeed to read her life from the expectations of Victorianism is to see truncations rather than continuity, incoherence rather than consistency, and disruptions rather than connections. The fact that critics of Besant's career and life focus on her "divided self," as William James calls it, suggests that the writing of her biography has never managed to surmount the age that she herself defied so assiduously. Nor has it succeeded in relating the apparently abrupt changes occurring in Besant to a larger set of historical developments no less dense and unpatterned in appearance.

Arthur Nethercot's description of Annie Besant as a woman of "many lives" has long remained history's definitive assessment of this complex, extraordinary woman whose life and career spanned nearly nine decades and at least three continents. Besant's own remarkable longevity (she lived from 1847 to 1933) gave further weight to the finality of this description. Every historian and biographer who has attempted to evaluate Annie Besant has felt compelled to account for the apparent incoherence of a life that went from one abrupt shift to another, from the most spirited defense of atheism and later socialism to an enthusiastic embrace of occultism. Although Besant passionately fought in behalf of birth control, workers' unionization, and women's suffrage in the earlier phase, by the latter phase seances, levitations, and table rapping had become as much a part of her activities as workers' rallies had been earlier.

For a long time, George Bernard Shaw's trenchant comment remained the standard assessment of Annie Besant, accentuating as it did the absence of any consistency of thought in her intellectual development. "Mrs. Besant," wrote Shaw magisterially, "is a woman of swift decisions. She sampled many movements and societies before she finally found herself, and her transitions were not gradual, she always came into a movement with a bound and was preaching the new faith before the astonished spectator had the least suspicion that the old one was shaken. People said, 'She will die a Roman Catholic,' which was their way of expressing the extreme of mutability for an Englishwoman."[4] More uncharitably yet, Shaw described her as akin to an actress playing a variety of roles on the stage, no single role being a more accurate representation of the person playing it than another:

> Like all great public speakers she was a born actress. She was successively a Puseyite Evangelical, an Atheist Bible-smasher, a Darwinian secularist, a Fabian Socialist, a Strike Leader, and finally a Theosophist, exactly as Mrs. Siddons was a Lady Macbeth, Lady Randolph, Beatrice, Rosalind, and Volumnia. She "saw herself" as a priestess above all. That was how Theosophy held her to the end. There was a different leading man every time: Bradlaugh, Robertson, Aveling, Shaw, and Herbert Burrows. That did not matter.[5]

Though Shaw averred an abiding affection and respect for Besant that never diminished despite his unremitting disapproval of her conversion to theosophy, succeeding biographers have taken their cue from his mordant analysis and emphasized Besant's inherent intellectual and emotional instability. Besant's radical break with materialism and socialism and her embrace of theoso-

1. Annie Besant in her youth c. late 1860s

phy have been ascribed to a host of personal limitations: her failed romances; an obsession with father-figures ("new male idols") to compensate for a father who died when she was three;[6] a neurotic disposition; and a stunning naïveté that belied her intellectual capabilities. Commentators have tended to see Annie Besant's career as entirely a series of disconnected transformations. Geoffrey West, Besant's first biographer, wrote in 1930 that by converting to theosophy Besant unequivocally turned her back on her former convictions held as an atheist, freethinker, and socialist: "It is undeniable that in Theosophy Mrs. Besant has increasingly rejected her earlier ideals, denied what, *at her most masculine, her most modern, her most significant*, she stood for. If this criticism of Theosophy is to be accepted, then it must be accepted too that the spiritual pilgrimage of Mrs. Besant has by her own highest ideals ended in spiritual failure."[7]

Needless to say, the representation of Annie Besant's conversion as an abandonment of the progressive markers of masculinity and modernity does even less justice to her intellectual shifts than the attribution of romantic entanglements. Besant was lampooned on numerous occasions by critics who proclaimed that "like most women, [she] was at the mercy of her last male acquaintance for her views."[8] Even where it was conceded that "she passed

2. Annie Besant at the Theosophical Society, Madras, c. 1900

through cyclical phases," it was also said that "she sought matching men."[9] The fact that Besant's most recent biographer, Anne Taylor, who is well positioned to take a more critical perspective, also concludes that love interests largely governed Besant's attraction to differing ideologies indicates the degree to which the biographical fallacy has succeeded in thwarting any attempt to place Besant's intellectual shifts and religious conversion in a context larger than her own personal travails.[10]

Writing her own autobiography, Annie Besant, on the other hand, placed her doctrinal shifts within a continuum of sameness and considered theosophy as the natural heir of challenges to religious orthodoxy, even though she could embrace theosophy only after a brief sojourn through socialism.[11] Socialism and theosophy never appeared to Besant as opposite movements, even though they may have had little in common philosophically, largely because each responded to material reality in ways that were appropriate to their specific relation to history. Catherine Wessinger, one of the few critics who heeds Besant's self-analysis, describes her doctrinal variations as being held together by a structure of "ultimate concern."[12] Although Wessinger restricts this structure too narrowly to one of sacrifice and service, her larger point is more important, for it appropriately suggests the presence of running threads in Bes-

3. Annie Besant lecturing in Madras, c. 1910s

ant's life and work that need to be considered in any assessment of her conversion. Indeed, only after reading Besant's life story from her own perspective does the biographer Arthur Nethercot concede that, despite his authoritative account of her disjointedly leading "many lives," Besant herself saw an evolutionary progression in her thought, a "series of just causes, each of which, in her own mind, grew naturally and reasonably out of its apparently antithetical predecessor."[13]

On the surface, Besant's anti-Christian stance would seem to be the chief "just cause" uniting such vastly different thought systems as socialism and theosophy. And indeed commentators have long stressed the early bonds between freethought and theosophy forged on a shared antipathy to orthodox Christianity. For instance, a collection of Besant's atheistic writings constitutes a volume named *The Origins of Theosophy*.[14] The title presupposes that Besant's freethought phase prepared the ground for her subsequent avowal of an alternative religion like theosophy, which rejected traditional Christianity. Even this rejection was not entirely categorical since theosophy still selectively preserved some aspects of Christianity's gnostic mysticism. It was widely believed by theosophists, under Madame Blavatsky's tutelage, that Christian sources were to be found not only in the teachings of Jesus but also in the origins from which Christ drew them, and that the traces of the earlier teachings, especially those of the Kabala (a term used by Blavatsky to cover all esoteric knowledge from the Vedas onward), had been effaced by being grafted on to Christianity. In turn, when Christianity was hijacked by powerful political forces, it was turned into a dogmatic theology that bore no resemblance to its mystical forebear. Again under Blavatsky's formative influence, theosophists maintained that mainstream Christianity had dispensed with long, endless views of time, cycles, and evolution and replaced them with finite genealogies of human history, like those recorded in Genesis. As a result, the teaching of the mysteries was lost forever, and it became a paramount goal of theosophy to recover them. Annie Besant was not unaffected by Blavatsky's thinking on the subject, and Besant's own work, *Esoteric Christianity*, grew out of her attempt to find new resources of meaning in the mysteries of Christianity, which she had come to despise in its most orthodox, institutional forms.

Besant's profound dissatisfaction with Christianity is too much a part of her amply documented biography to bear elaborate repetition here. It is well known that her anti-Christian stance caused her early separation from her husband and brought her to freethought as its most eloquent speaker and writer. Equally a part of public knowledge is the fact that Besant experienced extreme personal alienation from doctrinal creeds and endured the civil disabilities to which dissent was subject, disabilities such as losing custody of her children because as an agnostic she was deemed to be an unfit mother. Yet despite the compelling power of these biographical details, her opposition to Christianity took place in a much broader context than that of her own spiritual disillusionment and conjugal disappointment. Her perception of a logical hierarchy in her thought asserted an intellectual affinity between the impulses that drove her to atheism and then to alternative religions like theosophy. Though this assumption is not necessarily shared by the large majority of her critics and commentators, it does invite inquiry into the source of those impulses and their relation to historical forces within and outside Britain. Indeed, Besant's projection of her private epiphanies on a public canvas—her lifelong staging of belief on the lecture platform, in the law courts, and in pamphlet literature—broadened the scope of her conversion to include history, nation, and empire.

Besant's systematic ordering of ideas that cohered around specific events distanced her own psychological disposition as the backdrop to her final conversion to theosophy, even as she elusively spoke of a restless yearning for soul-satisfying answers to material problems of human existence. The effect of such contradictory assertions was, of course, to throw off her critics in their attempt to make sense of her conversion in the terms *they* had already decided in advance. Besant's impish response to Shaw's "wounded indignation" about her move to theosophy—she threw the doyen of vegetarian philosophy a little off guard by claiming that vegetarianism had enfeebled her mind—also prompted the irascible playwright to admit that the woman whom he had always chided for her lack of self-irony had at last "found her path and come to see the universe and herself in their real perspective."[15] Yet, despite the mischievous coyness and playful humor of her response to Shaw, in her numerous writings describing her conversion to theosophy Besant consistently maintained a calm steadiness of tone, signaling her refusal to bow down to accusations that she was impulsive, erratic, and unstable in her actions.

Inevitably, some strategic move is required of us as critics to pull away from the confines of Besant's biography and enter history. The relevant theoretical question is how conversion illuminates the manner in which this move takes place. What special function does conversion play in elucidating connections between disparate movements and events that cannot be performed as well by any other activity, such as historical and literary criticism? How does a focus on conversion facilitate the writing of life story *into* history rather than *as* history? When inquiry about the causes of individual conversions culminates in biographical reasons, as it often does in Annie Besant's case, such explanations isolate the convert from the course of historical developments. There is a real challenge in correlating conversion to these developments in order to showcase the points of transformation. This need not be done only in psychosocial terms but also more importantly in terms of the intertwined impact of historical events and intellectual trends on the departure of members from one fold into another. Behind all such questions is whether individual change can ever occur independently of drifts and currents in intellectual and political life, and whether the sorts of commitments made by individuals to new belief systems can at all be separated from their responsiveness to new and ever-changing historical conditions.

The challenge is augmented by the fact that there is also a slipperiness in Annie Besant's autobiography, where her account of how she moved into theosophy is deliberately vague and inconclusive. This is in stark contrast to the meticulous detail with which she recounts her socialistic years. The most she is willing to concede about her attraction to theosophy is that "this form of Pantheism appears to me to promise solution of some problems, especially problems in psychology, which Atheism leaves untouched," even as she also insists that the urgency of theosophy's appeal lies in its ability to tackle "some" problems without awaiting the transformation of the social order.[16] The slipperiness is particularly acute in Besant's allusion to psychology, which turns out to be a red herring since the frame of reference she sets up for her analysis is unequivocally sociological and political. So that while she discusses theosophy in terms of consciousness and its illumination of the animating principles of life, that discussion takes place within the frame of an evolving order of history whose development is not driven by principles of nature so much as it is quickened by political institutions.

I therefore suggest that biography's persistence in seeing Annie Besant's conversions as arbitrary and abrupt, and caused mainly by romantic disappointments and an excessive intellectual dependence on male authority figures, fails a historiography that might reveal, through Besant's conversions, a number of crucial but largely covert historical connections. Among these, the most important are the successive linkages between British secularism and Orientalism; between dissent from Christianity and imperialism; and between British support for Indian nationalism and race theory. I do not wish to appear as if I am restating a familiar and well-worn truism—that biography is a form of history. Rather, I want to suggest that individual conversions are an index of cultural change without themselves being subject to a crude form of historical determinism. Throughout this book I have been tracing instances of conversion as forms of activity—often oppositional—that alternatively are triggered by and shape the tendencies accruing around sociopolitical developments. If the advance of culture influences (and is influenced by) a progressively differentiated consciousness, it is also the case that the culture(s) in which an individual conversion occurs lends its own structural features to the content of this new consciousness. Crucial to this process is an elaboration of the full range of meanings of cultural forms and institutions to which the convert's sensibility subsequently gains unmediated access. What, therefore, appears to be a shift from one doctrinal affiliation to another may well reveal not continuity but rather points of overlap and convergence.

One simple fact is worth noting schematically as an abbreviated preamble to the extended argument that follows: Annie Besant's long and varied career, which in its diverse atheistic, secular, and socialist phases was marked by her active participation in the advocacy of birth control, workers' union strikes, and the relief of civil disabilities against religious dissenters, was simultaneously engaged with Ireland, India, Afghanistan, and with what she later called England's "great plan" with regard to her colonies.[17] Her shift from secularism to theosophy, through the detour of socialism, followed a trajectory that retraced the processes of national and imperial consolidation and the move toward the inevitable conferral of home rule to the colonies.[18] This move is not entirely surprising, given that Besant's secular identification, though opposed to the Anglican establishment, was also concurrent with crises in church-state relations in British national life, and these in turn with the secularization of colonial administration. (This process has already been elucidated at some length in Chapter One.) Neither Besant's contemporaries nor her subsequent biographers and critics have adequately acknowledged that her anti-orthodox, heretical position coalesces seamlessly into first an anticolonial and then an imperialist position. This happens largely through the agency of an intractable theory of human evolution embedded in theosophy, a religion that she embraced as an alternative to other minority religions available to her in England.

The anticolonialism of ideologies as disparate as secularism and theosophy was significantly qualified by the scientific foundationalism of race theory through which both were expressed. For this reason it is less interesting to explain, in biographical terms, why Annie Besant became a theosophist—the title of one of her own pamphlets—or even to debate whether Besant's membership in the National Secular Society and her subsequent leadership of the Theosophical Society in Madras are either continuous or discontinuous events in her life. Rather, the challenge lies in examining the common political grounds of both secularism and theosophy, especially considered within the intersecting discourses of religious dissent, decolonization, and evolutionary science.

Accordingly, this chapter assembles a number of related themes appearing in this book—on syncretism and conversion, nationalist ideologies, and the construction of alternative religious traditions—in order to reveal how emerging spiritual trends proclaiming "a universal brotherhood of man" are concurrent with theories of racial hierarchy in nineteenth-century culture. As one of the most influential of these movements, theosophy appeared primarily in response to imminent decolonization and home-rule appeals. Contextualized as an activity grounded in the domestic and international alignments of the nineteenth and early twentieth centuries, theosophy takes on a meaning far superseding its relegation to the ranks of an eccentric fringe movement. A focus on Annie Besant will permit us to see how her conversion to theosophy prepares the ground for the emergence of a relational model of the commonwealth, which spurns rule by force without fully surrendering the concept of empire. The idea of a common brotherhood appears to be a powerful mobilizing ideology of nationalist movements; however, in substance it has a far more potent role in facilitating the move toward a federation of nations as displaced empire.

The course of Besant's intellectual development makes strikingly evident that racial evolutionary theory answered more satisfactorily than any other theories the intellectual doubts that led her originally to atheism and socialism. If, as Besant discovered, the causes of suffering could not be explained by religious doctrines of atonement, recourse to the material sciences was inevitable in the search for more convincing answers. But though socialism ostensibly cleared doubts about the metaphysical origins of suffering by locating them definitively in conditions of inequality and material oppression, Besant was alienated from socialism's emphasis on the abstractness and impersonality of forces of social change, and suspected that socialism provided few explanations about how human beings participated in both oppression and its removal. Even Shaw noted that Fabian socialism would never be able to secure Besant permanently as a member unless it conducted her toward a religious philosophy that satisfied her persistent craving for humanistic principles.[19]

Besant's search for human agency in the material sciences may have failed to find a supportive religious framework, but it did draw her closer to theories offering the hope that racial evolution would produce superhuman agents endowed with the capacity to transform others and so promote social change. Paradoxically, however, principles of human evolution, although conducive to Besant's desire for active social intervention, also made her sympathetic to a new, more benevolent version of empire. This revision of empire subsumed the idea of a universal brotherhood within the triumphant culmination of the human race. Brotherhood constituted a philosophical counterpart to the endpoint of biological development in which diverse racial strains would gather together in one central unity as a family of nations. Besant's syncretic vision was receptive to the idea of the British empire as the quickening agent for a final triumphant orchestration of a great racial plan. If imperial conquest brought different races together in confrontation rather than accommodation, the threat of miscegenation and racial impurity was considerably thwarted by their sublimation into a cross-fertilization of language, history, culture, and literature. In an obvious displacement of sexual intermixing, the fusion of racial strains in international culture sanctioned the idea of a British commonwealth, or a community of nations joined together by a past history of expansive settlement. Simultaneously, this past history was also the catalyst for a regulated pattern of human evolution.

RELIGIOUS DISSENT AND RACIAL THEORY

The slippage from Besant's search for human agency in religious consciousness to her acceptance of the course of British imperial history occurs so effortlessly it is difficult to conceive how she could have arrived at a point so far from her thinking when she first set out to question Anglican doctrine. Why would an unrelenting, uncompromising critic like Annie Besant, who so consistently took an antigovernment stand by defying the Church of England establishment, publicly espousing freethought, courting blasphemy charges, spearheading labor strikes, and fighting for extension of the franchise to women, endorse Britain's international adventurism, albeit in a revised form (that is, as commonwealth rather than empire)? Is this a contradiction, a clear demonstration of conflicting interests between a socialist's desire for domestic reform and an English citizen's acceptance of Britain's international role? Or might Besant's conflictual stances be consistent with the pattern of domestic dissent in Britain?

First of all, it would be erroneous to assume that dissent at home necessarily precluded support of British imperialism, as the Governor Eyre controversy in Jamaica demonstrated only too clearly. For in that highly public event British intellectuals such as Carlyle and Dickens, who were known for their unremitting criticism of harsh conditions of capitalist labor in England, were not averse to defending Eyre's stern action against Jamaican blacks revolting against the arbitrary application of British power. Indeed, the support given to Governor Eyre by English social liberals disassociated conditions of labor in Britain from those in Jamaica, which was represented as a place legitimately requiring the harnessing of idle manpower to make hitherto uncultivated land yield both agricultural and industrial wealth.[20] Thomas Carlyle's "The Nigger

Question," for instance, reverberates with the figure of Adam in the Garden of Eden as the prototypical image of mankind's first agricultural laborer and industrious individual.

But what differentiates Annie Besant from these other liberal critics is that her position is not easily characterized by discrepancy between domestic and international stances—a disparity that is revealed only when the premises applying to "our" civilization fail to be applied to those civilizations placed lower on the scale. Indeed, what makes Besant so unusual in the literature is that it is difficult to accuse her of either equivocation or the hypocritical upholding of double standards, since she never applied one set of expectations to one people and a totally different set to another. Rather, Besant's position is distinguished by a certain continuity of intellectual assumptions. The continuity lies partly in her attempt to combine her enduring quest for salvation and her worldly commitment to the amelioration of disparate social conditions. Her search for salvation precipitated her break with Christianity (because she could not find Christian feeling in its orthodox forms), and at the same time kept her within Christianity's grip, since she could not seek salvation outside a religious framework.

Besant writes in her autobiography that "the teaching of social duty, the upholding of social righteousness, the building up of a true commonwealth— such would be the aims of the Church of the future."[21] The discreteness of intellectual and social movements in England, like religious nonconformity and socialism, left Besant uncertain about ever achieving significant outcomes through her social activism, since all these different movements developed institutions only relevant to themselves without showing any indication that they could merge into shared expressions of communal solidarity. She sought a larger, overarching institution committed to social righteousness, which could accommodate the concept of a church without becoming an ecclesiastical autocracy. For all its limitations, the idea of a commonwealth is her answer. To be successful, the commonwealth in her view required a centralized structure of administration both as a source of sustaining values and as the triumphant endpoint of the differential evolution of diverse races. Despite her keen suspicion of institutional forms of authority, she could not resist the allure cast by a center of emanating influence, given the inexorable thrust of her thinking on social duty as institutionally guaranteed and protected.

The trajectory from religious dissent to imperialist affirmation thus followed a certain logic that was at once streamlike and associative in its progress. It is not at all implausible to argue that the definers of British imperialism were not only intrepid explorers, settlers, and a managerial class of capitalists but also included anti-establishment figures like Annie Besant, whose dissent on social reform issues in England was, for various reasons, entirely compatible with Britain's international role. If there is any irony at all, it lies in the fact that in proportion to Besant's conscious rejection of establishment orthodoxy, her faithful adherence to principles of systematic questioning brought her to a

position where she affirmed those hegemonic structures of British institutions—including empire—that she had fiercely questioned at the onset of her
public career. The medium through which such affirmation was made possible
was a theory of racial development, which took over from socialist doctrine the
scientific principle that society was evolving toward social unity in ways that
were generalizable across races.

It is thus a mistake to focus so single-mindedly on Annie Besant's contradictions as if they have to be ironed out in order for us to make sense of her
public career. In other words, it is pointless to maintain that she had no imperialist interests because she was an anticolonialist, a socialist dissenter, president
of the Indian National Congress, and so forth. Besant's intellectual shifts were
occurring at a time when altering definitions of empire coincided with perceptions that home rule for the colonies was inevitable. Susceptible to currents of
thought yet by no means determined by them, Besant held to a point of reference that was inescapably historical. Even though she complicated matters by
mystically alluding to consciousness when discussing theosophical principles,
the evolution of spirit in an almost Hegelian sense was for her the truest definition of history.

In one of her most important works, *The Evolution of Society*, Annie Besant
isolates society as "an organism instead of a bag of marbles" in order to argue
that "if it be conceded that the health of the whole depends upon the healthy
functioning of every part, in correlation not in independence, then all that tends
towards integration will be recognised as of life, all that tends towards disintegration as of death."[22] The pamphlet transparently relies on an elaborate con-
ceit of society as an organism to convey the notion that biological and social
development are invariably cognate activities. As the basis of community
building and human mutuality, the social principle of integration is translated
into a form of biological aggregation. If the life principle is to carry out its
expected function, the ultimate goal will be a unity that forms the basis for
more complex human constructs such as society. Furthermore, such unity is
achieved first as an inexorable part of the process of biological development.
Conversely, the alternative—disintegration of the social fabric—is conceived
as a form of death itself, tending toward the extinction of the human species.
If the instinct of biology is to avoid precisely that dreaded outcome and so tend
toward the consolidation of the life principle, then society too must be driven
in similar, life-affirming directions. Therefore, if history is dotted with wars,
conquests, and civil tensions, these are not to be seen as deviations but as
essential steps toward a final unity that can only be understood as the fulfillment of a driving life force.

Besant proceeds to argue that "the further integration may be regarded as an
ideal to be embraced, or as a doom to be striven against, as a brotherhood to be
rejoiced in or as a slavery to be abhorred; but the believer in Evolution must
acknowledge that if Society is to endure, this further integration is inevitable."[23] This powerful, densely packed statement offers two versions of inte-

gration paralleling the distinctions between commonwealth and empire: the former, a model of a recovered unity that was earlier lost because of the forces of divisive historical change (tending toward death); and the latter, an aberrant development incorporating other peoples by subjugation and falsely terming the racial hierarchy set in place as a form of "unity." But significantly, Besant does not consider imperialism to be a stage that can be bypassed, nor even that it is desirable to do so, for she believes that the history of racial mixture set in motion by territorial expansion (admittedly by conquest) has a definite and even glorious end.[24] As the culmination of biological and social development, a harmonious federation of nation-societies will match a diverse variety of races, now no longer subsisting in a state of competitive tension but in mutual reconciliation.

In prophetic tones, Besant describes society "evolving towards a more generous brotherhood, a more real equality, a fuller liberty. It is evolving towards that Golden Age which poets have chanted, which dreamers have visioned, which martyrs have died for: towards that new Republic of Man, which exists now in our hope and our faith, and shall exist in reality on earth."[25] The operative word here, as in much else that Besant produced in her theosophical phase, is *brotherhood*, for she could not define liberty and equality in any other terms than as an equilibrium of societies achieved through a necessary cross between the races, or more precisely, between the cultures they produce. The racial slant of Besant's rhetoric allowed her to rationalize colonialism as an agent of cultural unity—as distinct from cultural transformation—even as her philosophical position remained fundamentally opposed to British appropriation of foreign territories and peoples.

Although undoubtedly having a long history in British discourse, the racial foundations of British anticolonialism, however, have a different twist in nineteenth-century debates. One influential line of thought tended to regard colonization as the source of an undesirable contamination of England's racial purity through miscegenation. For example, J. G. Herder's opposition to colonialism was premised less on liberal notions of the right to self-determination of peoples than on the dangers of disrupting the idea that the nation is unified around a racially homogeneous, similarly constituted group of people. On the other hand, the threatening aspects of interbreeding were muted when sexual intercourse took the form of cultural mixing. The cultural contact provided by colonialism offered the possibilities for the grafting of a new political society on the soil provided by colonized traditions and cultures. In British Orientalism, for instance, this theory of organicism conceived of political formation as part of a process of cultural synthesis, and the consolidation of British rule in India was ensured by a cultural policy that engrafted Western learning, literature, and science onto the Orientalist studies it had originally promoted.[26]

In a strikingly original and nuanced reading of Matthew Arnold's cultural politics, Robert Young has noted how widely English culture was accepted in the nineteenth century as a product of the polarities of races—Celtic and Teutonic, Aryan and Semitic—and of their differing ethnic characteristics.[27] Drawing on a wide range of ethnological writings, Young astutely observes that the delineation of English culture as the product of racial difference (Hellenic and Hebraic being metaphoric revisions of Celtic and Teutonic) displaced class conflict as the formative energy of culture. More importantly, such displacements allowed English culture to be written into world history as an ongoing struggle of races. The long view of culture as racial history, moving inexorably to the "disinterested" ascendancy of stronger strains, tended to obscure the localized evidence of class strife and absorb class warfare into the racialized discourses of evolutionary science.

In startlingly parallel ways Annie Besant, who was strongly influenced by both Matthew Arnold and Ernst Renan, attempted to forge through the theosophical movement a culture of universal brotherhood that was, at the same time, heavily marked by theories of racial fissures and regeneration. Her yoking of science and religion provided a racialist foundation to the evolution of religious cultures; the struggle of hybrid races initialed the move to the syncretic civilization that she and others heralded under the banner of a commonwealth-type model. And like Arnold, she metaphorised racial categories (termed "root races" in theosophical writing) to suggest that they were embedded in more abstract concepts, like geological time and migration. The importance of Arnold and Renan in the intellectual history of decolonization is evident in the crucial recovery of the Celts as survivors of English racial conflict. These same Celts, whom Arnold describes as persisting in English literature and culture as a spiritual counterpart to the "philistine" Anglo-Saxon,[28] are identified by the theosophical movement, with major branches in Ireland and India, as not only opposed to the Anglo-Saxon but being in fact Aryan.

The aryanizing of the Celts, who are attributed with racial supremacy, gave to theosophy—as a spiritual movement of anticolonialism—a decidedly elite brahmanical cast. Although this identification fueled the Indian nationalist movement (and the Irish as well to some extent, by contesting the stereotyped classification of Celts as non-Caucasian and "black"), it also consolidated an Orientalist tendency that valorized Aryanism—and Sanskrit literature—as the defining feature of "high" civilization, albeit as a result of racial struggle. As Malcolm Chapman points out, the association of Celtic culture with Indo-European languages emerged directly out of the scholarly and scientific study of language in the eighteenth and nineteenth centuries, promoted in Europe during a period of strident nationalism and nation building.[29] Since the Celts have a long history of being tied up in a discourse of race, language, and culture (which, as Chapman suggests, has indeed created them), it is equally valid to consider their placement within an Orientalist project of recovering classical Sanskrit and Aryanism.

If the selective rewriting and racial reinscription of both Indian and Irish cultures in the name of nationalism and anticolonialism requires one to move away from a strictly biographical focus when discussing an event like Annie Besant's conversion, it also obliges the critic to place her intellectual shifts from atheism to theosophy in the frame of national and international developments. Under a new global order of syncretic ambition, her transition from atheism to occultism takes place under the aegis of an overarching imperialist and racial doctrine, even as that very doctrine is either being denied or sublimated into mystical esotericism by organizations like the National Secular Society and the Theosophical Society. The not insubstantial numbers of freethinkers and members of the National Secular Society who became theosophists (Arthur Nethercot names several prominent defectors such as John Holmes and George Sexton) indicate that Besant's move was by no means idiosyncratic or exceptional and may have been part of a more general trend.[30] The steady trickle of people from one movement to another also reveals that theosophy was seen to offer more satisfying alternatives to the articulation of rational dissent, especially if, as seems to have been the widespread impression, dissent resulted in merely fragmenting English society into various local and regional alliances.

The conversion to minority or alternative religions evinced in all the individual case studies discussed thus far in this book establishes strong links between the struggle for essential rights and the rejection of secular ideologies because they are incapable of ensuring those rights. Of course, the question of whether these links are then channeled to serve other purposes—such as the call for restoration of church authority by John Henry Newman, or Besant's proposal of a commonwealth model displacing empire—casts a wider net for the study of conversion as cultural criticism, extending it in fact to the study of conversion as *cultural ideology*. In that spirit, I am proposing that Besant's conversions illuminate the successive ties between British secularism and Orientalism, between dissent from Christianity and imperialism, and between British support for Indian nationalism and race theory.

Of the various linkages, Orientalism's relation to secularism is the most familiar. Voltaire's sharp antagonism to Christianity led him to ancient Hindu writings for evidence of advanced religious systems; indeed, the French philosopher found a kind of proto-Christianity in Hindu idolatry, where even in the midst of polytheistic worship he could claim evidence of belief in a single God. His excavation of classical Hindu texts (such as the *Yajurveda*) shook the foundations of Christianity as revealed religion and introduced the European literati to a system of thought that not only contained concepts as sublime as those in the Judaeo-Christian tradition but, more importantly, challenged the unique truth claims of Western religion. Voltaire's *Essai sur les moeurs*, for instance, mocks the historical method of scholars influenced by Bossuet, who envisioned that the meaning of world history could more or less be deduced from sacred scripture. India had no place in this history, and it was partly Voltaire's aim to bring India and the rest of Asia into the world picture by laicizing its history.[31] By locating in ancient Hinduism everything that the west had claimed as its own unique spiritual insights, Voltaire's use of the same-ness-in-diversity theme proved to be the most potent weapon in challenging the exceptionalism of Christian doctrine.

British skeptics, freethinkers, and dissenters (ranging from Unitarians to Nonconformists) usurped Voltaire's method of attack. Sometimes they did so blindly and unthinkingly, for it is not likely they would have unanimously endorsed ancient Hinduism if pressed to do so. But there was something telling about the limited weapons available to English atheists. After all, it is of no small significance that Annie Besant first met Charles Bradlaugh, president of the National Secular Society and the first atheist to secure a seat in the English parliament, when he was delivering a lecture comparing Christ and the Hindu god Krishna.[32] This detail coheres in Besant's imagination, and years later she would translate Bradlaugh's secular perspective into a vastly different, Orien-talizing project and affirm the unity of world religions. Unlike Bradlaugh, who employed a comparative argument to undermine the claims to truth by all religions and not just Christianity, Besant drew upon the resources of compar-ative study to argue a pantheistic case for the existence of a divine conscious-ness underlying nature.

Besant's later redeployment of Bradlaugh's weapons against Christianity for her own, radically different purposes did not so much mark a break with secularism as signal her recognition that the insights of secularism could be invoked to construct a syncretic political and religious order. Her dependence on Orientalist scholarship for this purpose took her far beyond Bradlaugh's project of inculcating skepticism about Christianity. Orientalism also brought her closer to finding a meeting point between Christianity and other world religions, which increasingly engaged her attention in her attempt to accom-modate religious consciousness in a secular framework.

Dissent's relation to imperialism is far more subtle and more indirectly ar-ticulated, for it is mediated by scientistic explanations of human progress. The belief in the possibility of alleviating suffering and pain through science and reason, rather than through faith in the redemptive power of Christ's sacrifice, was perhaps the severest challenge to the doctrinal core of Christianity. Annie Besant's lifelong inner battle with Christ as a symbol of vicarious suffering caused her to remain aloof from spiritual justifications of pain, which appeared to be embodied in the doctrine of atonement.[33] She developed a scientific ap-proach to questions of pain that satisfied her more easily than did spiritual explanations; at times indeed, this approach often brought her close to the position of ancient stoics. Besant's scientific interest was cultivated by Edward Aveling, a fervent Darwinist under whom she studied science at the University of London. More than the scientific training he provided, however, the special mark of Aveling's influence lay in his speculative explorations of science and mysticism. The connections he forged between medieval alchemy and astrology and between psychology and ancient myth appealed to Besant's own sense that all branches of human knowledge had a hidden relation yet to be systematically explicated. But it was only after meeting Friedrich Büchner, leader of the German materialist movement whose *Mind in Animals* and *Force and Matter* she undertook to translate, that Besant found what had eluded her thus far: that the question of suffering could be framed successfully around the determination of matter. Under Büchner's influence, Annie Besant was drawn to the doctrine of monism as alone enabling her to come to terms with the ontology of suffering. The strict materialistic position of monism, which posited the idea of one substance and no separate God, appeared to settle the vexing paradox that the source of human suffering was a supposedly loving and merciful God. Thereafter, Besant found it easier to approach divinity as consciousness, neither separate from nor above the thinking, feeling subject.

However, although the materialism of this outlook certainly reinforced her atheism, she was led at the same time to regard suffering as a very substantive phenomenon which, when endured, served as witness to the human race's adaptability to the adversities of nature. The language of Darwinian struggle is unmistakable, even though it is transposed onto a metaphysics of the soul's salvation: "Those who never suffer must always remain weak, and only in the stress and the agony of the combat will the soul learn to endure."[34] Catherine Wessinger rightly attributes Besant's turn toward an adaptive meaning of suffering to the experience of extreme privations in her own life. Among the starkest of Besant's various travails were the social ostracism that beset her when she left her curate husband, followed by her battles to save her sickly child from death and then her profound loss in having to give up her young daughter in a long and well-publicized custody battle. But these experiences never stood alone in Besant's consciousness as mere biographical testimony to the fact of individual survival; rather, they were translated into social theory, which took a variety of hues as she journeyed from socialism to evolutionary science. Even though Besant's dedication to socialism derived from her commitment to alleviating human suffering by reforming the social conditions that produced it, there was a core part of her that still continued to see suffering as having an instrumental value in furthering the development of mankind as a whole, if not spiritually, then certainly as a species.

The enabling role of suffering in the progressive evolution of the human species took Besant far away from her original objection to the religious justification of pain. For she came to see suffering not as redemptive but as restorative, a self-regulating mechanism of social evolution that prepared the ground for both the uplifting of people from their debased social circumstances and the advanced movement of the human species toward a higher level of civilizational harmony: "Those are helping human evolution who are turning away from the life of the body and are training themselves in the life of the mind."[35] The enduring presence of suffering fit into a theory of history that increasingly absorbed Besant, and she was drawn to the view that human civilization is a product of conflict and strife between sects and races. The pain of enduring sectarian and racial struggle could not continue indefinitely, and Besant had sufficient faith to believe that, taken to its limits, civil strife would eventually lead to a universal brotherhood of man. Lest her faith be translated as ungrounded naïveté, Besant undertook a study of world histories to seek out a point of reference that marked the limits of human struggle, out of which a new consciousness about the meaning of that struggle would emerge. A number of elements drawn from socialism and evolutionary science coalesced in her thinking to offer a model of human progress that paralleled, and indeed even repeated by repudiation, the redemptive function of suffering in Christian salvation.

That dissent from Christianity is the starting point for the position thus arrived at needs to be reiterated sufficiently often if we are to see the ways that the idea of a universal brotherhood of man ran askew of some of its expected assumptions and turned radical dissent into a reactionary defense of hierarchy and racial categorization. For instance, Besant did not believe that racial struggle would result ultimately in a state of egalitarianism, nor was her idea of brotherhood necessarily premised on equality. On the contrary, she maintained that the concept of an equal brotherhood was possible only in an (unrealistically) abstract realm removed from history, time, and space. Given her reading of history as a series of struggles from which would emerge a new state akin to a global self-consciousness, it is not surprising that she would maintain that the materials for the construction of a brotherhood of man invariably come from racial differentiation, itself a product of historical evolution. Hierarchy is implicit in this conception of brotherhood, as clearly as are unequal relations between races and their unequal development.

For Besant firmly maintained that "humanity is brotherhood, but brotherhood does not mean identity, and brotherhood does not imply a flat dead level of absolute similarity and so-called equality. . . . The wise are not equal to the ignorant. . . . The genius of the Empire is to make every nation that you conquer feel that you bring them into the Imperial Family, that they and you from that time forward are brothers."[36] This remarkable statement offers as explicit a statement about the positive outcomes of Britain's international supremacy as one is likely to find anywhere in Besant's writings. But what distinguishes her position here is a radical qualification of brotherhood not as identity but as hierarchy. Furthermore, the family is refigured not as a reproductive unit of society but as the terminal site of biological and social development, the point at which the uncontrollable dynamism and robust vitality of sexual reproduction gives way to the calm if sterile state of "brotherhood."

The reproductive logic of the biological family is brought under control by the "Imperial Family," which, as a stunning new model of lateral rather than vertical development, offers a nonreproductive alternative to the endless proliferation of competing, divisive races in an age of increasing social complexity and modernity.

It is likely that Annie Besant's willful injection of a celibate, neo-Malthusian strain into theosophical doctrine is linked to her suppressed anger at Madame Blavatsky's condition that she abandon her earlier stance on birth control if she wished to be admitted into the Theosophical Society. Besant's famous work *The Laws of Population*, coauthored with Charles Bradlaugh, was criticized by Blavatsky for being inhospitable to an essential feature of theosophy: the theory of reincarnation. For if measures to control human population were instituted, they would reduce the numbers of bodies to which reincarnated souls must have access if there were to be a continuous and uninterrupted flow of the life cycle. (Blavatsky was utterly serious about this interpretation of reincarnation, no matter how absurd it might have sounded to Annie Besant at the time and certainly to modern readers.) By describing brotherhood as a state of nonreproduction, Besant may have sought to bring back her own commitment to population control, but she did so in a manner that was consistent with the syncretic goals of theosophy captured by its logo: "A Universal Brotherhood of Humanity without distinction of race, creed, sex, caste, or colour." At any rate, by the end of her pamphlet "brotherhood" loses whatever connotations of egalitarianism and fraternity it might have had and becomes instead a trope of institutional hierarchy and monastic discipline.[37] As in so much of Besant's writing, intellectual positions are reached not by a predetermined, carefully worked out intellectual strategy but rather by an associative, coalescent form of thinking that, as a method, is reminiscent of the final object of her quest: a confederation of nations that aggregates by extending one single cellular organism, the British nation, into the far reaches of the globe.

THEOSOPHY AND RACIAL MYTHOLOGY

Annie Besant's attraction to theosophy may well have been a fascination for the racial theories of Madame Blavatsky and other occultists like Colonel Olcott, A. P. Sinnett, and Charles Leadbeater. Theories of racial separation and the dominance of some races over others fed into a reading of history that was partly informed by Fabian socialism, but it produced a strange admixture of dialectical materialism, Darwinian science, and metaphysics, in which the progression toward syncretic realization followed the route of territorial expansion, conquest, and imperial rule. Some of Besant's pamphlets and longer works, such as *The Pedigree of Man* or *The Inner Government of Man*, appear to be merely derivative, borrowing wholesale from Blavatsky's *The Secret*

Doctrine an elaborate mythology of the evolution of races and sub-races. It was no secret that Besant's turn toward theosophy was dramatically quickened by her chance reading of Blavatsky's occult book, which is replete with recondite mythologies passing themselves off as histories of the ancient world. The book is also full of extravagant accounts of the evolution of races, which is narrated alongside an equally tendentious account of geological formation. But however powerful the work's influence, Besant kept a notably aloof perspective on Blavatsky's racial classification and adapted it to her own developing millenarian vision. In her reconstruction, the positivist legacy of secularism and socialism overrode pure metaphysical abstractions. This is particularly evident in Besant's reading of the historical spread of empires as a function of racial and biological differentiation. Observing that the evolution of races goes through cycles of growth, maturity and decay, Besant contended that

> you must look at the life of races as you look at the life of persons. Looking at the history of races in the past may guide us in our forecast as to the *role* of a race in the present. Each great division of the human race, each strongly marked type of racial character, has its own growth and development, its time of widespread empire, and then again its time of slow and gradual decay.[38]

The scientific, analytical tone of this passage, which draws on analogy, empirical observation, and historical reasoning, envelops and obscures the total speculativeness (and speciousness) of its chief point, which asserts the growth of empires in proportion to the strength of certain racial strains. The quality of *endurance*—once doctrinally contested by Besant but subsequently made metaphysically acceptable as an instrument of social and moral evolution—is translated into a racial trait, to which relations of domination and subordination in world history are then traced.

Besant describes colonial expansion and territorial conquest as a migration of races for the ultimate enrichment of the "Fifth Race." This sweep of time, measured in aeons and evolving land-masses, dissolves the political immediacy of imperialism. Besant remarks that the race of Teutons, who are classified in her scheme as the fifth sub-race of the Fifth Race, is

> now spreading over the world, [and] has occupied the greater part of North America, driving before it the old Atlantean stock; it has seized Australia and New Zealand, the remnants of still more ancient Lemuria, and the poor relics of that dying Race are vanishing before it. High is it rearing its proud head over the countries of the globe, destined to build a world-wide Empire, and to sway the destinies of the civilization.[39]

The intricate mythology of the five root-races and their various sub-races (the sixth is yet to come, or so say the theosophists) is drawn directly from the occultist writings of a score of theosophists heavily influenced by Blavatsky's commentary on *The Stanzas of Dzyan* in *The Secret Doctrine*. Despite individual differences between theosophists, there is remarkably little divergence in the evolutionary scheme they present. In fact, the impression of a lack of originality evoked by their common discourse works eerily on the reader, who is made to feel that this new mythology is virtually interchangeable with science, so strongly is its content fixed and closed to interpretation.

It is interesting that the theosophist Geoffrey Barborka's recent update of theosophical wisdom, *The Story of Human Evolution* (1979), follows Voltaire and specifically invokes Genesis in the preface to claim a biblical precedent for describing human evolution in inflated terms: "There were giants in the earth in those days; and also after that, when the sons of God came in unto the daughters of men, and they bare children to them, the same became mighty men which were of old, men of renown" (Genesis 6:4). The same extravagance is present in his utterly serious acceptance of the Leda myth as an accurate description of how the world was first populated by what Barborka, following the theosophical line, terms "the Third Race," or the "Egg-born Third" (a reference to the myth that, following Zeus's visit, Leda gave birth to eggs, and in due time human beings were hatched from the eggs). Madame Blavatsky had herself countered all charges of antiscientism in such types of descriptions by maintaining that no further proof was required than the evidence provided by history and tradition. She further insisted that the folk tales, oral storytelling, and legends of a culture encode the memory of racial evolution, and must therefore be accepted as seriously as empirically verifiable documents.

To recapitulate the evolutionary scheme briefly as presented in theosophy: the first two races are distinguished from the succeeding three in that they are self-born and sexless, their evolution being coterminous with the formation of land masses and oceans. Sexuality, differentiation, and identity commence with the third root-race. The disclaimer that the term root-race "has no connection with the ideas associated with ethnic groups or racial strains" is immediately nullified by the very language of classification and hierarchy.[40] Even without further detail, the admission that each race is associated with a particular homeland makes a mockery of the disclaimer. The First Race is described as having inhabited the never-changing North Pole; the Second Race, as arising in the Hyperborean or northern Asia; the Third Race, as subdivided between the areas called Southern Lemuria, which embrace Africa, southern Asia, and the Pacific islands, and Northern Lemuria, which consists largely of Europe; the Fourth Race, or the first real members of the "human species" who, in the seventh sub-race, inhabited the areas between China and Indonesia; and the Fifth Race, which is dispersed across the seven continents and each sub-race of which has inaugurated a settled civilization in each continent. According to modern theosophy, the Sixth Race is yet to come, and when it does, it is expected to appear first in (where else?) southern California![41]

The last sub-race of each root-race constitutes the first sub-race of the next root-race, so that the contributions of Chinese civilization (the seventh sub-race of the Fourth Race) provide the foundations for the variegated civilizations of all sub-races in the Fifth Race. Furthermore, each race is associated with a particular color, the surviving ones, expectedly, being yellow, brown, black, and red. Most compromising of all, though this esoteric mythology claims not to refer to ethnicity or racial strains, historical development is nonetheless accounted for in polygenetic terms. Ethnicized explanation clearly obviates theosophy's purported syncretic ambition of seeking oneness amidst diversity:

> While [esoteric philosophy] assigns to humanity a oneness of origin, in so far that its forefathers or "Creators" were all divine beings—though of different classes or degrees of perfection in their hierarchy—men were nevertheless born on seven different centres of the continent of that period. Though all were of one common origin, yet for reasons given their potentialities and mental capabilities, outward or physical forms, and future characteristics, were very different. Some superior, others inferior, to suit the Karma of the various reincarnating Monads which could not be all of the same degree of purity in their last births in other worlds. This accounts for the difference of races, the inferiority of the savage, and other human varieties.[42]

But although the racial mythology of Madame Blavatsky and other theosophists was so wildly extravagant as to be literally esoteric and virtually out of the bounds of credibility, Annie Besant's redescription of the same scheme was far more precise, recognizable, and perhaps even acceptable to those among her contemporaries who were familiar with Renan's work on racial typologies. Besant was first drawn to Renan through his work attacking Christianity, particularly *La Vie de Jesus*. But though Renan's name dropped out of her autobiography the closer she moved toward Fabian socialism and subsequently Blavatsky's occultism, her own movement from atheism to theosophy retraced Renan's movement from disbelief to scientific racialist doctrine. The language of agnosticism in both their writings develops into a language invoking notions of superior and inferior races, racial blending and racial purity, and the evolution of dominant racial traits. What is perhaps most striking about Besant's use of evolutionary science, marking her off somewhat from Blavatsky, Leadbeater, Sinnett, and others but bringing her closer to Renan and Matthew Arnold,[43] was her systematic reading of the evolution of races in terms of a cultural science that undergirds political relations, affecting such things as, for instance, the ideal conditions for the rule of one people by another and the limits of coercion where compatibility of racial types is absent:

> All those that I have mentioned to you as belonging to the fourth sub-race [termed Kelt] are emotional people. The reason why England and Ireland cannot get on

together is because England belongs to the Teutonic sub-race, in which the concrete mind is most developed, while the Kelts (the Irish are Kelts) belong to the
fourth sub-race and emotion is strong in them. Because the English are not imaginative enough to understand them, because in them the concrete scientific mind
is the dominant thing, they can never understand an emotional, impulsive people.
So they try to keep them by force. . . . They have not the common sense to rule
people according to their own type, and not according to a different type.[44]

In other words, colonial rule results when there is a lack of synchronicity
between races, a failure of understanding that makes its effects felt in abiding
differences of culture, language, and tradition. In the absence of racial unity,
argues Besant, these cultural differences can only be negotiated by the exercise
of force. The language of evolutionary science permeates this statement, as the
ultimate point of Besant's analysis is that the subordination of one group of
people to another is *racially* constituted, since each belongs to "a different
type." If colonial subjugation is a result of the polygenesis of civil society, then
the only possible condition for self-rule must be that of homogeneity. Only
when a society is truly composed of one single race will it ever attain a condition of self-governability; until then, peoples all over the world are subject to
control by others. But paradoxically, it is also through such control—through
cultural contact—that the possibilities for becoming one race are made real, so
that self-rule is a realizable goal only after societies pass through a history of
colonialist expropriation. It is by thus falling back on inexorable historical
(racial) evolution that Annie Besant provided a radically different twist to the
construction of a nationalist narrative, which conventionally sees alien rule as
a disruption—not fulfillment, as Besant does—of the imperatives of self-determination. The intriguing question is: to whose nationalism was Annie Besant
finally alluding, India's (as many believed) or England's?

Are we to understand from the above description that a polyracial society is
eternally subject to continuous civil warfare, unable to transcend itself to attain
a "universal brotherhood of man," Besant's choice phrase for her desired family of nations? Far from it. Elusively writing in *Britain's Place in the Great
Plan* that "the world's opportunity lies in this, that we are now at the transition
stage of human evolution, of racial evolution, in which the next step forward
is union and not persistence in division," Besant turns to India, with its racial
mixture resulting from a history of conquest and migration, as the exemplary
model for the new nation—one which provides an opportunity for ties to be
established "between the Nations."[45] That Besant's idea of the commonwealth
is a kind of racial melting pot makes sense only when it is understood that
imperial conquest, nomadism, and settlement are the means by which such
racial mixture is made possible. This occurs not necessarily through actual
miscegenation but through a cross-fertilization of language, history, culture,
and literature. In this respect Besant was far closer to Matthew Arnold than she

was to Blavatsky or the other occultists. Describing culture as the "middle region of intellect and of the higher tastes and emotions," she locates a higher spiritual quality in mental cultivation which transcends the animal-like competition for scarce resources that motivates colonialism and class warfare in the first place:

> For conflict between men is over when the desire turns to the intelligence, to the inner organ instead of to the outer things of sense. . . . The things of the tastes, the higher tastes, and of the intelligence are practically unlimited, and there is no conflict between men for them; for no man is the poorer because his brother is richly gifted artistically or intellectually; none has his own share diminished because his brother's share is greater. And so humanity progresses from competition to cooperation, and learns the lesson of Brotherhood.[46]

As in Besant's idiosyncratic use of brotherhood as sexual nonreproductiveness to recover her suppressed commitment to Malthusian population control, so here too Besant establishes continuity between her socialist principles and her theosophical program of cultural advancement, despite the apparent esotericism of the latter. If culture's special uniqueness lies in its inexhaustibility, its open availability to all peoples, its transcendence of the conditions of material oppression (which are grounded in inequitable distribution of resources) unites those of different classes and races. In the absence of competitive claims to cultural resources, which Besant regards strictly as a personal endowment rather than as institutionally guaranteed or controlled, the limits of class or race are more readily outstripped and the divisive tendencies of regional and local alliances muted. At once the product of a conflict of races and societies and the means of their unification, Besant's idea of culture takes on all the weight of a global political force. Though historical contact is its defining principle, culture's transhistorical character effaces the precise moments of such contact and renders world history subordinate to its dictates.

Similarly, Besant's use of reincarnated souls traversing through world history and world empires functions as a rhetorical device to argue for the fulfillment of a racial plan by imperial conquest:

> Now it is to us Theosophists significant and interesting that the bulk of the Souls to whom this offer is made have twice before builded an Empire and have carried its burden; for the majority of the Souls that made the Egyptian Empire lived again upon earth in the Roman Republic and Empire, and have been and are being born into the Anglo-Saxon, and indeed into the whole Teutonic, race. Men who wrought in the Rome on the Tiber are working now in the Rome on the Thames, and are again Empire-building.[47]

The reappearance of the same racial traits in more dominant forms and in future historical moments is encoded in the language of reincarnation. The recourse to mystical interpretation provides Besant necessary relief from hav-

ing to account for the recent history of imperialist appropriations of foreign
territory. On the same order of rhetorical strategy is the slide from territorial
expansion under an ascendant race to the inauguration of religious movements: "Wherever you find a new departure in spiritual matters there you find
it succeeded by a new departure in rule and in civilizing power."[48]

Besant's penchant for translation of the metaphysical into the political,
and vice versa, carries over into the way she turns the Hindu theory of the
self, internally conceived as multiply composed of knowledge, desire, and
action, into a description of cultural and educational influence. In this translation, the principle of knowledge is an external agent transforming rapa-
cious desires in animal-like man into a higher form of life. That principle of
knowledge comes from the outside in the person of a teacher or a wise ruler
or, very vaguely, as a "Force." Besant writes of such teachers that, "they
came because, without guidance from higher Beings, the intellect would
have gone wrong, plunged amid a world of passion and animal nature, with
which it was filled, to the great destruction of the forward evolution of human
beings."[49] Though diffused in the language of Hindu mysticism, this is the
rhetoric of colonial education, the capitalized "They" being the rulers and
the teachers, the men of advanced intellect, training, and civilization. The
teachers, the rulers, the self, the world, and the cosmos are at once undifferentiated and differentiated, internal and external. The naturalizing of outside
forces makes it difficult to distinguish who or what has agency. What seemingly has the power of causation is nature, but wise teachers and rulers who are
somehow apart from the rest of base mankind are also made interchangeable
with the force of nature. (Matthew Arnold's influence is unmistakable in this
instance, Besant's "Force" bearing comparison with Arnold's "aliens" in *Culture and Anarchy*).

I suggested earlier that, following an evolving pattern of racial differentiation, Besant's concept of brotherhood assumed hierarchy. Education was
Besant's chosen means of achieving a brotherhood whose inherent inequality
is counterbalanced by an identification with the nation. Besant's reading of
colonial domination as a rule necessitated by the non-negotiability of incompatible types also informs her analysis of educational reform. In order to avert
a proliferation of mismatched individuals wherever there is discrepancy between the culture of one's birth and the culture of one's education, she proposes (using the language of racial science) that Indian youth should be
molded and shaped "*after its own type*, to make the Mussalman a good Mussalman, the Hindu boy a good Hindu. . . . Only they must be taught a broad and
liberal tolerance as well as an enlightened love for their own religion, so that
each may remain Hindu or Mussalman, but both be Indian."[50] The move toward nationhood through a carefully designed education is part of the process
of diffusing the effects of coercion by alien British rule, just as education
prepares the way for a balanced, compatible relation between the races. Na-

tional consolidation is therefore less an antithesis than a perfection of colonial rule in that it has been prepared for and is part of the trajectory established by colonization.

Theosophy's fusion of east and west, as also its fusion of science and religion, philosophy and practical knowledge, presupposes a symbiotic relation between western and eastern nations. Besant's theory of education is premised on the idea that western development has so far outpaced itself that its materialism has been rendered hollow. But although the east may still be the preserve of ancient wisdom, it is doomed to stagnate because of its ineffectualness in dealing with its own wisdom. As the special contribution of the west to the east, the harnessing of spiritual energy to practical knowledge leads Besant to put forth a concept of empire as a mighty trust, charged with a religious obligation to bring forth a comity of nations. Despite her strong opposition to the forcible holding of subject peoples by alien rule, Besant was not immune to the narcotic pull of a messianic conception of empire. Her anticolonialism can go only so far as to decry the use of force in settling what was for her an issue of irremediable racial incompatibility. Beyond that, the call for home rule is reduced to a tame appeal to what she vaguely, mystically, calls "the end of individuality, the union of Life in others that once more it may be one."[51] Besant's conversion to theosophy, and her choice of India as the home where she would pursue her new religion, combine to invest alternative spiritual movements with the restorative power to redeem what England had long since lost.

THEOSOPHY, RACE, AND LITERARY NATIONALISM

When Annie Besant became involved with India's freedom struggle, her active participation in Indian nationalist politics was seen by her peers in the Theosophical Society as a conflict of interests. To such criticisms she retorted: "It is sometimes pretended that Theosophy has nothing to do with politics, and that in taking part in Indian politics, I have entered on a new line. The fact is conveniently ignored that, while labouring chiefly in religious propaganda and educational work, I used the light of Theosophy to illuminate political questions where great principles were involved."[52]

Besant's opposition to British imperialism was strongly informed by events in Ireland. She was encouraged to believe that there would be parliamentary settlement of the Irish problem, surely to be followed by peaceable concession to Indian home rule. But when home rule collapsed in Ulster, she took a more intransigent position toward the British Raj. She launched a campaign against British rule through speeches, cheap political pamphlets, and newspapers like *Commonweal* and *New India*, arguing that Indians were capable of governing themselves and taking responsibility for their political future. But all the time

that she courted arrest—and indeed she was briefly interned for causing political agitation in Madras and Calcutta presidencies—Annie Besant always
stressed that she opposed the British government for failing to live up to the
principles it stood for, and not because she sought the destruction of empire
itself. Her plea for Indian self-government *within* the empire was not quite the
same thing as a call for Indian independence from Britain, which more radical
Indian nationalists were seeking. Indeed, even in her most polemical pamphlets she was prone to using words like "dominion," "commonwealth," and
"federation of nations" as more favorable surrogates for empire.

Besant's persistent effort to distinguish between good imperialism and bad
imperialism considerably qualifies her support of Indian nationalism and opposition to British colonialism, despite such apparently contrary evidence as
her presidentship of the Indian National Congress and her internment by British authorities on charges of sedition.[53] This evidence is often cited as proof of
Besant's unremitting anti-imperialism. For instance, Peter Robb, who views
Annie Besant quite literally as an enemy of the British government, has argued
that Besant's activities in India challenged the British authorities to determine
whether the home-rule agitation was a revolutionary and seditious activity or
a political and constitutional one. Robb goes on to conclude that by releasing
Besant from internment, British officials sent out a message indicating the
exclusion of "Home Rulers" from the revolutionary category.

But if Besant argued for the inevitability of home rule on constitutional
grounds and thereby succeeded in securing acceptance for it by English liberals, howsoever grudgingly, it is also the case that her advocacy of decolonization did not necessarily feed into an Indian nationalist agenda and was, in fact,
premised on a different set of expectations. Among these was Besant's firm
belief that "liberty for India, but within the British Federation, was the goal for
which I was to work.... Dominion Status gives exactly what is wished—
Independence within India, with an equal and friendly link with Britain
through the Crown."[54] It is perhaps not coincidental that most of Besant's
pamphlets on home rule, which express her longing for classes to unite within
the nation and form a "real family, instead of warring fragments," were written
during the First World War.[55] Annie Besant often recalled how Blavatsky had
written as far back as 1889 that "the early years of the next century would see
many of the accounts of the Nations made up. . . . For one very clear result of
the . . . war is to bring Asia into new relations with Europe, and to establish her
in her old place of power in shaping the world's destinies."[56]

Not only Besant but also other theosophists developed a perspective on war
that emphasized its unique role in precipitating an emerging union of nations.
Most notable among them was James Cousins, leading poet of the Irish literary
renaissance whom Besant recruited to India from Ireland in 1915 to be the new
literary subeditor of her newspaper, *New India*. Cousins's appearance in India
was the source of mounting concern among the British authorities that the

Theosophical Society had turned political, even seditious. *New India* published a number of articles by Cousins, and one 1916 article in particular, praising the leaders of the Easter Rising in Dublin, brought him into open conflict with the government, causing Besant publicly to dismiss him. Cousins's consistent linking of literary and political concerns made him a key player in the literary nationalism of both Ireland and India. But although Cousins was deeply involved in the convulsive political debates of the day, his approach to these discussions was mediated by his engagement with literary issues. As a poet in Dublin, Cousins rejected romanticized reveries about the Irish past and, under the influence of Huxley and Darwin, was drawn to intellectual agnosticism and scientific determinism. But soon becoming interested in mystical experience, he turned to India as the practical site of a resolution between romance and realism that had long eluded him. Though eventually Cousins came to see India as the source of a spiritual revival throughout the world, India first offered him a way of working through problems in Irish literary nationalism—problems that he found difficult to resolve simply by mythologizing the Irish past. Such an approach seemed to him too local and narrow, and he found himself drawn to the larger project of establishing the common foundations of Irish-Indian culture as the first step toward the overthrow of colonial rule in both countries.

But Cousins did not stop at making Indian-Irish nationalism the driving quest of his literary criticism. Instead, he expanded his argument to emphasize that these two societies were in a process of transition and that their spiritual ties offered a prototype for a unity of humanity. Like Besant, Cousins fused the trend toward decolonization with the revival of spirituality worldwide, with India as the nodal point from which ties between nations would be forged. What began as Cousins's project to establish the foundations of Irish-Indian cultural history turned into a much larger work that merged with the theosophical goal of synthesizing all human thought, especially religion and science.

Cousins's description of war not as an opposition of contending forces but as a "vital cooperation between affinities in the vast process of human evolution," strongly informed Besant's own conviction that the world was being pushed, through strife and internecine warfare, to a common end that would dissolve all boundaries between nations.[57] When the demand for home rule is articulated within the configuration of a prospective federation built out of the fragments of war, the effect is less a dissolution than a *decentering* of empire. By this I mean that the commonwealth model, as Besant conceives it, expresses her yearning for an enduring unity between India and England, imaged as empire without colonial subordination. Her plea for home rule is, as she puts it, a "cry for freedom without separation."[58] The moment of decolonization for India is also the moment of its emergence into a federation of nations still held together by Britain at its center:

Great Britain is a model for the future Federation of the world. The world is not
yet ripe, because of the great differences between Races, to join them all together
in perfect Federation. But it is possible here [i.e., in India], where there are links,
which have been bonds of Empire and shall become links of Commonwealth if
you can bring about Union, Union between India and Britain, between East and
West, between Asia and Europe. It is not an Empire made by force but a commonwealth made by mutual goodwill and friendliness.[59]

Recent revisionist criticism of Annie Besant's role in Indian nationalism has
been unsparing in highlighting her imperialist interest in India. Her undis-
guised partiality for a brahmanical, aryanized Hinduism, along with her
dreams of restoring to India its lost Aryavarta, so clearly played into the strategic objectives of elite brahmanical Indian leaders that it was not difficult, either
for her contemporary detractors or later historians, to castigate her for her
involvement in "the most morbid aspects of Hindu revivalism."[60] Although
this is familiar ground to students of Indian nationalism and need not be rehearsed yet again, what still requires reiteration is that the support for Indian
nationalism by British anti-imperialists like Annie Besant shaped and refined
an emerging race theory that had a double edge in articulating both an elite
nationalist politics and a new literary consciousness.[61] For this is a moment of
discovery and revival of an indigenous heritage, at the same time that it is also
reactionary, elitist, and exclusionary. Singularly constituted as Aryan and Sanskrit, this literary and cultural heritage mobilizes nationalist politics along narrowly selective caste lines. Simultaneously, the recovery of Aryan roots re-
orders nationalist aspirations for modernity by locating modernity within a
resuscitated past. The significant move, of course, is that this past is now represented as having been fully evolved and advanced, and characterized by a
highly developed scientific temperament. The fusion of science and religion is
nowhere more effortlessly achieved than in refiguring indigenous culture as
embodying the full range of modern advances.

The wide-ranging effects of this double moment are felt not only in the
Indian literary renaissance but also the Irish cultural revival, particularly
through the influence of the theosophical movement. James Cousins describes
the resurgence of Irish literary pride as the discovery of a common Aryanism.
Emplotting literary history in terms analogous to Besant's and other theosophists' deployment of a racial scheme, Cousins traces the culture of the Celts
to an originary source in Asian religions, which had moved into Europe centuries before the birth of Christianity. Cousins subdivides these religions into
Aryan, Semitic, and Mongolian. Among the "cultural tendencies" left by these
older religions were Brehon laws that Cousins, citing Henry Maine's *Ancient
Institutions*, claimed had striking affinities to Vedic laws. Like Vedic laws that
were challenged by English law, Brehon laws and institutions were contested
and ultimately overthrown by the Roman law of England in the seventeenth

century. In Cousins's view the interweaving of Irish and Indian cultures gave racial continuity to their common struggle against British colonialism:

> So subtly, however had the Aryan influence intermingled with the culture of Ireland that when, once again, at the beginning of the twentieth century, the ancient Asian spirit touched Ireland through the philosophy of India, as conveyed to it through the works of Edwin Arnold and the Theosophical Society, there was an immediate response. Two poets (AE and Yeats) found their inmost nature expressed in the Indian modes. They found also the spiritual truths that Asia had given to the world reflected in the old myths and legends of Ireland; and out of their illuminations and enthusiastic response arose the Irish Literary and Dramatic Revival whose influence at its height was purely spiritual.[62]

Contrary to many accounts of Irish-Indian cultural influences then widely prevalent, what distinguishes Cousins's description of ancient Hindu influence on the Celtic renaissance is that, far from understanding this interest solely in terms of the Orientalist scholarship now made available to Irish nationalist writers, Cousins insisted on an existing religio-racial mixture of Celt and Aryan. This unique mixture prepared the ground for the "discovery" of Asia's spiritual truths. The mythologies of the past are preserved and reproduced by what Cousins clearly regarded as a racial imagination. Hence he could argue that the literary revival of his time was an awakened memory of what had, in epigenetic terms, been suppressed by colonial rule.[63]

But what makes the new, animated literary spirit unique is that it could be joined both to the purposes of nationalism and anticolonialism *and* a selective recasting and racial reinscription of a mythologized history as the "high" civilization of the Aryans. That both movements can accommodate an active anti-Christian spirit establishes their strong links with religious dissent. But the trajectory of dissent also would appear to suggest that the syncretic order it aimed to achieve is characterized by a necessary (racial) inequality, tempered only by the quest for national identification. Neither Besant nor Cousins ever relinquished their conviction that the struggle of hybrid races constituted the dynamic principle of literary and cultural change. Nor did they lose hope that this powerful struggle would precipitate the move to an eventual unity of political societies. If the sentiments of anticolonialism and imperialism become virtually indistinguishable, their blurring can be partly attributed to the racial doctrine that animates both, a doctrine that by the time of the Home Rule League offered striking ways of articulating the complex attitudes toward national and imperial consolidation.

Part Three

THE IMAGINED COMMUNITY

CHAPTER SEVEN

Conversion to Equality

WHO SPEAKS FOR WHOM?

Despite the British inclination to treat the sectarian differences between religious faiths in India as a purely internal affair, in much the same way that judicial decisions in England tended to treat questions involving religion as entirely a matter for the ecclesiastical establishment, the clamor for self-rule by Indians turned these religious differences into a political matter. An obvious case in point is the great controversy over the communal awards sanctioned by the Government of India Acts of 1909, 1919, and 1935, which gave Muslims separate electorates in the legislatures and established the grounds for the pursuit of political power on sectional lines.[1]

On the same principle, Bhimrao Ramji Ambedkar, leader of the untouchable (or *dalit*) community in India, demanded separate electorates for the untouchables.[2] If Muslims were given this privilege as a significant religious minority, he argued, untouchables as a minority oppressed by caste equally deserved a similar guarantee of self-representation to protect their own interests against the encroachments of Hindu majority rule. Born in 1891 into a Maharashtrian Mahar untouchable family, Ambedkar remained mired in the discriminatory caste politics of his time until his scholastic excellence came to the recognition of the Maharaja Gaekwad of Baroda, who undertook to sponsor his studies. Overcoming virtually insuperable obstacles of caste prejudice, Ambedkar rose to become one of the most highly educated Indians of his time, with a Ph.D. in political science from Columbia University and further advanced work in law and economics at the London School of Economics.[3] Ambedkar's academic achievements, however, did not exempt him from the disdain of caste Hindus. Returning to India to work in a law office, Ambedkar suffered the humiliation of clerks hurling files at him to avoid being defiled by his touch. Inflamed by these experiences of extreme indignity, he threw himself into the uplifting of the untouchables; not, however, by working for reform within Hinduism but by asserting the rights of untouchables to full equality before the law. Momentarily forgetting his own indictment of colonialism's denial of popular participation, he called the right to equality the only positive legacy of British colonialism.[4] Ambedkar's uncompromising appeal to principles of political liberty overrode what might have easily been a more modest project of eliminating the civil disabilities under which untouchables suffered daily harassment.

Rejecting the identification of untouchables with Hindus—a classification that both caste Hindus and British administrators were eager to retain—Ambedkar challenged the authority of other religious constituencies to usurp the untouchables' right of self-representation. His categorical assertion that only untouchables could speak for themselves was, not unexpectedly, violently denounced as a divisive tactic aimed at driving a wedge within the anticolonial movement and alienating masses of Indians from their nationalist leaders. Over the objections of members of the Indian National Congress, who clamored for a united India to throw off the British yoke, Ambekdar refused to yield and only reluctantly agreed to a compromise solution when Gandhi threatened to go on a hunger strike to protest Ramsay Macdonald's communal award, which had provisionally acceded to the untouchables' demand for separate electorates in 1932. The compromise agreement, known as the Poona Pact, made provisions for the reservation of seats for untouchables in exchange for Ambedkar's conceding to joint rather than separate electorates. Macdonald's communal award had granted untouchables seventy-eight seats in the legislature, along with the right to elect their own candidates as well as vote for general seats. Under the Poona Pact, they were granted a hundred and forty-eight seats, with 18 percent reservation in the central legislature. Only untouchables could be candidates for these seats; however, their right to elect their own candidates was withdrawn, the disheartening implication for untouchables being that their representation would still remain in the hands of the majority community, since their legislators would be chosen by the general electorate.[5]

Many critics are of the opinion that Ambedkar's famous declaration in 1935, announcing his intention to leave the Hindu fold and convert to another faith, can be traced to his intense frustration and anger over failing to secure self-representation for untouchables. However, his twenty-year decision to convert to Buddhism (his actual conversion only materialized in 1956, a few weeks before his death) developed in much more complex ways than conveyed by this description. Such a representation, in reducing his renunciation of Hinduism to political frustration, conceives of conversion as reactionary, apolitical, solipsistic, and separatist. Drawing on Ambedkar's writings on culture and religion, I shall argue that, despite his disappointment with the aborted demand for separate electorates, his conversion was less a rejection of political solutions than a rewriting of religious and cultural change into a form of political intervention. Such intervention was important not simply in demographic terms (that is, creating a numerically significant constituency distinct from Hinduism), but more so in terms of creating a new mythology around which the political identity of dalits could be mobilized. This mythology offered an alternative to mobilization around a structure of electoral reform that was flawed from the start because of its derivation from brahmanical and colonialist ideologies.

As a dissenter bent on dismantling an oppressive caste system, Ambedkar fulfilled the historical role of dissent not only to question hateful religious dogma but also unbuckle the consolidating ambitions of the secular state within which former religious orthodoxies are subsumed. The deliberateness with which he planned his conversion, all the time negotiating with Hindu leaders for legal measures against untouchability and courting Muslim, Sikh, and Christian organizations, while simultaneously developing formidable scholarship in Buddhist studies and writing his own version of the *Dhammapada*, indicates that his conversion was far from being a knee-jerk reaction to failed political solutions, as mass conversions tend to be read. Ambedkar's vast body of work on Buddhism, conversion, and caste ideology attempted to steer a steady course between a separatist, sectarian stance and an unconditional citizenship function in which the identity of untouchables would be subsumed within Hinduism. This chapter will consider the significance of Ambedkar's conversion and examine its implications for the possibilities of nationhood, at the time of decolonization, for a social class denied access to political power through self-representation, yet seeking a course of action that *preserved* rather than eradicated difference. As more than one scholar of modern Indian history has noted, consciousness of difference is often considered the privilege of the upper classes and castes, but recent history has shown that the victims of religious difference invoke religion to stake their own claims to identity: "Precisely those who should seek obliteration of the divisions and disparities that characterise the deeply hierarchical nature of the caste system are found to use it the most, hoping to undermine it . . . and do precisely what the larger secular order has failed to provide: a society free of exploitation and oppression and indignities."[6]

Ambedkar's conversion in the twentieth century ranks with John Henry Newman's in the previous one with respect to the centrality of conversion as a form of political and cultural criticism. Utterly different from one another in terms of class origin, personal history, and ideological disposition, Newman and Ambedkar nevertheless denote formidable figures whose conversions were as public as their participation in the political life of their respective nations. And while, for both, conversion was a clear political statement of dissent against the identities constructed by the state (through legislation, for example), they were not merely reacting to centralized authority in the name of asserting difference but, more fundamentally, were exploring the possibilities offered by conversion (especially to "minority" religions) in developing an alternative epistemological and ethical foundation for a national community. Without straining the comparison too much, the correspondence partly lies in the fact that Newman's conversion to Catholicism and Ambedkar's to Buddhism sought to reclaim cultural identities located at an originary point (pre-Reformation Catholicism in Newman's case, the triumph over caste-ridden Brahmanism by Buddhism in Ambedkar's), defined as the historical model for enlightened nationhood.

For both figures, conversion was a deliberate and calculated public decision, a performative gesture of recasting selfhood in history, though refracted at different points in time in their lives. Newman converted relatively early and spent the rest of his life ceaselessly talking and writing about it; Ambedkar, on the other hand, spent most of his life tirelessly expatiating on his impending decision (his opponents preferred to say his *threat*) to leave Hinduism, but his conversion occurred only toward the end of his life. Whereas Newman spent his post-Catholicism years recasting the content, form, and narrative structure of his conversion, giving it a shape quite distinct from its beginnings in the ironic reversals of his earlier political positions, Ambedkar reflected, planned, and prepared for his conversion for several decades before he actually performed his public ceremony of initiation to Buddhism, along with thousands of his followers. That period of preparation is less a period of uncertainty or hesitation than a careful working out of alternative possibilities for dalit emancipation. Indeed, just as in writing about Newman's conversion the critic finds herself returning insistently to certain paradigmatic moments and events, such as Catholic emancipation, Whately's writings on disestablishment, and the reform legislation of the English parliament, an analysis of Ambedkar's long-drawn-out conversion brings the critic back repetitively to earlier events and debates—centrally, his confrontation with Gandhi on electoral representation for dalits. The recurrent traversing of the same ground is an effect of the non-linearity and recursivity of both Newman's and Ambedkar's conversions, made doubly visible by a certain amount of critical self-reflexiveness on their part that clearly, too, is an effect of their conversions.

And so I close this book with an analysis of a (postcolonial) figure who brings us back full circle to the role of conversion in unraveling the complex relations among nation, religion, culture, and emancipatory legislation. The issue of legislative reform is crucial, and I must return to the place where I began, even if that means reiterating the simultaneity of Anglicization in India and parliamentary bills to enfranchise religious minorities in England. The relation between the two events is neither causal nor incidental, yet a connection exists which suggests that crucial issues of citizenship and subjecthood have always been played out between the twin poles of culture and religion. The removal of civil disabilities in preparation for citizenship is not necessarily equivalent to the acculturation of subjects, although they may take place at the same time. Few reformers fought as hard for lifting the stigma against untouchability as Ambedkar did, but he was also acutely aware that when the issue of legal eradication of disabilities supersedes, or at best subsumes, the issue of full political equality and full guarantee of rights, the effect is likely to be one of acculturation, or induction into the norms, values, and ideologies of the modern, "tolerant" state. As we saw earlier in Chapter Three, the British manipulation of colonial law produced a restrictive, rights-based discourse that aimed to protect converts against caste disabilities but did not extend further to incorporating converts' subjectivity. There, too, the effect is one of a conditional insertion of disenfranchised individuals into the modern liberal state, not a recognition of converts' self-defined, self-chosen status. Ambedkar's special mission aimed to puncture the false certainties of those nationalists, like Gandhi, who made the removal of civil disabilities their paramount goal—a goal that would have been unobjectionable were it not that it threatened to become a moral substitute for ensuring the self-representational rights of untouchables.

Since national independence, the material locus of ideological debate on the shape of Indian modernity has been confined to the contradiction between the principles of "hierarchy"—and the occlusion of human rights based on norms of pollution-purity-patriarchy—and the principles of "differentiation," or the accommodating system of governance of a nonhierarchical society whose vision of human rights is based on secular, liberal, and egalitarian principles.[7] Such a world-view envisions not the disappearance of stratification but what has been described as its "transformation into components of a pluralistic society in which invidious hierarchy is discarded while diversity is accommodated."[8] Viewed thus, so the argument goes, differentiation as it is expressed through compensatory discrimination policy is not antithetical to secularism; on the contrary, it enhances secularism by weakening the edge of hierarchic distinctions. But through his conversion, Ambedkar shifted the focus of debate away from ideological oppositions that left secular philosophies intact, and he produced a critique of secular differentiation as an ideology consistent with, rather than an alternative to, a social philosophy based on hierarchy. By moving the debate to this other fundamental site of contradiction, Ambedkar sought to expose the wide gap between the secular commitment to the removal of civil disabilities and the secular state's persistent functioning within a majoritarian ethic. His primary objective thus lay in demonstrating that modern secularism was essentially a universalist world-view stalling the processes of enfranchisement and creating the conditions for partial, rather than full, citizenship.

A pattern of similarity emerges in the driving forces of Newman's and Ambedkar's conversions as critiques of the failure of secular ideologies to extend full political rights. But if disingenuousness underlies Newman's conversion, because he uses the mantle of electoral reform (nonreflexively endorsed as the ideal embodiment of people's will) and espouses popular radicalism to

launch a crusade against religious emancipation, Ambedkar's own conversion
marks the structural and conceptual inadequacy of electoral reform as derived
from preexisting forms of governance. Ambedkar's slow but careful dismantling of the flawed structure of electoral politics in postcolonial India—
achieved less by critique than by conversion—belies the primacy accorded
by Newman to the extension of the franchise, especially since Newman does
not acknowledge the electoral system's structural links to the hegemonies of
class, state, and religion. Newman mistakenly believed that the democratization process was autonomous, and it led him to make all sorts of miscalculations about a parallel "extraconstitutional" source of agency in the people (see
above, pp. 57–58). Because popular agency was at the same time fraught with
anarchic potential, Newman looked toward foundational religious authority as
a corrective.

Ambedkar, on the other hand, regarded with great suspicion all attempts to
portray democratization as a process independent of caste manipulation (hence
his dissatisfaction with joint electorates). But his skepticism did not lead him
to seek dalit empowerment in extralegal or extraconstitutional sources, but
rather led him to find ways of writing dalit agency into and thus *reconstituting*
constitutional process. The issue to be analyzed is *not*, as one recent commentator maintains, how Ambedkar's "sense of alienation contribute[d] to his
constructive role in formulating a constitution which could ensure India's
emergence as a secular, egalitarian and liberal-democratic state."[9] Such a formulation persists in seeing the secular, egalitarian state as a static goal of dalit
emancipatory practice, which reaches out to claim what is out there in an unchanging, predetermined form. Rather, the recovery of dalit agency through
conversion to Buddhism suggests alternative conceptions of nation and community that resist being encompassed by preexisting, received forms of the
state and its apparatuses.

One of the most powerful literary expressions of the political impetus initiated by Ambedkar is the short story by dalit writer Waman Hoval, "The
Storeyed House."[10] This highly compressed story uses the metaphor of the
storeyed house to suggest different levels of expansion of dalit empowerment
within a self-constituting framework. Hoval offers in parable form what Ambedkar delineated in numerous political tracts and speeches. Hoval's protagonist Bayaji is a Mahar (dalit) laborer who, on superannuation, returns to his
village after working in Bombay for thirty-five years in the dockyard. With his
gratuity of twenty-five hundred rupees, he decides to build a two-storeyed
house so that his large family would no longer have to eat in turns or sit
crowded, "knocking our knees together" (*SH*, 158). The news of his intended
house construction is not well received by the upper castes, for only one other
storeyed house stands in the village, and it belongs to Kondiba Patil, a caste
Hindu, who rebukes Bayaji for daring to presume that he had social mobility:
"Do you aspire to an equal status with us by building this house? The poor

should remain content with their cottage, understand?" (*SH*, 158). Bayaji is restricted to building a small house having only three sections: a front veranda, a back veranda, and a living area in the middle. Threatened with dire consequences if he were to violate these regulations, Bayaji abandons his plans for a storeyed house. Or so it seemed.

> The conventional three portioned house was taken up. Work was resumed and the walls rose rapidly. The middle portion was a little elevated and a small first storey fixed up there with a wooden flooring. This part could be reached by stairs rising from the kitchen. No one could guess from the outside that there was a first storey to the house. Bayaji had to make the best of things (*SH*, 159).

Not only does Bayaji construct the hidden storey but when the house is completed he throws a housewarming party to which Patil and his cronies also come, driven there by only one, all-consuming thought: "This untouchable worm has got a swollen head. He needs proper handling" (*SH*, 160). As Buddhist chants rise in a chorus of devotion, circles of flames also begin to envelop the house. Bayaji rushes up to the raised storey and pulls out the pictures of Ambedkar and Buddha adorning its walls, but he does not escape quickly enough and becomes a burning torch as the staircase itself comes crashing down with the flaming house. The village officers' certification of his death as "the result of an accident due to a petromax flare-up" (*SH*, 161) is received, however, not with resigned acceptance by Bayaji's family but a determined energy to expose its lie, as his sons begin digging the earth with spades soon after the funeral: "We're starting on a house, not one with a concealed first floor but a regular two-storeyed house" (*SH*, 162).

This terse but multilayered story uses space in a remarkably original way to suggest a number of things. The most important of these is the rejection of regulated space—not just the preassigned space of ritual pollution—as the first step in the reclamation of full political rights. That rejection has already commenced for untouchables with the assumption of a Buddhist identity that informs not only the structure and form of community organization and residential living (the public building in the untouchables' settlement is named Buddha Vihar) but also modes of social relations. Bayaji's address to a caste Hindu with a simple "Greetings" rather than the usual subservient salutation meets with a severe rebuke: "Do you think you can become a Brahmin merely by saying 'Greetings'? Can you forget your position simply because you've turned Buddhist?" (*SH*, 156). The interesting slippage here, of course, is between "Brahmin" and "Buddhist," the conversion of the untouchables to Buddhism being regarded not as their departure from the Hindu fold but as their wrongful usurpation of Brahmin identity.

The forbidden second floor, constructed as a crypto-loft rising from the kitchen, presents itself in appearance as a Buddhist shrine infused with "a pious and holy ambience" (*SH*, 160), an effect enhanced by the images of the

Buddha as well as the pictures of noteworthy dalit figures like Ambedkar, Karmaveer Bhaurao Patil, and Jyotiba Phule decorating its walls. The rising tones of the chant sung in the housewarming ceremony, "Take to heart the sweet advice of Bhimaraya and bow down to Buddha for the emancipation of the whole world. I fly to the refuge of Lord Buddha" (*SH*, 160), create a community distinct from but not separate from the general community of the village, as evident in the mixed assemblage of guests, including high-caste Hindus, whom Bayaji invites to witness what is now freely displayed as his open flaunting of caste norms.

For what Bayaji has done is to reorient space and make the attempted neutralization of the spaces permitted him—the front and back verandas—into communal zones of active collective participation, where guests are accommodated, given due hospitality, and encouraged to join in devotional celebration. Patil's ominous warning to Bayaji that he confine himself to the front and back verandas, with a third restricted space in between as his sole living quarters, is as much a negation of dalit identity as it is also a ruling of control and constriction. As empty, nonlivable space, verandas are the borders of the house wherein regulation occurs; their open, unprotected character makes the house peculiarly vulnerable to official scrutiny. But Bayaji turns these borders from signifying the limits within which he is allowed to function—disarmed and disenfranchised—into sites of potential transformation of social relations; women, for instance, are not withdrawn from public gaze but seated in the front veranda. Nor does he succumb to the regressively separatist compulsion of turning his verandas into exclusionary markers of distance from the rest of the village. Rather, he establishes their continuity with the community organization of Buddhist converts and village elders alike, to all of whom he extends his hospitality under the welcoming embrace of the *pandal*, or ceremonial canopy.

A complex of motives governs Bayaji's impulse to build and that of caste Hindus to destroy. The Hindus' fearful response to Bayaji's conversion, which is construed as aspiration to brahmanical status, is on the same order as their perception that Bayaji's second storey competes for the sharing of power held exclusively by village high castes. Bayaji's Buddhism and the storeyed house crystallize in the caste oppressor's imagination as identical affronts, having their roots in the same impulse to undermine caste Hinduism. As for Bayaji's motives, he claims he is driven to expand by the need for more space, but he also learns that "need" should not be the sole rationale for extending his house and encounters the validity of staking claims to legitimate expansion on the basis of "rights." By the time he constructs his secret loft, his action is clearly no longer based on need alone but deliberately defies proscribed limits, even as it also stays within those limits by removing his transgression from public view. The functional sign-system of the second storey too accretes in meaning. The loft carves out a sacred space that competes with, if it does not entirely displace, the dining area for which he originally set out to build his house. The newly created, shrinelike storey is also that part of the house that Bayaji poignantly attempts to salvage when the flames of the arson consume him.

By means of parable the story exposes the contradictions of postcolonial, secular democracy. Under the democratic regime of the modern Indian state, the conditional assent to dalit enfranchisement mandates that whatever growth occurs in their power and position must be unseen and not challenge the ruling classes. Bayaji's sons, however, will have no part in it. The full transition from needs to rights is marked by their resumption of the murdered Bayaji's house building. This time, however, they will not settle for partial structures invisible from the outside; rather, they establish as their unconditional goal nothing less than a complete second storey, built entirely from the foundations of their home and fully visible to all. Hoval's story replays in imaginative terms the central dynamics of dalit emancipation, and the figure central to it who is both icon and exemplar—B. R. Ambedkar—is accorded the tribute of having raised the stakes for full restitution of rights.

AMBEDKAR AND THE INDIAN NATIONAL CONGRESS

"Mahatmaji, I have no country."[11] These words of exasperation and barely disguised fury were uttered by Ambedkar as he left his first meeting with Gandhi in 1931, a meeting marked by a confrontational intransigence on Gandhi's part to the claims of untouchables on the sharing of political power with the Indian National Congress. Ambedkar's frustrations in throwing his lot with the movement for national independence, while simultaneously fighting for the autonomy of untouchables against the incorporative tendencies of a Brahmin-dominated Indian National Congress, appeared to take the form of split loyalties, which his opponents were swift to exploit as evidence of a factional streak in him.[12] Ambedkar's inflammatory speeches denouncing the caste system rather than the British for having crippled India were, for evident reasons, construed as antinationalist. His public burning of the Hindu code of ethics, the *Manusmriti*, was intended to show that the main enemy of untouchables was Hinduism, not British colonialism. Among Ambedkar's critics perhaps the most scathing was C. Rajagopalachari, who blatantly described Ambedkar's demand for separate electorates for the untouchables as an antinational tactic that undermined the unified efforts of the Indian National Congress to gain independence from Britain. In an openly hostile and partisan attack, Rajagopalachari maintained that Ambedkar was never interested in the political incorporation of dalits into the Indian nation state and that he opposed constitutional provisions for including dalits in the new schedules (from which derives the official appellation of untouchables as "scheduled castes") because he wanted to keep them "isolated." Even more inflammatory was Rajagopalachari's charge that Ambedkar chose passive gestures like conversion, which clearly derailed the dalit platform from real political emancipation, in order to protect his own hold over those whose debased condition was the *raison d'être* of his leadership function. Rajagopalachari saw Ambedkar's resistance to the social reform measures of the Indian National Congress as no different from the apprehension of "Christian and Muslim proselytizers" about reform movements in Hinduism, since such reform would eradicate the exclusionary tendencies from which other religious groups had long benefited in their pursuit of new members.[13]

The main thrust of Rajagopalachari's polemic, however, was directed at what he called Ambedkar's manipulation of the dalit agenda in order to undermine the manifesto of political freedom on which the Indian nationalist movement was based. Without directly alluding to Ambedkar's impending conversion, Rajagopalachari intimated that his separatist demands were divisive because they undermined the Indian National Congress's struggle against British colonialism and indeed capitulated to colonialist manipulation of dissident voices in the Indian subcontinent. Similarly, other critics too, following Rajagopalachari's line, interpreted Ambedkar's declaration to leave Hinduism, made soon after that disastrous meeting with Gandhi, as a petulant response to the compromise formula of reserving seats for dalits rather than allowing them to elect their own representatives, as he had demanded. A number of pamphlets appeared, purportedly by untouchables but sounding suspiciously like Indian National Congress propaganda, which rejected Ambedkar's "pseudo theories" of dalit liberation and denounced him as a stooge of the British, while praising Gandhi's nonpartisanship.[14]

The privileging of Gandhi as an emblem of nonpartisan feeling has, as its inverse, the demonization of Ambedkar as a purveyor of sectarian politics. The view that "the national hagiography in India has rarely conceded a space for Ambedkar alongside Gandhi" is borne out by the amazing excision of Ambedkar from several well-known literary works about untouchability.[15] One of the best known of these, Mulk Raj Anand's *Untouchable* (1935), is written in the time period of Ambedkar's quarrels with Gandhi over the communal award and published in exactly the same year as Ambedkar's decision to convert. The novel is said to have educated the conscience of its English readers about the moral evils of assigning ritual pollution to untouchables and rendering them outsiders, but it makes no mention of Ambedkar at all. Instead, the novel celebrates Gandhi as the savior of the untouchables, whose message of cleanliness and purity is destined to redeem them as "children of God." Anand interprets the complex issues of electoral representation being negotiated in the 1930s from Gandhi's exclusive viewpoint, which interprets separate electorates as a divisive British strategy. In adopting Gandhi's perspective, Anand's narrative alienates and marginalizes the assertion of dalit will, and totally ignores the debate initiated by Ambedkar on the same issue:

"I have emerged," [Gandhi] said slowly . . . "from the ordeal of a penance, under-taken for a cause which is as dear to me as life itself. The British Government sought to pursue a policy of divide and rule in giving to our brethren of the depressed classes separate electorates in the Councils that will be created under the new constitution. I do not believe that the bureaucracy is sincere in its efforts to elaborate the new constitution. But it is one of the conditions under which I have been released from gaol that I shall not carry on any propaganda against the government. So I shall not refer to that matter. I shall only speak about the so-called 'Untouchables,' whom the government tried to alienate from Hinduism by giving them a separate legal and political status."[16]

Unsurprisingly, many of Gandhi's speeches appearing in the novel are taken verbatim from his political writings. It is significant that in the passage just quoted Gandhi admits his political activism has been so circum-scribed by the British government that he can address only the issue of untouchability. Constrained from participating in the agitation for self-rule, he nonetheless continues to fight British colonialism, but now by first making himself representative of the dalits, then selectively appropriating the political demands made by Ambedkar, and finally turning them into issues about the reform of Hinduism. Gandhi's usurpation of the dalit struggle as portrayed in Anand's novel cannot but make readers turn back with renewed interest to a speech Ambedkar delivered in 1927 at Mahad, where he publicly burned the Hindu codebook of social ethics, the *Manusmriti*, and defiantly threw the gauntlet before those who presumed to speak for and act in behalf of untouch-ables: "The task of removing untouchability and establishing equality that we have undertaken, we must carry out ourselves. Others will not do it. Our life will gain its true meaning if we consider that we are born to carry out this task and set to work in earnest."[17] It was also at Mahad that Ambedkar, along with other dalits, demonstrated the people's will to exercise their common civic right to draw public water.

Mulk Raj Anand's description of the untouchable Bakha's expanding vision of an all-embracing unity, which dissolves caste barriers through the mediating influence of Gandhi, partakes of the language of transcendental mysticism, its lofty and liberal sentiments beclouding the possibilities of real political change for untouchables:

There was an insuperable barrier between himself and the crowd, the barrier of caste. He was part of a consciousness which he could share and yet not under-stand. He had been lifted from the gutter, through the barriers of space, to partake of a life which was his, and yet not his. He was in the midst of a humanity which included him in its folds and yet debarred him from entering into a sentient, living, quivering contact with it. Gandhi alone united him with them, in the mind, be-cause Gandhi was in everybody's mind, including Bakha's. Gandhi might unite them really. Bakha waited for Gandhi (*U*, 231).

The most devastating line in this already troublesome passage is the last one, which inscribes Bakha's expected transformation into the trajectory of a Gandhian passive revolution. Bakha's state of anticipation for Gandhi, reiterated in the title of R. K. Narayan's novel *Waiting for the Mahatma*, is represented as not merely a temporal point in the spatialized narrative between "departure" and "arrival" (to use Partha Chatterjee's terms), but an internalization of the projected Gandhian goal of reforming Hinduism to accommodate untouchables.[18] The phrase "in the mind" already depoliticizes the interventionary role of Gandhi, just as Bakha's being lifted "through the barriers of space" detaches him from the material world in which real change is produced. The historical realities of exclusion conceived as physically established and enforced (that is, the denial of entry into temples and Brahmin households) are transmuted into a vague, metaphysical yearning to enter the debarred space of "a sentient, living, quivering contact with [humanity]."

The Penguin edition of *Untouchable* includes an admiring preface by E. M. Forster. It is not surprising that Anand's expansive, metaphysical ambience should have appealed to Forster's own sense of cosmic inscrutability. Forster's preface laces unabashed liberal sentiment ("[The book] has gone straight to the heart of its subject and purified it") with a thin crust of orientalist condescension ("Indians, like most Orientals, are refreshingly frank").[19] Far more unsettling is Forster's narrowing down of the voices that can most suitably author a work on untouchability: "*Untouchable* could only have been written by an Indian, and by an Indian who observed from the outside. No European, however sympathetic, could have created the character of Bakha, because he would not have known enough about his troubles. And no Untouchable could have written the book, because he would have been involved in indignation and self-pity."[20] Forster's dismissal of the untouchable's right to literary self-representation might likewise be dismissed summarily as a thoughtless, insensitive response, were it not for the fact that within that same historical moment, when negotiations were underway for the eventual transfer of power to Indians, untouchables were very much the ground on which fierce debate about electoral representation was fought. The argument that untouchables would not have the necessary aesthetic distance to represent their lives reenacts in literary terms—and in terms of the claims to author one's own narrative—the simultaneous foreclosure of the issue of separate electorates for untouchables. The advocacy of issues involving religious reform, like temple entry and eradication of caste stigmas, brings Gandhi into the center stage, while it simultaneously pushes out both Ambedkar and the demand for self-representation that he made his cause. At the same time that the Poona compromise pact was being forged by Gandhi, the novel produces its own narrative compromise whereby untouchables are resituated solidly within the Hindu fold, a fold that it describes as purged of its casteist features but nonetheless remains intact in structure.

Ambedkar fares no better in Shanta Rameshwar Rao's more recent novel, *Children of God* (1976); he is nowhere to be seen in this work written in English about a female untouchable's encounters with caste prejudice and the beginnings of mobilization of her low-caste community. Instead, Gandhi is the looming figure of importance in their lives. His undertaking of a fast to "atone for the sins of those who put up barriers between people and called their brothers untouchable," while drawing the curiosity of dalits to hear what he has to say, interestingly also introduces a note of skepticism about fasting as atonement.[21] The dalits in the novel clearly see fasting as a false and dishonest appropriation of their experience of gnawing hunger, leave alone an inappropriate strategy of political intervention.[22] Despite its own ideological emphases, a slight undercurrent of resistance marks this work, as it also marks *Untouchable* at one or two points, as when a baffled Bakha observes that "he could not quite understand what fasting had to do with helping the low-castes. 'Probably [Gandhi] thinks we are poor and can't get food . . . so he tries to show that even he doesn't have food for days'" (*U*, 141). Bakha also momentarily expresses his alienation from Gandhi's exhortation to untouchables that they observe sanitary hygiene: "Now the Mahatma is blaming us, Bakha felt. 'That is not fair!'" (*U*, 148). But as in *Untouchable*, where Bakha immediately appends the last quoted line with a conciliatory wish to "forget the last passages that he had heard" (*U*, 148), in Rameshwar Rao's novel the skepticism does not extend so far as to nullify Gandhi's surrogate untouchability. Instead, the dalits' initiative for forming themselves into a political constituency is pulled into the agenda set by Gandhi—in this case, the demand for lifting the ban on temple entry and the right to worship as Hindus. In taking its name from Gandhi's patronizing term for untouchables, *Children of God* reveals its own ideological interests in preserving the national hagiography.[23] The novel's occlusion of Ambedkar is consistent with a certain tradition of writing about untouchability that has roots in the antagonistic rhetoric of the Indian National Congress, which responded to Ambedkar's threat of splitting the leadership with disdain and fear.

DELIBERATING CONVERSION

To return, therefore, to the nationalist debates: although Rajagopalachari's diatribe was too vested in his own brahmanical position to be taken as an objective appraisal of Ambedkar's motives, his trenchancy did raise disturbing questions about Ambedkar's anomalous conversion, seemingly so contrary to the revolutionary potential of the dalit movement. Put on the defensive on all too many occasions, Ambedkar gave lengthy disquisitions on the inequities of caste society as a way of explaining his desire to move out of Hinduism, but he never directly addressed the question of why he chose conversion as his method of mobilizing dalits. For twenty years, he kept people guessing as to which religion he, along with his dalit supporters, was going to convert. In 1956, just a few weeks before he died, Ambedkar led one of the largest mass conversions witnessed in modern history and, by formally adopting Buddhism, fulfilled his promise that though he had no choice in being born a Hindu, he was resolved not to die as one.

Ambedkar's momentous conversion on October 16, 1956 at Nagpur (symbolically chosen as the land of the Nagas, who were ancient converts to Buddhism), was preceded by two decades of frantic maneuvers by Hindu political leaders to persuade him not to leave Hinduism and to work for change within the Hindu structural fold. Ambedkar's unshakable resolve to convert was blatantly read as a crude and vindictive attempt to split Hinduism, as well as disable the consolidating strength of the dalit movement. The cynicism with which his resolution was received accentuated the point that, by converting to Buddhism, Ambedkar and his followers sought the identity of a distinct religious minority group that had no special, favored status under the law, though under the earlier personal law officially recognized by the British, Buddhism was categorized as an offshoot of Hinduism, as were Sikhism and Jainism.[24] But in his speech at Nagpur on October 15, 1956, on the eve of what has come to be known as the "Great Conversion," Ambedkar defended himself against charges that by leading his followers away from their now constitutionally recognized status as "untouchables," he was gravely disadvantaging them at a time when compensatory legislation was being considered for the officially named "scheduled castes." None of his opponents had the courage to deny that conversion to Buddhism offered Ambedkar a way out of the hateful hold of caste prejudice. Nevertheless, they tried to press upon him that his renunciation of Hinduism was invariably at the cost of also renouncing new measures incorporating the dalit classes under the schedules proposed by the Indian Constitution, in the writing of which Ambedkar himself was a key figure.

Why then, in this secular climate of emancipatory legislation, did Ambedkar choose conversion as his favored mode of leading the dalits to political equality, while many of his own followers preferred a combination of organizational strength and constitutionalist methods to promote upward social mobility? And why Buddhism in particular rather than the more obvious alternatives, Islam or Christianity? Most important of all, why did Ambedkar reject the Marxist model of fighting social inequities and take what must surely appear on the surface to be a regressive step in turning to religion for liberating purposes? After all, the Marxist route was the chosen alternative of many groups similarly oppressed by caste discrimination, particularly in south India; the iconoclast Periyar E.V.R. Naicker launched his anticaste "Self-Respect" movement in Madras presidency under the banner of atheism, and denounced all religions as essentially discriminatory.

Recent critical approaches to Ambedkar's conversion are as disparate as his contemporaries' interpretations of his motives. By and large, the split is straight down the line, dividing the private from the public, the spiritual from the political. Critics like Gail Omvedt see Ambedkar's religious conversion as purely reactive, a mode of mass mobilization of dalits to retrieve them from the hostility of caste Hindus on the one hand and, on the other, the refusal of political groups like the Communist party to regard caste and religious oppression as distinctly separate from class factors.[25] In this reading, Ambedkar's conversion is a political stunt, albeit a highly successful one, which altered forever the demographic equation between religious groups. The population of Buddhists in India increased dramatically with the mass conversions of dalits, from the figure of 141,426 given in the 1951 Census to 3,206,142 in the 1961 Census.[26] Most mass conversions, including the 1981 large-scale conversions of scheduled caste groups to Islam in the southern town of Meenakshipuram, continue to be attributed to political motivation and the desire for social mobility.[27]

At the other extreme are interpretations of Ambedkar's conversion as an entirely spiritual event connected to the discovery of moral truths that had the power to liberate oppressed dalits. Critics who take this view are prone to emphasize Ambedkar's early-childhood influences, particularly pious parents who enveloped his life with the music and poetry of Hindu saints in the belief that Marathi saint-poets like Moropant, Mukteshwar, and Tukaram were saviors of the poor and the lowly. Rosalind O'Hanlon's comprehensive study of Jyotirao Phule traces the lines of influence of these saint-poets on the formation of a collective religious sensibility in dalit homes.[28] Of particular appeal was the devotional bhakti school of Kabir, which sought to abolish the inflexibility of the caste system and initiate an unmediated relation between devotee and deity.

The cultural mythology of dalit households often borrowed from archetypal images of the past in which religious dissenters were central figures. One such powerful image for a dalit liberation theology is provided by Nandanar, the "dalit martyr" of twelfth-century south India who, claiming the right to worship as an equal, inaugurated an activist tradition of protest from below against the Hindu refusal to admit untouchables into temples.[29] The *Periyapuranam*, a medieval Tamil epic of Shaivite hagiography, records the history of Nandanar as a worshiper in the bhakti tradition of personal devotion who repudiated the "right" of caste Hindus to debar him, as a member of the despised Pulaiya caste, from participating in temple worship because of his ritual impurity.[30] As the backbone of the production process, the Pulaiyas formed the major labor force in the village of Adanur where Nandanar was born. And yet they had no share either in the wealth created through their labor or in the right of worship in the Shiva temple where they performed hereditary services, including the supplying of skin coverings and leather straps for making temple drums. Nandanar was consumed by restless ambition to transgress the physical boundaries preventing untouchables from securing darshan, or gaining sight of the divine image. However, his goal was not confined to entering the Shiva temple in his own village. His drive extended also to the forbidden space of ritual worship in other places, from the Shivaloganadar temple at Tiruppungur to the Nataraja temple in Chidambaram. Nandanar's extended geographical pursuit of his right to worship recasts the traditional pilgrimage of Hindu life into a form of active political resistance.

But there is an interesting twist to this tale of transgression. When Nandanar's story "enters" (the pun is deliberate) the Tamil literary tradition, the rebel-activist of history is made to undergo a "conversion": he becomes a mythological figure who gains access to direct, unmediated worship only after his caste-oppressed, "impure" Pulaiya body enters a fire-bath, turns to ashes, and emerges from the sacrificial fire as a Brahmin sage. His purification is dramatically staged as semiosis, the sacred thread and tuft of hair atop his head iconically signifying his transformation into a Brahmin:

> "To get rid of this birth," the Lord said,
> Divine into a fire,
> and come out with the chest adorned
> by the thread of three strands,
> and come forward."[31]

The baptismal ordeal by fire, with its obvious parallels to the (foiled) Sita story in the Hindu epic *The Ramayana*, establishes the links between the oppression of dalits and women, even as it leaves intact the bhakti tradition of celebrating personal, unmediated devotion without altering the caste (and patriarchal) structure. For dalits, the perplexing challenge presented by the Nandanar story—of both reclaiming history and dismantling the coercive hold of mainstream literary narrative—is suspended, however, by critical approaches that rewrite Nandanar into a spiritual tradition consonant with bhakti, or a tradition of religious feeling that emphasizes the individual's personal relationship to God.

Another historical model for the definitive possibilities of realizing a compassionate, egalitarian religion is the central one of the emperor Ashoka, whose conversion to Buddhism in the third century B.C. is seen as marking the beginnings of an era of tolerance, justice, and service to humanity. Ambedkar's uncanny sense of the symbolic led him to choose October 16 as the date of his conversion, since this date is traditionally associated with Ashoka's conversion to Buddhism. Ambedkar's position in the constitution-drafting committee enabled him to press for the incorporation of the Buddhist wheel of law (the *dharma chakra*) in the national flag, as well as the adoption by the Constituent Assembly of the lions from an Ashokan pillar at Sarnath as the

4. B. R. Ambedkar, chief architect of the Indian constitution, presents a copy of the completed constitution to the prime minister and the president of India. From a popular poster; photo courtesy of Christopher Queen

national emblem. Ambedkar is often referred to in this literature as the "Ashoka of modern India," whose rejection of militant solutions to caste oppression and embrace of a nonviolent religious ethic are "a triumph of the spiritual side of this noble and sensitive soul."[32]

Whether the focus is on the literary or the historical tradition, either line of scholarly inquiry seeks to reclaim Ambedkar from the main role assigned him by history as chief architect of the Indian constitution and political leader of the untouchables. This move places him instead as one of the most significant interpreters and practitioners of Buddhism in recent times. Yet this approach too is flawed in many respects. The relevance of Ambedkar's conversion to the construction of his cherished national community, most visibly in his writing of the Indian constitution, remains marginalized, as is all too clear in the divorce between Ambedkar the politician and Ambedkar the commentator of Buddhist texts.[33] This split continues to be observed by modern scholars of Indian history in their own work.

Linking his two roles, one of the most compelling interpretations of Ambedkar's conversion is offered by Christopher Queen, who reads both Ambedkar's life and his conversion as a move from premodernity to modernity. From being a lowly untouchable whose "destiny" it was to endure the strictures of Hindu caste society, Ambedkar *chose* to leave Hinduism and embrace Buddhism, and in that act, Queen suggests, he fulfilled one of the conditions of modernity: the exercise of individual choice based on reason, careful deliberation, and historical consciousness. The injunction toward skepticism is one that Ambedkar took very seriously, as when he wrote: "In his [the Buddha's] opinion nothing was infallible and nothing could be final. Everything must be open to re-examination and reconsideration, whenever grounds for re-examination and reconsideration arise."[34] Ambedkar was as meticulous as his predecessor John Henry Newman in exploring choices. We may recall how carefully and in what minute detail Newman considered the attractions of Roman Catholicism in an increasingly centralized and pluralistic England, where legislated identities usurped self-definitions. Likewise Ambedkar, after systematically studying available alternatives for creating an ethical nation that would guarantee fundamental rights to his fellow dalits, finally adopted Buddhism as the faith that met his complex requirements of reason, morality, and justice. But having announced his choice of Buddhism, Ambedkar, as Queen points out, "went on to become the paradigm of postmodern man, who is driven not only to choose a religious tradition, but to dismantle and reassemble it, with scraps of faith and practice from the past, the present, and the imagined future."[35]

The core of Ambedkar's "discovery" of Buddhism lies in his own rewriting of Buddhist precepts to achieve the goals of dalit emancipation; *The Buddha and His Dhamma* (1957) stands as his most complete exposition of an older tradition updated to suit the complex requirements of a modern, secular India. Richard Taylor's inspired comparison of Ambedkar's compilation of *The Buddha and His Dhamma* with his work on the Indian constitution suggests how both documents were carefully reassembled to express the religious and political life of the community: the first, from selectively highlighted Buddhist precepts; and the other, from aspects of American, British, and Indian law.[36] Although conversion to Buddhism, no doubt, is an important emphasis of the traditional text, Ambedkar makes it absolutely central to the reworked structure he gives the Buddha's teachings. Parts 6, 7, and 8 of Book II of *The Buddha and His Dhamma* are carefully reorganized to fall into symmetrical parts covering not only the conversion of "sinful" people like Brahmins, criminals, and other fallen beings, but also the conversion of women and oppressed social classes. Ambedkar's reinvented Buddhism has long been a troublesome issue to traditional Buddhists, who find missing in his commentary some of the fundamental precepts of Buddhism, such as the Four Noble Truths; karma and reincarnation; the emphasis on monasticism; the otherworldly dimensions of time and space; and the notion of suffering as the product of ego attachments. Right at the outset, in his introduction to *The Buddha and His Dhamma*, Ambedkar submits the Four Noble Truths to particularly strong attack; he describes their resigned attitude to sorrow as a product of Aryanism, which gives people nothing more than a "gospel of pessimism" that expects them to endure the gross injustices of their present existence. Ambedkar eliminates these "Truths" altogether, believing that of all the obstacles to the acceptance of Buddhism by non-Brahmins, none was a greater stumbling block than these Four Noble Truths.

Out of the Buddhism of the classical texts Ambedkar reconstructs a pragmatic code book of social morality that offers what he believed classical Marxism also offered, but without the stable structure of identity that a social ethic, on the other hand, was able to provide. For example, in a somewhat whimsical essay called "Buddha or Karl Marx," Ambedkar defends Buddhism as a precursor to Marxism in a number of respects, notably its emphasis on the abolition of private property, the linking of suffering with social exploitation and poverty, and the antipathy toward an otherworldliness that sanctions the endurance of poverty.[37] On this last point, he cites the Buddha's sermon to Anathapindika on the virtues of collective economic prosperity as an example of the Buddhist exhortation to followers to embrace a materialist ethic.

But in Ambedkar's reading, Buddhism parts company with Marxism in the latter's proven failure to change the moral disposition, even though it may succeed in altering the economic relations within society. In a neo-Gramscian definition of ideology, Ambedkar claimed that the Buddha's way "was to alter the disposition of men so that they would do voluntarily what they would not otherwise do." But despite his tendency (deliberate or otherwise) to describe Buddhism as an ideology rather than a religious system, Ambedkar saw little kinship between a Buddhist hermeneutic practice and Marxist critique. His increasing antipathy to Marxist rhetoric manifests itself even in his refusal to refer to Marxism by its own name; rather, Marxism is designated as "the Permanent Dictatorship." An unlikely mentor is invoked by Ambedkar to refute Marx, and in Thomas Carlyle he approvingly finds an alternative figure whose social criticism of economic disparities is buttressed by a call to spiritual values. Ambedkar, however, also takes issue with Carlyle for calling political economy a "pig philosophy," yet he uses that metaphoric description simultaneously against Marxism when he writes: "Carlyle was of course wrong. For man needs material comforts. But the Communist philosophy seems to be equally wrong, for the aim of their philosophy seems to be to fatten pigs as though men are no better than pigs. Man must grow materially as well as spiritually."[38]

Ambedkar's invocation of Carlyle is of more than incidental interest, since the spiritual values upheld by his nineteenth-century predecessor derive from what John Rosenberg describes as Carlyle's fitful move "from conversion to revolution."[39] This description understands political consciousness as a dialectical leap that shifts in focus from a selfhood overwhelmed by despair to an exploited underclass oppressed by material circumstance. But differences between Carlyle's conversion and that of Ambedkar are quite striking. For Carlyle, religious experience is newly translated in political terms, the "transcendental despair" of the self being experienced expansively as a social disorder. At the same time, he represents the French Revolution as the historical fulfillment of the individual struggle to gain legitimacy for new values and reorder social relationships. For Ambedkar, on the other hand, religious experience is *constitutively* political. The advent of the Buddha and the conversions of women, outcastes, and the rich alike to Buddhism in classical Indian history occur during a period of crisis brought on by corruption, material disparities, and widespread neglect of collective responsibilities. The spiritual impoverishment of brahmanical Hinduism produced not metaphysical despair but a profound sense of injustice, which Ambedkar clearly saw as the heart of the Buddhist conversion experience.

For Ambedkar, the idea of "moral disposition" was closely intertwined with notions of rational choice, cultural identity, and self-renewal. And indeed, his great fear was that a secular and materialist response to factors of class and caste annihilated dalits' consciousness of their own past, besides inducing a cultural paralysis that held them back from actively claiming an identity for themselves. One of Ambedkar's allies, Kisan Phagoji Bansod, who opposed his decision to convert in 1935, found him too obsessed with reclaiming culture and not sufficiently concerned with analyzing conditions of material oppression. However, by insisting that his opposition to Ambedkar's conversion did not signify an acceptance of Hinduism, Bansod's attack showed how necessary such defensive assertions were in a movement where the repudiation of casteism was considered possible only by conversion. Ambedkar was critical of the dalit tendency to combine with peasant movements, but he was equally rejecting of Gandhi's insistence that they remain within the Hindu fold. Ambedkar's alienation from both the materialist rhetoric of dalit ideology and the accommodating gestures of Hindu social reformers has been read by some critics as embodying the classic disjunction between the positions of a "troubled insider" and a "struggling victim."[40]

The appeal of the Buddha's *dhamma* for Ambedkar was, again, its emphasis on the element of rational choice. The Buddha's mode of instruction was not to compel people to act in ways not of their own choosing, but to alter their *disposition* so that they would be prepared, through a combination of rationality, morality, and social consciousness, to take action out of reasoned volition. Ambedkar described religion as a means of "universalizing" social values that "brings them to the mind of the individual who is required to recognize them in all his acts in order that he may function as an approved member of the society."[41] The potential of a Buddhist ethic for dalit praxis captured Ambedkar's imagination as no other social philosophy had. His most subversive, "antinational" statement at Yeola, where he first announced his decision to leave Hinduism, consisted of exhorting his dalit followers to regard their religious identity as something they had the right to choose, and not a fate to which they were irretrievably doomed. No other single statement of his roused Gandhi to anger in the same way, and he dismissed the claim that one may choose one's religious identity by retorting, "Religion is not like a house or a cloak, which can be changed at will. It is a more integral part of one's self than one's own body. . . . A change of faith . . . will not serve the cause which [Ambedkar and the untouchables] have at their heart, . . . especially when it is remembered that their lives for good or for evil are intervolved [*sic*] with those of caste Hindus."[42]

It is precisely the nature of this "intervolving" that Ambedkar sought to disentangle by converting to Buddhism and creating the basis for alternative nationalist politics, which took into account the double deracination that non-elite Indians suffered as victims of both caste and colonialism. The clearest demonstration of what Christopher Queen calls Ambedkar's postmodern technique of dismantling and reassembling is found in his 1948 publication, *The Untouchables*. Quite unlike the work of a trained political scientist, Ambedkar's monograph on the origins of untouchability shows little inclination to demonstrate a scientific temperament; rather, drawing on a typology that recalls mythological description, it retells the story of untouchability as a product of religious conflict. Gail Omvedt makes the important observation that, although Ambedkar subscribed to certain Marxist descriptions of ideology and economic relations, he reversed the base-superstructure model to give primacy to the superstructure, of which religious factors were fundamentally important.[43] Instead of falling back on a theory of caste oppression as determined by economic disparities, Ambedkar interpreted religious difference as having an equally material effect in explaining the nature of social oppression. Buddhism's attraction for him lay in the link it enabled him to draw between the advent of untouchability and the spread of Buddhism. In his treatise, the untouchables are recast as "Broken Men" who converted to Buddhism in 400 A.D. and were ostracized by caste Hindus following the conquest of Buddhism by brahmanism.[44] As Buddhists who showed no interest in venerating Brahmins or employing them as priests, these "Broken Men" were tyrannized by

Hindus, and were further made to feel impure because they continued to eat beef after the practice had been abolished in Hinduism. The determined refusal by the "Broken Men" to return to brahmanism when it triumphed over Buddhism, for which they were punished with the stigma of untouchability, creates for the dalits a history in which they are agents and not merely victims buffeted by the forces of economic change. In believing that conversion to Buddhism would restore to dalits an agency that untouchability had eroded, Ambedkar brilliantly provided a religious framework for a politics of dalit renewal. Indeed, one of his main objections to Gandhi's offer to "purify" Hinduism of its discriminatory practices, in exchange for Ambedkar's commitment to stay within the Hindu fold, was that such an offer assumed untouchability was a problem internal to Hinduism and confined active agency to caste Hindus. Ambedkar's conversion to Buddhism aimed at challenging precisely this assumption; to the extent that it unsettled the complacency of Hindu reformers, who believed the initiative for social change lay exclusively with them, it must certainly be adjudged successful.

Even more importantly, by reinserting the "central" chapter of the struggle for supremacy between Buddhism and brahmanism into the narrative history of India, in which both caste Hindus and those known henceforth as untouchables were key players, Ambedkar fundamentally challenged the Indian National Congress's representation of the dalit political demands as separatist, antinational, and therefore undermining of the struggle against British colonialism. On the contrary, as he affirmed in a speech delivered in 1944 before the Madras Rationalist Society, the ascendancy of brahmanism held back the empiricist and epistemological advances made by Buddhism toward laying the foundation for a "new and modern India." Just as certainly, brahmanism returned India to a more benighted scripturalism from which a truly moral, political community could not be forged. Ambedkar's explanation for the colonial subordination of India to England was precisely that the closed system of brahmanism prevented the consolidation of organic communities based on principles of justice and equality, which alone would have been able to resist colonial aggressiveness. Indeed, the crowning achievement of Ambedkar's writings was the identification of Buddhism with enlightened nationhood—a historical possibility that clearly existed in ancient India but was thwarted by Hindu casteism. The theory that the nation had failed to come into its own as a result of the tenacious hold of brahmanism enabled Ambedkar to turn to ancient Buddhism as the prototype of a rational, modern nation state and, in the process, identify himself as a loyal Indian. In much the same way that John Henry Newman turned to pre-Reformation Catholicism to recover the foundational structure of Englishness, Ambedkar turned to an originating moment in Indian history—the spread of Buddhism—to reclaim a redemptive cultural identity not only for dalits but for all Indians.

The modernism of Buddhism is reiterated in many dalit writings, but as the following passage by dalit intellectual and literary figure Baburao Bagul might illustrate, the relation between Buddhism and democracy is less persuasively argued than Buddhism's claims to rationality:

> Buddhism is dynamic, progressive, revolutionary and atheistic. Unlike theism and spiritualism, it cannot be the protagonist of a static absolutism. Buddha's philosophy could have led society to democracy with the help of its basic principles. And when democracy is internalised to form a part of consciousness, the common man cannot remain untouchable, neglected or contemptible even if there is economic inequality and even though power is in the hands of the rich. The ordinary human being can be an object of thought. This had happened in Buddhism. That is the reason why the neglected sections of society have found a place in *Ther* and *Therigathas*. The point is that mythical values orient consciousness and also art and literature.[45]

Bagul presents an interesting though flawed argument, which ironically ends up explaining the impeded progress of Buddhism in ancient India far more successfully than it does Buddhism's sustaining power. First, however, he ascribes a dynamism to Buddhism that is not merely confined to its adaptability to the demanding requirements of a complex modernity. Rather, Buddhism's appeal to dalits lies in the kinetic transfer of precepts of justice and equality, drawn from an ethical system of moral laws, to the political infrastructure of democracy. But Bagul's use of consciousness as the means by which democracy is made a personal ethic begs the question of why values of social justice can only be disseminated through the political system and not through the originating system of Buddhism itself, since it is through consciousness, after all, that he believes secular, egalitarian principles are internalized. Why are political forms at all necessary if "mythical [ethical?] values orient consciousness"? Having phrased his argument in these terms, Bagul cannot forestall the inference that Buddhism's role is dispensed with once it communicates its principles to the political system. This explains not so much Buddhism's relation to democracy as its decline and subsequent defeat by brahmanism.

For his part, Ambedkar tries to avoid the problem of consciousness altogether. His own disclaimer that his philosophy has roots in religion (specifically, the teachings of the Buddha) and not in political science seeks to revive Buddhism from a vanquished condition in Indian history. At the same time, in reading Buddhism as the ideal basis of modern Indian democracy, Ambedkar cannot fully escape the critical question of how the values of religion become the values of politics. Morever, he felt a profound need to project a conception of religion that is not purely foundational in a passive sense. After all, Hinduism survived so long precisely because its caste system buttressed a hierarchical system of governance. His search for a religious conception that also actively shapes the moral contours of government resulted in his issuing a call for reordered religious values with a new infusion of democratic principles, a process that he describes as a "conversion": "You must give a new doctrinal basis to your religion—a basis that will be in consonance with Liberty, Equality, and Fraternity, in short, with Democracy. It means a complete change in outlook and in attitude towards men and things. It means conversion."[46] Given Ambedkar's unease with religion as received dogma, it is no wonder that he preferred to refer to Buddhism not as a religion but as dhamma—as right relations between people in social and political life. Ambedkar's dhamma occupies a space between politics and religion that perhaps may have served his purposes of detaching religion from dogma, but also left unelaborated the precise means by which the norms of one sphere influenced the other.

THE AMBIVALENCE OF NATIONAL IDENTITY

But even while Ambedkar sought to rewrite Buddhism into a liberation theology for dalits, it is also clear that Buddhism was made to carry added cultural weight in order to establish the appropriateness of converting to this faith rather than Islam, Christianity, Sikhism, or Jainism, which are the other possibilities he considered. Though all his postures indicated an abiding and irreversible decision to sever himself and his fellow dalits from all ties that bound them to Hinduism, he was never able fully to unfasten the link that he believed existed between Hinduism and India. Just as much as John Henry Newman, Ambedkar was not able to escape the alluring discourse of nationality. At no time did Ambedkar seriously entertain Islam or Christianity as real choices; his writings and speeches abound with references to these as "foreign" religions, alien to India and further alienating to already deracinated subjects.[47] His dismissal of Islam and Christianity as religions that threatened to "denationalize" untouchables by extending the hold of foreign powers spurned transnational alliances as a mode of consolidating dalit power.

Apart from Buddhism, the only other religion Ambedkar seriously considered was Sikhism. But he also confessed he was drawn to this religion primarily because it was "in the interest of the country" and untouchables would not then have to forsake Indian culture if they converted.[48] Preserving "Indian culture," "Indianness," and "Indian nationality" must surely appear a strange ambition in one who bitterly told Gandhi, "I have no country." But although Ambedkar's twenty-year study of comparative religions to decide which religion he would embrace was undertaken almost like a scientific project—and conducted very publicly—the tenterhooks on which he kept Hindu leaders for years gradually disappeared when even they realized Ambedkar's ambiva-

lence in leaving not the Hindu fold but the fold of Indianness with which
Hinduism was so obstinately identified. When Ambedkar finally converted to
Buddhism in 1956, most Hindus breathed a sigh of relief, because in their view
Buddhism did not pose a threat or a challenge to the concept of a predominantly Hindu India, which Islam or Christianity certainly did. Many even went
so far as to argue, on the claim that the Buddha was the ninth incarnation of the
Hindu god Vishnu, that Ambedkar's conversion was perfectly compatible with
Hindu culture and tradition. It has been suggested that "the cooptation of Ambedkar into the Hindu fold is being carried out with considerable sophistica-
tion by the Hindutvawadi forces on the one hand and on the other some Buddhist groups are doing their best to strip Ambedkar's ideology of its political
content."[49] However, the implication that the spiritualization of Ambedkar's
Buddhism is both a strategy of Hinduization and a reversion to the same traditional Buddhist ethics Ambedkar rejected creates a false polarization between
religion and politics. Indeed, it was Ambedkar's special objective to undo
precisely this dichotomy.

If Hindus were so little ruffled by Ambedkar's final act, it would suggest
that the liberating potential of Buddhism for dalits held no such subversive
meaning for Hindus. Equally, it would suggest that the radical, revisionist
possibilities of Ambedkar's conversion were neutralized by his difficulties in
disentangling Hinduism from the concept "India." As an incomplete project,
his conversion was unable effectively to negotiate the split between religious
and national identity, despite its success in providing an ethics of cultural
self-renewal.

A striking example of the contradictions in Ambedkar's thought is his position on temple entry. Although there was already a significant split within
modern Hinduism between the Gandhian idealization of the temple and the
antitemple radicalism of Hindu intellectuals like Rabindranath Tagore, which
it would have been easy for Ambedkar to exploit, he was less interested in
combining with the iconoclasm of the latter group than in demanding access
to the structure symbolizing the very object that dalits were fighting against:
namely, Hinduism. The intense energies he poured into the temple-entry
movement were so obsessive that it is clear that at some crucial point the
struggle for temple entry was conflated into an act of reclaiming a *cultural*, not
religious, symbol representing the whole of India. An inherent ambivalence
that generally informed his attitude to Hinduism carried over into his fight to
gain dalits entry into the religious space of Hindu worship, where, it has to be
admitted, he was far less successful than when fighting a secular civil rights
issue like securing access to public water.

Ambedkar's other great ambivalence lay in his attitude toward authority,
particularly the authority of the state. On one hand, he was quite settled in the
conviction that the secular Indian state, emerging from the ashes of colonialism, was incapable of providing a positive cultural identity to the underclasses,

least of all by electoral means. Nor did he did believe that the problem of untouchability and caste discrimination could be solved through legislation or by getting representation in the legislature. His rejection of the state was complete insofar as he believed that untouchables would never secure their full rights within a political system dominated by a Hindu majority. Following the defeat of his demand for separate electorates for untouchables, Ambedkar turned his back on institutionalized social measures:

> Any electoral arrangement, I believe, cannot be a solution of the larger social problems. It requires more than any political arrangement and I hope that it would be possible for you to go beyond this political arrangement that we are making today [of joint electorates] and devise ways and means whereby it would be possible for the Depressed Classes not only to be part and parcel of the Hindu community but also to occupy an honorable position, a position of equality of status in the community.[50]

Elsewhere, in "States and Minorities," Ambedkar deplored the fact that throwing off the British yoke did not result in a value-based democratic society committed to equality but merely perpetuated the political structure of hierarchical constraints introduced by British colonialism: "The soul of Democracy is the doctrine of one man, one value. Unfortunately, Democracy has attempted to give effect to this doctrine only so far as the political structure is concerned by adopting the rule of one man, one vote. . . . It has left the economic structure to take the shape given by those who are in a position to mould it."[51]

Ambedkar's conversion, along with the conversions of his followers, sounded the death knell for any hopes that the state would be an agent for social change. Yet, despite his loss of faith in the secular state as a potential ally in the lifting of disabilities under which untouchables had labored for centuries, one of Ambedkar's primary objections to Marxist philosophy was its belief that the crowning moment of world history would witness the withering away of the state. The fear of anarchy as a successor to the ultimate dissolution of the state so gripped Ambedkar that he found himself reasserting the need for some system of authority to ensure the continuing presence of moral laws. Though he may have blandly believed that "the only thing which can sustain [class struggle] after force is withdrawn is Religion," it is ironic that the position ultimately affirmed by him maintained that the social values "universalized" by religion could only be protected by the state.[52] So that even as Ambedkar despaired of the state being the source of fundamental rights for untouchables, he turned to that self-same state to provide the stable authority through which the nation's moral life would be ensured.

The ambivalence toward state authority in Ambedkar's work reenacts a split between the *separatism* of his call for protection of dalits' rights and the *universalism* of his appeal for the dissemination of religious and social values, which the Buddhist dhamma embodied for him. On the issue of political representation, Ambedkar never yielded to the suggestion that dalits would be given the right to full political participation under the rule of a Hindu majority, no matter how democratic the existing political apparatus. And in tracing the disenfranchisement of untouchables to an indifferent British government that, "in the manner of the Chinese tailor who when given an old coat as a pattern, produced with pride an exact replica, rents, patches, and all," Ambedkar was scathing in his indictment of a double colonialism at work.[53] Some of Ambedkar's bitterest language is reserved for British rulers who, despite their reformist rhetoric, were never prepared to make the practice of untouchability a penal offense nor undertake the large-scale education of untouchables and place them in positions of authority.[54] By contrast, English-educated Indians, secular and cosmopolitan in their outlook, were disaffiliating themselves from their Hindu and Muslim belief systems while retaining their religious identities to organize themselves politically.

Ambedkar's litany of continuing civil disabilities under the British, which were now only further aggravated by the untouchables' having to pay taxes to the British for what Hindus refused to allow them to use, reveals the gross discrepancy between the British discourse of reform and Britain's accommodation of the hierarchical structure of Hindu society. It is no wonder that in his memorandum to the Round Table Conference, Ambedkar categorically demanded the total removal of all civil disabilities as the first right of citizenship, preceding all other electoral calculations or conferral of political power.[55] Ambedkar ripped apart the British ideology of partial assimilation of colonial subjects, especially those already secularized through English education, whose status as Hindus or Muslims had preemptively been neutralized rather than enfranchised. The colonial situation was, of course, unlike the case in nineteenth-century England, where the secularization process was set in motion by the lifting of punitive restrictions against non-Anglican groups. The stalled enfranchisement of colonial subjects had its most deleterious effects on the untouchables, who remained consigned to the status of subjects rather than citizens long after the first concessions in self-rule.

Ambedkar's sustained and uncompromising critique of brahmanism was not blind to the role of British colonialism in reinforcing brahmanical ideology. Indeed, one of the most persistent themes in his work is the collusion between brahmanism and colonialism in assuming to represent the general interests, while denying popular participation and thereby an order based on fundamental claims. His analogies between a colonial ideology that drained resources from the colony and a caste ideology that lived off the labor of outcaste groups are consistent with his rhetorical strategy of conflating disparate historical moments within a single frame, in order not only to illuminate the interchangeability of British colonialism and brahmanism but also expose the claims of an ideology negated by its own practices.

But Ambedkar's anticolonialism also veered off in independent directions, and did not—could not—participate in the ritual celebrations of a pure Indianness indulged in by nationalist narratives, of which the Indian village was a perfect example. For Gandhi, the village was the basis for building a republican society uncontaminated by colonialist ideology, but for Ambedkar, it was the black hole of Indian civilization. Gandhi's antimodern, anti-urban bias was oblivious to the fact that for the dalits, the village and the village *panchayat* (council) structure could never be an embodiment of justice. Equally, to remain in the village meant remaining tied to the same humiliating occupations that had so far been their fate.[56]

After the disaster of the separate electorates, Ambedkar was forced to rethink his strategies for dalit empowerment. At one level he now changed his tune to maintain that the dalits' right to equality was only realizable through their leaving the Hindu fold, even if that meant renouncing constitutional provisions for "scheduled castes" as certified members of Hinduism. But even as he contemplated this separatist move, he recast his idea of nationhood in a contrary direction. Based on an overarching unity of the religious values of brotherhood, equality, and freedom (which he found in the dhamma of Buddhism), Ambedkar's idea of the nation required a centralized, unitary state to prevent these values from becoming marginalized at best or becoming the exclusive preserve of a few at worst. A strong state is also essential to deter the relegation of morality to the realm of private experience, where religious values can well become the guarded possession of a separate religious group. In this description, Ambedkar was clearly thinking of the historical course of Hinduism, which he saw as having consolidated itself by patronizing a set of moral norms and institutionalizing them in the caste system. More importantly, the effect of Hindu casteism is the balkanization of communities which are thus derailed from organizing themselves into a modernizing nation.

Ambedkar's conversion to Buddhism, which shows all signs of having roots in a separatist impulse, is nonetheless the base from which he sought to reconstruct a national community. This move redefines rights not in terms of political franchise alone but primarily moral claims. Where Ambedkar parted company with Gandhi on what seemed to be a shared objective was in the latter's conviction that untouchability was a Hindu problem that had to be tackled within the terms of Hindu social reform. For Ambedkar, the moral horror of untouchability could only be abolished by an alternative religious framework from which were derived the social principles that recognized untouchability as a *moral* offense against India's historical mission as exemplar of rationality, justice, and right conduct. These values were ideally embodied in the figures of the Buddha and the emperor Ashoka. Ambedkar had earlier insisted on legislative measures against untouchability, and, while not abandoning the path of legislation altogether, he now acknowledged that legal measures did not alter the caste structure of Hinduism but merely established the limits of caste prejudice. If Ambedkar exhorted untouchables to leave Hinduism for cultural self-renewal, he conceived of that departure not as a withdrawal into an autonomous space but as a prerequisite to reclaiming India as the nation from which untouchables had been severed by political disenfranchisement. As is evident, Ambedkar's nationalism struggled to release itself from the stranglehold of Hinduism and relocate national identity in alternative religious systems, for which, as I suggested earlier, a new historical mythology of brahmanism, Buddhism, and "Broken Men" was pressed into service.

The construction of a moral community emerges as Ambedkar's most fundamental motive for conversion. As such, his departure from Hinduism cannot be said to be merely a reactive gesture. But the final goal of his conversion—the assertion of a "fundamental oneness of all things"[57]—enters into such a realm of abstraction that the vital link he seeks to establish between an ethics of social equality and a newly imagined modernized nation cannot altogether dispense with forms of authority derived from earlier political systems. He is firm in his conviction that political rights can issue only from a reconstructed community whose structural origin is neither the British system of limited representation nor the reformed system of Hinduism, purged of its casteist features. Indeed, one of Ambedkar's most radical gestures was to deny that the rights of untouchables would be adequately protected by a government characterized by structural continuity with previous systems of authority. However, although the Buddhist dhamma provided the moral authority for the reclamation of full rights by untouchables, Ambedkar could find no means of disseminating the values of the alternative ethical system he envisioned for India as a whole, other than by utilizing existing forms of centralized state authority.

This is not to say he conceived of a theocratic Buddhist state. Rather, in seeking to make the ethics of Buddhism part of the democratic principles of the modern nation state, Ambedkar was drawn back into the political apparatus of a parliamentary democracy in which such concepts as popular representation, electorates, and the franchise were already too fraught with hierarchical constraints to be viable. The translation of moral laws into political rights, for which conversion functions as a trope, is more completely worked out as a strategic maneuver of dissent, which required Ambedkar to go through a separatist route to attain a nation committed to the universalist principles of justice and equality. That the principal architect of the Indian constitution was obliged to traverse such a tortuous route to create the political charter of his ideal nation state suggests the vast gap between his vision and the collective aspirations that the written document was intended to reflect.

CHAPTER EIGHT

Epilogue: The Right to Belief

IF THE RIGHT to individual belief is the remaining, indeed only visible form of religion in modernity, the chief challenge lies in protecting that right without reducing religious subjectivity to sentiment or affect. In the absence of any acknowledgment of the centrality of belief in self-constitution, or what I have been describing as "worldliness," religion in the public sense of the word can have no meaning other than as an object of transgression. The most obvious instance, in my mind, is that of blasphemy. When offense is offered as proof of religion's public existence, then it confirms what Talal Asad has all along described as religion's universal definition in belief: not a form of dynamic activity capable of producing knowledge, but an ideological collection of propositions commanding assent.

It is on the site of blasphemy that religion's shifting definitions can most sharply be discerned. Once considered a relic of the benighted Middle Ages, the word blasphemy is enjoying something of a popular revival today. This is not because it has its own particular currency as an ongoing practice but because it has usefulness in providing an index of the uneven development of world societies. The presumed archaism of blasphemy is invoked to separate cultures of modernity from those of premodernity, as if to suggest that blasphemy is operative today only in the Third World. In addition, the term is deployed to measure the status of laws guaranteeing fundamental liberties of speech and the degree of tolerance that civil societies are inclined to show. It is no accident that two recent, identically titled books on blasphemy, David Lawton's *Blasphemy* and Leonard Levy's *Blasphemy*, though written from very different perspectives, culminate in the Rushdie affair as an exemplary case study to explicate the cultural meanings of blasphemy.[1] In both works the fatwa against Rushdie is the ostensible starting point for a retrospective view of the stages through which European history has passed, as well as the end point for the dangers posed to western society by religious fundamentalism, particularly militant Islamic fundamentalism. David Lawton specifically states at the outset that his interest in blasphemy was "re-awakened by the Rushdie affair" and proclaims that he does not "address this book to anyone who supports killing writers," as if all those who took offense with Rushdie's novel also endorsed his death penalty. Lawton's is a voice that speaks for an enlightened multiculturalism against what he calls the "perverted and already transcultured monoculturalism" of militant Muslims like Yusuf Islam and Doctor

Siddiqi.[2] The terms of the debate are clear and unambiguous, firmly establishing that prosecution of blasphemy and a tolerant society are incompatible propositions.

If blasphemy as a concept denotes the past of the European world, it is also put to use to mark the present of the non-European world. The narrative organization of Lawton's and Levy's works views blasphemy as helping to demarcate the west from the Islamic world far more usefully than any other signifier—cultural, geographical, or political. Leonard Levy's *Blasphemy: Verbal Offense against the Sacred from Moses to Salman Rushdie* lays bare its intended trajectory and, like David Lawton's book, traces the changing status of blasphemy in English law to argue that, although blasphemy has virtually disappeared as a prosecutable offense in the west, the Rushdie affair dramatically highlights a continuing history of medieval obscurantism in other parts of the world. As a linear narrative, Levy's book encourages one to believe that advanced societies have left behind medieval blasphemy prosecutions, along with other obsolete definitions of religion, law, and state. The emergence of western culture from the stranglehold of medieval inquisitions allows for a certain triumphalist note that simultaneously distances nonwestern societies. One could say that a similar sense of fascinated but distant horror marks the news media's obsession with Taslima Nasreen, the Bangladeshi feminist writer accused of blaspheming Islam in her novel *Lajja*. The continuing force of blasphemy as a functional concept in Islamic societies underlies the reading of efforts at internal social reform as a generalized form of apostasy, with effects not only on those societies themselves but on how Islam is represented and understood in non-Islamic societies.

Talal Asad's recent criticism that religion in contemporary parlance has become modernity's alienated self provides a useful framework to analyze the distancing of blasphemy from the present, even when blasphemy and its persecution exist at the heart of contemporary culture. For the controversy over recent events like Martin Scorsese's film version of Nikos Kazantzakis's *The Last Temptation of Christ*, the *Gay News*'s publication in 1976 of a homosexual poem about a Roman centurion's lust for the crucified Christ, and a short 1984 video about the erotic fantasies of St. Teresa de Avila makes abundantly clear that blasphemy is not only an operative concept in modern western culture but a litigious one as well. In *The Culture of Disbelief*, the legal scholar, Stephen L. Carter, delineates the flash points of a crisis in which blasphemy prosecutions periodically emerge as reminders that a secular culture has still to negotiate a viable relation with entrenched belief systems.[3] Inevitably too, blasphemy trials raise questions about how far freedom of speech can extend without infringing the rights of specific religious groups. Equally pressing is the extent to which the obligation to protect their rights leads in turn to an irreversible climate of censorship.

Given the persistence of religiously motivated prosecution cases in Anglo-American culture, however sporadic they may be, why do Salman Rushdie and Taslima Nasreen command the kind of rapt media attention that they do, disproportionate to the attention given to other blasphemy cases? Why, for instance, is James Kirkup, the author of the offending *Gay News* poem, not as familiar a name as Rushdie or Nasreen? An obvious reason for the passion evoked by Rushdie's and Nasreen's plight (and the one most often given) is the extremity of the punishment meted out to them, which is nothing less than the death sentence for impugning the Qur'an. But even the unreasonableness of a punishment in excess of the original crime insufficiently explains the absurdist quality of their torment. What is perhaps more difficult to grasp is the fact that their transgression consists of challenging what is put forth as irrefutable points of doctrine and creed. This charge does not surface in the same way in the other cases mentioned earlier, for their main offensiveness is described in legal briefs as the violation of norms of decency and the wounding of believers' sentiments. The intractableness of doctrinal positions, coupled with punitive threats that exceed the law, is not readily accommodated by the historical shift in emphasis from the *matter* of blasphemy (whose exclusive reference point remains the text) to the *manner* of its utterance (which can be arbitrated in the law courts).

The important distinction between manner and matter, the historical roots of which I shall return to shortly, is also what distinguishes blasphemy from heresy, even though the differences between the two terms have historically not been particularly clear-cut or self-evident. If blasphemers are defined as those who commit verbal offense in shocking, vile, and crude language or imagery but without necessarily attacking points of doctrine, heretics on the other hand are those whose alternative interpretations of fundamental religious truths substantially undermine the stable foundation on which those truths stand, regardless of whether the language they use is tasteless or not. Heresy is the site of competing interests and doctrines. When not resolved by expulsion and excommunication of the offending heretic, doctrinal conflict produces nothing short of the paradigm shifts that create new structures of knowledge. A simple, yet unacknowledged, notion is that blasphemers may blaspheme without undermining the content or truth of any proposition because blasphemy's enemy is not a text or a creed but a community, along with the codes and rules it employs to sanction membership within it. Blasphemy shades into heresy when the text is subsumed so entirely within the identity of a community that the community *is* the text. The move is akin to what Thomas Kuhn has described as the process by which scientific knowledge is made into a set of truths to which interpretive communities give their assent. It is not the demonstrable salience of a proposition that produces a community's acceptance of it but the community's commitment that determines what is to count as an acceptable "truth."[4]

In David Lawton's postmodern reading, blasphemy is a problematic discourse of belonging and community that proves to be anachronistic in a modern world characterized by (transgressive) conditions of displacement and migration. Lawton's psychoanalytic turn suggests a link between Freud and Rushdie as writers who could express their identities only by subverting the religion of the fathers through blasphemy. Freud defines blasphemy and heresy as religious phenomena manifested in the neurotic symptoms of individuals. For Freud, the history of religions contains repressions that subsequently survive in traditions of legends and folk tales, whose function as the repository of forgotten memory translates the past into that part of history which exerts claims on one's belief. When these repressions surface as conscious memory, they take the form of blasphemy, which becomes newly defined as the reappearance of the denials and repressions in one's history. By establishing blasphemy as a return to the primal scene, Freud accentuated its archaic, vestigial character, which, as a return to the scene of childhood, exposes the religious construction of human history.

But if blasphemy is an archaic concept that has no place in the modern world, it is also the case that the multitudinous responses to the chaos of modernity produce the new blasphemy of searching for origins where there are none, of seeking community where there can be no belonging. For the blasphemer, home is what is both rejected and sought, and it is in the pull between these dual impulses—"one belongs where one cannot be, and one is where one does not belong"—that Lawton, following Homi Bhabha, locates the subversive force of blasphemy.[5] Freud's exemplary figure of endless migration without return is the Egyptian Moses in *Moses and Monotheism*. Moses's hybrid condition—he is, after all, the Egyptian founder of the religion of the Jews—encapsulates the special condition of blasphemy as an act of self-alienation issuing from a desire, paradoxically, to belong or return (the two terms have an uncanny interchangeability in the conditions of modern life). In *The Satanic Verses* Rushdie's ambivalent representation of his protagonists' alienation from both the land of their birth and their adopted country poses migration and return as the central problematic around which blasphemy is determined. For even without his characters uttering a single word, it is apparent that, in an exaggerated sort of way, migration functions in the novel as a textual code for blasphemy, that is, for conditions of estrangement and loss of community that would place any utterance, innocent or malicious, outside the framework of known, familiar, and acceptable meanings.

Lawton puts his finger on a significant shift in the cultural meaning of blasphemy in modern religious history. The contradictions of belonging, home, and community transform what was once a marker of foreignness (in a notion deriving from the representation of Jews as the archetypal blasphemers, only adherents of another creed could blaspheme) into a signifier of betrayal from within, and then back again into an outsider's violation. The threat to a community perceiving itself to be under siege by its own members reintroduces punitive measures like excommunication and imposition of civil disabilities against verbal offense, measures that are customarily associated with the removal of heretics from community. The circularity of meanings is evident in the fact that whereas blasphemy is often a means of self-definition for blasphemers, it signifies their lack of cultural belonging in the communities they challenge, which condemn them to irreversible expulsion, and virtually to a state of foreignness.

From internal expressions of dissent, the construction of blasphemy as yet again foreign contributes to an endless polarization between religion and secularism, community and nation, nation and international community. When Salman Rushdie is defended by western literary figures and intellectuals, his dialogue with Islam is turned into a blasphemy sponsored by the non-Islamic world. This move is a measure of how difficult it is for Islam to reconcile the sense of betrayal from within to the internal coherence of the Muslim community. As Sara Suleri points out, Rushdie's "blasphemy" was made more hurtful to Muslims because of western intellectuals' reclamation of him as a secular figure, marking off believing Muslims as nonsecular or nonwestern (the two terms become virtually interchangeable).[6] If migration and displacement are transgressions in religious terms, the penalty for blasphemy, tragically and ironically, is for the blasphemer to transgress infinitely by being consigned to permanent exile. The mark of modernity is imprinted on these displaced meanings, the punitive force of which rejects any kind of assimilative will toward blasphemers. In earlier contexts, on the other hand, assimilation might have functioned as a pedagogical model of incorporation: in a process akin to conversion, the promise of assimilation has historically been used to influence heretics to embrace the positions of the religion they opposed.

Like blasphemy, conversion also bears the notations of geographical migration. It does so in two senses: first, in the more obvious sense associated with colonial periods, when missionaries traveled large distances to convert others to their own religion; and second, in the idea that conversion itself is a a crossing over, a migration or travel from one country, culture, religion, and identity to another. Jean-Luc Nancy's conception that the death of God brings about the movement of peoples and ideas is not inappropriate, though it is interesting that Nancy also locates the "return of the religious" in the moment of migration: "I suspect that one would need to move away, to find a place at some remove in order to say of the gods that they are the gods."[7] The mapping of space in narratives about conversion reveals the boundaries established by orthodoxy, as well as the heresies that are produced by the transgression of boundaries. Emplotting the spatial and spiritual aspects of religious change is virtually to map the coordinates of what would be described today as acts of border-crossing.

Modernity's complication of blasphemy is prefigured to some extent in the patterns of community consolidation and the diminishing role of conversion characterizing the histories of religious growth. This is about the only theme of interest in an otherwise unexceptional collection of essays, *Conversion to Christianity*, that purports to study the meanings of religious change.[8] In a volume that examines Christian conversion almost exclusively as an agent of transformation of nonwestern societies, the only essay to submit the history of early Christianity to the same sort of anthropological scrutiny is Howard Clark Kee's "From the Jesus Movement toward Institutional Church." The inclusion of this essay is crucial to understanding the extent to which, from the standpoint of a fledgling community aspiring to consolidate itself by establishing certain norms, conversion from one sect to another is as much an expression of blasphemy as it is of heresy. It is perhaps for this reason that narrowly conceived doctrines like anti-Trinitarianism assumed such an exaggerated importance in delineating the outlines of Christianity, and accounts for the far greater persecution of Unitarians than of Jews or Catholics.[9] By the fourth century the intradenominational rivalries in early Christianity were so sharp that both blasphemy and heresy blended with connotations of factionalism, sedition, schism, apostasy, and sacrilege.

Kee's own account suggests that the roots of these assocations lie in a change in the different connotations of "faith" from a meaning found in Paul's writings that stressed trust, reliance, and confidence in divine deeds, to a meaning enunciated in the subsequent deutero-Pauline writings that emphasized right belief or true doctrine. This reading conflicts with Leonard Levy's argument that the consolidating moment in Christianity occurred when Paul, in reinterpreting blasphemy to mean the denial and defamation of Christ's teachings, established a connection between heresy and blasphemy that persisted in Christian thought for at least fifteen centuries. This more narrowly conceived dogmatic emphasis disallowed the possibility that the Bible could be read as a composite book of different interpretations and authorship, or that what was "a cardinal reproach . . . to a particular doctrine" to one person might be sacred doctrine to another.[10] But whether the doctrinal emphases that conflate blasphemy and heresy are present in Paul's own writings or in those of his compositors, there is little doubt that dogmatism of religious opinion is a product of the post-Pauline creation of an institutional church carved out of a community of former Jews. Their sharpened doctrinal formulations paved the way for the sectarian divide of the fourth century on questions of Christ's divinity, as well as the Trinity.

The first great heresy to split the Church and challenge patristic orthodoxy—the Arian heresy—repudiated the doctrine of the Trinity and maintained the belief that Jesus was less than divine. Much later, in nineteenth-century England, these fourth-century heresies of the early church furnished

John Henry Newman with rhetorical weapons for waging war against the displacement of ecclesiastical authority by the state. Stephen Thomas's *Newman
and Heresy* shows that Newman employed rhetorical analogies between those
past heresies and the liberal forces of his own time to portray the consolidation
of the English state as a struggle of schismatic, sectarian forces ripping apart
the unified religious fabric of English life. Heresy, in Thomas's discerning
observation, becomes for Newman rather a rhetorical strategy than an alternative form of knowledge.[11] To some extent Newman's antistatism had its model
in the discourse of early Anabaptists, whose emulation of the primitive church
of the original apostles led to the doctrine that no true Christian could be a
genuine statist, Christianity being an entirely private affair in which the state
had no part. The rejection of state apparatuses like the civil courts and civil
magistrates had the unusual effect of making blasphemy an impossible category. It is an irony of ecclesiastical history that, with disestablishment, the
English state recovers blasphemy not as a religious but, rather, a political concept connoting separatism and treason; and "antinational" displaces "antire-
ligious orthodoxy" as a working definition of blasphemy.

For this reason, I have found Newman's rhetoric to be particularly trenchant
in pinpointing heresy not as an action against church and state as it was in an
earlier, more integrated era, but as a policy supported by the state. Newman's
is a rhetorical strategy no different from typical antisecularist critiques aimed
at dismantling power reinvested in the state from ecclesiastical bodies.
In Newman's shrewd rendering, heresy as treason against the state is newly
confounded by the state participating in its own subversion. By neutralizing
religious difference, parliamentary legislation to remove restrictions against
religious minorities represented the ultimate betrayal by the state. Newman's
conversion of the parliamentary discourse of religious enfranchisement into
the language of heresy allowed him to reintroduce principles of inclusion on
the basis of class and thus make religious or cultural pluralism unacceptable in
a philosophy of tolerance. That the fourth-century heresies of Christianity provided him with the metaphors for attacking the centralizing tendencies of the
state says a great deal about how "heresy" as a concept has been used both by
and against the state.

The semantic links between heresy and blasphemy began to crumble with
the great legislative decisions of the nineteenth century. In a major intellectual
shift brought on by disestablishment, national union, and the advent of a pluralistic society, the transition from the principle of "matter" to that of "manner" established a functional definition of modern blasphemy as an affront to
the religious sentiments of a community. The legal opinions of John Duke
Coleridge set a precedent for requiring a decency test in cases of alleged religious insult, which had less to do with evaluating the approximation of content
to accepted doctrine than with the acceptability of the form in which that content is expressed. Clearly class-marked, the decency test targeted levels of

language use, and those who were prosecuted most frequently were members of the lower classes who profaned in coarse, indecent language.

One of the most notorious cases in Victorian England, which came up for trial in 1857, concerned an eccentric artisan called Thomas Pooley, who held that potato rot could be cured by burning Bibles and dispersing their ashes over fields. Accused of writing "offensive words" against Christianity on a gate, he was sentenced to twenty-one months' imprisonment after a successful prosecution by John Duke Coleridge, whose fame ironically rested on his wide reputation as a great liberalizer of blasphemy laws. Leonard Levy writes, "When the law punished indecency or bad taste, it became a class weapon of the prosperous against the poor. The class that made and enforced the law had little sympathy for the different taste of the class that usually broke the law. No one prosecuted Matthew Arnold for his sarcasms against the Trinity in his *Literature and Dogma.*"[12]

The London *Spectator* sharply took up the issue and declared that "there must be something wrong in a law of blasphemy which punishes the vulgar man for saying in coarse language what it never thinks of punishing the refined man for saying in keen, sarcastic language."[13] The Pooley case widened the class divide and made blasphemy an offense by the poor, despite the fact that anti-Christian sentiments were just as common among the upper classes. The endorsement of high culture as an acceptable medium for expressing blasphemous thoughts is, of course, an issue that crops up in the Rushdie affair. It is significant that the suspicion of literary form as a screen for the enactment of class biases, immune to prosecution because literary language has privileged status, should have been articulated at the moment when the decency test—manner over matter—was urged as a principle of litigation. Already it is apparent that the class lines are firmly drawn, and the separation of blasphemy from heresy—and sentiment from creed—throws the weight of offense on the relative bluntness or refinement of language, now measured on a sliding scale running from direct polemic on one end to irony and satire on the other.

The new legislation of the nineteenth century clearly indicates that the concept of heresy derived from religion no longer pertains in the same degree. However, the space that religious orthodoxy occupied is taken over by culture, onto which are displaced the discriminations and exclusions that formerly established the grounds of religious heresy. Levy's references to Matthew Arnold are telling in this context, though Levy misses Arnold's strategic move in turning culture into religion's surrogate, replete with its own standards and orthodoxies, while simultaneously puncturing the dogmatic assertions of Christianity on certain points of doctrine such as the Trinity. David Lawton is a little closer to exploring the nature and implications of this displacement, dating the move from religious orthodoxy to cultural conformity as far back as the seventeenth century. An important observation that emerges in his account concerns the increasing distance between the opinions of intellectuals and the cultural norms upheld by state power. It is so wide at some points in European intellectual history that the marginalization of intellectuals and their views could produce nothing but a narrowing of community, which now no longer attempts to incorporate all members, as was the case when the ideology of the church prevailed, but rather functions as an "enclosed middle ground set against social and intellectual extremes and dedicated to their continued separation. What is held in common is law, in England common law, which becomes the expression of an exclusive rather than an inclusive ideal of community, an elevated abstraction from which comes the standard used to judge transgression."[14]

Where then does blasphemy stand in this artificially created middle space of culture and state power? Are a tolerant, secular society and prosecution for blasphemy mutually exclusive? Or does the fact that religious differences exist make blasphemy laws not only allowable in a tolerant society but necessary as well? From a committed position of multiculturalist relativism, David Lawton provides a textured analysis of the semiotic functions of blasphemy in exposing the latent resistances of dominant cultures to a more heterogeneous social make-up. But in dismissing blasphemy as a failed concept in a multicultural society, Lawton to my mind does not adequately acknowledge the extent to which blasphemy continues to function with its original religious associations precisely because it has been put to use to test the limits of a tolerant, multicultural society. For it cannot be gainsaid that blasphemy has retained currency as religious offense, though as a much looser concept. Its verbal excesses have a functional use in calling forth regulative measures of constraint in a deregulated environment where religious belief is left without protection. Without public awareness of verbal offense, tolerance could turn into laissez-faire and threaten modern civil society by turning its licenses against itself. If blasphemy is now more a discourse of rights than of creed or belief, it is a reflection of the extent to which culture has usurped the function of religion, religious difference itself being vociferously defended only because it signifies *cultural* difference.

Nor does Lawton account for a major historical shift in the function of blasphemy laws from one of protecting religious orthodoxy to that of establishing the boundaries of pluralism. While dispensing with the heretical connotations of religious slander, blasphemy, as "a difference of religious opinion" (which is what it has come to mean in its most watered-down, updated version), still leaves room for tolerant societies to hold on to a concept of religious offense that impugns communities rather than doctrine, and enables them to prosecute on that principle. Furthermore, its estrangement from secular culture has made the discourse of blasphemy a safer, more neutral ground for exploring intractable questions of freedom of speech, protection of minority rights, and mediation of racial bigotry. Secularized into a cultural code that monitors racial and ethnic slurs, even while maintaining religious offense as its ostensible subject, prosecution for blasphemy has been modernized and refurbished to regulate bigotry's excesses. Although blasphemy in a religious society provides an index of the degree to which religious opinion has become monolithic, the existence of blasphemy laws in a pluralistic society ideally acknowledges the obligation to protect difference (the very point on which the decency test of John Duke Coleridge remained deliberately vague), on the assumption that without legal recourse the individuality of community difference cannot be protected against the brutal affronts of verbal abuse.

However, although enabling communities to consolidate their defenses, the regulation of religious bigotry by legal action reverts to considering blasphemy as an offense committed by outsiders. The best illustration for this is the well-documented 1855 trial of a Catholic Redemptorist father, the Reverend Vladimir Petcherine, who was accused of burning the authorized version of the Bible in the presence of royal subjects. A Russian exile who had converted to Catholicism, Petcherine mobilized the people of Kingstown, a small Irish town, to burn copies of the Bible in a raging bonfire. Before the event actually occurred, however, local Protestants amassed at the site and confronted the Catholics congregated there, exchanging violent abuses with them. Petcherine was charged with blasphemy, though his role in actually burning bibles was never fully ascertained. In the trial conducted by the attorney-general and the solicitor-general, the prosecution made an impassioned appeal to what Lawton describes as the worst elements of xenophobia. The fact that Petcherine was not British opened up all sorts of unseemly associations, such as those between foreigner and fanatic, outsider and heretic. These links all helped to identify blasphemy as essentially an antinational act. Questions of modernity were also implicated in the defense of English nationhood, which is what the Petcherine trial was primarily all about. When exported to England, the antimodernism of Roman Catholicism was reported to have taken an antinational turn. Similarly, the appeal to lofty abstractions of progress and civilization denounced the bishoprics' "hierarchy of controls" as an excuse to reestablish antiquated concepts like heresy and excommunication—concepts that English law had already declared unenforceable.[15]

Though Petcherine was eventually acquitted, the case—and the passion it evoked against the "foreign hand"—indicates that modern blasphemy cases have been far more inclined to treat blasphemy as a form of foreign subversion than as internal dissent. This tendency is all too evident in the clashes of freethinkers and atheists, like Charles Bradlaugh, George William Foote, and Annie Besant, with mainstream Christianity. The perceived opposition of these freethinkers and dissenters to international imperialism and their espousal of nationalist struggles in Britain's colonies contributed in no small measure to the construction of blasphemy as antinational and foreign in origin. The fact that Hinduism and other eastern religions were often invoked by such figures to refute the exclusivity of Christian doctrine only proved that they had fallen into the embrace of a foreign-inspired paganism.

T. S. Eliot, flush in his own newfound Anglican consciousness that partly grew out of his reaction to the rise of European fascism, completely turned around this tendency to paganism by using it as a metaphor for the English state's "blasphemy." This was Eliot's allusion to England's persecution not of dissenters but of believing Christians, who were made minorities in their own land. "Becoming Christian" is, for Eliot, a matter of recognizing the moral anarchy of the secular path; and in *The Idea of a Christian Society*, the work that literary critics have liked least to comment on because it has unpalatable theocratic tendencies, Eliot insistently uses paganism as a catch-all term for England's self-alienation.[16] In its reaction against the banishment of religion to the ceremonial margins of society, his move resonates with what Stephen Thomas has described as John Henry Newman's diatribe against the state as the source of modern heresy. Equally, Eliot's attempt to recover belief as a component of civil society would make blasphemy, in turn, an offense that can only be committed within a community of belief. In other words, Eliot's idea of blasphemy would seek to reendow it with religious, rather than cultural, significance, thus restoring religion to the public sphere. Where there is blasphemy, Eliot wished it to be inferred, there must be belief.

Some critics may argue that a tolerant society requires blasphemy laws more than an intolerant society. In the absence of these laws, it can be taken for granted that the rights of a religious community to have their sentiments respected will dissolve into a mindless and anarchic cultural relativism. That would seem to be the import of an argument about toleration that has persisted since John Locke, who established certain basic distinctions between religious belief and atheism while minimalizing the content of acceptable doctrine. All the while, of course, he showed a relative lack of concern in condemning variant forms of religious belief or doctrinal differences. Even while he insisted that aberrant forms of belief should not be punished, Locke's introduction of morality as a principle of arbitration in blasphemy and heresy cases left him enough room to argue that downright attacks on the existence of God could not be treated with impunity. Such attacks, he maintained, were basically immoral and posed a threat to the state. "The business of laws," he wrote in *A Letter Concerning Toleration* (1689), "is not to provide for the truth of opinions, but for the safety and security of the commonwealth, and of every particular man's goods and person."[17]

Much of the same thinking informed Macaulay's proposal to protect all religions against insult. During his tenure in India he framed a blasphemy law that imposed a year's imprisonment for any verbal act deliberately aimed at hurting another person's religious feelings. Macaulay boasted that were he a judge in India, he would "have no scruple about punishing a Christian who should pollute a mosque."[18] Approvingly cited by Levy as an expression of high tolerance, Macaulay's claim was more in keeping with England's policy of religious neutrality in India, which was introduced to maintain a balance of power between the Indian elite and British rulers, than it was a genuine commitment to the principle of equal protection to all religions. Still, such legislation, which was offered as a model for England as well, reiterated Locke's reluctance to accommodate atheists in his tolerant society. To secularists like Charles Bradlaugh, on the other hand, the liberalization of blasphemy laws to protect all religions was merely a cover to impose punitive restraints against nonbelievers, such as forbidding them from holding seats in parliament (Bradlaugh was himself the first atheist to be admitted into parliament in 1882, after a long-drawn-out battle).

Although I do not wish to shift the focus of my argument to debate how best tolerance is to be defined, I do think that, amidst the great upheavals and transitions to a secular world-view, it was never fully established whether the aggrieved community whose sentiments were to be protected was majority or minority. This ambivalence has led to what Levy suggests is the central crisis in the Rushdie affair: could British Muslims legally claim that their religion had been blasphemed if provisions under English law existed only for prosecuting blasphemy against Christianity? By the test of decency Coleridge introduced in the nineteenth century, which acknowledged the reality that Christianity was no longer the law of the land, it would have appeared that all religions would be eligibile for protection. However, Coleridge had drawn a line in liberalizing the heretical connotations of blasphemy and merely acknowledged that although heresy was no longer punishable in a secular society, prosecution was still possible wherever verbal insult occurred under the label of blasphemy. Christianity still continued to be the reference point, and English law remained closed to admitting cases involving insult to other religions. A century later, it is telling that whatever support British Muslims garnered from intellectuals and religious figures in England was primarily out of an obligation to listen to the claims of cultural difference in an inescapably multicultural society. This, in my mind, marks an interesting change in how blasphemy legislation is regarded: not as an obligatory protection of religious sensibilities but rather of cultural difference. The sympathy for "wounded sentiments" is a permissible secular gesture that has the special virtue of not pandering to the religious absolutism on which those sentiments may be based. If tolerance is obliged to protect the rights of all communities, its privileging of the subjectivity of sentiment over the objectivity of creed steers clear of antiheretical presumptions while still holding fast to the ideal of cultural relativism.

But in all the debates and polemic that have appeared in the past several years, there has been very little discussion of belief as something that is not reducible to either sentiment or creed. These are the twin poles between which the discourse of blasphemy primarily remains confined. This polarization has been perpetuated by some who claim to be offended by Rushdie and who not only feel wounded in sentiment but also want blasphemy to revert to its earlier identification with heresy. But for many others such polarization has imposed an artificial constraint on a form of criticism that might provide creative ways of expressing belief, without necessarily invoking offense as proof of its existence. Despite his conservative stance on state centralization and established religion, John Henry Newman comes close to articulating what this criticism might look like when he propounds an idea of belief as disembodied subjectivity, severed from a closely guarded interpretive community that compels assent to given propositions on purely notional grounds. The connotations of dissent are much more coded in this notion of belief, howsoever subtly and surprisingly, than those of assent. At first glance such an understanding of belief smacks uncannily of heresy as I described it earlier. Its challenge to Kuhnian paradigms of knowledge and its potential to effect virtually revolutionary paradigm shifts appear to bear heretical connotations. And indeed one would not be far off the mark in deducing so, for Newman's "belief," in calling for a more direct, unmediated relation to experience, is as much an epistemological as a religious category. Primarily it is a form of dissent from consensus thinking and institutional definitions, which, when translated into critical practice, aims at disempowering notional assent to foundational premises.

Stephen L. Carter's *The Culture of Disbelief* is one among the gradually increasing numbers of popular books written in recent years that attempts to speak of belief without embarrassment or apology. Carter's book has been more polemical than most in challenging the complete banishment of religion from American public discourse, which he describes as symptomatic of another kind of fanaticism that has come to characterize the strict separation of church and state in America. As he also points out sardonically, when belief does reappear, it is usually in litigious or juridical contexts. Carter's description of the impossibility of true neutrality by the state rests on the fundamental paradox that the state takes a position on the status of belief systems whether it acts or not. When it does not intervene in certain practices such as drug abuse or animal mutiliation by believers of a particular faith, the state virtually assents to the truth value of these beliefs, just as much as when, by directly interceding, it declares these beliefs to be false. Inaction is, therefore, as much a form of action as direct intervention. But Carter's contentious project is weighed down by a cumbersome defensiveness that sidetracks him into lengthy arguments aimed at disengaging belief from fundamentalist associations. What these arguments prove more than anything else are the limitations of vocabulary and language, revealing how difficult it is for secular intellectuals to articulate a concept of religious belief—distinct from religious ideology—in and for a secular community.

No mode of criticism that fully accounts for belief as a form of knowledge has really emerged from the Rushdie controversy, despite the efforts of certain British religious figures like Keith Ward, a minister of the established church and professor of the philosophy of religion, to introduce a more innovative approach to the issue of blasphemy laws in modern society. Ward's views, which Levy calls "the best consequence of the Rushdie affair," were quite unusual even as they were also commonplace in other respects. I say they were unusual because, unlike so many other arguments made at the same time, Ward's disregarded both the claims of pluralism and the defense of rights and instead took the self-consciously Christian viewpoint that "it is profoundly *irreligious* to take offence when offence is offered." Espousing a turn-the-other-cheek philosophy, he continued,

> The most obvious way is to make it apparent that your religious faith is in fact admirable and estimable and is contributing to peace and reconciliation in the world. This is better than having a law which says, 'we are not going to let you insult us.' . . . The real defense of free speech is that it is for the sake of truth that we are prepared to put up with the abuses of it, because truth is so important that it is worth a few abuses in the hope of getting it.[19]

When Ward refers to "truth," he clearly does not mean creed or dogma but, rather, the experiential understanding of objects. But having moved beyond the polarity of sentiment and creed, Ward turns to a more conventional view of religious liberty as the disinterested pursuit of truth. He retains a naïve belief that individuals and communities can absorb offense without feeling either their religions or themselves threatened, and that ideas of truth can be pursued detached from the unequal relations that pertain in society. Ward's is still a majority position that is closed to the power differentials in a heterogeneous society, where tolerance is often the privilege of the dominant culture. The distinction between "majority" and "minority" religious cultures is not just a numerical one but a difference of inflection as well. For if the first term is unmarked in relation to the second, it explains why Ward is oblivious to the conditions of relative strength in a culture that permit some groups to absorb offense more readily than others. Preston King sums it up aptly when he describes liberty as a "socially guaranteed power" presenting or removing obstacles; liberty is also akin to tolerance in that the power to act or forbear is not generalized and in fact assumes inherent inequality.[20]

To be responsive to unequal power relations in multicultural societies and yet at the same time practice a form of criticism that would dispense altogether with offense as a measure of belief's existence: that is the real challenge emerging from the Rushdie affair. From this perspective, T. S. Eliot's yearning for a presecular age where blasphemy presents itself as a healthy sign of belief's presence is not simply a nostalgic fantasy but a dangerously flawed vision that has the potential to perpetuate a cycle of hostility and violence in the name of belief. Until the culture of modernity permits a critical discourse of belief to be unlocked from the closed problematic set forth in Eliot's imagined state, we are likely to continue seeing blasphemy as an outcome of belief, sometimes with tragic consequences. Just as surely, in the absence of timely critical interventions, we will continue to see blasphemy laws establish the boundaries of pluralistic societies, as regulative in their social function as cultural codes that monitor hate speech and racial bigotry.

Appendix

The Census of India, 1901

Name and Address of Persons Converted	Profession	Cause of Conversion	Former Caste
1. Mukta Muchini of Hydarpur, thana Baduria	Day-labourer	She fell in love with one Jhanu Sheik of her village, who converted her and afterwards married her	Muchi
2. Mukta Dassi of Kalutolla, Hassanabad	Ditto	She married a Mohammadan	Goala
3. Mathura Bania of Magrahat	Railway gateman	He fell in love with a Muhammadan girl and married her	Bania
4. Degambari Dasi, Magrahat	Day-labourer	She was a poor widow with two little children, and under the inducement of a rich Muhammadan she was converted with her two boys	Dhopa
5. Jasodia Talini, daughter of Ajitam Teli of Sonari, thana Mubarak, district Saran, aged 30 years	Mill-hand	She fell in love with her Muhammadan paramour, who converted her to his faith	Teli
6. Nanku Kalwar, alias Nanku Mian, son of Bissesswar Kalwar of Dalary, thana Madhubanjia, district Saran, aged 32 years	Ditto	Embraced the religion of Muhammad of his own accord	Teli
7. Dalu Mali, alias Dil Muhammad, son of Heta Mali of Belaganj, thana Belaganj, district Belaganj, aged 30 years	Ditto	Ditto	Mali

Name and Address of Persons Converted	Profession	Cause of Conversion	Former Caste
8. Mahadevya Chamarin, daughter of Nanker Chamar of Karai, thana Dildargunge, district Ajamgarh, aged 13 years	Nil	Married a Muhammadan while in sick-bed	Chamar
9. Lakpatia Bharin, alias Saliman Bibi, daughter of Narsing Bhar of Rajanpur, thana Mirganj, district Saran, aged 25 years	Mill-hand	Fell in love with her Muhammadan paramour, and was converted to his faith	Bhar
10. Jitu Kahar, alias Situ Mianson of Thakuri Kahar of Vikaran, thana Mirganj district. Saran, aged 45 years	Ditto	Embraced the Muhammadan religion of his own accord	Kahar
11. Nathia Bharia, daughter of Narsing Bhar of Rajanpur, thana Mirganj, district Saran, aged 30 years	Ditto	Fell in love with her Muhammadan paramour, who converted her to his faith	Bhar
12. Lakpatia Guraram, daughter of Kanta Gareri of Mubarakpur, thana Mohanta, district Shahabad, aged 30 years	Ditto	Ditto ditto	Gareri
13. Sundaria Ksharin, daughter of Thakur Kahar of Vikaran, thana Mirganj, district Saran, aged 50 years	Ditto	Embraced Muhammadanism of her own accord	Kahar

Name and Address of Persons Converted	Profession	Cause of Conversion	Former Caste
14. Andia Ksharin, daughter of Thakur Kahar of Vikaran, thana Mirganj, district Saran, aged 30 years	Ditto	Fell in love with her Muhammadan paramour, who converted her to his faith	Do.
15. Parameswar Kahar, alias Dil Muhammad, son of Bhagaban Kahar of Sandapur, thana Manjni, district Saran, aged 33 years	Ditto	Embraced Muhammadanism of his own accord	Do.
16. Thakur Dasi, alias Kusum Dasi, daughter of Biswanath Pal of Nayabasti, thana Barrackpore, aged 40 years	Nil	Fell in love with a Muhammadan and was converted	Kumhar (potter)
17. Prasanna Dasi, daughter of Tarini Ghose of Nayabasti, thana Barrackpore, aged 50 years	Nil	Embraced the Muhammadan religion after her son's conversion to that faith	Goala
18. Hara Devi, daughter of Dinanath Banerji of Nayabasti, thana Barrackpore, aged 40 years	Seller of wood	Owing to straitened circumstances, she embraced Muhammadanism	Brahman
19. Harani Dasi, alias Idia Bibi, daughter of Madhu Kaora of Nayabasti, thana Barrackpore, aged 40 years	. . . .	Fell in love with a Muhammadan paramour, and was converted to his faith	Kaora
20. Rajkumari Dass, daughter of Mati Ram Paraumanik of Nayabasti, thana Barrackpore, aged 60 years	Ayah	Ditto ditto	Napit

Name and Address of Persons Converted	Profession	Cause of Conversion	Former Caste
21. Behari Goala, alias Khodabox, son of Sewo Prasad Goala of Ujayini, thana Pabeganj, district Mirzapur, aged 25 years	Beggar	Owing to straitened circumstances, he embraced the Muhammadan religion	Goala
22. Lachman Pasi, son of Suku Pasi of Sadar Bezar, thana Barrackpore, aged 33 years	Lives on the sale-proceeds of his house property	Fell in love with a Muhammadan prostitute and became a convert	Pasi
23. Kokil Kaora, son of Bhadua Kaora of Chanak, thana Barrackpore, aged 40 years	Labourer	Ditto ditto	Kaora
24. Hari Bagdi, son of Kala Chand Bagdi of Chanak, thana Barrackpore, aged 33 years	Nil	Owing to his straitened circumstances, he became a convert to Muhammadanism	Bagdi
25. Mathura Goala, son of Dhani Ram Goala of Chanak, thana Barrackpore, aged 30 years	Nil	Ditto ditto	Goala
26. Habul Chandra Ghose, son of Haran Chandra Ghose of Sewli, thana Barrackpore, aged 30 years	Nil	Conviction of the truth of Muhammadism	Goala
27. Mahendra Napit, son of Radhanath Napit of Gambhirgachi, aged 35 years	Day-labourer	Joined a band of magicians; married the girl of one of them, and became a Muhammadan	Napit
28. Dasi Goalini, daughter of Kerun Mall of Durgapura, aged 33 years	Nil	Two years after the death of her husband, she fell in love with a Muhammadan named Soleman of Bandipur, and embraced Islam	Goala

Name and Address of Persons Converted	Profession	Cause of Conversion	Former Caste
29. Mookhada Dasi, wife of Nimchand Ghose of Kamdebgachi, aged 25 or 30 years	Nil	She embraced Muhammadanism when driven out of her father's house for her immoral character	Do.
30. Abhoya Dasi, wife of Nakul Ghose, Kharki, aged 33 or 32 years	Nil	She embraced Muhammadanism on account of her husband's ill-treatment	Do.
31. Dasi Bagdini, wife of Tustu Bagdi of Khamur, aged 20 or 25 years	Nil	She fell in love with Khosh Mondal of Madangram and afterwards married him	Bagdi
32. Satya Bagdini, wife of Puti Bagdi of Konami	Nil	Owing to her straitened circumstances, she embraced Muhammadanism	Do.
33. Bilashi Bagdini, widow of Hara Bagdi of Nischindapur, aged 35 or 36 years	Nil	Ditto ditto	Do.
34. Paran Tiyar, son of Natabar Tiyar of Kasimpur, aged 30 or 32 years	Nil	Owing to his straitened circumstances, he embraced Muhammadanism	Tiyar
35. Shebu Bagdi, alias Shamser Mundol of Chandigore, aged 30 or 35 years	Nil	Ditto ditto	Bagdi
36. Badan Ghose, son of late Ravan Ghose of Degha Nebodhin (present abode), aged 30 or 35 years	Nil	Fell in love with a Muhammadan woman and became a convert and married her	Goala

Name and Address of Persons Converted	Profession	Cause of Conversion	Former Caste
37. Kumi Dasi, wife of Nim Chand Ghose	Nil	She was enticed from the protection of her husband by a Muhammadan named Kedar Mandal, who converted her to his faith and married her	Do.
38. Punchi Dasi	Nil	She was enticed away by her Muhammadan paramour, Ohijuddi, and converted to his faith	Do.
39. A Bagdi woman at Bankura, in thana Dum-Dum	Nil	She was enticed away by a Muhammadan, who subsequently converted her and married her	Bagdi
40. Wife of Prem Chand Rajak, Rajarhat, thana Dum-Dum	Nil	She eloped with a Muhammadan, named Pusha Garwan, who subsequently converted and married her	Dhoba

Source: From *Report of the Census of India 1901: Bengal—Extracts from District Reports Regarding Causes of Conversion to Mohammadanism,* appendix II, vol. 6 (Calcutta: 1902).

Notes

Preface

1. Mumtaz Ali Khan, *Mass Conversions of Meenakshipuram* (Madras: Christian Literature Society, 1983) provides detailed sociological analysis of the event, including numerous case histories of low-caste groups converting to Islam in the Ramanathapuram district of south India.

2. Johannes Fabian, *Time and the Other: How Anthropology Makes Its Objects* (New York: Columbia University Press, 1983).

3. David Lawton, *Blasphemy* (Philadelphia: University of Pennsylvania Press, 1993), p. 144. Lawton's psychoanalytic approach to blasphemy in modern history focuses on Freud's construction of a developmental religious history, particularly as it appears in Freud's reading of the Wolf-Man case. From an analysis of this case, Lawton infers that for Freud religion, like perversion, is precultural and that the Wolf-Man's own childhood blasphemy is at once "a product and deliberate construction of Freud's own blasphemous system" (p. 145).

4. Ashis Nandy, "The Politics of Secularism and the Recovery of Religious Tolerance," in *Mirrors of Violence: Communities, Riots, and Survivors in South Asia*, edited by Veena Das (Delhi: Oxford University Press, 1990), p. 70.

5. Barbara Harlow, "Drawing the Line: Cultural Politics and the Legacy of Partition," *Polygraph* 5 (1992): 84–111. Edward W. Said also provides a moving account of the law of return as a religiously motivated policy of partition and expulsion, in "Ideology of Difference," *Critical Inquiry* 12, no. 1 (1985): 38-58; reprinted in Edward W. Said, *The Politics of Dispossession: The Struggle for Palestinian Self-Determination* (New York: Pantheon, 1994).

6. Ritu Menon and Kamla Bhasin, "Recovery, Rupture, Resistance: Indian State and Abduction of Women during Partition," *Economic and Political Weekly*, April 24, 1993: WS7. See also Urvashi Butalia, "Community, State and Gender: On Women's Agency during Partition," *Economic and Political Weekly*, April 24, 1993: WS12–WS24.

7. Menon and Bhasin, "Recovery, Rupture, Resistance," p. WS6.

8. Quoted in Veena Das, "The Composition of the Personal Voice: Violence and Migration," *Studies in History* 7, no. 1 (1991): 65–77. More partition testimonies of the inner lives of women are included in Veena Das, *Critical Events: An Anthropological Perspective on Contemporary India* (Delhi: Oxford University Press, 1995).

9. Susan Harding, "Representing Fundamentalism: The Problem of the Repugnant Cultural Other," *Social Research* 58 (Summer 1991): 375. I am grateful to Saba Mahmood for directing my attention to this article.

10. Rustom Bharucha, *The Question of Faith*, Tracts for the Times, no. 3 (Delhi: Orient Longman, 1993), p. 3.

11. Ibid., p. 7.

12. Ibid., p. 8.

13. Works on belief, comparative religion, and religious nationalism by such scholars as Talal Asad, Rustom Bharucha, and Peter van der Veer typically address postcolo-

nial situations, and their rejection of derivative discourses is part of an ongoing reexamination of religion's representation in the official discourse of the west. But revisionist work on religion is obviously not confined to postcoloniality, and in recent years critical interventions in American scholarship, albeit of a different order and not always in disinterested ways, have sought to rethink the polarities of religion and secularism. Stephen L. Carter's *The Culture of Disbelief* (New York: Basic Books, 1993), a very different work no doubt from the ones I have described earlier, has undertaken a polemical foray into the diminished status of religion in American society. His book describes the expulsion of belief from public discourse as evidence of the fanaticism that has come to characterize the strict separation of church and state in America. Written in a similar spirit of challenge and reconciliation, Jim Wallis's *The Soul of Politics: A Practical and Prophetic Vision for Change* (Maryknoll, NY: Orbis Books, 1994) likewise exhorts secular intellectuals to rethink belief as a form of consciousness having less to do with a body of doctrine narrowly aligned with political ideology than with self-directed transformation.

14. Nandy, "The Politics of Secularism," p. 73.

15. Talal Asad, *Genealogies of Religion: Discipline and Reasons of Power in Christianity and Islam* (Baltimore: Johns Hopkins University Press, 1993).

16. Ibid., p. 45.

17. Ibid., p. 46.

18. Ibid., p. 39.

19. Ernest Gellner, *Postmodernism, Reason, and Religion* (London: Routledge, 1992).

Chapter One
Cross Currents

1. See, for example, my *Masks of Conquest: Literary Study and British Rule in India* (New York: Columbia University Press, 1989), which examines the patterns of decision making about the colonial curriculum in English. The book argues that the introduction of English education in India had far more to do with certain historical conditions in England, such as the constraints of church-state relations, than a monolithic imposition of cultural will. When the genealogy of English studies is described by means of historical cross-referencing, it yields two conclusions: first, English literature was taught earlier in India than England; and second, the later institutionalization of English in the home country is related in large part to the hold of Christian culture on English civil society. England's religious culture provided a structure of Christian values that—in colonial India—could only be officially communicated through secular instruction, of which English literature was an important medium.

2. Max Weber, *The Sociology of Religion*, translated by Ephraim Fischoff (1922; Boston: Beacon Press, 1963). Weber describes the bureaucratic attitude toward religion as an "elimination of all those emotional and irrational manifestations of personal religion" (p. 90).

3. There is a host of works on European secularization that one can draw upon: the works of Max Weber himself; Bryan Wilson, *Religion in Secular Society* (London:

Watts, 1966); Peter Berger, *The Sacred Canopy* (New York: Anchor Books, 1967); Reinhart Koselleck, *Futures Past: On the Semantics of Historical Time*, translated by Keith Tribe (Cambridge: MIT Press, 1985); Carl Schmitt, *Political Theology*, translated by George Schwab (Cambridge: MIT Press, 1985); and Karl Lowith, *From Hegel to Nietzsche*, translated by David E. Green (1964; rpt. New York: Columbia University Press, 1991). But none of these works discusses the specific impact of European imperial expansion on the historical production of secular culture. This is not to dismiss them but to acknowledge their methodological limitation.

4. See Peter van der Veer, *Religious Nationalism: Hindus and Muslims in India* (Berkeley and Los Angeles: University of California Press, 1994).

5. Thomas B. Macaulay, "Minute on Indian Education, 2 February 1835," in *Macaulay: Poetry and Prose*, edited by G. M. Young (Cambridge: Harvard University Press, 1967), p. 729. See also my *Masks of Conquest* (pp. 144–45) for an analysis of Macaulay's separation of cultural and religious concerns.

6. This phase of colonial cultural history is outlined in my *Masks of Conquest*, pp. 23–44.

7. Israel Finestein, *Jewish Society in Victorian England* (London: Valentine Mitchell, 1993), pp. 79–92.

8. M.C.N. Salbstein, *The Emancipation of the Jews in Britain: The Question of the Admission of the Jews to Parliament, 1828–1860* (East Brunswick, NJ: Associated University Presses, 1982), p. 78.

9. Finestein, *Jewish Society in Victorian England*, p. 85. See also David Katz, *Jews in the History of England 1485–1850* (Oxford: Clarendon Press, 1994), pp. 293–95.

10. Ibid., p. 83.

11. Thomas B. Macaulay, "Civil Disabilities of the Jews," *Edinburgh Review* (January 1830); reprinted in *Selections from the Edinburgh Review*, vol. 5, edited by Maurice Cross (Paris: Baudry, 1835), p. 207–8. See also Thomas B. Macaulay, "Parliamentary Reform, I: A Speech Delivered in the House of Commons on the 2d of March, 1831," in *Macaulay: Poetry and Prose*; this speech makes an impassioned plea in behalf of disabilities relief but registers Macaulay's opposition to universal suffrage.

12. Thomas B. Macaulay, "Gladstone on Church and State," in *Macaulay: Poetry and Prose*, p. 656.

13. Macaulay, "Minute on Indian Education," in *Macaulay: Poetry and Prose*, pp. 723–24.

14. Salbstein, *Emancipation of the Jews in Britain*, p. 40.

15. Ibid.

16. Ibid., p. 41.

17. Macaulay, "Gladstone on Church and State," in *Macaulay: Poetry and Prose*, p. 613.

18. Ibid., p. 615.

19. Robert Pattison, *The Great Dissent: John Henry Newman and the Liberal Heresy* (New York: Oxford University Press, 1991), p. 6.

20. Ibid., p. 6.

21. Antony Lentin, "Anglicanism, Parliament, and the Courts," in *Religion in Victorian Britain: Controversies*, vol. 2, edited by Gerald Parsons (Manchester: Manchester University Press, 1988), p. 32.

22. Richard J. Helmstadter, "The Nonconformist Conscience," *Religion in Victorian Britain: Interpretations*, vol. 4, edited by Gerald Parsons (Manchester: Manchester University Press, 1988. See also K.S Inglis, "Patterns of Religious Worship in 1851," *Journal of Ecclesiastical History* 11, no. 1 (1960): 74–86; and W.S.F. Pickering, "The 1851 Religious Census—a Useless Experiment?" *British Journal of Sociology* 18, no. 4 (1967): 382–407. Jeffrey Cox, in *The English Churches in a Secular Society, Lambeth 1870–1930* (New York: Oxford University Press, 1982), provides tables of church attendance in Lambeth in 1851, indicating the steep decline of Anglican attendance (p. 297).

23. It is true, as John Wolffe points out, that Tractarians also found it possible to regard the Church of England as Catholic, indicating a rapprochement between Catholicism and Anglicanism that diminished the Roman element. See John Wolffe, *God and Greater Britain: Religion and National Life in Britain and Ireland 1843–1945* (London: Routledge, 1994), p. 36.

24. See Ali Asghar Engineer's *The Shah Bano Controversy* (Delhi: Orient Longman, 1990) for comprehensive source material on the case. For more on Shah Bano, see also Gayatri Chakravorty Spivak's brief intervention in *Outside in the Teaching Machine* (New York: Routledge, 1993); and Zakia Pathak and Rajeswari Sundar Rajan, "Shahbano," *Signs* 14 (Spring 1989): 558–577.

25. Graham Pechey, "On the Borders of Bakhtin: Dialogization, Decolonization," *Oxford Literary Review* 9, nos. 1–2 (1987): 59–85.

26. Edward W. Said, *Culture and Imperialism* (New York: Knopf, 1993). See also Suvendrini Perera, *Reaches of Empire: The English Novel from Edgeworth to Dickens* (New York: Columbia University Press, 1991).

27. Ernest Gellner, *Postmodernism, Reason, and Religion* (London: Routledge, 1992).

28. Two recent scholarly works fitting this description are Gyanendra Pandey, *The Construction of Communalism in Colonial North India* (Delhi: Oxford University Press, 1990), and Sandria Freitag, *Collective Action and Community: Public Arenas and the Emergence of Communalism in North India* (Berkeley and Los Angeles: University of California Press, 1989).

29. Maria Edgeworth, *Harrington*, vol. 7 of *Tales and Novels*, 20 vols. (1817; rpt. New York: Harper and Brother, 1856).

30. Ibid., p. 154.

31. I am grateful to Neville Hoad for suggesting a line of thought that places the anti-Semitism of the novel against the backdrop of subaltern representations.

32. Michael Ragussis, "Representation, Conversion, and Literary Form: *Harrington* and the Novel of Jewish Identity," *Critical Inquiry* 16 (Autumn 1989): 135.

33. Charles Dickens, *Barnaby Rudge* (1841; rpt. London: Penguin, 1986), p. 354.

34. Ibid., pp. 354–55.

35. Steven Marcus, *Dickens: From Pickwick to Dombey* (New York: Basic Books, 1965), pp. 171–72.

36. Dickens, *Barnaby Rudge*, p. 233.

37. Simon During, "Literature—Nationalism's Other? The Case for Revision," in Homi Bhabha, ed., *Nation and Narration* (London: Routledge, 1990), p. 142.

38. Dickens, *Barnaby Rudge*, p. 689.

39. Valentine Cunningham, *Everywhere Spoken Against: Dissent in the Victorian Novel* (Oxford: Clarendon Press, 1975), p. 83.

40. Dennis Walder, *Dickens and Religion* (London: George Allen, 1981), p. 91.

41. Sydney (Lady Morgan) Owenson, *Luxima the Prophetess* (London: Charles Westerton, 1859). First published as *The Missionary* in 1811. Cited in the text as *L*.

42. Two popular novels that illustrate the continuing power of Anglican ideology among the British readership are Cyril Dennehy's *Flower of Asia* (London: Burns and Oates, 1901) and Alice Perrin's *Idolatry* (London: Chatto and Windus, 1909). Even though both works, like much popular English fiction about Indian converts, claim their primary target to be a polytheistic Hinduism, the "Papist" fear that looms large in all of them suggests that Hinduism functions as a displaced form of Roman Catholicism. In *Idolatry* Perrin disapproves of the Jesuit strategy of disguise and accommodation to win converts, claiming that "to practice our religion in Oriental fashion would seem to be an acceptance of Hindu methods which could not well be tolerated by the Church" (p. 322). In Dennehy's novel, on the other hand, while the Church of England struggles to ward off its sectarian rivals, the heroine Kesur is nonplussed by the conflict between Roman Catholic and Anglican missionaries, and asks with incredulity: "Are you not both English?" (p. 152).

43. Nigel Leask, *Anxieties of Empire: British Romantic Writers and the East* (Cambridge: Cambridge University Press, 1993).

44. M. Mainwaring, *The Suttee; or, the Hindu Converts*, 3 vols. (London: A.K. Newman, 1830).

45. Owenson, *Luxima*, p. 264. Emphasis in original.

46. Salbstein, *Emancipation of the Jews in Britain*, p. 42.

47. George Eliot, *Daniel Deronda* (1876; Oxford: Oxford University Press, 1984), p. 450.

48. Ibid., p. 456.

49. See Robert Young, *Colonial Desire: Hybridity in Theory, Culture, and Race* (London: Routledge, 1995), for a provocative reading of Matthew Arnold that situates his cultural politics in contemporary race theories.

50. Attitudinal conversion enters the conceptual apparatus of several recent postmodern students of religion, among whom David Krieger gives one of the most useful accounts of "methodological conversion" as a means of overcoming impasses between religious communities. Krieger draws heavily on religious conversion as a metaphor for a theory of knowledge to suggest the conceptual means by which the gaps between different cultural metanarratives might be bridged, "to deal with the problem of how global thinking—the general validity of knowledge, the universality of norms and a more than merely local solidarity with fellow humans and with nature—is possible in a radically pluralistic world and a postmodern context" (p. 223). See his "Conversion: On the Possibility of Global Thinking in an Age of Particularism," *Journal of the American Academy of Religion* 58, no. 2 (1990): 223–43.

Attitudinal conversion occupies the attention of several modern historians, as well. At the close of a wide-ranging essay on perceptions of Islamic conversions by different groups in South Asia, Peter Hardy speculates whether these perceptions are not themselves essays in conversion, in that they encourage conversion to particular conceptions of relationships between Hindus and Muslims. See his "Modern European and Muslim Explanations of Conversion to Islam in South Asia: A Preliminary Survey of the Literature," in Nehemia Levtzion, ed., *Conversion to Islam* (New York: Holmes and Meier, 1979).

51. Benjamin Disraeli, preface to *Tancred: Or the New Crusade* (1847; New York

and London, M. Walter Dunne, 1904), quoted in Daniel R. Schwartz, *Disraeli's Fiction* (London: Macmillan, 1979), p. 84.

52. Salbstein, *Emancipation of the Jews in Britain*, p. 173. See also David Cesarani, ed., *The Making of Modern Anglo-Jewry* (London: Basil Blackwell, 1990); and David S. Katz, *The Jews in the History of England 1485–1850* (Oxford: Clarendon Press, 1994).

53. Quoted in Sarah Bradford, *Disraeli* (London: Weidenfeld and Nicolson, 1982), p. 183.

54. Benjamin Disraeli, *Coningsby* (1844; rpt. London: Penguin, 1989), p. 239. Emphasis added.

55. Ibid.

56. Ibid., p. 146.

57. Ibid., 270.

58. Michael Ragussis, *Figures of Conversion: "The Jewish Question" and English National Identity* (Durham: Duke University Press, 1995).

59. Disraeli, *Coningsby*, p. 273.

60. Ragussis, *Figures of Conversion*, p. 188.

61. J. C. Winslow, *Narayan Viman Tilak: The Christian Poet of Maharashtra* (Calcutta: Association Press, 1923), p. 17.

62. *Abhang* no. 160; ibid., p. 58.

63. Ibid., p. 60.

64. Quoted ibid., p. 58.

65. See Muhammad Mohar Ali, *The Bengali Reaction to Christian Missionary Activities 1833–1857* (Chittagong: Mehrub Publications, 1965).

66. Robin Horton, "African Conversion," *Africa* 41, no. 2 (1971): 85–108; idem, "On the Rationality of Conversion," *Africa* 45, no. 3 (1975): 219–35, and "On the Rationality of Conversion, Part II," Africa 45, no. 4 (1975): 373–99. Horton entered into a debate with several scholars contesting his theory of African modernity, and Humphrey Fisher, in "Conversion Reconsidered: Some Historical Aspects of Religious Conversion in Black Africa," *Africa* 43, no. 1 (1973): 27–40, offered a hard-hitting critique of Horton's description of Africanist Christian movements. Deryck Schreuder and Geoffrey Oddie, "What is 'Conversion'? History, Christianity, and Religious Change in Colonial Africa and South Asia," *Journal of Religious History* 15 (December 1989): 496–518, attempt to sift through some of the salient arguments emerging from the debate, though they tend at times to misapply perceptions deriving from the African situation to South Asia.

67. Terence Ranger, "The Local and the Global in Southern African Religious History," in *Conversion to Christianity: Historical and Anthropological Perspectives on a Great Transformation*, edited by Robert W. Hefner (Berkeley and Los Angeles: University of California Press, 1993).

68. Klaus K. Klostermaier, *Indian Theology in Dialogue* (Madras: Christian Literature Society, 1986), provides an informative account of recent trends in the relations of the Indian Christian community to other religious groups. A. J. Appaswamy is among the most consistent of the reinterpreters of Indian Christianity; his interpretation of the Christian message in terms of bhakti places Christianity within the framework of Ramanuja's Visitadvaita. A. J. Appaswamy, *The Gospel and India's Heritage* (Madras: Christian Literature Society, 1942).

69. Enumerating the studies that follow this tired pattern would be a lengthy and tedious exercise, but it is discouraging that even as recent a work as Robert Hefner's edited volume *Converson to Christianity* confines itself to these same questions without questioning the relationship between conversion and modernity. As a corrective to an unwavering pattern of scholarship on the subject, the numerous authors in *Conversion to Modernities: The Globalization of Christianity*, edited by Peter van der Veer (New York and London: Routledge, 1996) seek to steer questions away from cultural transformation toward a study of cultural transactions.

70. See Homi Bhabha, *The Location of Culture* (London: Routledge, 1994); Richard Fox Young, *Resistant Hinduism: Sanskrit Sources on Anti-Christian Apologetics in Early Nineteenth-Century India* (Vienna: DeNobili Research Library, 1981); Vicente Rafael, *Contracting Colonialism: Translation and Christian Conversions in Tagalog* (Ithaca: Cornell University Press, 1989).

71. See my "Raymond Williams and British Colonialism," *Yale Journal of Criticism* 4, no. 2 (1991): 47–66.

Chapter Two
A Grammar of Dissent

1. Talal Asad, in *Genealogies of Religion* (Baltimore: Johns Hopkins University Press, 1993), reconstructs religion's detachment from knowledge production as the moment when religion in Europe was delineated as a universal system.

2. Edward W. Said, *The World, the Text, and the Critic* (Cambridge: Harvard University Press, 1983), p. 290.

3. John Henry Newman, *Loss and Gain: The Story of a Convert*, edited by Alan G. Hill (1848; rpt. Oxford: Oxford University Press, 1986), p. 62. Hereafter cited in the text as *LG*.

4. This last question is addressed with subtlety and insight by Gayatri Chakravorty Spivak in "The Burden of English," in *Orientalism and the Postcolonial Predicament*, edited by Carol Breckenridge and Peter van der Veer (Philadelphia: University of Pennsylvania Press, 1993). Spivak argues that, although colonial transactions sought to shape natives by eliciting assent to the intended transformation, this assent was not consistent along the lines of race, gender, and class. Drawing on analogies between colonial subjects and the implied reader of texts, Spivak suggests that for readers (and subjects) to give a simple assent to the text is virtually to participate in the violence perpetuated by it. But she also sees the stratification on lines of gender and class as enabling the critic to give a divided assent to texts, which are thus turned against themselves.

5. See K. S Inglis, "Patterns of Religious Worship in 1851," *Journal of Ecclesiastical History* 11, no. 1 (1960): 74–86; and W.S.F. Pickering, "The 1851 Religious Census—a Useless Experiment?" *British Journal of Sociology* 18, no. 4 (1967): 382–407.

6. Robert Pattison, *The Great Dissent: John Henry Newman and the Liberal Heresy* (New York: Oxford University Press, 1991), p. 6.

7. John Reed, *Victorian Will* (Athens: Ohio State University Press, 1989), p. 110.

8. Ibid.

9. For contemporary versions of this argument, with particular reference to postcolo-

nial societies, see Ashis Nandy, "The Politics of Secularism and the Recovery of Religious Tolerance," in *Mirrors of Violence: Communities, Riots, and Survivors* in South Asia, edited by Veena Das (Delhi: Oxford University Press, 1990).

10. Hugh McLeod, *Religion and the Working Class* (London: Macmillan, 1984), p. 36. See also Deryck W. Lovegrove, *Established Church, Sectarian People: Itinerancy and the Transformation of English Dissent, 1780–1830* (Cambridge: Cambridge University Press, 1986), which details the growing use of Sunday schools by preachers and teachers for the purpose of alienating the minds of the young from the established clergy.

11. McLeod, *Religion and the Working Class*, p. 23.

12. Ibid.

13. E. P. Thompson, *Witness against the Beast: William Blake and the Moral Law* (Cambridge: Cambridge University Press, 1993), p. xix.

14. Charles Dickens, *Barnaby Rudge* (1841; London: Penguin, 1986).

15. The Five Mile Act took its name from the fact that it excluded a nonjuror from teaching, preaching, or living within five miles of a place where he had served as minister.

16. In *Apologia Pro Vita Sua* (1864; New York: Doubleday, 1956), Newman refers to an essay by Whately, "Letters on the Church by an Episcopalian," as having left a profound impression on him. Whately upholds the basic tenets of disestablishment in this essay, the two most important being, from Newman's point of view, the non-interference in temporal matters by the Church and in spiritual affairs by the State; and the retaining of revenues and property by the Church (p. 134). Hereafter cited in the text as *Apo*.

17. Stephen Thomas, *Newman and Heresy* (Cambridge: Cambridge University Press, 1992), p. 4.

18. *The Letters and Diaries of John Henry Newman*, vol. 2, edited by Ian Ker and Thomas Gornall (Oxford: Clarendon Press, 1979), p. 128; also quoted in Ian Ker, *John Henry Newman: A Biography* (Oxford: Oxford University Press, 1988), p. 34.

19. *The Letters and Diaries of John Henry Newman*, vol. 4, edited by Ian Ker and Thomas Gornall (Oxford: Clarendon Press, 1980), p. 35.

20. Thomas, *Newman and Heresy*, p. 38.

21. Ibid., p. 3.

22. John Henry Newman, *Historical Sketches*, vol. 1 (London: Pickering, 1889), p. 340; quoted in Ker, *John Henry Newman*, p. 82.

23. Ker, *John Henry Newman*, p. 109.

24. Quoted ibid.

25. Benedict Anderson, *Imagined Communities* (1983; 2d rev. ed. London: Verso, 1992).

26. See Charles Stewart and Rosalind Shaw, eds., *Syncretism/Anti-Syncretism* (London: Routledge, 1994) for diverse essays on this subject. See also my "Beyond Orientalism: Syncretism and the Politics of Knowledge," *Stanford Humanities Review* 5, no. 1 (1995): 19–34.

27. I am grateful to David Lipscomb for helping out with this phrase. Worldliness, of course, is a concept central to Edward Said's thought: the textual engagement with history that Said emphasizes as a way of resisting both critical systems and dominant

orthodoxies has its counterpart, I might suggest, in Newman's understanding that belief interacts with history. With little damage to Newman's intention, the word "belief" is possibly interchangeable with Said's "texts" in a passage where Said refers to "the connection between texts and the existential actualities of human life, politics, societies, and events. The realities of power and authority—as well as the resistances offered by men, women, and social movements to institutions, authorities, and orthodoxies—are the realities that make texts possible, that deliver them to their readers, that solicit the attention of critics." See Said, *The World, The Text, and the Critic*, p. 5.

28. John Henry Newman, *An Essay in Aid of a Grammar of Assent* (Notre Dame: University of Notre Dame Press, 1979), p. 330. Hereafter cited in the text as *GA*.

29. John Henry Newman, *An Essay on the Development of Christian Doctrine* (1878; 6th ed., rpt. Notre Dame: University of Notre Dame Press, 1989), p. 186 (hereafter cited as *Christian Doctrine*); cited in Edward Thomas, "Newman's Social and Political Thinking," in Ian Ker and Alan G. Hill, eds., *Newman after a Hundred Years* (Oxford: Clarendon Press, 1990), p. 165.

30. Newman, *Christian Doctrine*, p. 45.

31. Pattison, *The Great Dissent*, p. 153.

32. Alan Crowley, "The Performance of the *Grammar*: Reading and Writing Newman's Narrative of Assent," *Renascence* 43, nos. 1–2 (1991): 137–57.

33. John Coulson, *Religion and Imagination* (Oxford: Clarendon Press, 1981), p. 35.

34. In a response from the floor to an earlier version of this paper, which was first presented at the University of Warwick, Edward Said addressed the question of authority in terms of Newman's own biography. Said suggested that Newman was so driven by anarchic, egotistical impulses that authority constituted for him the only stable structure that would both contain and shape those impulses in more creative ways. This argument contextualizes Newman's turn to a foundational religious history in an interesting way, though I would also argue that Newman's projection of biography into history is consistent with the public nature of his conversion.

35. Asad, *Genealogies of Religion*. See also Alan M. Olson, "Postmodernity and Faith," *Journal of the American Academy of Religion* 58, no. 1 (1990): 37–53; David J. Krieger, "Conversion: On the Possibility of Global Thinking in an Age of Particularism," *Journal of the American Academy of Religion* 58, no. 2 (1990): 223–43. Specifically on Newman, see Alan Crowley, "The Performance of the *Grammar*"; Jonathan Loesberg, *Fictions of Consciousness: Mill, Newman, and the Reading of Victorian Prose* (New Brunswick and London: Rutgers University Press, 1986); Gerard Casey, *Natural Reason: A Study of the Notions of Inference, Assent, Intuition, and First Principles in the Philosophy of John Henry Cardinal Newman* (New York: Peter Lang, 1984).

36. Pattison, *The Great Dissent*, p. v.

37. John Henry Newman, *The Idea of a University* (1873; Notre Dame: University of Notre Dame Press, 1982), p. 190. Hereafter cited in the text as *Idea*.

38. Pattison, *The Great Dissent*, p. 206.

39. Thomas, *Newman and Heresy*, p. 5.

40. Alan G. Hill, "Originality and Realism in Newman's Novels," in *Newman after a Hundred Years*, p. 26. The disarray in which English Protestantism found itself, amidst widespread conflict between Tractarians and Evangelicals, encouraged efforts

by the English Catholic community to prove their Englishness to the general population. This theme is explored in depth by John Wolffe, *God and Greater Britain: Religion and National Life in Britain and Ireland 1843–1945* (London: Routledge, 1994).

41. W. Ralls, "The Papal Aggression of 1850: A Study in Victorian Anti-Catholicism," in *Religion in Victorian Britain: Interpretations,* vol. 4, edited by Gerald Parsons (Manchester: Manchester University Press, 1988), p. 116.

42. See D. G. Paz, *Popular Anti-Catholicism in Mid-Victorian England* (Stanford: Stanford University Press, 1992), for a comprehensive discussion of the extent to which anti-Catholicism was at the center of political life during the nineteenth century, which Paz meticulously links to the Irish Question.

43. Lester Kurtz, in *The Politics of Heresy: The Modernist Crisis in Roman Catholicism* (Berkeley and Los Angeles: University of California Press, 1986), discusses in detail Catholicism's response to modernity, one part of which was its partial assimilation of the doctrine of evolution and scientific progress. It should also be added, however, that celibacy and English nationalism were not necessarily opposed concepts for Newman, and that sexual renunciation offered a way of conserving himself for public service. This becomes for Newman the needed authority he was seeking.

44. Pattison, *The Great Dissent,* p. 39. Pattison also describes the earnest pilgrimages of many young men eager to meet Newman as the man who inspired them to make their tryst with "the Scarlet Woman," as the Catholic Church was then described. One fervent admirer was Oscar Wilde, "a violent Papist," who in Reading Gaol sent for Newman's books, including the *Apologia, The Idea of a University,* and *A Grammar of Assent.* See also Paz, *Popular Anti-Catholicism.*

Chapter Three
Rights of Passage

1. As I write, modern India has entered a new phase of a controversial debate over the drafting of a uniform civil code, provisionally mandated in Article 44 of the Indian Constitution. The debate has been freshly ignited by the May 21, 1995, decision of the Supreme Court of India, holding that a Hindu husband cannot end his first marriage by converting to Islam. The decision echoes an earlier controversial ruling in 1985, in which the Supreme Court expressed concern over the government's inaction in bringing about a uniform code and, in what has now become the infamous Shah Bano judgment, ordered Shah Bano's Muslim husband to pay her maintenance support, contrary to the prerogative to refuse alimony he claimed under Muslim personal law. The ensuing storm led to the repeal of the judgment through an enactment of the Indian Parliament. But in a repeat performance, the Supreme Court has now concluded, in response to Sarla Mudgal's suit against her husband, that the plurality of personal laws in the country necessitates a uniform civil code. Its more hardline position in this case throws the position of religious minorities in India once again into uncertainty. The 1995 judgment unequivocally lays the blame for the stalled move toward a uniform code squarely on minorities. Justice Kuldip Singh, who delivered the main judgment, ominously declared that "those who preferred to remain in India after partition fully knew that the Indian leaders did not believe in two-nation or three-nation theory and that in the Indian Republic there was to be only one nation—the Indian nation—and no community could

claim to remain a separate entity on the basis of religion. . . . The Hindus along with Sikhs, Buddhists, and Jains have forsaken their sentiments in the cause of the national unity and integration; some other communities would not." (*The Hindu*, Madras, May 28, 1995).

Sarla Mudgal's case is not an uncommon one, and some of the nineteenth-century cases I allude to in this chapter also tread on the uncertain ground between marriages of convenience and those of conviction. The legal dimension in Mudgal's case is clearly above controversy: her Hindu husband wants to remarry, but he cannot get a divorce either because his wife does not want to give it to him or he does not want to go through the complicated proceedings. He converts to Islam, as does his new female companion, and the two get married under Islamic law. And it is presumed that the first marriage is over. The dissolution of the first marriage and the validity of the second one are the two points of law that have come up before the Supreme Court.

The ruling has made it clear that the first marriage is not dissolved just through the conversion of the husband, and he is obliged to obtain a divorce to remarry. Nor can he marry again under any other religious law unless he has obtained a divorce from the first wife. The Supreme Court has gone a step further by declaring that since the second marriage contracted through conversion is void, the husband can be prosecuted for bigamy. Feminist scholars like Vasudha Dhagamwar and Seema Mustafa are of the view that the Supreme Court's position will bring relief to a large number of women. Indeed, among feminist activists Dhagamwar is confident that the uniform civil code can be kept separate from religious ceremonies and rituals, and she believes that the code will increase the rights of women. She asks, "Which woman would object to a code that gives her equal property rights, protection from polygamy, protection from arbitrary divorce? Which orphan child would not wish for a home? Which child would like to be debarred from its inheritance because the father has converted to Islam?" (Vasudha Dhagamwar, "Who's Afraid of the Uniform Code?" *The Hindu*, Madras, June 18, 1995).

But for other feminist critics, the equation between the uniform civil code and gender justice is not always so clearcut, and Seema Mustafa suggests, quite rightly I believe, that arguments for the uniform code ignore progressive and secular efforts made by minority communities toward gender equity. (See Seema Mustafa, "Whose Code, to Whose Good? *The Hindu*, Madras, May 28, 1995.) When such efforts, which we must assume are made in good faith, are preempted by the call for uniformity of laws, it is not surprising to see that the demand for gender equality is turned into a sectarian issue, and that even the unarguable legal aspect of bigamy in the Sarla Mudgal case is turned into a religious controversy.

This is precisely what the vice president of the Muslim Personal Law Board, Kalbe Sadiq, managed to achieve. In an interview in Hyderabad, Sadiq admitted that Islam does not accept conversion for the sake of marrying a woman. But he insisted that the Supreme Court's ruling that upheld the validity of the first Hindu marriage even after Islamic conversion is not acceptable to the Muslim community, as it is opposed to the Islamic Shariat. This, despite the authoritative opinion of Asaf A. A. Fyzee in *Outlines of Muhammedan Law*, where he affirms that a non-Muslim lawfully married in accordance with his own law cannot dissolve his marriage by mere conversion to Islam, and that a marriage performed according to one scheme of personal law cannot be destroyed by the mere adoption of another faith by one of the spouses; (see Tahir Mahmood,

"Islamic Law and State Legislation on Religious Conversion in India," in *Islam and Public Law: Classical and Contemporary Studies*, edited by Chibli Mallat (London: Graham and Trotman, 1993). As Seema Mustafa writes, "One can only hope that the Muslim Personal Law Board takes as mature a view of the judgment and does not create a meaningless controversy by citing the wishes of the 'community' to perpetuate injustice and deny women their basic rights."

2. National Archives of India (hereafter NAI), Home Department—Public Proceedings, nos. 73–78, Letter from T. E. Slater to the Secretary to the Government of India, September 1876, p. 705. Emphasis added.

3. Julian Saldanha, *Conversion and Indian Civil Law* (Bangalore: United Theological College, 1981), p. 121. See also C. A. Moore, ed., *The Status of the Individual in East and West* (Honolulu: University of Hawaii Press, 1968).

4. India Office and Library Records (hereafter IOLR), Board's Collections, Bengal Despatches, India Political Department, draft no. 669, no. 33, 17 August 1853, p. 1,345.

5. Dicey's classic text is *A Digest of the Law of England with Reference to the Conflict of Laws* (London: Stevens and Sons, 1896); its overriding premise is that the conflict of laws must begin with laws defined strictly according to the authority they derived from the sovereign in whose territory they were enforced. G. W. Bartholomew, in "Private Interpersonal Law," *International and Comparative Law Quarterly* 1 (July 1952): 325–44, directly applies choice-of-law rules and private interpersonal law to cases of conversion. The classic case is Khambatta v. Khambatta, in which a Scottish woman married in Scotland a Muslim whose residence was in India. Both husband and wife went to live in India, and the wife then converted to Islam. After her conversion, her husband divorced her by pronouncing *talaq*, the triply uttered statement that connotes dissolution of a marriage in Islam. The woman later remarried under the Special Marriage Act. But her second husband, contesting a suit for dissolution of his marriage to her, subsequently claimed that, since her first marriage was contracted in Scotland, her conversion had no impact—and the pronouncement of *talaq* no validity—and, therefore, she was still married to her first husband. This meant of course that the second husband was not officially married to her at all. The substantive basis of his bewildering claim was that the territory where civil contracts are made overrides religious identity. See Bartholomew, "Private Interpersonal Law," pp. 333–34.

6. Bartholomew, "Private Interpersonal Law," p. 327.

7. Saldanha, *Conversion and Indian Civil Law*, p. 19. Queen Victoria's proclamation of religious liberty in 1858 suggests a return to the Orientalist policy of the Hastings era, though I would argue that its sentiments are much closer to the emancipatory rhetoric of mid-nineteenth-century England. Declared Victoria: "We disclaim alike the right and desire to impose our convictions on any of our subjects. . . . We will that generally in framing and administering the law due regard be paid to the ancient rights, usages, and customs of India." Quoted in Robert Lingat, *The Classical Law of India* (Berkeley and Los Angeles: University of California Press, 1973), p. 136.

8. Standish G. Grady, *A Treatise on the Hindoo Law of Inheritance, Comprising the Doctrines of the Various Schools with the Decisions of the High Courts of the Several Presidencies of India, and the Judgments of the Privy Council on Appeal* (London: Wildy and Sons, 1868), p. 26. Hereafter cited as *Hindoo Law of Inheritance*.

9. NAI, Home Department—Legislative, Draft of Law Commission, 25 January 1845. The relevant clauses, numbers 11 and 12, state: "Provided always, that no Hindoo

or Mahommedan shall, in consequence of any thing in this Act contained, by renouncing the Hindoo or Mahommedan religion, lose any rights or property or deprive any other person of any rights or property. And it is hereby enacted, that so much of the Hindoo and Mahommedan Law as inflicts forfeiture of rights or property upon any party renouncing, or who has been excluded from the communion of either of those Religions, shall cease to be enforced as Law in the Courts of the East India Company."

10. IOLR, Board's Collections, Legislative Department, no. 12 of 1851, draft 875 (F/2436): Memorial from the Hindoo inhabitants of Bengal praying for the repeal of Act XXI of 1850. Saldanha, in *Conversion and Indian Civil Law*, however, notes that the force of the Caste Disabilities Removal Act was considerably diluted in post-Independence India (p. 131). Its reversal in the Hindu Adoption and Maintenance Act of 1956 is evident in that everything was geared to protecting Hindus and punishing "apostates" from Hinduism. The same 1956 act also reverses the attempt in 1850 to protect converts' guardianship rights. The act provided that, upon conversion, the Hindu cedes to his or her spouse the right of guardianship. See also Marc Galanter, *Law and Society in Modern India* (Delhi: Oxford University Press, 1989), pp. 147–61, and his *Competing Equalities* (1984; rpt. Delhi: Oxford University Press, 1993) for further analysis of reversals of the Caste Disabilities Removal Act in post-Independence legislation.

11. Popular English novels about conversion include M. Mainwaring, *The Suttee: or, the Hindoo Converts* (London: A.K. Newman, 1830); Sydney Owenson (Lady Morgan), *Luxima the Prophetess* (London: Charles Westerton, 1859); Philip Meadows Taylor, *Seeta* (London: Kegan Paul, 1872); J. Campbell Oman, *Where Three Creeds Meet* (London: Grant Richards, 1898); Cyril Dennehy, *Flower of Asia* (London: Burns and Oates, 1901); Sara J. Duncan, *Set in Authority* (London: Constable, 1906); Alice Perrin, *Idolatry* (London: Chatto and Windus, 1909), *The Anglo-Indians* (London: Methuen, 1912), *The Mound* (London: Methuen, 1922); Fanny Penny, *The Romance of a Nautch Girl* (London: Swan Sonnenschein, 1898), *The Outcaste* (London: Chatto and Windus, 1912), *A Question of Colour* (London: Hodder and Stoughton, 1928); Henry Bruce, *The Temple Girl* (London: John Long, 1919); Mary Ann Scharlieb, *Yet a More Excellent Way* (London: W. Gardner, 1929).

12. For example, British authorities had great difficulty in arriving at a decision to determine the rightful heirs to the property of a Hindu woman converted to Roman Catholicism who died intestate in Cochin. Two nephews claimed the property, but because it was uncertain whether the property was acquired before the woman's conversion or after, the case dragged on for years. If the property were acquired before the conversion, the nephews would be sole heirs according to Hindu law; if after, the property could devolve only on those who professed Christianity. Being Hindus, the nephews were not then entitled to inherit. Even when—on the advice of the pundits who were employed to interpret Hindu law for British judges—the Sadr Diwani Adalat (or appeals court) decided to rule in favor of the nephews, the government at Madras hesitated to take final action until it could obtain information from the governor-general in Calcutta whether any rule or precedent existed in Bengal that determined the succession to property in cases of conversion from Hinduism. IOLR, Board's Collections, Legislative Department, no. 21 of 1844, 4 November 1843, para. 43; Tamil Nadu Archives, Madras Judicial Consultations, vol. 472, no. 40, 21 March 1843; vol. 502a, no. 41, 10 March 1846; vol. 515, no. 45, 1 September 1846.

13. William James, *The Varieties of Religious Experience* (1902; New York: New American Library, 1958), p. 157.

14. See Jennifer Nedelsky, "Law, Boundaries, and the Bounded Self," *Representations* 30 (Spring 1990): 162–89, for a compelling discussion of the notion of rights as boundaries, which suggests a link between liberty and the security provided by law and government.

15. See Robert M. Doran, *Psychic Conversion and Theological Foundations: Toward a Reorientation of the Human Sciences*. American Academy of Religion Studies in Religion, no. 25 (Ann Arbor: Scholars Press, 1981), p. 24.

16. Richard McKeon, "The Individual in Law and in Legal Philosophy in the West," in Charles A. Moore, ed., *The Status of the Individual in East and West* (Honolulu: University of Hawaii Press, 1968), p. 453.

17. Although a uniform criminal code was developed for British India, the personal laws of the two major communities, Hindus and Muslims, continued to be administered in British courts where issues of marriage, divorce, inheritance, adoption, and so on, were involved, the assumption being that these were too closely intertwined with Hinduism or Islam to be amenable to a common civil code derived from English law. For all practical purposes, Buddhists, Jains, Parsis, and Sikhs all came under Hindu law. See J. Duncan Derrett, *Religion, Law, and the State in India* (London: Faber and Faber, 1968); A. C. Banerjee, *English Law in India* (Atlantic Highlands, NJ: Humanities Press, 1984); and Marc Galanter, *Law and Society in Modern India* for historical background to the administering of personal laws in British India. Derrett and Galanter are especially informative in showing how the application of personal laws reflects assumptions about the structure of Indian society that still guide modern Indian law.

18. Lingat, *The Classical Law of India*, p. 139.

19. Galanter, *Law and Society in Modern India*, p. 120.

20. IOLR, Board's Collections, Judicial Department, no. 12 of 1844, 8 July 1844, draft 866 (F/4/2065) (cited hereafter as IOLR, Judicial 1844); Tamil Nadu Archives, Madras Judicial Consultations, vol. 472, nos. 22–30, 2 July 1844 (cited hereafter as TNA, Madras Judicial 1844).

21. Fanny Penny's novel *The Outcaste* is the first attempt to tell the story of Ananda's conversion from his point of view. Transparently based on the Ananda Row case, with meticulous details drawn from the 1844 records—even the hero's name Ananda remains the same—the novel opens by unfolding events through Ananda's eyes. But the novel abruptly shifts from spiritual biography to social criticism. The second half of the book is almost wholly taken up by the English teachers and missionaries who shelter Ananda, as they reflect abstractly on the legal challenges facing the British in fighting the civil disabilities of native converts. By this point, Ananda has faded into an abstraction, a faceless "native" whose expulsion from Hindu society provides the occasion for deliberations on the extension of English law into territories not yet controlled by the British.

22. IOLR, Madras Judicial Despatches (F/4/2065), 27 November 1844, p. 986.

23. Lata Mani, "The Production of an Official Discourse on Sati in Early Nineteenth Century Bengal," in *Europe and Its Others*, vol. 1, edited by Francis Barker et al. (Colchester: University of Essex, 1985). Mani characterizes the movement toward British abolition of sati as a simultaneous process of accommodation and censure.

24. IOLR, Board's Collections, Legislative Department, no. 10 of 1852, draft 859; F/4/2481 (1 May 1852), p. 4.

25. Ibid., p. 5.

26. IOLR, Judicial 1844, p. 65.

27. Ibid., p. 15.

28. Ibid., p. 52.

29. Section 9, Regulation 7, Bengal Code, 1832; IOLR, Judicial 1844, p. 148.

30. Lata Mani has brilliantly shown a similar process at work in the British outlaw-ing of sati, where women are constituted as the ground for the redefinition of Hindu tradition as scripturally derived. See Lata Mani, "Contentious Traditions: The Debate on Sati in Colonial India," *Cultural Critique* 7 (Fall 1987): 119–56.

31. Derrett, *Religion, Law, and the State in India*, p. 52.

32. Interestingly, in novels dealing with the subject of conversion from Hinduism, the plight of the hapless widow receives extraordinary emphasis, acting as a prelude and background to the visual enactment of sati. Among some of the more extraordinary nineteenth-century novels on this subject are Owenson's *Luxima the Prophetess* and Mainwaring's *The Suttee, or The Hindoo Converts*.

33. IOLR, Judicial 1844, p. 15.

34. Gayatri Chakravorty Spivak, "The Burden of English," in *Orientalism and the Postcolonial Predicament*, edited by Carol Breckenridge and Peter van der Veer (Phila-delphia: University of Pennsylvania Press, 1993).

35. IOLR, Judicial 1844, p. 30.

36. Ibid., p. 2,032.

37. Julian Saldanha is surely right to point out that the Caste Disabilities Removal Act only preserved the natural rights of converts and left untouched the question of succession applicable after conversion. Such legislation was intended less to favor con-verts than to "prejudice the fundamental peculiar social and religious rights of the caste and family from which the apostate is cut off." See Julian Saldanha, *Civil and Ecclesi-astical Law in India* (Trichinopoly: Catholic Truth Society, n.d.), p. 22.

38. NAI, Home Department—Public Proceedings, nos. 73–78, September 1876, p. 702. Hereafter cited as NAI, Home Department 1876.

39. The issue of baptism is a crucial one, because Huchi's lack of baptism at the time of her marriage to Appiah is treated by the courts as placing her firmly within the Hindu fold. The missionaries found themselves in a closed situation, since the baptism that marked their formal attainment of a soul for Christianity had to be negotiated so that a "confession of faith" should suffice.

40. NAI, Home Department 1876, cross-examination of Huchi, pp. 729–30. Such assertions play on the multiple dictionary meanings of *testimony* as: the evidence given by a witness under oath; the evidence given in support of a fact or statement; proof; and open declaration or profession of faith.

41. Ibid., p. 730

42. NAI, Home Department 1876, cross-examination of Appiah, p. 748.

43. NAI, Home Department 1876, cross-examination of Huchi, p. 731. Whether the marriage ceremony of *sobana prastha* was performed or not before Huchi became a Christian was the crucial issue before the judges in the case. The ceremony that Huchi describes in her testimony is referred to as part of the "preliminary ceremonies of marriage," involving the Hindu ritual of walking seven steps around the sacrificial fire and tying the *tali*, or betrothal symbol (NAI, Home Department 1876, no. 74, p. 707). According to Huchi's testimony, during the six months when she was imprisoned in her mother-in-law's house (at which time she reached puberty), plans were underway to

perform the *sobana prastha*, which is defined as the ceremony marking readiness for consummation—the ultimate pronouncement of marriage. Huchi hints that it is when she learned that the *sobana prastha* was to take place soon that she decided to take refuge with the English schoolteacher and seek missionary assistance. In the court depositions there was considerable confusion about what constituted marriage: the missionaries, receiving advice "from high authority" (p. 708), were encouraged to seek annulment of Huchi's marriage on the assumption that Hindu marriages consist of two parts: the first (prepubertal) marriage ceremony and, following the girl's attainment of puberty, *sobana prastha*.

However, just as aware as government officials that such quibbling could violate Hindu religious liberties, they refrained from making a distinction between nuptials of betrothal and ceremonies of consummation, instead emphasizing liberty of conscience. In one legal opinion, the former ceremony, according to Hindu law, "constitute[d] a binding and irrevocable marriage" (p. 711). For her part, claiming that *sobana prastha* had not been performed, Huchi sought a provision in law declaring that "Hindu marriages (before the ceremony of *sobana prastha* has been performed) shall become void on either party ceasing to be a Hindu" (p. 710). Appiah, on the other hand, claimed that *sobana prastha* had been performed and that his marriage to Huchi was fully solemnized—a claim received with incredulity by Huchi's mother, who remarked that *sobana prastha* is an openly celebrated ceremony, not one performed in secret, and that if there had such been such a ceremony the girl's parents certainly would have known about it.

44. Ibid.

45. Ibid., p. 733.

46. NAI, Home Department 1876, cross-examination of the Inspector of Police, p. 736.

47. NAI, Home Department 1876, cross-examination of Huchi, p. 733.

48. Ibid.

49. NAI, Home Department 1876, cross-examination of Appiah, p. 750.

50. Grady, *Hindoo Law of Inheritance*, p. 8. Grady cites Hindu law to the effect that the husband had the option of either separating completely from his wife or replacing her with another woman, the first wife still continuing to be legally bound to him.

51. The Native Converts' Marriage Dissolution Act of 1866 made provisions for such eventualities, where unconverted spouses could file for dissolution of the marriage when their partner's loss of caste threatened them with a similar fate. This act, like so much else in British civil legislation, was designed to enable unconverted persons to retain their membership in caste society. If he so chose, Appiah could have appealed to the provisions of this act, especially since by his own admission he had no intention of taking Huchi back as his wife but only as his prostitute. Huchi's (ultimately misguided) appeal to the Native Converts' Marriage Dissolution Act may also have been motivated in part by the wish that Appiah would invoke it to release her from the marriage. See William Theobald, ed., *Acts of the Legislative Council of India, 1866–1867*, vol. 8 (Calcutta: Thacker, Spink, 1867), p. 247.

52. It might well be asked whether a different conclusion can be drawn wherever the situation was reversed, and the convert was the husband rather than the wife; whether the power to end the marriage in such cases shifted from the husband to the unconverted

wife; and whether this does not dispute my earlier contention and conclusively prove, to the contrary, that it was not so much patriarchal structures that were affirmed but the exclusive right of unconverted spouses to continue or discontinue a marriage. The available records, however, suggest that in the instances where converts were men, their wives were invariably persuaded to convert along with them, whatever reservations the wives might have had. One of the most moving testimonies of the agonizing decision to convert is by Lakshmibai Tilak, wife of the Christian convert Narayan Viman Tilak, who resisted for a long time and eventually gave in, virtually conceding that hers was Hobson's choice—either to remain unconverted and lose her husband (in which case she would be shunned by Hindu society and treated as a widow, as Ananda Row's wife pointed out) or to convert and thereby renounce the religion with which she had deep emotional and cultural ties. See P. S. Jacob, *The Experiential Response of N. V. Tilak* (Madras: Christian Literature Society, 1979).

53. In a related case in Bengal involving yet another female convert, Ram Kumari, who argued that her civil death dissolved her first marriage, the Calcutta High Court ruled that civil death pertained only to civil rights, "but we find no authority in Hindu law for the position that a degraded person or an apostate is absolved from all civil obligations incurred before degradation or apostasy." See *Collection of the Decisions of the High Courts and the Privy Council on the Hindu Law of Marriage and the Effect of Apostasy after Marriage up to March 1891* (Madras: Scottish Press, 1891), p. 13.

54. NAI, Home Department 1876, cross-examination of Huchi, p. 733.

55. Ibid., p. 757.

56. Ibid., p. 759.

57. Ibid., p. 760.

58. Ibid., p. 706.

59. Ibid., p. 705.

60. Dadaji v. Rakhmabai, suit no. 139 of 1884; *Indian Law Reports*, Bombay Series, vol. 9 (1885): 529–35, and vol. 10 (1886): 301–13. The case even received literary attention, as no less a writer than Rudyard Kipling satirized it in a poem, "In the Case of Rukhmibhaio," which mocked Indian reformers' call for self-rule as premature, since they were incapable of redressing Rakhmabai's plight:

> Gentleman reformers, you have heard the story
> Weighed the woman's evidence—marked the man's reply.
> Here's a chance for honour, notoriety and glory!
> Graduates of culture will you let that chance go by?

In *Early Verse by Rudyard Kipling, 1879–1889: Unpublished, Uncollected, and Rarely Collected Poems*, edited by Andrew Rutherford (Oxford: Clarendon Press, 1986), p. 374..

61. Uma Chakravarti, "Law, Gender, and the Colonial State," unpublished manuscript; Sudhir Chandra, "Whose Laws? Notes on a Legitimising Myth of the Colonial Indian State," *Studies in History* 8, no. 2 (1992): 187–211. See also Janaki Nair, *Women and Law in Colonial India* (New Delhi: Kali for Women, 1996), pp. 73–75, for a brief commentary on the Rakhmabai case.

62. Chandra, "Whose Laws?" p. 192.

63. See Mary Lyndon Shanley, *Feminism, Marriage, and the Law in Victorian En-*

gland, 1850–1895 (Princeton: Princeton University Press, 1989), chap. 5, for an account of these debates. Shanley also points out that parliamentary interest in the age of consent issue came out of widespread alarm at the rise in child prostitution and pornography. Attempts to control the burgeoning child-sex trade resulted in acts like the Criminal Law Amendment Act, which "reflected an expanded definition of childhood as well as a new impulse to use state authority to control sexual behavior" (p. 152). Deborah Gorham has written on W. T. Stead's (Annie Besant's one-time friend) pornographic foray, where she argues that the Victorian reaction to such offensive publications has to be understood in a larger context "of other legal definitions that relate to the boundaries that a society draws between childhood, youth, and maturity" (p. 363). See Deborah Gorham, "The 'Maiden Tribute of Modern Babylon' Reexamined: Child Prostitution and the Idea of Childhood in Late-Victorian England," *Victorian Studies*, 21 (Spring 1978): 353–79.

64. Carole Pateman, *The Sexual Contract* (Stanford: Stanford University Press, 1988), p. 48.

65. NAI, Home Department 1876, Letter from the Legislative Department to the Foreign Department, p. 2.

66. NAI, Home Department 1876, Letter from the Foreign Department to the Legislative Department, p. 3.

67. NAI, Home Department 1876, p. 712.

68. James Fitzjames Stephen's counsel was sought not long after he returned from India in 1872 as legal member of council, where he carried out codification of law in a post-Mutiny setting. In 1873–1874, immediately after his return to England, he prepared a bill consolidating acts relating to the government of India, but the bill was never passed into law. His signed response to Huchi's petition is dated 24 July 1875.

69. NAI, Home Department 1876, p. 712.

70. Leslie Stephen, *Life of Sir James Fitzjames Stephen* (London, 1895), p. 242; quoted in K.J.M. Smith, *James Fitzjames Stephen: Portrait of a Victorian Rationalist* (Cambridge: Cambridge University Press, 1988), p. 126.

71. Smith, *James Fitzjames Stephen*, p. 134.

72. Gayatri Chakravorty Spivak, "Can the Subaltern Speak?" in *Marxism and the Interpretation of Culture*, edited by Cary Nelson and Lawrence Grossberg (Urbana and Chicago: University of Illinois Press, 1988), p. 302.

73. *Reports of Cases Heard and Determined by the Judicial Committee and the Lords of H.M. Most Honourable Privy Council, on Appeal from the Supreme and Sudder Dewaney Courts in the East Indies*, vol. 9 (London: V. and R. Stevens, 1864), p. 205. Hereafter cited as *Reports of Cases Heard by the Privy Council*.

74. The official correspondence repeatedly emphasizes that although the terms "East Indian" or "Eurasian" merely indicated persons of mixed European and Indian blood, the question of whether any particular individual would ordinarily be recognized as East Indian depended on the circumstances and habits of life. NAI, Home Department—Public Proceedings A, nos. 84–85, April 1882.

75. NAI, Home Department—Ecclesiastical Proceedings, nos. 13–18, June 1874.

76. Grady, *Hindoo Law of Inheritance*, p. 320.

77. John Taylor Coleridge was, of course, the nephew of the poet Samuel Taylor Coleridge. After a career in law distinguished more by literary taste and classical knowledge than legal learning, Coleridge was appointed to serve on the Privy Council

from 1858 to 1876, where his knowledge of ecclesiastical law proved to be of great service in a number of judicial pronouncements. Lord Kingsdown (Thomas Pemberton-Leigh) was especially experienced in minutiae of Indian land tenures and, though sharing an equal weight with his colleagues on the bench from 1844 to 1864, bore the burden of preparing and formulating decisions, which were regarded as models of judicial expression during his time. See *The Dictionary of National Biography*, edited by Leslie Stephen and Sidney Lee, vols. 4 and 15 (1917; rpt., London: Oxford University Press, 1973).

78. A running complaint in the Privy Council's deliberations was the absence of an effective law of the land, leaving large numbers of non-Hindu or non-Muslim communities in British India, such as the Armenians, the Portuguese, and the French, without a law of their own to determine their civil cases. The judges pointed to the example of French Christians in Pondicherry, for whom succession was governed by French law, as well as the example of those living in Portuguese-held territory who were governed by Portuguese law (*Reports of Cases Heard by the Privy Council*, p. 224). In 1865, two years after the final decision on Abraham v. Abraham was taken, the Indian Succession Act was passed extending English law to native Christians. But the civil courts in British-controlled districts recorded more cases of exemptions from the exercise of this act than its application. See Saldanha, *Conversion and Indian Civil Law*, pp. 97–104.

79. *Reports of Cases Heard by the Privy Council*, p. 217. There were other restrictions built into the application of English law. In Rallo v. Smith, which came up in the Bombay courts in 1868 involving an East Indian with a European great-grandfather, it was stated that "descendants of British subjects resident in a foreign country . . . are generally considered in three generations to lose their nationality, and with their nationality their legal status as subjects of their original country." See *Collection of the Decisions of the High Courts and the Privy Council on the Law of Succession and Maintenance* (Madras: Scottish Press, 1892), p. 35.

80. The exact wording is as follows: "The convert may renounce the old law by which he was bound, as he renounced his old religion, or, if he thinks fit, he may abide by the old law, notwithstanding he has renounced the old religion. For though the profession of Christianity releases the convert from the trammels of the Hindoo law, yet it does not of necessity involve any change of the rights or relations of the convert in matters in which Christianity has no concern, such as his rights and interests in, and his power over the property. The convert, though not bound as to such matters either by the Hindoo law or by any other positive law, may, by his course of conduct after his conversion, have shown by what law he intended his rights to be governed. He may do so either by attaching himself to a class which in this respect has adopted and acted upon some particular law or by having himself observed some past law, family usage, or custom." See Grady, *Hindoo Law of Inheritance*, p. 319.

81. Ibid., p. 324. Emphasis added.

82. Ibid., p. 323. Emphasis added. Marc Galanter points out that, although the Indian Succession Act of 1865 reversed Abraham v. Abraham, modern Indian courts are still divided about whether the Hindu rule of inheritance is applicable to Christian families who continue to be joint after conversion. For instance, in 1954 the Supreme Court ruled that "if the individual desires and intends to retain his old social and political ties, if the old religion is tolerant of the new faith and does not excommunicate the convert,

the conversion has no effect." Quoted in Galanter, *Law and Society in Modern India*, p. 106.

83. *Reports of Cases Heard by the Privy Council*, p. 230. James Nelson, one of the severest critics of the Abraham v. Abraham decision, argued that the case only proved the determination of the British law courts to secure a Sanskritic base for the law administered in India, and that it showed clearly to what extent the Sadr Diwani Adalat was prepared to go in forcing Sanskrit-based law upon non-Hindu inhabitants. See James Nelson, *A View of the Hindu Law as Administered by the High Court of Judicature at Madras* (Madras: Higginbotham, 1877), p. 28.

84. *Reports of Cases Heard by the Privy Council*, p. 244.

85. Ibid., p. 217.

86. Ibid., p. 244. In fact, the final judgment settled Francis's claim as "just remuneration" to him for services rendered.

Chapter Four
Silencing Heresy

1. A. B. Shah, ed., introduction to *The Letters and Correspondence of Pandita Ramabai* (Bombay: Maharashtra State Board for Literature and Culture, 1977), p. xi. Hereafter cited as *Correspondence*.

2. Letter from Pandita Ramabai, Poona, to Sister Geraldine, C.S.M.V., Wantage, December 11, 1893, in *Correspondence*, p. 308.

3. In *Home and Harem: Nation, Gender, Empire, and the Cultures of Travel* (Durham: Duke University Press, 1996), Inderpal Grewal points out the difficulties of positioning Ramabai within the critiques of Hindu patriarchy, since this discourse was also deployed by English missionaries to achieve their own aim of Christian conversion (p. 180). Arguing that there were no "neutral spaces" for articulating the problems and oppressions of Hindu women, Grewal maintains that Ramabai's genius lay in appropriating the rhetoric of the colonial state and missionaries to construct her own independent agency. Much the same is argued by Antoinette Burton in *Burdens of History: British Feminists, Indian Women, and Imperial Culture, 1865–1915* (Chapel Hill: University of North Carolina Press, 1994): resistance to the imperialist gestures of British women, she maintains, spurred Ramabai to an acute self-consciousness (p. 32). Teresa Hubel, in *Whose India? The Independence Struggle in British and Indian Fiction and History* (Durham: Duke University Press, 1996), also conjoins Ramabai's critique of imperialism and Hindu patriarchy. My own argument has a considerably different focus, for my suggestion is that Ramabai's agency is constitutive of her developing religious sensibility, and not a mere strategy appropriated from her colonial mentors. Her critiques of colonialism not only aimed to dismantle Hindu patriarchy but also served to create her own ideal religious system in which her critical sensibility remained intact.

4. Pandita Ramabai, *The High-Caste Hindu Woman* (Philadelphia, Press of the J. B. Rogers Printing, 1888), p. 103. See also Meera Kosambi, "Women, Emancipation, and Equality: Pandita Ramabai's Contribution to Women's Cause," *Economic and Political Weekly*, October 29, 1988: WS38-WS49, for a thorough treatment of Ramabai's social activism.

5. Quoted in S. M. Adhav, *Pandita Ramabai* (Madras: Christian Literature Society, 1979), p. 15. It is interesting that four decades earlier, in 1841, John Henry Newman made the argument that a completely Protestant document like the Thirty-Nine Articles still made room for the English clergy to accept their vocation on the authority of the Church of Rome. In denying the exclusionary intents of the articles, Newman made the claim that the interpretive possibilities of the document allowed for its being brought in harmony with the Book of Common Prayer. "The Protestant Confession was drawn up with the purpose of including Catholics; and Catholics now will not be excluded. What was an economy in the reformers, is a protection to us. What would have been a perplexity to us then, is a perplexity to Protestants now. We could not then have found fault with their words; they cannot now repudiate our meaning." John Henry Newman, "Remarks on Certain Passages in the Thirty-Nine Articles," in *Religion in Victorian Britain: Sources*, vol. 3, edited by James R. Moore (Manchester: Manchester University Press, 1988), p. 13.

6. Letter from Pandita Ramabai to Sister Geraldine, September 22, 1885, in *Correspondence*, p. 88.

7. Letter from Sister Geraldine to Pandita Ramabai, October 1885, in *Correspondence*, p. 104.

8. E. P. Thompson, *Witness against the Beast: William Blake and the Moral Law* (Cambridge: Cambridge University Press, 1993), p. 10.

9. Letter from Sister Geraldine to Pandita Ramabai, October 1885, in *Correspondence*, p. 103.

10. Letter from Sister Geraldine to Pandita Ramabai, in answer to objections she made to the Catholic faith, October 5, 1885, in *Correspondence*, p. 91.

11. Letter from Pandita Ramabai to Sister Geraldine, May 12, 1885, in *Correspondence*, p. 61.

12. Letter from Pandita Ramabai to Canon Butler, July 3, 1885, in *Correspondence*, p. 74.

13. See letter from Sister Geraldine, in Wantage, to Pandita Ramabai, in Poona, December 14, 1896, in *Correspondence*, p. 339: "It is that I *hold* the Faith which the Church has taught for nearly nineteen centuries, and *you choose* for yourself a spurious production: that *I have been willing to learn from the Church*, and you are unwilling to 'hear the Church.' And our Lord says of such: 'If any man neglect to hear the Church, let him be unto thee as a heathen man and a publican.' " Emphasis in original.

14. Letter from the Rev. Mother, C.S.M.V., to an Exterior Sister, C.S.M.V., November 1, 1883, in *Correspondence*, p. 20.

15. Letter from Sister Geraldine, Wantage, to Pandita Ramabai, Cheltenham, May 10, 1885, in *Correspondence*, p. 53.

16. Letter from Pandita Ramabai, Cheltenham, to Sister Geraldine, Wantage, May 12, 1885, in *Correspondence*, p. 59.

17. Letter from Dorothea Beale, Cheltenham, to Sister Geraldine, Wantage, May 8, 1885, in *Correspondence*, p. 49.

18. Pandita Ramabai, *My Testimony* (1907: 10th ed. Kedgaon: Ramabai Mukti Mission, 1977), p. 17; quoted in Meera Kosambi, "Indian Response to Christianity, Church and Colonialism: Case of Pandita Ramabai," *Economic and Political Weekly*, October 24, 1992: p. WS-62.

19. Ibid.

20. Letter from the Rev. Mother, C.S.M.V., to an Exterior Sister, C.S.M.V., November 1, 1883, in *Correspondence*, p. 19.

21. Ram Bapat, "Pandita Ramabai: Faith and Reason in the Shadow of the East and West," in *Representing Hinduism: The Construction of Religious Traditions and National Identity*, edited by Vasudha Dalmia and H. von Stietencron (Delhi: Sage Publications, 1995), p. 226.

22. Pandita Ramabai, *My Testimony*, pp. 18–20; quoted ibid., p. 227.

23. Bapat, "Pandita Ramabai," p. 228.

24. Ramabai, *My Testimony*; quoted in Bapat, p. 227.

25. Bapat, "Pandita Ramabai," p. 227.

26. Letter from Dorothea Beale to the Bishop of Bombay in England, May 22, 1884, in *Correspondence*, p. 42.

27. Letter from Sister Geraldine, London, to Dorothea Beale, Cheltenham, January 1886, in *Correspondence*, p. 114.

28. Letter from Pandita Ramabai, Cheltenham, to Sister Geraldine, Wantage, May 12, 1885, in *Correspondence*, p. 59.

29. Letter from Sister Geraldine, Wantage, to Pandita Ramabai, Cheltenham, May 10, 1885, in *Correspondence*, p. 53.

30. Letter from Pandita Ramabai, U.S.A., to Dorothea Beale, Cheltenham, May 22, 1887, in *Correspondence*, p. 176. Emphasis added.

31. Letter from Pandita Ramabai, Cheltenham, to Canon Butler, Wantage, July 3, 1885, in *Correspondence*, p. 74. A Sanskrit and Marathi scholar, Father Nehemiah Goreh (Nilakanta Shastri) was, like Ramabai, a Chitpavan Brahmin who converted to Christianity. Ramabai had occasion to know him in Poona in the years prior to her departure for England. She often claimed that he was one of the few people to whom she could confide her religious doubts and questions; while in England, she frequently corresponded with him for clarification about points of Christian doctrine.

32. Sister Geraldine, "Apologia Pro Opere" (1917), in *Correspondence*, p. 3.

33. Letter from Pandita Ramabai, Cheltenham, to Sister Geraldine, Wantage, November 7, 1885, in *Correspondence*, p. 112.

34. Letter from Pandita Ramabai to Sister Geraldine, July 1884, in *Correspondence*, p. 25.

35. Sister Geraldine, "Apologia Pro Opere," in *Correspondence*, p. 4.

36. Letter from Pandita Ramabai to Dorothea Beale, June 21, 1885, in *Correspondence*, p. 157.

37. Letter from Pandita Ramabai to Sister Geraldine, September 20, 1885, in *Correspondence*, p. 86.

38. Letter from Sister Geraldine to the Dean of Lincoln, July 1, 1885, in *Correspondence*, p. 71.

39. Letter from Pandita Ramabai to Sister Geraldine, September 20, 1885, in *Correspondence*, p. 87.

40. Shah, introduction to *Correspondence*, p. xxxiii.

41. David Lawton, *Blasphemy* (Philadelphia: University of Pennsylvania Press, 1993), p. 126.

42. Ibid.

43. Letter from Dorothea Beale to the Rev. Canon William Butler, Wantage, July 1885, in *Correspondence*, p. 78.

44. Letter from Pandita Ramabai to Sister Geraldine, June 1885, in *Correspondence*, p. 70.

45. Letter from Pandita Ramabai to Dorothea Beale, September 1, 1885, in *Correspondence*, p. 136.

46. Letter from Pandita Ramabai to Dorothea Beale, 30 June, 1885, in *Correspondence*, p. 128.

47. Ibid.

48. Letter from Pandita Ramabai to Dorothea Beale, November 29, 1885, in *Correspondence*, p. 160.

49. Letter from Dorothea Beale to Sister Geraldine—Proposal for Ramabai to leave at midsummer, April 22, 1885, in *Correspondence*, p. 32. Emphasis in original.

50. Letter from Sister Geraldine to Pandita Ramabai, October 1855, in *Correspondence*, p. 96.

51. Sister Geraldine, "Apologia Pro Opere," in *Correspondence*, p. 4.

52. Letter from Dorothea Beale to the Rev. Canon William Butler, Wantage, July 1885, in *Correspondence*, p. 79. Emphasis in original.

53. Letter from Pandita Ramabai to Sister Geraldine, March 25, 1885, in *Correspondence*, p. 37. Ramabai came to know Max Müller quite well when she was in England, and was invited to visit his home at Oxford, where he was then a professor of comparative philology. Though he admired her vast learning in Sanskrit and Hinduism, he deplored her Christian conversion, writing in an 1895 letter from Oxford: "What I feared when Ramabai became a Christian, has happened: She has impaired her power of doing useful work among her countrymen. Her native friends do not quite trust her, her European friends do not always remember what they owe to her. In all essentials, Ramabai had been a Christian even while she was still a Brahmin; and when she openly professed herself a Christian, it was because she felt the necessity of belonging to some communion, to be one with her friends. . . . I did not persuade Ramabai to become a Christian, because I know she *was* a Christian in heart, which is far better than a Christian by profession." Quoted in Adhav, *Pandita Ramabai*, p. 12.

54. Bapat, "Pandita Ramabai," p. 227.

55. Hugh McLeod, *Religion and the Working Class in Nineteenth-Century Britain* (London: Macmillan, 1984), p. 36.

56. Letter of Pandita Ramabai to Dorothea Beale, February-March 1886, in *Correspondence*, p. 170.

57. Ibid.

58. See, for instance, Christopher Queen, "Ambedkar, Modernity, and the Hermeneutics of Buddhist Liberation," in *Dr. Ambedkar, Buddhism and Social Change*, edited by A. K. Narain and D. C. Ahir (Delhi: B.R. Publishing, 1994).

59. Letter from Sister Geraldine, Bath, to Pandita Ramabai, October 1885, in *Correspondence*, p. 102. Emphasis added.

60. Rachel Bodley, introduction to *The High-Caste Hindu Woman*, p. i.

61. Letter from Pandita Ramabai, Cheltenham, to Canon Butler, Wantage, July 3, 1885, in *Correspondence*, p. 74.

62. Ibid., p. 76.

63. John Henry Newman, *An Essay in Aid of a Grammar of Assent* (Notre Dame: University of Notre Dame Press, 1979), p. 166.

64. Letter from Pandita Ramabai to Sister Geraldine, October 15, 1885, p. 107.

65. Letter from Sister Geraldine, at Bath, to Pandita Ramabai, October 1885, in *Correspondence*, p. 106.

66. Letter from Pandita Ramabai to Sister Geraldine, November 7, 1885, in *Correspondence*, p. 112.

67. Gyan Prakash, introduction to *After Colonialism: Imperial Histories and Postcolonial Displacements* (Princeton: Princeton University Press, 1995), p. 6.

68. Letter from Pandita Ramabai to Sister Geraldine, October 15, 1885, in *Correspondence*, p. 108.

69. See my *Masks of Conquest: Literary Study and British Rule in India* (New York: Columbia University Press, 1989).

70. Letter from Dorothea Beale, Penshurst, to Sister Geraldine, April 22, 1885, in *Correspondence*, p. 32.

71. Letter from Dorothea Beale, Cheltenham, to Sister Geraldine, April 1885, in *Correspondence*, p. 33.

72. Letter from Dorothea Beale, Penshurst, to Sister Geraldine, April 22, 1885, in *Correspondence*, p. 32.

73. Letter from Pandita Ramabai to Dorothy Beale, November 29, 1885, in *Correspondence*, p. 159.

74. Letter from Pandita Ramabai to Sister Geraldine, May 12, 1885, in *Correspondence*, pp. 60–61.

75. Ibid.

76. Letter from Dorothea Beale, Cheltenham, to Sister Geraldine, Wantage, May 8, 1885, in *Correspondence*, p. 49.

77. British administrators themselves feared that the introduction of English education created self-alienation and false independence in the colonized population. See my *Masks of Conquest*, pp. 142–65.

78. Letter from Pandita Ramabai, Cheltenham, to Sister Geraldine, Wantage, July 1884, in *Correspondence*, p. 25.

Chapter Five
Ethnographic Plots

1. Peter van der Veer, "Ayodhya and Somnath: Eternal Shrines, Contested Histories," *Social Research* 59 (Spring 1992): 96.

2. J. F. Seunarine, in *Reconversion to Hinduism through Suddhi* (Madras: Christian Literature Society, 1977), describes the rituals of purification prescribed by reconversion to Hinduism. See also Kenneth Jones, "Religious Identity and the Indian Census," in *The Census in British India: New Perspectives*, edited by N. Gerald Barrier (Delhi: Manohar, 1981), for a discussion of reconversion as an important variable in census taking, reflecting the shifts in the relative strength of different religions (p. 81).

3. Vidya Dehejia, "Shaivite and Vaishnavite Art: Pointers to Sectarian Tensions?" Unpublished paper.

4. On this point, Peter van der Veer's anthropological fieldwork in Surat offers some insights: he argues, for instance, that the discourse of tolerance and communal harmony is related to the eclipse of the themes of Hindu participation and the influence of Hinduism from the debate about Sufi ritual. See Peter van der Veer, *Religious Nationalism:*

Hindus and Muslims in India (Berkeley and Los Angeles: University of California Press, 1994), pp. 33–43. See also my "Beyond Orientalism: Syncretism and the Politics of Knowledge," *Stanford Humanities Review* 5, no. 1 (1995): 19–34, for a discussion of the complex interweaving of syncretic ideologies and identity politics in postcolonial societies.

5. Peter Hardy, "Modern European and Muslim Explanations of Conversion to Islam in South Asia: A Preliminary Survey of the Literature," in *Conversion to Islam*, edited by Nehemia Levtzion (New York: Holmes and Meier, 1979).

6. The question of what produced changes in the strength of any religion was settled by reference to three causes: the reproductive power of a religion's adherents, migration, and conversion. By the 1890s Muslims had grown twice as rapidly as Hindus, and the census asks the question: "How far is this due to the conversion of Hindus and how far to the greater fecundity of Muslims?" See *Report of the Census of India 1901: The Lower Provinces of Bengal and Their Feudatories*, vol. 6, part 1 (Calcutta, 1902), p. 156. Hereafter cited as *Census of India 1901*, vol. 6.

7. Benedict Anderson, *Imagined Communities* (1983; 2nd rev. ed., rev., London: Verso, 1992), p. 163.

8. Ibid., p. 167.

9. *Report of the Census of Bengal, 1872* (Calcutta, 1873), paragraphs 348 to 354. For example: "The real explanation of the immense preponderance of the Musalman religious element in this portion of the delta is to be found in the conversion to Islam of the numerous low castes which occupied it. . . . If further proof were wanted of the position that the Musalmans of the Bengal delta owe their origin to conversion rather than to the introduction of foreign blood, it seems to be afforded in the close resemblance between them and their fellow-countrymen who were still from the low castes of Hindus. That both are originally of the same race seems sufficiently clear, not merely from their possessing identically the same physique, but from the similarity of the manners and customs which characterise them."

10. Khondkar Fazli Rabi, *The Origins of the Musalmans of Bengal* (1895; rpt. Dacca: Society for Pakistan Studies, 1970), p. 43. See also Rafiuddin Ahmed, *The Bengal Muslims 1871–1906: A Quest for Identity* (Delhi: Oxford University Press, 1981) for a complex exploration of the construction of Muslim identity. Ahmed argues that a dominant feature of the nineteenth-century campaigns of Islamization in Bengal was the attempted rejection of virtually all that was Bengali in the life of a Muslim as something that was "incompatible with the ideas and principles of Islam" (p. 106).

11. *Census of India, 1901*, vol. 6, p. 166.

12. Ibid. Rafiuddin Ahmed, in *The Bengal Muslims*, maintains that the Muslim community's claims to family names and alien origins, by way of removing the stigma of their local descent, "were helped by certain government measures . like census classification" (p. 184). Although it is true that the census did elicit the names by which Muslims called themselves, this should not be taken to mean that it accepted the foreign origins that those names connoted. On the contrary, it often contested their authenticity, incredulously dismissing, for instance, the number of self-proclaimed "Shekhs" as being more than twenty times the estimated population of "Arabia" at that time.

13. H. H. Risley, *The Tribes and Castes of Bengal*, vol. 1 (Calcutta: Bengal Secretariat Press, 1891), pp. xxii-xxxvii.

14. *Census of India 1901*, vol. 6, p. 167. Emphasis added.

15. The ritual of shuddhi contributed greatly to the increase of Hindu-Muslim antagonism. For many Muslims, the infamous pork test of the Shuddhi Sabha was taken as the ultimate insult to their religious adherence. But there were many communities and individuals who manifested dual types of behavior, and they were targeted as ripe candidates for shuddhi. For instance, the religious status of the Malkanas, in the western part of what was then called the United Provinces, was a confused one. Their culture showed the influence of Islam, even to the point of using Muslim functionaries in some of their ceremonies. At the same time they retained many Hindu practices. However, in the census they tended to declare themselves Muslims. Several unsuccessful attempts to reconvert them had been made between 1907 and 1910, but as J.T.F. Jordens points out, "the decisive break-through came in 1922 when the Hindu Rajputs in their Kshatriya Upkarini Sabha passed a resolution in support of receiving the Malkanas, and permitting them to be reunited with the Rajput Hindu brotherhood after purification" (p. 158). See J.T.F. Jordens, "Reconversion to Hinduism, the Shuddhi of the Arya Samaj," in *Religion in South Asia*, edited by Geoffrey Oddie (Delhi: Manohar, 1977).

16. Anderson, *Imagined Communities*, p. 166.

17. *The Census of India 1901*, vol. 6, p. 166.

18. *Report of the Census of India, 1901: Bengal—Extracts from District Reports Regarding Causes of Conversion to Muhammadanism*, appendix II, vol. 6, pp. x–xix.

19. Michael Ragussis, *Figures of Conversion: "The Jewish Question" and English National Identity* (Durham: Duke University Press, 1995), p. 104.

20. Ibid.

21. Walter Scott, *Ivanhoe: A Romance* (1819; rpt. Boston and New York: Houghton Mifflin, 1923), p. 3. Edward A. Freeman, on the other hand, regarded the Norman Conquest as no more than a "temporary overthrow of our national being" (p. 3). In Freeman's view, the Norman invasion affected English culture but did not eradicate England's Saxon heritage, which in fact survived remarkably well and eventually absorbed the Normans in the national blood stream. See Edward A. Freeman, *The History of the Norman Conquest of England*, vol. 1 (Oxford: Clarendon Press, 1870).

22. Ragussis, *Figures of Conversion*, p. 105.

23. Robert Young, *Colonial Desire: Hybridity in Theory, Culture, and Race* (London: Routledge, 1995), p. 112.

24. Bernard Cohn, "The Census, Social Structure and Objectification in South Asia," in *An Anthropologist among the Historians and Other Essays* (Delhi: Oxford University Press, 1987), p. 243.

25. See, for example, Ronald Inden, *Imagining India* (Oxford: Basil Blackwell, 1990); and Nicholas B. Dirks, "Castes of Mind," *Representations* 37 (Winter 1992): 56–78.

26. The list is virtually inexhaustible, but among the more important ones are the following: M. Mainwaring, *The Suttee; or, the Hindoo Converts* (London: A.K. Newman, 1830); Sydney Owenson (Lady Morgan), *Luxima the Prophetess* (London: Charles Westerton, 1859); Philip Meadows Taylor, *Seeta* (London: Kegan Paul, 1872); Krupabai Sattianadhan, *Saguna* (Madras: Srinivasa, Varadachari, 1895) and *Kamala's Letters to Her Husband* (Madras: English Publishing House, 1902); William Hunter, *The Old Missionary* (London: Henry Frowde, 1895); J. Campbell Oman, *Where Three Creeds Meet* (1915; rpt. London: Grant Richards, 1898); Cyril Dennehy, *Flower of Asia* (London: Burns and Oates, 1901); Alice Perrin, *Idolatry* (London: Chatto and Windus,

1909); Fanny Penny, *The Outcaste* (London: Chatto and Windus, 1912) and *The Swami's Curse* (London: Hodder and Stoughton, 1922); A. Madhaviah, *Clarinda* (1915; rpt. Madras: Christian Literature Society, 1992); Henry Bruce, *The Temple Girl* (London: John Long, 1919); Dhan Gopal Mukerji, *Caste and Outcaste* (London: Dent, 1923); Mary Ann Scharlieb, *Yet a More Excellent Way* (London: W. Gardner, 1929); J. Chinna Durai, *Sugirtha* (London: Hulbert, 1929); Kaveri Bai, *Meenakshi's Memoirs* (Madras: Natesan, 1937).

27. See, for instance, a nineteenth-century sketch entitled "A Jew Turning to a Christian," which is part of the collections of the Jewish Theological Seminary; in Ragussis, *Figures of Conversion*, p. 55.

28. Ahmed, *The Bengal Muslims*, p. 184.

29. Cf. *The Census of India, 1901*, vol. 6, which describes Hinduism as "not so much a form of religious belief as a social organization. . . . A man's faith does not greatly matter so long as he recognizes the supremacy of the Brahmans and observes the restrictions of the Hindu caste system" (p. 152).

30. Ibid., p. 172.

31. Ibid., p. 166.

32. Although S.A.A. Rizvi states that Muslim commentators usually give an "altogether exaggerated account of proselytisation," claiming pride in Islam for winning scores of Hindu followers (p. 17), Peter Hardy suggests a more ambivalent reading. Hardy proposes that although there was a certain amount of exaggerated self-glorification among recorders of Muslim history, Muslim historians were interested in showing how Islam expanded less through force and chance than through the missionary zeal of sufis and pirs. See S.A.A. Rizvi, "Islamic Proselytisation, Seventh to Sixteenth Centuries," in *Religion in South Asia*, edited by Geoffrey Oddie; and Hardy, "Modern European and Muslim Explanations."

33. The Bharatiya Janata Party's insistence on eliminating separate personal laws for Muslims relating to marriage, divorce, and inheritance rights, as well as on developing a common civil code by which Hindus and Muslims would be governed alike, functions within a rhetoric of reclamation of Muslims as Hindus.

34. "Ayodhya Temple," *The Hindu*, Madras, December 10, 1990.

35. Ashis Nandy, "The Politics of Secularism and the Recovery of Religious Tolerance," in *Mirrors of Violence: Communities, Riots, and Survivors in South Asia*, edited by Veena Das (Delhi: Oxford University Press, 1990), p. 70.

36. David J. Krieger, "Conversion: On the Possibility of Global Thinking in an Age of Particularism," *Journal of the American Academy of Religion* 58, no. 2 (1990): 223–43. See also Alan M. Olson, "Postmodernity and Faith," *Journal of the American Academy of Religion* 58, no. 1 (1990): 37–53. And see Michael C. Banner, *The Justification of Science and the Rationality of Religious Belief* (Oxford: Oxford University Press, 1990) for an illuminating analysis of the problematic opposition between the "rationality" of science and the "irrationality" of religious belief and the circularity of paradigm conflicts to which this gives rise.

37. Krieger, "Conversion," p. 227.

38. Ibid., p. 223.

39. Susan Bayly, *Saints, Goddesses and Kings: Muslims and Christians in South Indian Society 1700–1900* (Cambridge: Cambridge University Press, 1989). See also Robin Horton, "African Conversion," *Africa* 41, no. 2 (1971): 85–108; and Deryck

Schreuder and Geoffrey Oddie, "What is 'Conversion'? History, Christianity and Religious Change in Colonial Africa and South Asia," *Journal of Religious History* 15 (December 1989): 496–518.

40. Hardy, "Modern European and Muslim Explanations," p. 99.

Chapter Six
Conversion, Theosophy, and Race Theory

1. Annie Besant, *An Autobiography* (1893; rpt. Madras: Theosophical Publishing House, 1939), p. 66; also quoted by William James in *The Varieties of Religious Experience* (1902; New York: New American Library, 1958), p. 142.

2. Besant, *Autobiography*, p. 66.

3. Ibid., p. 98.

4. James Cousins, *The Annie Besant Centenary Book* (Madras: Theosophical Publishing House, 1947), p. 85.

5. George Bernard Shaw, *An Autobiography 1856–1898*, edited by Stanley Weintraub (New York: Weybright and Talley, 1969), p. 142.

6. Catherine Wessinger, *Annie Besant and Progressive Messianism (1847–1933)* (New York: E. Mellen, 1988), p. 4.

7. Geoffrey West, *The Life of Annie Besant* (London: G. Howe, 1933); quoted in Wessinger, *Annie Besant and Progressive Messianism*, p. 4. Emphasis added.

8. Roger Manvell, *The Trials of Annie Besant and Charles Bradlaugh* (New York: Horizon Press, 1976), p. 173.

9. David Tribe, *One Hundred Years of Freethought* (London, 1967); quoted in Manvell, *The Trials of Annie Besant*, p. 173.

10. Anne Taylor, *Annie Besant: A Biography* (Oxford: Oxford University Press, 1992).

11. Besant, *Autobiography*. Her pamphlet, *Why I Became a Theosophist* (London: T. Scott, 188?), is a reply to freethinkers' criticisms of her conversion to theosophy; in this speech she charges the Freethought movement with setting up a "new orthodoxy," "a new infallibility, as indefensible, less venerable, than that of Rome" (p. 4).

12. Wessinger, *Annie Besant and Progressive Messianism*, p. 57.

13. Arthur Nethercot, *The First Five Lives of Annie Besant* (Chicago: University of Chicago Press, 1960), p. 12.

14. J. Gordon Melton, ed., *The Origins of Theosophy: Annie Besant—The Atheist Years* (New York: Garland Publishing, 1990).

15. Shaw, *Autobiography*, p. 142.

16. Besant, *Autobiography*, p. 321.

17. See, for instance, the following pamphlets by Annie Besant: *India and the Empire* (London: Theosophical Publishing House, 1914); *How India Wrought for Freedom* (London: Theosophical Publishing House, 1915); *India: a Nation. A Plea for Indian Self-Government* (London: Theosophical Society Committee and E. C. Jack, 1916); *Home Rule and the Empire* (Madras: Commonweal Office, 1917); *Britain's Place in the Great Plan* (London: Theosophical Publishing House, 1921); *India as She Was and as She Is* (Madras: New India, 1923); *India Bond or Free? A World Problem* (London: Putnam, 1926); *England, India, and Afghanistan: a Plea for the*

Weak against the Strong (Madras: Theosophical Publishing House, 1931); *The India that Shall Be* (Madras: Theosophical Publishing House, 1940); *Theosophy and Imperialism* (n.p., n.d.).

18. S. R. Mehrotra, "Mid-Victorian Anti-Imperialists and India," *Indian Economic and Social History Review* 13 (June 1976): 251–67, and Peter Robb, "The Government of India and Annie Besant," *Modern Asian Studies* 10, no. 1 (1976): 107–30, provide useful contextual material for examining the distinctions between various strands of British anti-imperialism and the multiple meanings of "home rule" for British colonial authorities.

19. Shaw, *Autobiography*, p. 140.

20. See Catherine Hall, *White, Male, and Middle-Class* (Cambridge: Polity Press, 1992) for a probing analysis of the Morant Bay uprising. Robert Young, in *Colonial Desire: Hybridity in Theory, Culture, and Race* (London: Routledge, 1995), notes that Arnold's refusal to take sides presaged his own critical position of disinterestedness, articulated so strikingly in *Culture and Anarchy*.

21. Besant, *Autobiography*, p. 300.

22. Annie Besant, *The Evolution of Society* (London: Freethought Publishing, 1886), p. 3.

23. Ibid., p. 3.

24. Similarly, as the frequently anthologized pieces on British India show, Karl Marx affirmed the historical necessity of imperialism as part of a mode of production, "march of history" narrative. Yet at the same time it does not seem enough to cite these essays alone, for it is evident that scholars are not agreed about whether the articles are representative of Marx's overall position. I do not want to enter the debate here, but I do want to distinguish Marx's position from Annie Besant's in one vital respect: Besant's argument about imperialism as a necessary stage in world history did not have only an instrumentalist goal. She believed that British imperialism permitted forms of cultural contact that allowed for the refinement of Aryan principles and enabled Europe to rediscover its lost self in Asia. Her universal brotherhood was essentially the recovery of a former unity that had even feudal overtones; in this respect she may have been closer to Thomas Carlyle than to Marx. See Karl Marx, "The British Rule in India" and "The Future Results of British Rule in India," in *The Marx-Engels Reader*, edited by Robert Tucker (New York: 1972; 2d rev. ed., W. W. Norton, 1978).

25. Besant, *The Evolution of Society*, p. 24.

26. See my *Masks of Conquest: Literary Study and British Rule in India* (New York: Columbia University Press, 1989), p. 33.

27. Young, *Colonial Desire*, chap. 3.

28. Ibid., p. 81.

29. Malcolm Chapman, *The Celts: The Construction of a Myth* (London: Macmillan, 1992), p. 19.

30. Nethercot, *The First Five Lives of Annie Besant*, p. 194.

31. A paper delivered at Columbia University by Dorothy Figuera in 1991, "Tolerance as *Humanität*," helped in clarifying these ideas.

32. Besant, *An Autobiography*, p. 116.

33. See Annie Besant, *On the Deity of Jesus of Nazareth by the Wife of a Beneficed Clergyman*, edited by Rev. Charles Voysey (London: T. Scott, 1873) and *On the Atonement* (London: T. Scott, 1874).

34. Annie Besant, *Pain: Its Meaning and Use* (Madras: Theosophical Publishing House, 1961), p. 18.

35. Ibid., p. 12.

36. Besant, *Britain's Place in the Great Plan*, p. 23.

37. See Mary Clawson, *Constructing Brotherhood: Class, Gender, and Fraternalism* (Princeton: Princeton University Press, 1989) for a dense, sociological construction of brotherhood as an institution involving artisans and other laboring classes. In a seminar at Wesleyan where an early version of this chapter was presented, Henry Abelove raised useful questions about the (a)sexual connotations of Besant's use of "brothers."

38. Annie Besant, *The Secret of Evolution* (Harrogate: Theosophical Publishing Committee, 19?), p. 5.

39. Annie Besant, *The Pedigree of Man* (Benares and London: Theosophical Publishing Society, 1904), pp. 150–51.

40. Geoffrey Barborka, *The Story of Human Evolution* (Madras: Theosophical Publishing House, 1979), p. 18.

41. See Charles Leadbeater, *The Beginnings of the Sixth Root Race* (Madras: Theosophical Publishing House, 1920).

42. *The Stanzas of Dzyan*, II:249; quoted in Barborka, *The Story of Human Evolution*, p. 52. See also Joscelyn Godwin, *The Theosophical Enlightenment* (Albany: State University of New York Press, 1994), for an overview of a wide assortment of theosophical themes, ranging from initiates to animal magnetism.

43. See Young, *Colonial Desire*, chap. 3, "The Complicity of Culture: Arnold's Ethnographic Politics," for a thoughtful reading of Arnold's idea of culture as racially composed.

44. Annie Besant, *The Inner Government of the World* (Madras: Theosophical Publishing House, 1920), p. 47.

45. Besant, *Britain's Place in the Great Plan*, p. 31.

46. Besant, *Pain*, p. 13.

47. Besant, *Theosophy and Imperialism*, p. 7.

48. Ibid., p. 3.

49. Besant, *The Inner Government of the World*, p. 21.

50. Annie Besant, *The Birth of New India: A Collection of Writings and Speeches on Indian Affairs* (Madras: Theosophical Publishing House, 1917), p. 36. Emphasis added.

51. Ibid., p. 51.

52. *New India*, April 21, 1915; quoted in Josephine Ransom, *A Short History of the Theosophical Society* (Madras: Theosophical Publishing House, 1938), p. 414.

53. There are a number of studies that attempt to reevaluate Annie Besant's role in Indian nationalism. Although Prabha Dixit's journalistic piece, "Annie Besant Devalued?" in *The Illustrated Weekly of India* (July 10–16, 1977): 36–39, trenchantly critiques Besant's manipulation of the Indian National Congress and propagation of a false ideal of India as spiritual and otherworldly, there are other studies that question the extent of her influence on Indian nationalist politics. For background history, see Mehrotra, "Mid-Victorian Anti-Imperialists and India"; Robb, "The Government of India and Annie Besant"; and Gerald Studdert-Kennedy, *British Christians, Indian Nationalists, and the Raj* (Delhi: Oxford University Press, 1991). Anne Taylor's recent biography reviews unpublished material to illuminate further the strained relations between Besant and other Indian nationalists, especially Tilak and Gandhi.

54. *The Theosophist*, January 1929, p. 341; quoted in Ransom, *A Short History of the Theosophical Society*, p. 408.

55. Besant, *The Birth of New India*, p. 51.

56. *The Theosophist*, February 1915, p. 475; quoted in Ransom, *A Short History of the Theosophical Society*, p. 413.

57. James Cousins, *War: A Theosophical View* (London: Theosophical Publishing Committee, 1914), p. 15.

58. Besant, *Home Rule and the Empire*, p. 10.

59. Besant, *Britain's Place in the Great Plan*, p. 53.

60. Studdert-Kennedy, *British Christians, Indian Nationalists, and the Raj*, p. 170.

61. Partha Chatterjee, in *The Nation and Its Fragments* (Princeton: Princeton University Press, 1994), offers a detailed, provocative analysis of how this double consciousness informed Bengali politics, culture, and letters.

62. James Cousins, *The Cultural Unity of Asia* (Madras: Theosophical Publishing House, 1922), pp. 7–8; also James Cousins, *The Renaissance in India* (Madras: Ganesh, 1917).

63. James Cousins, *The Wisdom of the West: an Introduction to the Interpretive Study of Irish Mythology* (London: Theosophical Publishing Society, 1912), p. 15.

Chapter Seven
Conversion to Equality

1. Separate electorates referred to the representation of religious minorities by legislators comprising only members of that minority. The provision of such representation remained a persistently obstinate problem in the first few decades of the twentieth century. Apart from the 1909 act, the Government of India Acts of 1919 and 1935 provided separate electorates also for Sikhs and Christians. Census figures regarding population size acquired new significance in the debates (and anxiety) about separate electorates.

2. The matter of terminology is evidently an important one, and the term for social groups who in the past used to be referred to simply as "untouchables" has gone through a number of christenings. Gandhi's term *harijan*, or children of God, was categorically rejected by Ambedkar as patronizing. In his own writings Ambedkar used the term "depressed classes," and subsequent commentary has agreed on the term *dalit*. For purposes of consistency I will use the word *dalit* to refer to untouchables, though I will revert occasionally to the term "untouchables" where it is specifically used in a text from which I may be quoting or paraphrasing, or whenever I refer to the historical context in which the word was widely used. In his review of dalit literary movements, Arjun Dangle writes that dalit means "masses exploited and oppressed economically, socially, culturally, in the name of religion and other factors." See Arjun Dangle, "Dalit Literature: Past, Present, and Future," in *Poisoned Bread: Translations from Modern Marathi Dalit Literature*, edited by Arjun Dangle (Bombay: Orient Longman, 1992), p. 265.

3. Dhanajay Keer, *B. R. Ambedkar: Life and Mission* (Bombay: Popular Prakashan, 1962) recounts in detail the series of events that brought Ambedkar under the patronage of the Maharaja Gaekwad of Baroda.

4. B. R. Ambedkar, "The Untouchables and the Pax Britannica," in *Dr. Babasaheb Ambedkar: Writings and Speeches*, vol. 12 (Bombay: Education Department, Government of Maharashtra, 1993), p. 146. Hereafter this and other volumes in the series cited as *Writings and Speeches*.

5. See Ravinder Kumar, "Ambedkar, Gandhi, and the Poona Pact," Occasional Papers in Society and History, no. 20, Nehru Memorial Museum, New Delhi, 1985, for a discussion of the intricate issues involved in the negotiations.

6. Rajni Kothari, "Rise of the Dalits and the Renewed Debate on Caste," *Economic and Political Weekly*, June 25, 1994: 1,589.

7. Some of these distinctions are brought out in M. S. Gore, *The Social Context of an Ideology: Ambedkar's Political and Social Thought* (Delhi: Sage Publications, 1993).

8. Marc Galanter, *Law and Society in Modern India* (Delhi: Oxford University Press, 1992), p. 206. See also his *Competing Equalities* (1984; rpt. Delhi: Oxford University Press, 1994) for a sobering assessment of post-Independence India's compensatory discrimination policies. Oliver Mendelsohn and Upendra Baxi's edited volume, *The Rights of Subordinated Peoples* (Delhi: Oxford University Press, 1994), contains valuable essays on the contradiction I have noted above; Oliver Mendelsohn and Marika Vicziany's essay, "The Untouchables" (pp. 64–116) is particularly rich in data drawn from educational and demographic statistics, which confirm the wide gap between secular, compensatory principles and the actual status of dalits in contemporary India. For an ethnographic perspective, see R. S. Khare, "The Body, Sensoria, and Self of the Powerless: Remembering/"Re-Membering" Indian Untouchable Women," *New Literary History* 26, vol.1 (1995): 147–68, records village women's perceptions of the constitutive contradictions of Indian democracy.

9. Yogendra Singh, "Dalit Definitions," *The Hindu* (Madras), June 18, 1995.

10. Waman Hoval, "The Storeyed House," translated by M. D. Hatkanagalekar, in *Poisoned Bread*. Cited hereafter in the text as *SH*.

11. See B. R. Ambedkar, *What Congress and Gandhi Have Done to the Untouchables*, vol. 9 of *Writings and Speeches* (Bombay: Education Department, Government of Maharashtra, 1991), for a complete set of documents that trace the conflict between the two leaders over separate electorates for untouchables.

12. Ambedkar, *What the Congress and Gandhi Have Done to the Untouchables*.

13. C. Rajagopalachari, *Ambedkar Refuted* (Bombay: Hind Publications, 1946), p. 35.

14. *Gandhi or Ambedkar, by a Harijan*, edited by Dakshayani (Madras: Velayudhan Gandhi Era Publications, 1945), p. 9.

15. Valerian Rodrigues, "Between Tradition and Modernity: The Gandhi-Ambedkar Debate," in *Dr. Ambedkar, Buddhism and Social Change*, edited by A. K. Narain and D. C. Ahir (Delhi: B. R. Publishing, 1994), p. 137.

16. Mulk Raj Anand, *Untouchable*, preface by E. M. Forster (1935; London: Penguin Books, 1940), pp. 145–46. Hereafter cited in the text as *U*.

17. B. R. Ambedkar, "Speech at Mahad, December 25, 1927," in Dangle, ed., *Poisoned Bread*, p. 231.

18. Partha Chatterjee, *Nationalist Thought and the Colonial World* (Delhi: Oxford University Press, 1986).

19. E. M. Forster, preface to *Untouchable*, pp. v, vi.

20. Ibid., p. vii.

21. Shanta Rameshwar Rao, *Children of God* (1976; rpt. Calcutta: Orient Longman, 1992), p. 149.

22. The power of Mahasweta Devi's short stories about tribal dalits derives in large part from her uncompromising depiction of hunger: her relentless descriptions of the physical assault made on the human body by deprivation of food contrast sharply with the metaphysical rhetoric of fasting associated with Gandhi. See *Of Women, Outcastes, Peasants, and Rebels: A Selection of Bengali Short Stories*, edited by Kalpana Bardhan (Berkeley and Los Angeles: University of California Press, 1992); and Mahasweta Devi, *Imaginary Maps*, translated by Gayatri Chakravorty Spivak (London: Routledge, 1995).

23. No issue so stirred up controversy as Gandhi's naming of untouchables as *harijans*, or children of God. "Mere change of name, like 'Harijan,' meant to give a new identity, did not help in the eradication of untouchability. The new label in fact sealed the Untouchables more effectively in their own category. It did not give them self-respect but made them only objects of compassion for the liberal Hindus." See A. K. Narain, "Dr. Ambedkar, Buddhism, and Social Change—A Reappraisal," in *Dr. Ambedkar, Buddhism, and Social Change*, p. 91.

24. See Julian Saldanha, *Conversion and Indian Civil Law* (Bangalore: Theological Publications in India, 1981).

25. Gail Omvedt, *Dalits and the Democratic Revolution: Dr. Ambedkar and the Dalit Movement in Colonial India* (New Delhi: Sage Publications, 1994). See also her *Dalit Visions* (Bombay: Orient Longman, 1995).

26. Bhagwan Das, "Ambedkar's Journey to Mass Conversion," in *B. R. Ambedkar*, edited by Verinder Grover (New Delhi: Deep and Deep Publications, 1993), p. 609. See also Ravinder Kumar, "Ambedkar, Gandhi, and the Poona Pact"; and Keer, *B. R. Ambedkar: Life and Mission*.

27. Mumtaz Ali Khan, *Mass Conversions of Meenakshipuram* (Madras: Christian Literature Society, 1983).

28. Rosalind O'Hanlon, *Caste, Conflict, and Ideology: Jyotirao Phule and Low-Caste Protest in Western India* (Cambridge: Cambridge University Press, 1990).

29. S. Manickam, *Nandanar the Dalit Martyr* (Madras: Christian Literature Society, 1990).

30. Shaivism refers to one of the two major, rival sects of brahmanical Hinduism, the other sect being Vaishnavism. Both are devotional cults in the worship of male Hindu deities, Shiva and Vishnu, respectively. Among their primary differences are conflicting perceptions of godhead, the origins of sin and evil, and the nature of incarnation.

31. G. Vanmikanathan, ed., *The Periyapuranam by Sekkizhaar*, English version (Madras: Ramakrishna Math, 1985), p. 561.

32. V. R. Lakshminarayanan, "Dr. Ambedkar's Contribution to the Revival of Buddhism in India," in *Buddhist Themes in Modern Indian Literature*, edited by J. Parthasarathi (Madras: Institute of Asian Studies, 1992), p. 40.

33. See B. R. Ambedkar, *Writings and Speeches*, vol. 13 (Bombay: Education Department, Government of Maharashtra, 1994) for his complete collection of drafts, minutes, and notes made during the course of his writing of the constitution.

34. B. R. Ambedkar, *The Buddha and His Dhamma*, vol. 11 of *Writings and*

Speeches (Bombay: Education Department, Government of Maharashtra, 1992), p. 89.

35. Christopher Queen, "Ambedkar, Modernity, and the Hermeneutics of Buddhist Liberation," in *Dr. Ambedkar, Buddhism and Social Change*, p. 100.

36. Richard Taylor, "The Ambedkarite Buddhists," in *Ambedkar and the Neo-Buddhist Movement*, edited by T. S. Wilkinson and M. M. Thomas (Madras: Christian Literature Society, 1972), p. 146.

37. B. R. Ambedkar, "Buddha or Karl Marx," in *Writings and Speeches*, vol. 3 (Bombay: Education Department, Government of Maharashtra, 1989), p. 457.

38. Ibid., p. 461.

39. John D. Rosenberg, *Carlyle and the Burden of History* (Oxford: Clarendon Press, 1985), pp. 11–12.

40. D. R. Nagaraj, *The Flaming Feet: A Study of the Dalit Movement* (Bangalore: South Forum Press, 1993).

41. B. R. Ambedkar, "Away from the Hindus," in *Writings and Speeches*, vol. 5 (Bombay: Education Department, Government of Maharashtra, 1989), p. 409. Reprinted in B. R. Ambedkar, *Christianizing the Untouchables* (Madras: Dalit Liberation Education Trust, 1994).

42. Quoted in Keer, *B. R. Ambedkar: Life and Mission*, p. 255. See also M. K. Gandhi, *The Removal of Untouchability* (Ahmedabad: Navajivan Publishing House, 1954), pp. 135–64.

43. Omvedt, *Dalits and the Democratic Revolution*, p. 229.

44. B. R. Ambedkar, *The Untouchables: Who Were They and Why They Became Untouchables* (New Delhi: Amrit Book Co., 1948), p. 76.

45. Baburao Bagul, "Dalit Literature Is but Human Literature," in Dangle, ed., *Poisoned Bread*, p. 281.

46. B. R. Ambedkar, "Castes in India," in *Writings and Speeches*, vol. 1, p. 78.

47. See B. R. Ambedkar, "The Condition of the Convert," in *Writings and Speeches*, vol. 5. Reprinted in *Christianizing the Untouchables*.

48. Das, "Ambedkar's Journey to Mass Conversion," p. 609.

49. Gopal Guru, "Hinduisation of Ambedkar in Maharashtra," *Economic and Political Weekly*, February 16, 1991, p. 339. "Hindutva" refers to a mass movement mobilized by communal organizations to establish a Hindu state. Its momentum accelerated in the 1980s and reached a climax with the destruction of the Babri mosque at Ayodhya in December 1992. See Tapan Basu et al., *Khaki Shorts and Saffron Flags: A Critique of the Hindu Right*, Tracts for the Times, no. 1 (Delhi: Orient Longman, 1993), for a useful critique of the forces of Hindutva.

50. Quoted in Das, "Ambedkar's Journey to Mass Conversion," p. 595.

51. B. R. Ambedkar, "States and Minorities," in *Writings and Speeches*, vol. 1, p. 412. Quoted in Omvedt, *Dalits and the Democratic Revolution*, p. 240.

52. Ambedkar, "Buddha or Karl Marx," p. 460.

53. Ambedkar, "The Untouchables and the Pax Britannica," p. 145.

54. Ibid., p. 146.

55. B. R. Ambedkar and Rao Bahadur Srinivasan, *A Scheme of Political Safeguards for the Protection of the Depressed Classes in the Future Constitution of a Self-Governing India, Submitted to the Indian Round Table Conference* (London: A. C. Phillips, n.d.)

56. See R. S. Khare, *The Untouchable as Himself* (Cambridge: Cambridge University Press, 1984) for an empirical and theoretically informed anthropological study of a Chamar untouchable community in Lucknow.

57. B. R. Ambedkar, "Buddha or Karl Marx," p. 460.

Chapter Eight
Epilogue

1. Leonard W. Levy, *Blasphemy: Verbal Offense against the Sacred from Moses to Salman Rushdie* (New York: Knopf, 1993); David Lawton, *Blasphemy* (Philadelphia: University of Pennsylvania Press, 1993).

2. Lawton, *Blasphemy*, p. 7.

3. Stephen Carter, *The Culture of Disbelief* (New York: Basic Books, 1993).

4. Thomas Kuhn, *The Structure of Scientific Revolutions*, 2nd edition (Chicago: University of Chicago Press, 1970). See also Michael C. Banner, *The Justification of Science and the Rationality of Religious Belief* (Oxford: Clarendon Press, 1990), which extends Kuhn's understanding of how interpretive communities govern scientific knowledge to a consideration of the controlled growth of religious knowledge. One of the more interesting series on television to appear in recent years, the BBC's "Heretics," employs the language of religious heresy to describe scientific innovation and its resistance by mainstream establishments.

5. Lawton, *Blasphemy*, p. 179.

6. Sara Suleri, *The Rhetoric of English India* (Chicago: University of Chicago Press, 1992), p. 190.

7. Jean-Luc Nancy, *The Inoperative Community*, translated by Peter Connor (Minneapolis: University of Minnesota Press, 1991), p. 114.

8. Robert W. Hefner, ed., *Conversion to Christianity: Historical and Anthropological Perspectives on a Great Transformation* (Berkeley and Los Angeles: University of California Press, 1993).

9. See Levy, *Blasphemy: Verbal Offense*, p. 227.

10. Ibid., p. 32.

11. Stephen Thomas, *Newman and Heresy* (Cambridge: Cambridge University Press, 1992), p. 3.

12. Ibid., p. 484. See also Timothy J. Toohey, "Blasphemy in Nineteenth-Century England: The Pooley Case and Its Background," *Victorian Studies* 30, no. 3 (1987): 315–33. Arguing that the Pooley case became a crucial test case for distinguishing between rationality and eccentricity as the bases for freedom of expression, Toohey's essay moves toward the conclusion that, after the Pooley case, "England slowly moved out of an age when men were successfully prosecuted for blasphemy. If sane they were reasonable enquirers, if insane they needed treatment" (p. 316).

13. Quoted in Levy, *Blasphemy: Verbal Offense*, p. 484.

14. Lawton, *Blasphemy*, p. 120.

15. Lester Kurtz, *The Politics of Heresy: The Modernist Crisis in Roman Catholicism* (Berkeley and Los Angeles: University of California Press, 1986), p. 147.

16. T. S. Eliot, *The Idea of a Christian Society, and Other Writings* (1939; rpt. London: Faber and Faber, 1982), pp. 54–55. See also his *After Strange Gods* (London: Faber and Faber, 1934).

17. John Locke, *A Letter Concerning Toleration*, edited by James Tully (1689; rpt., Indianapolis: Hackett Publishing, 1983), p. 46.

18. *The Works of Lord Macaulay*, 8 vols., edited by Lady Trevelyan (London, 1866), speech of April 17, 1833, vol. 8, pp. 104–5; quoted in Levy, *Blasphemy: Verbal Offense*, p. 494.

19. Levy, *Blasphemy: Verbal Offense*, p. 566.

20. Preston King, *Toleration* (London: George Allen and Unwin, 1976), p. 25.

Select Bibliography

Documentary Sources

Unpublished Sources, Including Official Papers

INDIA OFFICE AND LIBRARY RECORDS, LONDON

Board's Collections, Judicial Department, no. 28 of 1824, draft 276; F/4/724 (4 January 1822).

Board's Collections, Madras Despatches, Judicial Department, vol. 70 (8 September 1824).

Board's Collections, Madras Despatches, vol. 82 (3 April 1833).

Board's Collections, India and Bengal Despatches, Political Department, vol. 41 (27 March 1839).

Board's Collections, Legislative Department, no. 21 of 1844 (4 November 1843).

Board's Collections, Judicial Department, no. 12 of 1844, draft 866; F/4/2065 (8 July 1844).

Madras Judicial Despatches (F/4/2065), 27 November 1844.

Board's Collections, Madras Despatches, vol. 103 (2 December 1844).

Board's Collections, Legislative Department, no. 12 of 1851, draft 875; F/2436 (25 July 1851): Memorial from the Hindoo inhabitants of Bengal. . . .

Board's Collections, Bengal Despatches, India Ecclesiastical Department (10 March 1852).

Board's Collections, Legislative Department, no. 10 of 1852, draft 859; F/4/2481 (1 May 1852).

Board's Collections, Bengal Despatches, India Political Department, no. 33 of 1853, draft no. 660 (17 August 1853).

Board's Collections, Legislative Department, no. 17 of 1854, despatch 520; F/4/2/2557 (7 December 1853).

Board's Collections, Madras Despatches, Ecclesiastical Department, vol. 123 (26 September 1855).

Board's Collections, Madras Despatches, Ecclesiastical Department, vol. 125 (23 July 1856).

Board's Collections, Madras Despatches, vol. 128 (24 February 1857).

Board's Collections, India Public Consultations, no. 9 of 1857 (16 May 1857).

TAMIL NADU ARCHIVES, MADRAS

Madras Judicial Consultations, vol. 472, no. 40 (21 March 1843).

Madras Judicial Consultations, vol. 472, nos. 22–30 (2 July 1844).

Madras Judicial Consultations, vol. 502a, no. 41 (10 March 1846).

Madras Judicial Consultations, vol. 506 (28 July 1846).

Madras Judicial Consultations, vol. 515, no. 45 (1 September 1846).

Madras Judicial Consultations, vol. 517, nos. 22–25 (5 January 1847).

SCHOOL OF ORIENTAL AND AFRICAN STUDIES, LONDON

Council on World Missions (London Missionary Society)—South India—Tamil—Incoming Papers (1817–1860).

Council on World Missions (London Missionary Society)—South India—Canarese—Incoming Papers (1817–1825).

Sadhu Singh Letters, Council on World Missions (London Missionary Society)—India—Personal.

Government Printed Sources

NATIONAL ARCHIVES OF INDIA, DELHI

Home Department—Legislative, Draft of Law Commission (25 January 1845).

Foreign Department—Political Consultation, no. 2355 (December 1847).

Home Department—Judicial Consultation, no. 13 (20 May 1859).

Home Department—Judicial Consultation, nos. 9–11 (July 1859).

Home Department—Ecclesiastical Consultations, nos. 11–17 (11 May 1860).

Home Department—Ecclesiastical Proceedings, nos. 3–4 (October 1870).

Home Department—Public Proceedings A, nos. 442–444 (March 1872).

Home Department—Ecclesiastical Proceedings, no. 37 (November 1872).

Home Department—Ecclesiastical Proceedings, nos. 13–18 (June 1874).

Home Department—Judicial Proceedings, no. 101 (February 1875).

Home Department—Public Proceedings, nos. 73–78 (September 1876).

Home Department—Public Proceedings, nos. 33–34 (July 1878).

Home Department—Public Proceedings A, nos. 84–85 (April 1882).

REPORTS

Collection of the Decisions of the High Courts and the Privy Council on the Hindu Law of Marriage and the Effect of Apostasy after Marriage up to March 1891. Madras: Scottish Press, 1891.

Collection of the Decisions of the High Courts and the Privy Council on the Law of Succession and Maintenance. Madras: Scottish Press, 1892.

First Report of H. M. Commissioners Appointed to Prepare a Body of Substantive Law for India. London: n.p., 1864.

Grady, Standish G. A Treatise on the Hindoo Law of Inheritance, Comprising the Doctrines of the Various Schools with the Decisions of the High Courts of the Several Presidencies of India, and the Judgments of the Privy Council on Appeal. London: Wildy and Sons, 1868.

Indian Law Reports, Bombay Series, vol. 9 (1885): 529–35, and vol. 10 (1886): 301–13.

Note of Cases in the Court of the Recorder and in the Supreme Court of Judicature at Madras (1798–1816). 3 vols. Madras: Asylum Press, 1816.

Report of the Census of Bengal, 1872. Calcutta, 1873.

Report of the Census of India 1901: Madras, vol. 15, part 1. Calcutta, 1902.

Report of the Census of India 1901: The Lower Provinces of Bengal and Their Feudatories, vol. 6, part 1. Calcutta, 1902.

Report of the Census of India, 1901: Bengal—Extracts from District Reports Regarding Causes of Conversion to Muhammadanism, appendix II, vol. 6. Calcutta, 1902.

Reports of Cases Heard and Determined by the Judicial Committee and the Lords of H.M. Most Honourable Privy Council, on Appeal from the Supreme and Sudder Dewaney Courts in the East Indies, vol. 9. London: V. and R. Stevens, 1864.

Theobald, William, ed. Acts of the Legislative Council of India, 1866–1867, vol. 8. Calcutta: Thacker, Spink, 1867.

Primary Sources

Pamphlets, Speeches, and Tracts

Ambedkar, Bhimrao Ramji. *Annihilation of Caste.* 1936; rpt. Bangalore: Dalit Sahitya Akademi, 1987.

———. "Away from the Hindus." *Writings and Speeches*, vol. 5. Bombay: Education Department, Government of Maharashtra, 1989.

———. *The Buddha and His Dhamma*, vol. 11 of *Writings and Speeches*. Bombay: Education Department, Government of Maharashtra, 1992.

———. "Buddha or Karl Marx." *Writings and Speeches*, vol. 3. Bombay: Education Department, Government of Maharashtra, 1989.

———. "Castes in India." *Writings and Speeches*, vol. 1. Bombay: Education Department, Government of Maharashtra, 1979.

———. *Christianizing the Untouchables.* Madras: Dalit Liberation Education Trust, 1994.

———. "The Condition of the Convert." *Writings and Speeches*, vol. 5. Bombay: Education Department, Government of Maharashtra, 1989.

———. "States and Minorities." *Writings and Speeches*, vol. 1. Bombay: Education Department, Government of Maharashtra, 1979.

———. "The Untouchables and the Pax Britannica." *Writings and Speeches*, vol. 12. Bombay: Education Department, Government of Maharashtra, 1993.

———. *The Untouchables: Who Were They and Why They Became Untouchables.* New Delhi: Amrit Book Co., 1948.

———. *What Congress and Gandhi Have Done to the Untouchables*, vol. 9 of *Writings and Speeches*. Bombay: Education Department, Government of Maharashtra, 1991.

———. *Why Go for Conversion?* 1936; rpt. Bangalore: Dalit Sahitya Akademi, 1984.

———. *Dr. Babasaheb Ambedkar: Writings and Speeches*, vols. 1 to 14. Bombay: Education Department, Government of Maharashtra, 1979–1995.

Ambedkar, B. R., and Rao Bahadur Srinivasan. *A Scheme of Political Safeguards for the Protection of the Depressed Classes in the Future Constitution of a Self-Governing India, Submitted to the Indian Round Table Conference.* London: A. C. Phillips, n.d.

Besant, Annie. *Ancient Wisdom.* 1897; rpt. Madras: Theosophical Publishing House, 1939.

———. *Atheism and Its Bearing on Morals.* London: Freethought Publishing, 1887.

———. *An Autobiography.* 1893; rpt. Madras: Theosophical Publishing House, 1939.

———. *The Birth of New India: A Collection of Writings and Speeches on Indian Affairs.* Madras: Theosophical Publishing House, 1917.

———. *Britain's Place in the Great Plan.* London: Theosophical Publishing House, 1921.

———. *Dharma.* Madras: Theosophical Publishing House, 1918.

———. *England, India, and Afghanistan: A Plea for the Weak against the Strong.* Madras: Theosophical Publishing House, 1931.

———. *Esoteric Christianity.* Madras: Theosophical Publishing House, 1914.

———. *The Evolution of Society.* London: Freethought Publishing, 1886.

Besant, Annie. *For the Crown and against the Nation*. London: Freethought Publishing, 1886.

———. *Home Rule and the Empire*. Madras: Commonweal Office, 1917.

———. *How India Wrought for Freedom*. London: Theosophical Publishing House, 1915.

———. *India: a Nation. A Plea for Indian Self-Government*. London: Theosophical Society Committee and E.C. Jack, 1916.

———. *India and the Empire*. London: Theosophical Publishing Society, 1914.

———. *India as She Was and as She Is*. Madras: New India, 1923.

———. *India Bond or Free? A World Problem*. London: Putnam, 1926.

———. *The India that Shall Be*. Madras: Theosophical Publishing House, 1940.

———. *The Inner Government of the World*. Madras: Theosophical Publishing House, 1920.

———. *Liberation or Salvation*. Madras: Theosophical Publishing House, 1961.

———. *The Masters*. Madras: Theosophical Publishing House, 1912.

———. *The Necessity for Reincarnation*. Madras: Theosophical Publishing House, 1920.

———. *On the Atonement*. London: T. Scott, 1874.

———. *On the Deity of Jesus of Nazareth by the Wife of a Beneficed Clergyman*, edited by Rev. Charles Voysey. London: T. Scott, 1873.

———. *Pain: Its Meaning and Use*. Madras: Theosophical Publishing House, 1961.

———. *The Path of Discipleship*. Madras: Theosophical Publishing House, 1910.

———. *The Pedigree of Man*. Benares and London: Theosophical Publishing House, 1904.

———. *The Political Status of Women*. 2d ed. London: C. Watts, 1885.

———. *The Secret of Evolution*. Harrogate: Theosophical Publishing Committee, 19?).

———. *A Selection of the Social and Political Pamphlets of Annie Besant*. New York: Augustus Kelley, 1970.

———. *Seven Great Religions*. 1896; rpt. Madras: Theosophical House, 1966.

———. *The Seven Principles of Man*. Madras: Theosophical Publishing House, 1931.

———. *A Study in Consciousness*. 1907; rpt. Madras: Theosophical Publishing House, 1938.

———. *Theosophy and Imperialism*. N.p., n.d.

———. *Theosophy and the Theosophical Society*. Madras: Theosophical Publishing House, 1931.

———. *Thought Power*. Madras: Theosophical Publishing House, 1952.

———. *The Universal Textbook of Religion and Morals*. Madras: Theosophical Publishing House, 1909.

———. *Why I Became a Theosophist*. London: T. Scott, 188?

Besant, Annie, and H. P. Blavatsky. *The Nature of Memory*. Madras: Theosophical Publishing House, 1935.

The Besant Privy Council Appeal: Full Arguments and Judgment. Madras: Law Weekly Office, 1914.

Blavatsky, H. P. *The Original Programme of the Theosophical Society*. Madras: Theosophical Publishing House, 1931.

———. *Two Books of the Stanzas of Dzyan*. Madras: Theosophical Publishing House, 1940.

Bonner, Hypatia Bradlaugh. *Charles Bradlaugh*. London: T. Fisher, Unwin, 1908.

Braidwood, J. *True Yokefellows of the Mission Field: The Life and Labours of the Rev. John Anderson and the Rev. Robert Johnston traced in the Rise and Development of the Madras Free Church.* London: J. Nisbet, 1862.

Buchanan, Claudius. *Christian Researches in Asia.* London: G. Sidney, 1812.

Carey, William. *An Enquiry into the Obligations of Christians to Use Means for the Conversion of the Heathens.* Leicester: Ann Ireland, 1792.

———. *The Garo Jungle Book.* rpt. Garo Hills, Assam: Garo Baptist Convention, 1919.

Cousins, James H. *The Bases of Theosophy.* Madras: Theosophical Publishing House, 1913.

———. *The Cultural Unity of Asia.* Madras: Theosophical Publishing House, 1922.

———. *New Ways in English Literature.* Madras: Ganesh, 1920.

———. *The Renaissance in India.* Madras: Ganesh, 1917.

———. *Samadarshana (Synthetic Vision): A Study in Indian Psychology.* Madras: Ganesh, 1925.

———. *A Study in Synthesis.* Madras: Ganesh, 1934.

———. *War: A Theosophical View.* London: Theosophical Publishing Committee, 1914.

———. *The Wisdom of the West: An Introduction to the Interpretive Study of Irish Mythology.* London: Theosophical Publishing Society, 1912.

———. *Work and Worship: Essays on Culture and Creative Art.* Madras: Ganesh, 1922.

Cousins, James H., and Margaret E. Cousins. *We Two Together.* Madras: Ganesh, 1950.

Cust, Robert N. *Essay on the Prevailing Methods of the Evangelisation of the Non-Christian World.* London: Luzac, 1894.

Dakshayani, ed. *Gandhi or Ambedkar, by a Harijan.* Madras: Velayudhan Gandhi Era Publications, 1945.

Davies, Charles Maurice. *Heterodox London; or, Phases of Free Thought in the Metropolis.* London: Tinsley Brothers, 1874.

Dicey, Arthur. *A Digest of the Law of England with Reference to the Conflict of Laws.* London: Stevens and Sons, 1896.

Dubois, Abbé J. A. *Letters on the State of Christianity in India; in which the Conversion of the Hindoos is Considered as Impracticable ... To which is added a vindication of the Hindoos, male and female, in answer to a severe attack upon both by the Reverend ***.* London: Longman, Hurst, Rees, Orme, Brown and Green, 1823.

Gandhi, Mohandas. *The Removal of Untouchability.* Ahmedabad: Navajivan Publishing House, 1954.

Hoole, Elijah. *Personal Narrative of a Mission to South India from 1820–1828.* London: Longman, Rees, Orme, Brown and Green, 1829.

Jones, John P. *India's Problem Krishna or Christ.* New York: Fleming H. Revell Company, 1903.

Kaye, John W. *Christianity in India: An Historical Narrative.* London: Smith, Elder, 1959.

Keshub Chunder Sen in England: Diaries, Sermons, Addresses, and Epistles. 1871; rpt. Calcutta: Writers Workshop, 1980.

Keshub Chunder Sen's Lectures in India. London: Cassell, 1901.

Kingsmill, Joseph. *British Rule and British Christianity in India.* London: n.p., 1859.

Leadbeater, Charles. *The Beginnings of the Sixth Root Race*. Madras: Theosophical Publishing House, 1920.

Locke, John. *A Letter Concerning Toleration*, edited by James Tully. 1689; rpt., Indianapolis Hackett Publishing, 1983.

Macaulay, Thomas B. "Civil Disabilities of the Jews." *Edinburgh Review* (January 1830). Reprinted in *Selections from the Edinburgh Review*, vol. 5, edited by Maurice Cross. Paris: Baudry, 1835.

————. *Macaulay: Poetry and Prose*, edited by G. M. Young. Cambridge: Harvard University Press, 1967.

Malabari, Behramji. *The Hindu Child-Widow*. Bombay: Voice of India, 1887.

Melton, J. Gordon, ed. *The Origins of Theosophy: Annie Besant—The Atheist Years*. New York: Garland Publishing, 1990.

Mill, James. *History of British India*. With Notes by Horace Hayman Wilson. 6 vols. 1817; rpt. London: Piper, Stephinson, and Spence, 1858.

Morris, John Brande. *An Essay towards the Conversion of Learned and Philosophical Hindus*. London: J.G.F. and J. Rivington, 1843.

Nelson, James. *A View of the Hindu Law as Administered by the High Court of Judicature at Madras*. Madras: Higginbotham, 1877.

Olcott, Henry Steel. *Applied Theosophy and Other Essays*. Madras: Theosophical Publishing House, 1975.

Oman, John Campbell. *The Brahmans, Theists, and Muslims of India*. London: T. Fisher Unwin, n.d.

Rajagopalachari, C. *Ambedkar Refuted*. Bombay: Hind Publications, 1946.

Risley, H. H. *The Tribes and Castes of Bengal*, vol. 1. Calcutta: Bengal Secretariat Press, 1891.

Smith, George. *The Conversion of India*. London and Edinburgh: J. Murray, 1893.

Smith, William. *Dwij: The Conversion of a Brahman to the Faith of Christ*. London: James Nisbet, 1850.

Strange, Thomas. *Elements of Hindu Law Referable to British Judicature in India*. London: Payne and Foss, 1825.

Sundar Singh, Sadhu. *With and without Christ*. London: Cassel, 1929.

The Theosophy of Mrs. Besant, including Account of the Recent Lawsuits. Mysore: Wesleyan Mission Press, 1913.

Underwood, Alfred C. *Conversion: Christian and Non-Christian*. London: Allen and Unwin, 1925.

Novels, Essays, Letters, and Diaries

Abbott, Anstice. *Indian Idylls*. London: Elliott Stock, 1911.

Anand, Mulk Raj. *Untouchable*. Preface by E. M. Forster. 1935; London: Penguin Books, 1940.

Bai, Kaveri. *Meenakshi's Memoirs*. Madras: Natesan, 1937.

Baldwin, Olivia A. *Sita: A Story of Child-Marriage Fetters*. New York: Revell, 1911.

Besant, Walter. *The Revolt of Man*. Edinburgh and London: William Blackwood, 1891.

Brayne, Frank Lugard. *Socrates in an Indian Village*. London: Oxford University Press, 1929.

Bruce, Henry. *The Bride of Shiva*. London: John Long, 1920.

————. *The Native Wife, or Indian Love and Anarchism*. London: John Long, 1909.

————. *The Temple Girl*. London: John Long, 1919.

Carus, Paul. *Amitabha: A Story of Buddhist Theology*. Chicago: Open Court, 1906.

Chinna Durai, J. *Sugirtha*. London: Hulbert, 1929.

Dangle, Arjun, ed. *Poisoned Bread: Translations from Modern Marathi Dalit Literature*. Bombay: Orient Longman, 1992.

Dennehy, Cyril. *Flower of Asia*. London: Burns and Oates, 1901.

Dickens, Charles. *Barnaby Rudge*. 1841; London: Penguin, 1986.

Disraeli, Benjamin. *Coningsby*. 1844; rpt. London: Penguin, 1989.

————. *Tancred: Or the New Crusade*. 1847; rpt. New York and London: M. Walter Dunne, 1904.

Duncan, Sara J. *Set in Authority*. London: Constable, 1906.

Edgeworth, Maria. *Harrington*, vol. 7 of *Tales and Novels*, 20 vols. 1817; rpt. New York: Harper and Brother, 1856.

Eliot, George. *Daniel Deronda*. 1876; Oxford: Oxford University Press, 1984.

Eliot, T. S. *After Strange Gods*. London: Faber and Faber, 1934.

————. *The Idea of a Christian Society, and Other Writings*. 1939; rpt. London: Faber and Faber, 1982.

Fraser, William A. *Caste*. London: Hodder and Stoughton, 1922.

Garbe, Richard. *The Redemption of the Brahmin*. Chicago: Open Court, 1894.

Goldsack, William. *Ghulam Jabbar's Renunciation*. Madras: Christian Literature Society, 1913.

Hunter, William W. *The Old Missionary*. London: Henry Frowde, 1895.

Longley, Pearl Dorr. *The Rebirth of Venkata Reddi*. Philadelphia: Judson Press, 1939.

Madhaviah, A. *Clarinda; A Historical Novel*. 1915; rpt. Madras: Christian Literature Society, 1992.

Mainwaring, M. *The Suttee; or, the Hindoo Converts*. 3 vols. London: A. K. Newman, 1830.

Mayo, Katherine. *Slaves of the Gods*. London: Jonathan Cape, 1929.

Mukerji, Dhan Gopal. *Caste and Outcaste*. London: Dent, 1923.

Newman, John Henry. *Apologia Pro Vita Sua*. 1864; New York: Doubleday, 1956.

————. *An Essay in Aid of a Grammar of Assent*. Notre Dame: University of Notre Dame Press, 1979.

————. *An Essay on the Development of Christian Doctrine*. 1878; 6th ed., Notre Dame: University of Notre Dame Press, 1989.

————. *Historical Sketches*, 3 vols. London: Pickering, 1889.

————. *The Idea of a University*. 1873; Notre Dame: University of Notre Dame Press, 1982.

————. *The Letters and Diaries of John Henry Newman*. Vols. 1–5, edited by Ian Ker and Thomas Gornall. Oxford: Clarendon Press, 1978–81.

————. *Loss and Gain: The Story of a Convert*, edited by Alan G. Hill. 1848; rpt. Oxford: Oxford University Press, 1986.

Oman, J. Campbell. *Where Three Creeds Meet*. London: Grant Richards, 1898.

Owenson, Sydney (Lady Morgan). *Luxima the Prophetess*. 1811; rpt. London: Charles Westerton, 1859. Originally published as *The Missionary*.

Pegg, Eleanor. *Star Maiden: A Tale of South India*. London: Sheldon Press, 1926.

Penny, Fanny. *Caste and Creed*. 2 vols. London: White, 1890.

———. *The Mound*. London: Methuen, 1922.

———. *The Outcaste*. London: Chatto and Windus, 1912.

———. *The Romance of a Nautch Girl*. London: Swan Sonnenschein, 1898.

———. *The Swami's Curse*. London: Hodder and Stoughton, 1922.

Perrin, Alice. *The Anglo-Indians*. London: Methuen, 1912.

———. *Idolatry*. London: Chatto and Windus, 1909.

Ramabai, Pandita. *The High-Caste Hindu Woman*. Philadelphia, n.p., 1888.

———. *The Letters and Correspondence of Pandita Ramabai*. edited by A. B. Shah. Bombay: Maharashtra State Board for Literature and Culture, 1977.

Rameshwar Rao, Shanta. *Children of God*. 1976; rpt. Calcutta: Orient Longman, 1992.

Sattianadhan, Krupabai. *Kamala*. Madras: Srinivasa Varadachari, 1894.

———. *Kamala's Letters to Her Husband*. Madras: English Publishing House, 1902.

———. *Saguna: A Story of Native Christian Life*. Madras: Srinivasa Varadachari, 1895.

Scharlieb, Mary Ann Dacomb. *Yet a More Excellent Way*. London: W. Gardner, 1929.

Scott, Walter. *Ivanhoe: A Romance*. 1819; rpt. Boston and New York: Houghton Mifflin, 1923.

Taylor, Philip Meadows. *Seeta*. London: Keegan Paul, 1872; rpt. New Delhi: Asian Educational Services, 1989.

———. *Tara: A Mahratta Tale*. 1863; rpt. New Delhi: Asian Educational Services, 1986.

Thompson, Edward. *An Indian Day*. New York: Knopf, 1927.

———. *Night Falls on Siva's Hill*. London: Heinemann, 1929.

Vanmikanathan, G., ed. *The Periyapuranam by Sekkizhaar*, English version. Madras: Ramakrishna Math, 1985.

Secondary Sources

Adhav, S. M. *Pandita Ramabai*. Madras: Christian Literature Society, 1979.

Ahmed, Rafiuddin. *The Bengal Muslims 1871–1906: A Quest for Identity*. Delhi: Oxford University Press, 1981.

Ali, Muhammad Mohar. *The Bengali Reaction to Christian Missionary Activities, 1833–1857*. Chittagong: Mehrub Publications, 1965.

Anderson, Benedict. *Imagined Communities: Reflections on the Origin and Spread of Nationalism*. London: Verso, 1983; 2d. rev. ed., 1992.

Arnold, T. W. *The Preaching of Islam: A History of the Propagation of the Muslim Faith*. 1914; 1896; rpt. Lahore: Shirkat-Qualam, 1956.

Asad, Talal. *Genealogies of Religion: Discipline and Reasons of Power in Christianity and Islam* (Baltimore: Johns Hopkins University Press, 1993).

Banerjee, A. C. *English Law in India*. Atlantic Highlands, NJ: Humanities Press, 1984.

Banerjee, Brojendra Nath. *Religious Conversions in India*. New Delhi: Harnam Publications, 1982.

Banner, Michael C. *The Justification of Science and the Rationality of Religious Belief*. Oxford: Clarendon Press, 1990.

Bapat, Ram. "Pandita Ramabai: Faith and Reason in the Shadow of the East and West."

In *Representing Hinduism: The Construction of Religious Traditions and National Identity*, edited by Vasudha Dalmia and H. von Stietencron (Delhi: Sage Publications, 1995).

Barborka, Geoffrey. *The Story of Human Evolution*. Madras: Theosophical Publishing House, 1979.

Bartholomew, G. W. "Private Interpersonal Law." *International and Comparative Law Quarterly* 1 (July 1952): 325–44.

Bayly, Susan. *Saints, Goddesses and Kings: Muslims and Christians in South Indian Society 1700–1900*. Cambridge: Cambridge University Press, 1989.

Bebbington, D. W. *Evangelicalism in Modern Britain: A History from the 1730s to the 1980s*. London: Unwin Hyman, 1989.

Bhabha, Homi. *The Location of Culture*. London: Routledge, 1994.

Bhalla, Alok, and Sudhir Chandra. *Indian Responses to Colonialism in the Nineteenth Century*. New Delhi: Sterling, 1993.

Bharucha, Rustom. *The Question of Faith*. Tracts for the Times, no. 3. Delhi: Orient Longman, 1993.

Bradford, Sarah. *Disraeli*. London: Weidenfeld and Nicolson, 1982.

Bulliet, Richard. *Conversion to Islam in Medieval Times*. Cambridge: Harvard University Press, 1987.

Burns, R. I. "Christian-Islamic Confrontation in the West: The Thirteenth-Century Dream of Conversion." *American Historical Review* 76, no. 5 (1971): 1,386–1,434.

Burton, Antoinette. *Burdens of History: British Feminists, Indian Women, and Imperial Culture, 1865–1915*. Chapel Hill: University of North Carolina Press, 1994.

Butalia, Urvashi. "Community, State and Gender: On Women's Agency during Partition." *Economic and Political Weekly*, April 24, 1993: WS12–WS24.

Carter, Stephen L. *The Culture of Disbelief*. New York: Basic Books, 1993.

Casey, Gerard. *Natural Reason: A Study of the Notions of Inference, Assent, Intuition, and First Principles in the Philosophy of John Henry Cardinal Newman*. New York: Peter Lang, 1984.

Cesarani, David, ed. *The Making of Modern Anglo-Jewry*. London: Basil Blackwell, 1990.

Chadwick, Owen. *The Victorian Church*. 2 vols. 1966; rpt. London: SCM Press, 1987.

Chandra, Sudhir. "Whose Laws? Notes on a Legitimising Myth of the Colonial Indian State." *Studies in History* 8, no. 2 (1992): 187–211.

Chapman, Malcolm. *The Celts: The Construction of a Myth*. London: Macmillan, 1992.

Chatterjee, Partha. *Nationalist Thought and the Colonial World*. Delhi: Oxford University Press, 1986.

——— . *The Nation and Its Fragments*. Princeton: Princeton University Press, 1994.

Clawson, Mary Ann. *Constructing Brotherhood: Class, Gender, and Fraternalism*. Princeton: Princeton University Press, 1989.

Cohn, Bernard. "The Census, Social Structure and Objectification in South Asia." In Bernard Cohn, *An Anthropologist among the Historians and Other Essays*. Delhi: Oxford University Press, 1987.

Correia-Afonso, John, S.J. *Jesuit Letters and Indian History 1542–1773*. Bombay: Oxford University Press, 1969.

Coulson, John. *Religion and Imagination*. Oxford: Clarendon Press, 1981.

Cousins, James, ed. *The Annie Besant Centenary Book*. Madras: Theosophical Publishing House, 1947.

Cox, Jeffrey. *The English Churches in a Secular Society: Lambeth 1870–1930*. New York: Oxford University Press, 1982.

Crowley, Alan. "The Performance of the *Grammar*: Reading and Writing Newman's Narrative of Assent." *Renascence* 43, nos. 1–2 (1991): 137–57.

Cunningham, Valentine. *Everywhere Spoken Against: Dissent in the Victorian Novel*. Oxford: Clarendon Press, 1975.

Das, Bhagwan. "Ambedkar's Journey to Mass Conversion." In *B. R. Ambedkar*, edited by Verinder Grover. New Delhi: Deep and Deep Publications, 1993.

Das, Sisir Kumar. *The Shadow of the Cross: Christianity and Hinduism in a Colonial Situation*. New Delhi: Munshiram, 1974.

Das, Veena. "The Composition of the Personal Voice: Violence and Migration." *Studies in History* 7, no. 1 (1991): 65–77.

———. *Critical Events: An Anthropological Perspective on Contemporary India*. Delhi: Oxford University Press, 1995.

Dennett, D. C. *Conversion and Poll Tax in Early Islam*. Cambridge: Harvard University Press, 1950.

Derrett, J. Duncan. *Dharmashastra and Juridical Literature*. Wiesbaden: n.p., 1973.

———. *Religion, Law, and the State in India*. London: Faber and Faber, 1968.

Devadason, E. D. *A Study on Conversion and Its Aftermath*. Madras: Christian Literature Society, 1982.

Dirks, Nicholas B. "Castes of Mind." *Representations* 37 (Winter 1992): 56–78.

Dixit, Prabha. "Annie Besant Devalued?" *Illustrated Weekly of India* 98 (July 10–16, 1977): 37–39.

Doran, Robert M. *Psychic Conversion and Theological Foundations: Toward a Reorientation of the Human Sciences*. American Academy of Religion Studies in Religion, no. 25. Ann Arbor: Scholars Press, 1981.

During, Simon. "Literature—Nationalism's Other? The Case for Revision." In Homi Bhabha, ed., *Nation and Narration*. London: Routledge, 1990.

Dutta, Pradip Kumar. "'Dying Hindus': Production of Hindu Communal Common Sense in Early 20th Century Bengal." *Economic and Political Weekly*, June 19, 1993: 1,305–19.

Eaton, Richard M. "Conversion to Christianity among the Nagas, 1876–1971." *Indian Economic and Social History Review* 21, no. 1 (1984): 1–44.

Engineer, Ali Asghar. *The Shah Bano Controversy*. Delhi: Orient Longman, 1990.

Fabian, Johannes. *Time and the Other: How Anthropology Makes Its Objects*. New York: Columbia University Press, 1983.

Farquhar, J. N. *Modern Religious Movements in India*. London: Macmillan, 1915.

———. *An Outline of the Religious Literature of India*. 1920; rpt. Delhi: Motilal Banarsidas, 1967.

Fernandes, Walter. *Caste and Conversion Movements in India: Religion and Human Rights*. New Delhi: Indian Social Institute, 1981.

Finestein, Israel. *Jewish Society in Victorian England*. London: Valentine Mitchell, 1993.

Fisher, Humphrey. "Conversion Reconsidered: Some Historical Aspects of Religious Conversion in Black Africa." *Africa* 43, no. 1 (1973): 27–40.

Forrester, Duncan B. *Caste and Christianity: Attitudes and Policies on Caste of Anglo-Saxon Protestant Missions in India*. London Studies on South Asia, no. 1. London and Dublin: Curzon Press, 1979.

Freeman, Edward A. *The History of the Norman Conquest of England*, vol. 1. Oxford: Clarendon Press, 1870.

Freitag, Sandria. *Collective Action and Community: Public Arenas and the Emergence of Communalism in North India* (Berkeley and Los Angeles: University of California Press, 1989).

Freud, Sigmund. *Moses and Monotheism*. Translated by Katherine Jones. 1939; rpt. New York: Vintage, 1967.

Frykenburg, R. E. "The Impact of Conversion and Social Reform upon Society in South India under the Late Company Period . . . with special reference to Tinnevelly." In C. E. Philips and M. D. Wainwright, eds., *Indian Society and the Beginnings of Modernization* (London: School of Oriental and African Studies, 1976).

Galanter, Marc. *Competing Equalities*. 1984; rpt. Delhi: Oxford University Press, 1994.

————. *Law and Society in Modern India*. Delhi: Oxford University Press, 1989.

Gellner, Ernest. *Postmodernism, Reason, and Religion*. London: Routledge, 1992.

Godwin, Joscelyn. *The Theosophical Enlightenment*. Albany: State University of New York Press, 1994.

Gomes, Michael. *Theosophy in the Nineteenth Century: An Annotated Bibliography*. New York: Garland Library, 1994.

Gore, M. S. *The Social Context of an Ideology: Ambedkar's Political and Social Thought*. Delhi: Sage Publications, 1993.

Gorham, Deborah. "The 'Maiden Tribute of Modern Babylon' Reexamined: Child Prostitution and the Idea of Childhood in Late-Victorian England." *Victorian Studies* 21 (Spring 1978): 353–79.

Grewal, Inderpal. *Home and Harem: Nation, Gender, Empire, and the Cultures of Travel*. Durham: Duke University Press, 1996.

Gupta, Brijen K. *India in English Fiction, 1800–1970: An Annotated Bibliography*. Metuchen, N.J.: Scarecrow Press, 1973.

Guru, Gopal. "Hinduisation of Ambedkar in Maharashtra." *Economic and Political Weekly*, February 16, 1991; 339–41.

Hardgrave, Robert. *Nadars of Tamilnadu*. Berkeley and Los Angeles: University of California Press, 1944.

Harding, Susan. "Representing Fundamentalism: The Problem of the Repugnant Cultural Other." *Social Research* 58 (Summer 1991): 373–93.

Hardy, Peter. "Modern European and Muslim Explanations of Conversion to Islam in South Asia: A Preliminary Survey of the Literature." In *Conversion to Islam*, edited by Nehemia Levtzion. New York: Holmes and Meier, 1979.

Harlow, Barbara. "Drawing the Line: Cultural Politics and the Legacy of Partition." *Polygraph* 5 (1992): 84–111.

Hawkins, Anne Hunsaker. *Archetypes of Conversion: The Autobiographies of Augustine, Bunyan, and Merton*. London and Toronto: Associated University Presses, 1985.

Hefner, Robert W., ed. *Conversion to Christianity: Historical and Anthropological Perspectives on a Great Transformation*, Berkeley and Los Angeles: University of California Press, 1993.

Helmstadter, Richard J. "The Nonconformist Conscience." In *Religion in Victorian Britain: Interpretations*, vol. 4, edited by Gerald Parsons. Manchester: Manchester University Press, 1988.

Helmstadter, Richard J., and Paul T. Phillips, eds. *Religion in Victorian Society: A Sourcebook of Documents*. Lanham: University Press of America, 1985.

Hill, Alan G. "Originality and Realism in Newman's Novels." In *Newman after a Hundred Years*, edited by Ian Ker and Alan G. Hill. Oxford: Clarendon Press, 1990.

Hilton, Boyd. *The Age of Atonement: The Influence of Evangelicalism on Social and Economic Thought, 1795–1865*. Oxford: Clarendon Press, 1988.

Horton, Robin. "African Conversion," *Africa: Journal of the International African Institute* 41, no. 2 (1971): 85–108.

———. "On the Rationality of Conversion." *Africa: Journal of the International African Institute* 45, no. 3 (1975): 219–35.

———. "On the Rationality of Conversion, Part II." *Africa: Journal of the International African Institute* 45, no. 4 (1975): 373–99.

Hubel, Teresa. *Whose India? The Independence Struggle in British and Indian Fiction and History*. Durham: Duke University Press, 1996.

Hudson, Dennis. "Christians and the Question of Caste: The Veḷḷāla Protestants of Pāḷaiyankōttai." In *Images of Man: Religion and Historical Process in South Asia*, edited by Fred Clothey. Madras: New Era, 1982.

———. "Hindu and Christian Theological Parallels in the Conversion of H. A. Kṛṣṇa Piḷḷai, 1857–1859." *Journal of the American Academy of Religion* 40 (June 1972): 191–206.

Inden, Ronald. *Imagining India*. Oxford: Basil Blackwell, 1990.

Inglis, K. S. "Patterns of Religious Worship in 1851." *Journal of Ecclesiastical History* 11, no. 1 (1960): 74–86.

Jacob, P. S. *The Experiential Response of N. V. Tilak*. Madras: Christian Literature Society, 1979.

Jaffrelot, Christophe. "Hindu Nationalism: Strategic Syncretism in Ideology Building." *Economic and Political Weekly*, March 20, 1993: 517–24.

James, William. *The Varieties of Religious Experience*. 1902; New York: New American Library, 1958.

Jay, Elizabeth. *Faith and Doubt in Victorian Britain*. London: Macmillan, 1986.

Jones, Kenneth, ed. *Religious Controversy in British India*. Albany: State University of New York Press, 1992.

———. "Religious Identity and the Indian Census." In *The Census in British India*, edited by N. Gerald Barrier (Delhi: Manohar, 1981).

Jordens, J.T.F. "Reconversion to Hinduism, the Shuddhi of the Arya Samaj." In *Religion in South Asia*, edited by Geoffrey Oddie. Delhi: Manohar, 1977.

Katz, David S. *The Jews in the History of England 1485–1850* Oxford: Clarendon Press, 1994.

Keer, Dhanajay. *B. R. Ambedkar: Life and Mission*. Bombay: Popular Prakashan, 1962.

Ker, Ian. *John Henry Newman: A Biography*. Oxford: Oxford University Press, 1988.

Khan, Mumtaz Ali. *Mass Conversions of Meenakshipuram*. Madras: Christian Literature Society, 1983.

Khare, R. S. "The Body, Sensoria, and Self of the Powerless: Remembering/'Re-

Membering' Indian Untouchable Women." *New Literary History* 26, no. 1 (1995): 147–68.

————. *The Untouchable as Himself.* Cambridge: Cambridge University Press, 1984.

King, Preston. *Toleration.* London: George Allen and Unwin, 1976.

Klostermaier, Klaus K. *Indian Theology in Dialogue.* Madras: Christian Literature Society, 1986.

Kooiman, Dick. *Conversion and Social Equality in India: The London Missionary Society in South Travancore in the 19th Century.* New Delhi: Manohar, 1989.

Kooiman, Dick, Otto van den Muijzenberg, and Peter van der Veer, eds. *Conversion, Competition and Conflict: Essays on the Role of Religion in Asia.* Amsterdam: Free University Press, 1984.

Kosambi, Meera. "Indian Response to Christianity, Church and Colonialism: Case of Pandita Ramabai." *Economic and Political Weekly*, October 24, 1992: WS61–WS71.

————. "Women, Emancipation, and Equality: Pandita Ramabai's Contribution to Women's Cause." *Economic and Political Weekly*, October 29, 1988: WS38–WS49.

Kothari, Rajni. "Rise of the Dalits and the Renewed Debate on Caste." *Economic and Political Weekly*, June 25, 1994: 1, 589–94.

Krieger, David J. "Conversion: On the Possibility of Global Thinking in an Age of Particularism." *Journal of the American Academy of Religion* 58, no. 2 (1990): 223–43.

Kuhn, Thomas. *The Structure of Scientific Revolutions.* 2d ed. Chicago: University of Chicago Press, 1970.

Kumar, Ravinder. "Ambedkar, Gandhi, and the Poona Pact." Occasional Papers in Society and History, no. 20. New Delhi: Nehru Memorial Museum, New Delhi, 1985.

Kuriakose, M. K., ed. *History of Christianity in India: Source Materials.* Madras: Christian Literature Society, 1982.

Kurtz, Lester R. *The Politics of Heresy: The Modernist Crisis in Roman Catholicism.* Berkeley and Los Angeles: University of California Press, 1986.

Lakshminarayanan, V. R. "Dr. Ambedkar's Contribution to the Revival of Buddhism in India." In *Buddhist Themes in Modern Indian Literature*, edited by J. Parthasarathi. Madras: Institute of Asian Studies, 1992.

Latourette, Kenneth Scott. *A History of the Expansion of Christianity.* 5th ed., New York: Harper and Brothers, 1939.

Lawton, David. *Blasphemy.* Philadelphia: University of Pennsylvania Press, 1993.

Leask, Nigel. *Anxieties of Empire: British Romantic Writers and the East.* Cambridge: Cambridge University Press, 1993.

Lehmann, Arno E. *It Began at Tranquebar: A History of the First Protestant Mission in India*, translated by M. J. Lutz. Madras: Christian Literature Society, 1956.

Lentin, Antony. "Anglicanism, Parliament, and the Courts." In *Religion in Victorian Britain: Controversies*, vol. 2, edited by Gerald Parsons. Manchester: Manchester University Press, 1988.

Levtzion, Nehemia, ed. *Conversion to Islam.* New York: Holmes and Meier, 1979.

Levy, Leonard W. *Blasphemy: Verbal Offense against the Sacred from Moses to Salman Rushdie.* New York: Knopf, 1993.

Lewis, Donald M. *Lighten Their Darkness: The Evangelical Mission to Working-Class London, 1828–1860.* Contributions to the Study of Religion, no. 19. Westport, CT: Greenwood Press, 1986.

Lightman, Bernard. *The Origins of Agnosticism: Victorian Unbelief and the Limits of Knowledge*. Baltimore: Johns Hopkins University Press, 1987.

Lingat, Robert. *The Classical Law of India*. Berkeley and Los Angeles: University of California Press, 1973.

Livingston, James. *Matthew Arnold and Christianity*. Columbia: University of South Carolina Press, 1986.

Loesberg, Jonathan. *Fictions of Consciousness: Mill, Newman, and the Reading of Victorian Prose*. New Brunswick and London: Rutgers University Press, 1986.

Lorenzen, David N., ed. *Religious Change and Cultural Domination*. Mexico: Colegio de Mexico, 1981.

Lovegrove, Deryck W. *Established Church, Sectarian People: Itinerancy and the Transformation of English Dissent, 1780–1830*. Cambridge: Cambridge University Press, 1986.

Lovett, Richard. *The History of the London Missionary Society 1795–1895*. 2 vols. London: Henry Frowde, 1899.

Machin, G.I.T. *Politics and the Churches in Great Britain, 1869–1921*. Oxford: Clarendon Press, 1987.

MacKillop, Ian. *The British Ethical Societies*. Cambridge: Cambridge University Press, 1986.

Madan, T. N. *Muslim Communities of South Asia: Culture and Society*. New Delhi, 1976.

Mahmood, Tahir. "Islamic Law and State Legislation on Religious Conversion in India." In *Islamic and Public Law: Classical and Contemporary Studies,* edited by Chibli Mallat. London: Graham and Trotman, 1993.

Maison, Margaret. *The Victorian Vision: Studies in the Religious Novel*. New York: Sheed and Ward, 1961.

Malmgreen, Gail, ed. *Religion in the Lives of English Women, 1760–1930*. London: Croom Helm, 1986.

Mani, Lata. "Contentious Traditions: The Debate on Sati in Colonial India." *Cultural Critique* 7 (Fall 1987): 119–56.

———. "The Production of an Official Discourse on Sati in Early Nineteenth Century Bengal." In *Europe and Its Others*, vol. 1, edited by Francis Barker et. al. Colchester: University of Essex Press, 1985.

Manickam, Sundaraj. *Nandanar the Dalit Martyr*. Madras: Christian Literature Society, 1990.

———. *The Social Setting of Christian Conversion in South India: The Impact of the Wesleyan Methodist Missionaries on the Trichy-Tanjore Diocese with Special Reference to the Harijan Communities of the Mass Movement Area 1820–1947*. Wiesbaden: Franz Steiner Verlag, 1977.

Manvell, Roger. *The Trials of Annie Besant and Charles Bradlaugh*. New York: Horizon Press, 1976.

Marcus, Steven. *Dickens: From Pickwick to Dombey*. New York: Basic Books, 1965.

Matthew, A. *Christian Missions, Education, and Nationalism: From Dominance to Compromise 1870–1930*. Delhi: Anamika Prakashan, 1988.

McClintock, Anne. *Imperial Leather: Race, Gender, and Sexuality in the Colonial Contest*. New York: Routledge, 1995.

McKeon, Richard. "The Individual in Law and in Legal Philosophy in the West." In

The Status of the Individual in East and West, edited by Charles A. Moore. Honolulu: University of Hawaii Press, 1968.

McLeod, Hugh. *Religion and the Working Class in Nineteenth-Century Britain*. London: Macmillan, 1984.

Mehrotra, S. R. "Mid-Victorian Anti-Imperialists and India." *Indian Economic and Social History Review* 13 (June 1976): 251–67.

Mendelsohn, Oliver and Upendra Baxi, eds. *The Rights of Subordinated Peoples*. Delhi: Oxford University Press, 1994.

Menon, Ritu, and Kamla Bhasin. "Recovery, Rupture, Resistance: Indian State and Abduction of Women during Partition," *Economic and Political Weekly*, April 24, 1993: WS2–WS11.

Mews, Stuart, ed. *Religion and National Identity: Studies in Church History*. Oxford: Clarendon Press, 1982.

Moore, James R. *Religion in Victorian Britain: Sources*, vol. 3. Manchester: Manchester University Press, 1988.

Moorhouse, Geoffrey. *The Missionaries*. Philadelphia: J.B. Lippincott, 1973.

Mullen, Shirley. *Organized Free Thought: The Religion of Unbelief*. New York: Garland, 1987.

Nagaraj, D. R. *The Flaming Feet: A Study of the Dalit Movement*. Bangalore: South Forum Press, 1993.

Nair, Janaki. *Women and Law in Colonial India*. New Delhi: Kali for Women, 1996.

Nancy, Jean-Luc. *The Inoperative Community*, translated by Peter Connor. Minneapolis: University of Minnesota Press, 1991.

Nandy, Ashis. "The Politics of Secularism and the Recovery of Religious Tolerance." In *Mirrors of Violence: Communities, Riots, and Survivors in South Asia*, edited by Veena Das. Delhi: Oxford University Press, 1990.

Nedelsky, Jennifer. "Law, Boundaries, and the Bounded Self," *Representations* 30 (Spring 1990): 162–89.

Neill, Stephen. *A History of Christianity in India, 1707–1858*. Cambridge: Cambridge University Press, 1985.

Nethercot, Arthur. *The First Five Lives of Annie Besant*. Chicago: University of Chicago Press, 1960.

Nock, A. D. *Conversion: The Old and the New in Religion from Alexander the Great to Augustine of Hippo*. Oxford: Clarendon Press, 1933.

Norman, Edward R. *Anti-Catholicism in Victorian England*. London: Allen and Unwin, 1968.

O'Hanlon, Rosalind. *Caste, Conflict, and Ideology: Jyotirao Phule and Low-Caste Protest in Western India*. Cambridge: Cambridge University Press, 1990.

Oddie, Geoffrey A. "Anti-Missionary Feeling and Hindu Revivalism in Madras: The Hindu Preaching and Tract Societies, 1886–1891." In *Images of Man: Religion and Historical Process in South Asia*, edited by Fred Clothey. Madras: New Era, 1982.

Oddie, Geoffrey A. *Religion in South Asia: Religious Conversion and Revival Movements in South Asia in Medieval and Modern Times*. 1977; 2d rev. ed., New Delhi: Manohar, 1991.

Olney, James. *Metaphors of Self*. Princeton: Princeton University Press, 1972.

Olson, Alan M. "Postmodernity and Faith." *Journal of the American Academy of Religion* 58, no. 1 (1990): 37–53.

Omvedt, Gail. *Dalit Visions*. Tracts for the Times, no. 8. Bombay: Orient Longman, 1995.

———. *Dalits and the Democratic Revolution: Dr. Ambedkar and the Dalit Movement in Colonial India*. New Delhi: Sage Publications, 1994.

Pandey, Gyanendra. *The Construction of Communalism in Colonial North India*. Delhi: Oxford University Press, 1990.

Parsons, Gerald, and James R. Moore, eds. *Religion in Victorian Britain*. 4 volumes. Manchester: Manchester University Press, 1988.

Pascoe, E. F. *Two Hundred Years of the S.P.G.: An Historical Account of the Society for the Propagation of the Gospel in Foreign Parts, 1701–1900*. London: S.P.G., 1901.

Pateman, Carole. *The Sexual Contract*. Stanford: Stanford University Press, 1988.

Pathak, Zakia, and Rajeswari Sundar Rajan. "Shahbano." *Signs* 14 (Spring 1989): 558–77.

Pattison, Robert. *The Great Dissent: John Henry Newman and the Liberal Heresy*. New York: Oxford University Press, 1991.

Paz, D. G. *Priesthoods and Apostasies of Pierre Connelly: A Study of Victorian Conversion and Anti-Catholicism*. Lewiston, NY: E. Mellen Press, 1986.

———. *Popular Anti-Catholicism in Mid-Victorian England*. Stanford: Stanford University Press, 1992.

Pechey, Graham. "On the Borders of Bakhtin: Dialogization, Decolonization." *Oxford Literary Review* 9, nos. 1–2 (1987): 59–85.

Peel, J.D.Y. "Syncretism and Religious Change." *Comparative Studies in Society and History* 10 (January 1968): 121–41.

Perera, Suvendrini. *Reaches of Empire: The English Novel from Edgeworth to Dickens* (New York: Columbia University Press, 1991).

Pickering, W.S.F. "The 1851 Religious Census—a Useless Experiment?" *British Journal of Sociology* 18, no. 4 (1967): 382–407.

Pickett, J. Waskom. *Christian Mass Movements in India*. New York: Abingdon Press, 1933.

Potts, Daniel E. *British Baptist Missionaries in India 1793–1837*. Cambridge: Cambridge University Press, 1967.

Powell, A. A. "Muslim Reaction to Missionary Activity in Agra." In *Indian Society and the Beginnings of Modernization c. 1830–1850*, edited by C. E. Philips and M. D. Wainwright. London: School of Oriental and African Studies, 1976.

Prakash, Gyan, ed. *After Colonialism: Imperial Histories and Postcolonial Displacements*. Princeton: Princeton University Press, 1995.

Queen, Christopher. "Ambedkar, Modernity, and the Hermeneutics of Buddhist Liberation." In *Dr. Ambedkar, Buddhism and Social Change*, edited by A. K. Narain and D. C. Ahir. Delhi: B. R. Publishing, 1994.

Qureshi, I. H. "Muslim India before the Mughals." In *Cambridge History of Islam*, vol. 2, edited by P. M. Holt, Ann K. S. Lambton, and Bernard Lewis. Cambridge: Cambridge University Press, 1970.

Rabi, Khondkar Fazli. *The Origins of the Musalmans of Bengal*. 1895; rpt. Dacca: Society for Pakistan Studies, 1970.

Rafael, Vicente. *Contracting Colonialism: Translation and Christian Conversions in Tagalog*. Ithaca: Cornell University Press, 1989.

Ragussis, Michael. *Figures of Conversion: "The Jewish Question" and English National Identity*. Durham: Duke University Press, 1995.

―――. "Representation, Conversion, and Literary Form: *Harrington* and the Novel of Jewish Identity." *Critical Inquiry* 16 (Autumn 1989): 113–43.

Ralls, W. "The Papal Aggression of 1850: A Study in Victorian Anti-Catholicism." In *Religion in Victorian Britain: Interpretations*, vol. 4, edited by Gerald Parsons. Manchester: Manchester University Press, 1988.

Ranger, Terence. "The Local and the Global in Southern African Religious History." In *Conversion to Christianity: Historical and Anthropological Perspectives on a Great Transformation*, edited by Robert W. Hefner. Berkeley and Los Angeles: University of California Press, 1993.

Ransom, Josephine. *A Short History of the Theosophical Society*. Madras: Theosophical Publishing House, 1938.

Ray, Aswini K. "India's New Secular Activism: Exploding Some Myths." *Economic and Political Weekly*, May 15, 1993: 968–73.

Reed, John R. *Victorian Will*. Athens: Ohio State University Press, 1989.

Rizvi, S.A.A. "Islamic Proselytisation, Seventh to Sixteenth Centuries." In *Religion in South Asia*, edited by Geoffrey Oddie. Delhi: Manohar, 1977.

Robb, Peter. "The Government of India and Annie Besant." *Modern Asian Studies* 10, no. 1 (1976): 107–30.

Rodrigues, Valerian. "Between Tradition and Modernity: The Gandhi-Ambedkar Debate." In *Dr. Ambedkar, Buddhism and Social Change*, edited by A. K. Narain and D. C. Ahir. Delhi: B. R. Publishing, 1994.

Roland, Joan. *Jews in British India: Identity in a Colonial Era*. Hanover and London: University Press of New England, 1989.

Rosenberg, John D. *Carlyle and the Burden of History*. Oxford: Clarendon Press, 1985.

Rosman, Doreen M. *Evangelicals and Culture*. London: Croom Helm, 1984.

Rowell, Geoffrey. *The Vision Glorious: Themes and Personalities of the Catholic Revival in Anglicanism*. Oxford: Clarendon Press, 1983.

Royle, Edward. *Radicals, Secularists, and Republicans: Popular Freethought in Britain, 1866–1915*. Manchester: Manchester University Press, 1980.

―――. *Victorian Infidels: The Origins of the British Secularist Movement, 1791–1866*. Manchester: Manchester University Press, 1974.

Said, Edward W. *Culture and Imperialism*. New York: Knopf, 1993.

―――. "Ideology of Difference," *Critical Inquiry* 12, no. 1 (1985): 38–58. Reprinted in Edward W. Said, *The Politics of Dispossession: The Struggle for Palestinian Self-Determination*. New York: Pantheon, 1994.

―――. *The World, the Text, and the Critic*. Cambridge: Harvard University Press, 1983.

Salbstein, M.C.N. *The Emancipation of the Jews in Britain: The Question of the Admission of the Jews to Parliament, 1828–1860*. East Brunswick, NJ: Associated University Presses, 1982.

Saldanha, Julian. *Civil and Ecclesiastical Law in India*. Trichinopoly: Catholic Truth Society, n.d.

―――. *Conversion and Indian Civil Law*. Bangalore: Theological Publications in India, 1981.

Schreuder, Deryck and Geoffrey Oddie. "What is 'Conversion'? History, Christianity and Religious Change in Colonial Africa and South Asia." *Journal of Religious History* 15 (December 1989): 496–518.

Schwartz, Daniel R. *Disraeli's Fiction*. London: Macmillan, 1979.

Seunarine, J. F. *Reconversion to Hinduism through Suddhi*. Madras: Christian Literature Society, 1977.

Shanley, Mary Lyndon. *Feminism, Marriage, and the Law in Victorian England, 1850–1895*. Princeton: Princeton University Press, 1989.

Sharpe, Eric J. *Not to Destroy but to Fulfil: The Contribution of J. N. Farquhar to Protestant Missionary Thought in India before 1914*. Uppsala: Gleerup-Lund, 1965.

Shaw, George Bernard. *An Autobiography 1856–1898*, edited by Stanley Weintraub. New York: Weybright and Talley, 1969.

Shepherd, William C. "Conversion and Adhesion." In *Religious Change and Continuity*, edited by Harry M. Johnson. San Francisco: Jossey-Bass, 1979.

Smith, Donald Eugene. *India as a Secular State*. Princeton: Princeton University Press, 1963.

Smith, K.J.M. *James Fitzjames Stephen: Portrait of a Victorian Rationalist*. Cambridge: Cambridge University Press, 1988.

Spivak, Gayatri Chakravorty. "The Burden of English." In *Orientalism and the Post-Colonial Predicament*, edited by Carol Breckenridge and Peter van der Veer. Philadelphia: University of Pennsylvania Press, 1993.

———. "Can the Subaltern Speak?" In *Marxism and the Interpretation of Culture*, edited by Cary Nelson and Lawrence Grossberg. Urbana and Chicago: University of Illinois Press, 1988.

———. *Outside in the Teaching Machine*. New York: Routledge, 1993.

Stanley, Brian. *The Bible and the Flag: Protestant Missions and British Imperialism in the Nineteenth and Twentieth Centuries*. Leicester: Leicester University Press, 1990.

Stocking, George. *Victorian Anthropology*. New York: Free Press, 1987.

Studdert-Kennedy, Gerald. *British Christians, Indian Nationalists, and the Raj*. Delhi: Oxford University Press, 1991.

Suleri, Sara. *The Rhetoric of English India*. Chicago: University of Chicago Press, 1992.

Taylor, Anne. *Annie Besant: A Biography*. Oxford: Oxford University Press, 1992.

Taylor, Richard. "The Ambedkarite Buddhists." In *Ambedkar and the Neo-Buddhist Movement*, edited by T. S. Wilkinson and M. M. Thomas. Madras: Christian Literature Society, 1972.

Thomas, Edward. "Newman's Social and Political Thinking." In *Newman after a Hundred Years*, edited by Ian Ker and Alan G. Hill. Oxford: Clarendon Press, 1990.

Thomas, Stephen. *Newman and Heresy*. Cambridge: Cambridge University Press, 1992.

Thompson, E. P. *The Making of the English Working Class*. 1963; rpt. New York: Vintage, 1966.

———. *Witness against the Beast: William Blake and the Moral Law*. Cambridge: Cambridge University Press, 1993.

Thompson, H. P. *Into All Lands: The History of the Society for the Propagation of the Gospel in Foreign Parts 1701-1950*. London: S.P.C.K., 1951.

Toohey, Timothy. "Blasphemy in Nineteenth-Century England: The Pooley Case and Its Background." *Victorian Studies* 30, no. 3 (1987): 315–33.

Van der Veer, Peter. "Ayodhya and Somnath: Eternal Shrines, Contested Histories." *Social Research* 59 (Spring 1992): 85–109.

———, ed. *Conversion to Modernities: The Globalization of Christianity.* New York and London: Routledge, 1996.

———. *Religious Nationalism: Hindus and Muslims in India.* Berkeley and Los Angeles: University of California Press, 1994.

Viswanathan, Gauri. "Beyond Orientalism: Syncretism and the Politics of Knowledge." *Stanford Humanities Review* 5, no. 1 (1995): 19–34.

———. *Masks of Conquest: Literary Study and British Rule in India.* New York: Columbia University Press, 1989.

———. "Raymond Williams and British Colonialism." *Yale Journal of Criticism* 4, no. 2 (1991): 47–66.

Walder, Dennis. *Dickens and Religion.* London: George Allen, 1981.

Wallis, Jim. *The Soul of Politics: Practical and Prophetic Vision for Change.* Maryknoll, NY: Orbis Books, 1994.

Weber, Max. *The Sociology of Religion,* translated by Ephraim Fischoff. 1922; Boston: Beacon Press, 1963.

Wessinger, Catherine. *Annie Besant and Progressive Messianism (1847–1933).* New York: E. Mellen, 1988.

West, Geoffrey. *The Life of Annie Besant.* London: G. Howe, 1933.

Wink, André. *Al Hind: The Making of the Indo-Islamic World.* Leiden: E. J. Brill, 1990.

Winslow, J. C. *Narayan Viman Tilak: The Christian Poet of Maharashtra.* Calcutta: Association Press, 1923.

Wolffe, John. *God and Greater Britain: Religion and National Life in Britain and Ireland 1843–1945.* London: Routledge, 1994.

Young, Richard Fox. *Resistant Hinduism: Sanskrit Sources on Anti-Christian Apologetics in Early Nineteenth-Century India.* Vienna: DeNobili Research Library, 1981.

Young, Robert. *Colonial Desire: Hybridity in Theory, Culture and Race.* London: Routledge, 1995.